A HISTORY OF PERUVIAN LITERATURE

LIVERPOOL MONOGRAPHS IN HISPANIC STUDIES
7

A HISTORY OF PERUVIAN LITERATURE

JAMES HIGGINS

X
FRANCIS CAIRNS

Published by Francis Cairns (Publications) Ltd
c/o The University, P.O. Box 147, Liverpool L69 3BX, Great Britain
and
27 South Main Street,Wolfeboro, New Hampshire 03894, U.S.A.

First published 1987

British Library Cataloguing in Publication Data

Higgins, James
    A history of Peruvian literature.—
    (Liverpool monographs in hispanic studies,
    ISSN 0261-1538; 7)
    1. Peruvian literature—History and
    criticism   2. Quechua literature—History
    and criticism
    I. Title   II. Series
    860.9´86885   PQ8311

    ISBN 0-905205-35-9

Library of Congress Cataloging-in-Publication Data

Higgins, James, 1939-
    A history of Peruvian literature.

    (Liverpool monographs in Hispanic studies ; 7)
    Bibliography: p.
    Includes indexes.
    1. Peruvian literature—History and criticism.
    2. Quechua literature—History and criticism.
    I. Title.   II. Series.
    PQ8311.H53 1987   860´.9´985   86-26819
    ISBN 0-905205-35-9

Printed in Great Britain by
Redwood Burn Ltd, Trowbridge, Wiltshire

CONTENTS

Foreword ix

1 THE NATIVE TRADITION: Quechua Literature
from Pre-Columbian Times to the Present Day 1

2 THE COLONIAL EXPERIENCE
I. Prose and Drama in the Colonial Period 21
II. Poetry in the Colonial Period 41

3 INDEPENDENCE AND THE SEARCH FOR
LITERARY EXPRESSION (1821-c. 1925)
I. Fiction in the Republican Era 63
II. Drama and Poetry in the Republican Era 83

4 THE BIRTH OF A LITERATURE (c.1915-c.1941)
I. Regionalist Fiction and the Establishment of a
Novelistic Tradition 111
II. The Poetic Avant-Garde 144

5 THE BLOSSOMING (c.1940-c.1970)
I. The New Narrative 191
II. Poetry Pure and Impure 236

6 THE CONTEMPORARY THEATRE 293

7 FRESH GROWTH
I. The New Narrative Mark II 307
II. The New Poetry 326

Glossary 365
List of Abbreviations 367
Bibliography 369
Index of Principal Authors 375
Index of Principal Works 377

Acknowledgements

Grateful acknowledgement is due to the British Academy
and to the Centre for Latin-American Studies, University
of Liverpool, for grants which enabled me to make
research visits to Peru in preparation for this book.

FOREWORD

The motivation behind this book is quite simply a wish to share with others my personal enthusiasm for Peru and its literature. It is perhaps an inevitable consequence of the economic, political and cultural dominance of the developed nations that the literature of small, underdeveloped and peripheral countries should be fated to remain little known in the world at large, but to a considerable extent it is so for reasons that have nothing to do with literary quality and it is my hope that the following pages will succeed in persuading at least a few readers that Peruvian literature has much to offer. It is true, of course, that recent decades have seen a growing interest in Latin American literature both in Europe and in the United States, but, while that is a welcome development, the tendency to treat the continent as a whole and to concentrate attention on major figures has the inevitable effect of giving a somewhat distorted view of the literature — and the reality — of individual nations. One of my main concerns, therefore, has been to demonstrate that, while Peru has much in common with other Latin American countries and has participated in continent-wide literary movements, its literature also has its own distinctive character reflecting its distinct national reality.

Two factors in particular must be taken into account in any attempt to arrive at an appreciation of Peruvian literature. Firstly, Peru is a former colony and a part of the underdeveloped Third World and geographically it is isolated on the periphery of Western culture. In a very real sense, therefore, Peruvian writers have had to contend with conditions which conspire against creativity. One of the main themes of this book, in fact, is the general poverty of the cultural scene, Peru's backwardness in relation to the developed world, and in particular the lack of a publishing infrastructure to stimulate literary activity.[1] In such circumstances the surprising thing is not that much Peruvian literature has been amateurish and outdated but that so much of originality and quality has been written. Indeed, perhaps the most admirable thing about Peruvian writers has been their dedication to literature in an adverse cultural environment, an attitude epitomised in the early sixteenth century, at a time when the country was still a frontier society, in works of two anonymous poetesses exalting the virtues of poets and poetry.[2] In the colonial period and in the nineteenth century that attitude threw up isolated figures of stature such as Caviedes and Ricardo Palma, and in the twentieth century it brought about a widespread professionalism in the sense of a genuine literary awareness and expertise, first in poetry and the short story and later in the novel. In Vallejo, Arguedas and Vargas Llosa Peru has produced figures in the front rank of world literature, and in addition it can boast a host of writers, particularly poets, of whom any country would be proud, and it is only its theatre which, because of the particularly adverse conditions it has had to face, has failed to develop in line with the other genres. Furthermore, despite the obvious disadvantages of Peru's geographical isolation, it could be argued that its peripheral position has served as a stimulus to innovation in that its major writers have shown a greater willingness to experiment than they perhaps would have done had they been at the centre of the Western cultural tradition. It is precisely that willingness to experiment which portends well for the future of Peruvian literature.

A second factor to be borne in mind is that Peru is not a unified nation but a country made up of different regions and racial groups, each with its distinct cultural tradition. In that respect a particularly revealing image of Peru is provided by Mario Vargas Llosa in *La Casa Verde*, a novel whose fragmented narrative structure mirrors the reality of a country which is not only fragmented by geography but divided by levels of development and by culture, race and class.[3] Hence, except in pre-Columbian times when it took the form of the oral literature of the Quechua people, Peruvian literature cannot be regarded as a national literature in the sense of one which is the expression of a coherent national identity. Rather it is a literature in

[1] See particularly pp. 319-20.   [2] See p. 44.   [3] See pp. 225-28.

which diverse cultural traditions coexist in conflictive tension. After the Conquest the vast majority of colonial writers saw Peru as an outpost of Spain and shared the mother country's cultural values, and since Independence many writers have continued to regard themselves as belonging to the Western cultural tradition and to look to Europe for their standards. At the same time, the native tradition has remained very much alive, in Quechua in the form of a flourishing oral culture, and in Spanish in the shape of colonial works expressing the vision of the vanquished and of modern *indigenista* writing vindicating the rights and values of the Indian population. In the years leading up to and following Independence attempts were made to shrug off the colonial heritage and to create a distinctively national literature, but for the most part this limited itself to works reflecting the values of the *criollo* middle classes of Lima. Subsequently, however, there was to emerge an important corpus of literature depicting provincial life, particularly that of the sierra, and vindicating regional culture. More recently, various marginal sectors of Peruvian society have claimed or been given a voice, and the emergence in the seventies of a significant number of writers from humble backgrounds points to a growing "democratisation" of the literary scene. The literature of Peru, therefore, is that of a country whose national identity is still in the process of being forged. For, as José María Arguedas depicts it in *El zorro de arriba y el zorro de abajo*, Peru is a melting-pot that is still on the boil.[4]

Despite its title, this book is not intended to duplicate the exhaustive detail of histories of Peruvian literature which already exist in Spanish, such as those of Luis Alberto Sánchez and Augusto Tamayo Vargas, to which it owes a considerable debt.[5] It is conceived, above all, as an introduction to Peruvian literature and is deliberately selective, limiting itself to a discussion of the main writers, works and trends. Many writers who would merit a place in a more comprehensive history are either omitted or relegated to footnotes, and in the main those who fall into the latter category are not cited in the indexes, which are restricted to authors and works that have been allotted at least a minimum of discussion. My main criterion has been one of utility, in the sense of providing as much information as possible for a public unfamiliar with Peruvian

---

[4] See pp. 218-20.

[5] See Luis Alberto Sánchez, *La literatura peruana: derrotero para una historia cultural del Perú*, 5 vols., 5th ed. (Mejía Baca, 1981); Augusto Tamayo Vargas, *Literatura peruana*, 2 vols. (San Marcos, 1965).

literature. The authors discussed receive fuller treatment than is usual in literary histories. A general bibliography is furnished at the end, and for each author a separate bibliography is provided in the footnotes, the editions cited being the most accessible and the critical material being as exhaustive as possible, except in the case of major figures like Vallejo, Arguedas and Vargas Llosa, where I have been obliged to be selective. All quotations in Spanish are accompanied by an English translation, and included at the end is a glossary of terms requiring some knowledge of Peru or of Hispanic culture.

A few words should be said to clarify the terms "literature" and "Peru" as used in this book. For the most part I have confined myself to the major genres — fiction, poetry, theatre —, but I have also discussed the histories and chronicles of the early colonial period and the nineteenth-century costumbrist sketch, I have briefly referred to the writings of influential essayists, and I have treated Quechua oral culture as literature. As for Peru, it is a country whose geographical extension has undergone considerable variations in the course of its history. For the pre-Columbian period I have regarded Peru as synonymous with the Inca Empire. For the post-Conquest period, on the other hand, I use the term in the main to refer to the territory occupied by the modern Republic rather than to the larger Vice-royalty of Peru of which it once was a part, for the reason that my concern is to trace the development of the national literature of the country which we now know as Peru. Excluded from this book, therefore, are writers such as Ercilla and Olmedo who, despite their links with Peru, more properly belong to the national literature of other countries.

It will no doubt strike readers as a curious anomaly that the opening chapter should present extracts of Quechua literature in Spanish translation. That anomaly is one of which I am acutely conscious, but it is also one which lies at the heart of Peruvian cultural life. For it is a regrettable fact that, since Quechua is primarily an oral language and one with which few educated Peruvians are familiar, printed editions of Quechua literature are to be found much more readily in Spanish translation than in the original tongue.

Some readers may feel, too, that disproportionate attention has been devoted to the modern period. This, I would emphasise, is not due to any prejudice that the literature of earlier periods is somehow less relevant, and, indeed, I hope to have established quite clearly the existence and importance of literary tradition. Rather it is because the flourishing of Peruvian literature in terms of both quantity and quality begins effectively only in the twentieth century. And, moreover, given the scarcity of studies of the work of many modern writers and the lack of a coherent overall view of Peruvian twentieth-century literature, that is perhaps the area where the average reader most requires information and guidance.

There is also a certain amount of arbitrariness in my division of Peruvian literature into periods and in my classification of authors in relation to those periods. Thus, for example, I have chosen to place Martín Adán's poetry in the post-avant-garde era, though he began his literary career in the avant-garde context. And in the case of Mario Vargas Llosa I have opted to view his work as the culmination of the new narrative of the fifties, when he could have been regarded equally legitimately as the fictional counterpart of the new poetry of the sixties. No doubt there are many other classifications no less debatable, but I trust that most readers will have the good sense to appreciate that such arbitrariness is inevitable in a book of this nature.

In the sections of the book devoted to poetry I have made generous use of quotations, in the belief that these convey the feel of the poets' work more effectively than any words of mine could ever do. The translations accompanying the quotations are my own, though I have consulted other versions where they exist. My translations, I must stress, have no pretensions to be poetry. For the most part I have sacrificed considerations of rhyme and metre, and my concern has been quite simply to convey as far as possible the sense and spirit of the original.

With regard to the bibliographies, the place of publication of all books mentioned is Lima, unless otherwise stated. Journals are either well-known international reviews or published in Lima. A list of abbreviations used is provided at the end of the book.

A further point requiring clarification is the term "white", which occurs through the book in phrases such as "the white man", "white culture", "the white ruling classes". Though a misnomer, it is used as convenient shorthand to refer to the dominant sectors of Peruvian society, which, while originally European, have, of course, long since ceased to be so.

Finally, I would like to express my gratitude to countless friends and colleagues, both Peruvians and Peruvianists, who over the years have given me the benefit of their knowledge and contributed to the making of this book. In particular, I am indebted to Edmundo

Bendezú and Luis Monguió, who had the kindness to read drafts of the first and second chapter respectively and offered invaluable guidance. Last but by no means least, my thanks are due to Rosemary Morris and Sandie Murphy for the patience and efficiency with which they prepared the typescript for press.

James Higgins

University of Liverpool

CHAPTER 1

THE NATIVE TRADITION:
Quechua Literature from Pre-Columbian Times to the Present Day

Quechua was the official language of the Inca Empire of Tahuantin-suyo, which embraced not only present-day Peru but also Bolivia, Ecuador and parts of Colombia, Chile and Argentina. The Incas developed a civilisation which was highly complex and sophisticated in many respects, yet curiously they appear to have possessed no written phonetic language. However, they had a vigorous oral culture which, as Edmundo Bendezú has argued, only a narrow ethnocentrism would deny classification as literature.[1] That literature, it should be emphasised, was not merely folkloric, but was the creation of artists who had a recognised role in society. The *amautas*, the learned men of the Empire, were philosophers, historians and poets as well as teachers and counsellors of the nobility, and as state functionaries they produced a literature which propagated the values of the Inca ruling class. In particular, they commemorated the great

[1] Edmundo Bendezú Aybar, ed., *Literatura quechua* (Caracas: Biblioteca Ayacucho, 1980), pp. xv-xx. On Quechua literature see José Alcina, *Poesía americana precolombina* (Madrid: Prensa Española, 1968); José María Arguedas, *Formación de una cultura nacional indoamericana* (Mexico City: Fondo de Cultura Económica, 1975); id., *Señores e indios. Acerca de la cultura quechua* (Buenos Aires: Arca/Calicanto, 1976); Abraham Arias-Larreta, *Literaturas aborígenes de América* (Kansas City: Indo-américa, 1968); Edmundo Bendezú, *op. cit.*; José Cid Pérez and Dolores Martí de Cid, eds., *Teatro indio precolombino* (Madrid: Aguilar, 1964), pp. 11-116; Mario Florián, *La épica inkaika* (Lima S.A., 1980); Jesús Lara, *La poesía quechua*, 2nd ed. (Mexico City: Fondo de Cultura Económica, 1979); id., *La literatura de los quechuas* (La Paz: Juventud, 1980).

events and figures of Inca history, celebrated occasions of political and social importance and composed hymns to the tutelar gods. In contrast the *haravecs* were popular poets whose lyrics conveyed the sentiments of the community, though it is also believed that they sometimes collaborated in the work of the *amautas*. All these artists have remained anonymous, for, in keeping with the authoritarian and communal nature of Inca society, their task was not to produce personal works of art but to interpret and express official ideology or the collective consciousness. Their works were preserved and transmitted by oral tradition, not simply in a haphazard fashion, but also, it seems, more methodically by the *quipucamayocs*, the state archivists.[2] They were recited, sung or performed publicly in the open air on the great feasts of the Inca calendar and in the course of collective labours and were often accompanied by music and dancing.

The lack of written texts and the determination of the Spanish authorities to eradicate manifestations of the defeated culture which might hinder the process of evangelisation made it inevitable that most of this pre-Columbian literature should disappear after the collapse of the Inca Empire. What has survived is a small corpus of texts collected by sixteenth- and seventeenth-century chroniclers, whose versions are in all likelihood adulterated.[3] These range from myths explaining the origins of the Incas and their Empire and chapters of official Inca history to lyrics singing the joys and pains of love. Among the most interesting are hymns and prayers expressing the religious sentiments of pre-Columbian man. Though some are directed to minor gods such as the Sun and the Moon, Inca religion

[2] The *quipucamayocs* kept official records by means of *quipus*, coloured strings which served as a mnemonic device. These were used mainly to record statistics, but also, it is thought, as a method for memorising poems, histories, legends and laws.

[3] See Bendezú, p. x. Meriting special mention is a collection of tales and legends from the locality of Huarochirí; see *Dioses y hombres de Huarochirí. Edición bilingüe. Narración quechua recogida por Francisco de Avila (¿1598?)*, ed. Pierre Duviols and trans. José María Arguedas (Museo Nac. de Historia/Instituto de Estudios Peruanos, 1966). For selections of Quechua literature see the above-cited works by Alcina, Bendezú and Lara. See also José María Arguedas, ed., *Poesía quechua* (Buenos Aires: Editorial Universitaria, 1965); Francisco Carrillo, ed., *Poesía y prosa quechua*, 2nd ed. (Biblioteca Universitaria, 1968); Winston Orrillo, ed., *Antología general de la prosa en el Perú*, I (Ecoma, 1971); Mario Razzeto, ed., *Poesía quechua* (Havana: Casa de las Américas, 1972); Sebastián Salazar Bondy, ed., *Poesía quechua* (Buenos Aires: Arca/Galerna, 1968). The low level of literacy among Quechua-speakers and the ignorance of Quechua in cultured circles are reflected in the fact that the most accessible collections are in Spanish. For that reason all quotations in this chapter are in that language. Since there are often different versions of the same text, I have indicated my source.

appears to have evolved, in cultured circles at least, towards an abstract monotheism, for the deity most frequently invoked is Viracocha, the supreme God, creator and governor of the universe. Many such compositions display a high degree of intellectual sophistication in that they involve philosophical speculation about the nature of the divinity and express a passionate mystical yearning that the immaterial Viracocha might reveal himself to man:

¡Ah Wiraqocha, de todo lo existente el poder!
"Que éste sea hombre,
que ésta sea mujer" (dijiste).
Sagrado ... señor,
de toda luz naciente
el hacedor.
¿Quién eres?
¿Dónde estás?
¿No podría verte?
¿En el mundo de arriba
o en el mundo de abajo
o a un lado del mundo
está tu poderoso trono?
"¡Jay!", dime solamente
desde el océano celeste
o de los mares terrenos en que habitas.
Pachacamac,
creador del hombre,
Señor, tus siervos,
a ti,
con sus ojos manchados
desean verte.
Cuando pueda ver,
cuando pueda saber,
cuando sepa señalar,
cuando sepa reflexionar,
me verás,
me entenderás.

El sol, la luna,
el día, la noche,
el verano, el invierno
no están libres,
ordenados andan:
están señalados
y llegan
a lo ya medido.
¿Adónde, a quién
el brillante cetro
enviaste?
"¡Jay!", dime solamente,

escúchame
cuando aún
no esté cansado,
muerto.   (Arguedas)

(Oh Viracocha, power behind all that exists!
"Let this be man,
let this be woman," you said.
Sacred ... lord,
maker
of all light that dawns.
Who are you?
Where are you?
Might I not see you?
Is your powerful throne
in the world of above
or in the world of below
or beyond the world's edge?
From the celestial ocean
or the earthly seas wherein you dwell,
speak to me, say but "I hear!".
Pachacamac,
creator of man,
Lord, your servants
wish to see you
with their tainted eyes,
you.
When I am able to see,
when I am able to know,
when I am able to point,
when I am able to reflect,
you will see me,
you will understand me.

The sun, the moon,
day, night,
summer, winter
are not free,
they move to order;
they are designated
and arrive
at the appointed time.
Where, to whom
did you send
the shining sceptre?
Speak to me, say but "I hear!",
hear me
while I am still
not worn out,
dead.)

However, while such compositions are an indication of the sophistication of the Inca court, Andean society was essentially a rural society living close to the earth and bound together by a communal spirit, and the world of the ordinary peasant is more truly reflected in choral songs sung in accompaniment to some collective agricultural task or in intervals of rest from such labours. These songs allude directly to the task at hand and have the form of a double chorus in which the men take the lead and the women respond. Their function was obviously recreational in that they served to lighten the burden of physical toil, but it is possible that they also had a magical or religious basis and were conceived as ritual acts of propitiation. The Indian's close identification with nature is evident in the common parallel between the cultivation of the soil and human reproduction, as in a *haylli* (song of triumph) celebrating the sowing of the seed in the womb of Pachamama, the Earth Mother:

> *Los hombres*:
> ¡Ea, el triunfo! ¡Ea, el triunfo!
> ¡He aquí el arado y el surco!
> ¡He aquí el sudor y la mano!
>
> *Las mujeres*:
> ¡Hurra, varón, hurra!
>
> *Los hombres*:
> ¡Ea, el triunfo! ¡Ea, el triunfo!
> ¿Dónde está la infanta, la hermosa?
> ¿Dó la semilla y el triunfo?
>
> *Las mujeres*:
> ¡Hurra, la simiente, hurra!
>
> *Los hombres*:
> ¡Ea, el triunfo! ¡Ea, el triunfo!
> ¡Sol poderoso, gran padre,
> ve el surco y dale tu aliento!
>
> *Las mujeres*:
> ¡Hurra, Sol, hurra!
>
> *Los hombres*:
> ¡Ea, el triunfo! ¡Ea, el triunfo!
> ¡Al vientre de Pachamama,
> que da vida y fructifica!
>
> *Las mujeres*:
> ¡Hurra, Pachamama, hurra!
>
> *Los hombres*:
> ¡Ea, el triunfo! ¡Ea, el triunfo!
> ¡He aquí la infanta, la hermosa!

> *Las mujeres*:
> ¡He aquí el varón y el sudor!
> ¡Hurra, varón, hurra!   (Lara)

> (*The men*:
> Hey, the triumph! Hey, the triumph!
> Here's the plough and the furrow!
> Here's the sweat and the hand!

> *The women*:
> Hurray, man, hurray!

> *The men*:
> Hey, the triumph! Hey, the triumph!
> Where is the princess, the beautiful one?
> Where is the seed and the triumph?

> *The women*:
> Hurray, the seed, hurray!

> *The men*:
> Hey, the triumph! Hey, the triumph!
> Powerful Sun, great father,
> behold the furrow and into it infuse your breath!

> *The women*:
> Hurray, Sun, hurray!

> *The men*:
> Hey, the triumph! Hey, the triumph!
> Into the womb of Pachamama,
> which gives life and bears fruit!

> *The women*:
> Hurray, Pachamama, hurray!

> *The men*:
> Hey, the triumph! Hey, the triumph!
> Here's the princess, the beautiful one!

> *The women*:
> Here's the man and the sweat!
> Hurray, man, hurray!)

It has also been established that theatrical representations were performed in Inca times. Initially Inca theatre appears to have been religious in character and to have been a combination of dialogued recitation and mime, but in the latter years of the Empire it evolved into a drama of some sophistication. Plays were performed in the open air and without scenery, so that changes of location followed one another without interruption throughout the work. As in the Greek theatre, a chorus intervened at crucial points in the action. Unfortunately, despite the many claims made on behalf of *Ollantay*, no authentic pre-Columbian play has survived. However, the existence of theatre in Inca times seems to be confirmed by the fact that a play on the death of Atahualpa was represented by Indians in Potosí in 1555, various versions of which continued to be performed in different parts of Peru and Bolivia throughout the colonial period and even down to modern times.

A version believed to belong to the sixteenth century exists in written form under the title *Tragedia del fin de Atawallpa*.[4] The core of the action is made up of Atahualpa's premonitions of catastrophe, two parleys between his envoys and the invaders, and the seizure and execution of the Inca. An original feature is that in all encounters between Indians and Spaniards the latter do not speak but merely move their lips and an interpreter translates for them. The historical facts are treated with a considerable degree of licence. Atahualpa is not garrotted but beheaded and in a kind of epilogue the Spanish King, appalled by his subordinate's actions, orders that Pizarro be executed, his corpse burned and all memory of him obliterated. The play reveals a tendency, also present in *Ollantay*, to subordinate characterisation to plot, so that for the most part the Indians are defined by their role and the Spaniards are little more than stereotypes of arrogance and greed. Only in the presentation of Atahualpa himself do we encounter anything approaching a rounded figure. His changing states of mind are convincingly portrayed and, again as in *Ollantay*, the interventions of the chorus include some fine lyrical passages. However, the most interesting aspect of the play is the Indians' response to their conquerors. The unease and uncertainty provoked by the news of the invasion is conveyed by Atahualpa's dreams, and the Incas' bewilderment in face of an alien culture symbolised by their inability to decipher the written message sent by Almagro. Demoralisation at the collapse of their world and helplessness in face of the new situation are reiterated in the farewell speeches of Atahualpa's entourage as he prepares to go to his death, and an impotent hatred of the conquerors is voiced in the curses heaped on Pizarro. Finally, a hunger for justice is expressed in the wish-fulfilling epilogue where the Spanish King wreaks punishment on the murderer of the Inca.

---

[4] *Tragedia del fin de Atawallpa*, ed. Jesús Lara (Cochabamba, Bolivia: Imprenta Universitaria, 1957). The Spanish version is to be found in the more accessible *Teatro indoamericano colonial*, ed. José Cid Pérez and Dolores Martí de Cid (Madrid: Aguilar, 1973) and *Teatro quechua colonial*, ed. Teodoro L. Meneses (Edubanco, 1983).

The Indians' reaction to the traumatic experience of the Conquest is also expressed in another work dating from the early years of the colonial period. One of the most moving of all Quechua poems, the "Elegía al poderoso Inca Atahualpa" is a lament on the execution of Atahualpa in 1533.[5] The Inca's death is lamented not merely as the demise of a monarch but as the extinction of the world order, and the earth and the elements are represented as sharing the people's anguished shock. There is bitterness in the reference to the rapaciousness and treachery of the Spanish conquistadores, but, above all, the poem voices the desolation that henceforth was to become a dominant note of Quechua verse, the bewildered desolation of a whole race suddenly orphaned in a world turned cruelly alien:

> Bajo extraño imperio, aglomerados los martirios,
> y destruidos;
> perplejos, extraviados, negada la memoria,
> solos;
> muerta la sombra que protege,
> sin tener a quién o a dónde volver,
> estamos delirando.   (Arguedas)

> (Under foreign rule, torment piled upon torment,
> destroyed;
> perplexed, astray, denied memory,
> alone;
> dead the shade that protects,
> with no one or nowhere to turn to,
> we are raving.)

Significantly, the first book printed in Peru was a catechism of 1584 translated into Quechua and Aymara for the instruction of the Indians.[6] For while on the one hand the Spanish authorities took measures to stamp out ideologically dangerous manifestations of Inca culture, on the other the clergy adopted Quechua as a medium for catechising the natives. As part of that process pre-Columbian religious verse was superseded by a corpus of Catholic hymns, some of which seem to have been modelled on the pattern of the former. Thus, "Eternamente viviente Dios" invokes the Christian God in terms which echo Inca hymns to Viracocha:

---

[5] See Mercedes López-Baralt, "The Quechua Elegy to the All-powerful Inka Atawallpa: A Literary Rendition of the Inkarrí Myth", *Latin American Indian Literatures*, 4 (1980), 79-85.

[6] For a facsimile of the original edition, see *Doctrina Christiana y Catecismo para instrucción de los Indios, y de las demás personas que han de ser enseñadas en nuestra santa fe*, ed. José Tamayo Herrera, 2 vols. (Petroperú, 1984).

Tú, el hacedor del Sol, el embellecedor de la Luna,
Tú, que cuentas las infinitas estrellas,
Tú, que cuentas todo lo contable y existente,
llamándolos por su nombre [...]

Las aves que vuelan, los peces que en el agua viven con
        hirviente apariencia,
los cuadrúpedos, los seres reptantes,
los insectos, las hormigas, todo ser viviente,
que sean dijiste.   (Arguedas)

(You, maker of the Sun, embellisher of the Moon,
You, who reckon the infinite stars,
You, who reckon all things that exist and are countable,
calling them by their name [...]

The birds that fly, the fish that live in the water in swarming
        abundance,
the quadrupeds, the reptiles,
the insects, the ants, every living being,
"Let them be," you said.)

Others introduce a new note into Quechua culture, for while pre-Columbian religious verse tended to be characterised by an attitude of joyful gratitude towards the Creator, the colonial hymns often evoke a wrathful God and preach the sombre doctrine that happiness can be attained only in the next world and only by resignation to the miseries of this and absolute submission to the divine will:

El furor del Señor Todopoderoso
desde ahora que se aplaque, como el agua al fuego,
que todos los pecados
con lágrimas de sangre se laven [...]

¡Llora, oh hombre! ¡Sufre, oh corazón!
Y llorando así, en ondas, en ondas,
quebranta a Jesús, gana su amor,
acércate suavemente a sus brazos.

Y ya sostenido por tu Señor,
a El y sólo a El entrégate.
Para el implorante, para el cargado de culpas que clama,
El, únicamente El, es la dicha y la alegría.   (Arguedas)

(Henceforth let the fury of the All-powerful Lord
be placated, as water placates fire,
let all sins
be washed with tears of blood [...]

Weep, oh man! Suffer, oh heart!
And thus weeping, in waves, in waves,
mollify Jesus, win his love,
softly approach his arms.

And now sustained by your Lord,
surrender to Him and to Him alone.
For the suppliant, for the guilt-laden sinner who cries out,
He, and only He, is happiness and joy.)

The theatre, which in Inca times had served as a medium of ideological indoctrination, was likewise taken over by the missionaries as an instrument for propagating the Christian faith. However, its main cultivators appear not to have been Spaniards but natives assimilated into the new order. Three such plays have been conserved.[7] The earliest, believed to belong to the first half of the seventeenth century, is *El pobre más rico* by Gabriel Centeno de Osma, a Cuzqueñan priest about whom nothing is known. Similar in theme but markedly inferior in quality is *Usca Paucar*, the work of an unidentified eighteenth-century author. The third, *El hijo pródigo*, was written in the seventeenth century by the famous Juan de Espinosa Medrano (1632-88), nicknamed El Lunarejo. A native whose exceptional talents and erudition elevated him to a position of relative status in colonial society, the latter was appointed professor of Arts in the Seminary of San Antonio in Cuzco at the age of eighteen and later became canon of Cuzco Cathedral. His masterly command of the Spanish language earned him a wide reputation as a preacher and his sermons were published under the title of *La novena maravilla* in 1695. He was also an accomplished writer and among his various activities translated Virgil into Quechua, wrote plays in Spanish as well as in his native tongue and penned a celebrated defence of the poetics of Góngora. More than any other colonial figure, Espinosa Medrano was the epitome of the cultivated Indian who, while retaining a pride in his race, had become almost totally identified with the culture of the conquerors.

The date of *El pobre más rico* has proved impossible to establish with any precision, for, if, on the one hand, the fact that the characters retain customs from Inca times would seem to place it fairly early in the seventeenth century, on the other, certain parallels with *El mágico prodigioso* and *La vida es sueño* point to the influence of Calderón de la Barca, which would make it much later. The play is a three-act *auto sacramental* (eucharistic play) set in Cuzco. Its protagonist, Yauri Ttitu, an impoverished member of the Inca nobility driven by despair to thoughts of suicide, signs over his soul to the Devil when the latter tempts him with promises of riches and

---

[7] All three plays are included in the above-cited *Teatro indoamericano colonial* and *Teatro quechua colonial*.

earthly happiness. He becomes the lover of a young widow, Cori Umiña, but money and pleasure fail to bring him contentment and he remains weary of life, though he himself is unable to understand the cause of his disenchantment. At the end of five years he leaves his beloved to surrender himself to the Devil as agreed, but voices urge him to go instead to the church of Our Lady of Belén and he is guided there by a guardian angel. Meanwhile, the abandoned Cori Umiña has succumbed to despair and the Devil endeavours to snatch her soul by tempting her to commit suicide, but she, too, is summoned to the church by the strange voices. There the final show-down takes place. The Devil comes claiming the souls of the lovers, but he is left thwarted when they call on the Virgin for protection. The pair swear to love each other in the Christian faith and the play ends with the homily that true riches are those of the spirit.

Centeno de Osma was obviously familiar with Spanish literature and, though the play conserves certain features of pre-Columbian drama such as the use of a chorus and traditional Quechua images, it is essentially a work in the tradition of the Golden-Age theatre with distinctively Indian characters. In the presentation of those characters it is much more sophisticated than the *Tragedia del fin de Atawallpa*, for not only are the protagonists portrayed as figures of considerable complexity but even minor figures such as the lovers' servants stand as personalities in their own right. But, above all, the author's aim is to propagate Christian ideas and to win over the Indian nobility and people to the new religion, and the message put across is that the source of their woes is not so much material poverty arising out of the loss of past glories as ignorance of the God of the Church in whom true happiness lies.

Written later and directed at a different generation, *El hijo pródigo* has few points of contact with the Inca past either in form or in subject-matter. As the title indicates, it is a version of the biblical parable of the prodigal son and, apart from the language and certain images, motives and allusions, it is very much a mystery play in the Spanish tradition based on allegory of the type favoured by Calderón and other Baroque dramatists. However, Espinosa Medrano's dramatic craft goes beyond that of a mere imitator and the symbolism is developed with estimable mastery. The protagonist, 'Hurin Saya, is the Christian who turns his back on God in his desire for excitement and pleasure. He is accompanied on his wanderings by his servant, the *gracioso* (fool) U'ku, who symbolises the body, and by a young man, Huaina 'Kari, who is the embodiment of youth.

He meets up with Mundo, a man of the world whose two servants represent the fleeting nature of earthly pleasures, and a trio of courtesans headed by Aicha, the incarnation of voluptuousness. Between them they drain him of his wealth and his health and then repudiate him and he is deserted, too, by Huaina 'Kari, the companion of his youth. In his abjectness he becomes the servant of the Devil, tending the swine of sin, till at last he heeds the word of God personified in Diospa Simin and returns symbolically to the bosom of the Lord. The play thus preaches the vanity of the things of the world in contrast to the comfort and fulfilment to be found in the Christian religion.

However, by far the most interesting of Quechua dramas is *Ollantay*, a play reputed to have been performed in front of Tupac Amaru during his abortive rebellion in 1780. In 1816 a manuscript copy was discovered among the papers of a Father Antonio Valdez and since then other copies have come to light.[8] The action of the play spans a period of eleven years at the end of the reign of Pachacutec (1438-71) and the beginning of that of his son, Tupac Yupanqui (1471-93). Ollantay, an illustrious warrior chief from the region of Antisuyo and the Empire's foremost general, has a secret love affair with Cusi-Coyllur, though Inca law forbids unions between members of the royal family and ordinary mortals. Driven on by his passion, he comes out into the open and asks the Inca for his daughter in marriage. The Emperor refuses and orders his daughter to be imprisoned in the convent of the Virgins of the Sun, where some months later she gives birth to a daughter. Thinking her dead and fearing arrest, Ollantay withdraws into the mountains, where he rises in rebellion and repulses the troops sent to subjugate him, but shortly after Tupac Yupanqui's accession to the throne, his fortress is captured by treachery and he is brought before the new monarch. Instead of executing him, however, the Inca magnanimously spares his life, restores his honours and privileges and even appoints him to the office of governor of Antisuyo, and when he learns of Cusi-Coyllur's imprisonment, he sets her free and gives the lovers his permission to marry.

According to one school of thought, *Ollantay* is a pre-Columbian

[8] For the most accessible Spanish version and general introduction, see *Teatro indio precolombino*, ed. José Cid Pérez and Dolores Martí de Cid (Madrid: Aguilar, 1964). For a bilingual edition see *Ollantay*, ed. Guillermo Ugarte Chamorro (CAP, 1973). For an English version see *Ollanta*, trans. Clements R. Markham (London: Trubner and Co., 1871). To date there is no critical edition listing variants found in the several manuscripts.

work which was written down after the Conquest and which, despite adulterations, has remained substantially intact. However, it is more likely that it is the creation of a colonial writer, perhaps Father Valdez himself, who has reworked a traditional epic theme, possibly on the basis of some lost Inca drama. Certainly the technical and stylistic influence of Spanish Golden-Age theatre is evident in the division of the play into scenes, in the presence of a *gracioso* (fool) and in the preciosity of much of the diction, and the themes of rebellion and thwarted love give it a distinctly pre-romantic flavour. The happy ending accords ill with what is known of the ruthlessly authoritarian Inca regime and is at variance with other versions of the Ollantay legend, where the rebel is mercilessly punished for his offences against the state. Above all, in view of the propagandistic character of official Inca literature, it is difficult to conceive that a pre-Columbian work would not only give expression to discontent against the state, but actually show rebellion rewarded.[9]

Given that *Ollantay* is first mentioned in the context of the rebellion headed by Tupac Amaru, it may be regarded as a manifestation of a resurgence of Indian "nationalism". In that sense it may usefully be compared to Macpherson's *Ossian* in that it appeals to native pride not only by evoking the heroes of a glorious past but by itself appearing to be a product of that past. The theme of rebellion is central to the play, of course. Though Ollantay's motivation is largely personal, his relationship with Cusi-Coyllur represents a challenge to Inca hegemony and he comes to embody the discontent of the subject peoples of Tahuantinsuyo and, thus, to stand as a symbol of revolt against oppressive overlords. There is a subversive message, too, in the defeat of the rebellion, for Tupac Yupanqui's magnanimity presents an image of benevolent Inca rule which contrasts with the Indians' experience of their Spanish masters (who were to show no such clemency to Tupac Amaru). It is hardly surprising, therefore, that the play was banned by the Spanish authorities.

Because of the play's uniqueness, its merits have sometimes been

[9] For an interesting, if dubious, interpretation of the play as a pre-Columbian work, see Gordon Brotherston, "*Ollanta* and the Literature of Tahuantinsuyu", *Bulletin of the Society for Latin American Studies*, 31 (1979), 95-111. Brotherston argues that since Ollantay's rebellion is shown to be doomed from the outset and the favours heaped on him are not conceded as a right but bestowed by the magnanimity of the Inca, the play conforms to the traditional didacticism of official Inca literature in that it simultaneously asserts the authority of the state and exalts the benevolence of the regime. Such an interpretation ignores that the audience is invited to sympathise with the rebel.

exaggerated and, though it might well be argued that it cannot properly be judged by European literary standards, it must be admitted that it has certain inherent weaknesses. In particular, the episodic development of the plot is accompanied by a sketchiness of characterisation. Thus, Pachacutec's motives are never explored, so that, coming as it does in the wake of effusive declarations of affection and without any sign of inner turmoil, his harsh treatment of his daughter and his favourite appears completely arbitrary. Similarly, in the case of Ollantay himself, he switches from the role of impassioned lover to that of political rebel so completely that he apparently gives no further thought to his lost love until the end of the play, and the indomitable hero of the earlier episodes displays remarkable submissiveness when brought before the Inca. Yet if characterisation suffers through its subordination to plot, the emotions and states of mind of the characters are often effectively and powerfully conveyed, particularly in the scenes expressing the anguish of the separated lovers. The play also contains three *harawis* (lyrics of a sad, nostalgic nature) which are amongst the most beautiful love songs in the Quechua language. The second, built around one of the classic motifs of Quechua poetry, presents the parted lovers as a pair of doves, one of whom has strayed and been lost:

Dos queridas palomitas
tienen pesar, se entristecen,
gimen, lloran, palidecen,
con un inmenso dolor.
Ambas fueron sepultadas
de la nieve en la espesura,
y cuya guarida dura
era un árbol sin verdor.

(Two loving doves
sadly grieve,
wanly they moan and weep
with immense sorrow.
Both were buried
in the thick snow,
and a tree without verdure
was their hard refuge.

La una a su compañera
perdióla súbitamente,
un día que fue inocente
su mantención a buscar.
Al pedregal va tras ella
pero la encuentra ya muerta
empezando, al verla yerta,
triste en su lengua a cantar:

One unexpectedly
lost its mate
one day it innocently
went in search of food.
It sought it out among the rocks
but found it already dead
and seeing it lying there,
sadly it began to sing:

—¡Corazón! ¿dó están tus ojos?
¿Y ese tu pecho amoroso?
¿Dó tu corazón virtuoso
que con ternura me amó?
¿Y dónde tus dulces labios

"Sweetheart, where are your eyes,
and where your loving breast?
Where your virtuous heart
that loved me so tenderly?
And where are your sweet lips

que adivinaban mis penas?	that divined my sorrows?
Sufriré, pues, mil condenas;	I shall suffer a thousand woes,
ya mi dicha concluyó.	now that my happiness is ended."
Y la infeliz palomita	And the unhappy dove
de peña en peña vagaba	wandered from crag to crag
y nada la consolaba	and nothing consoled it
ni calmaba su pesar:	or calmed its grief:
vuela al valle preguntando	it flew to the valley
por su amor a una paloma;	and asked about its love;
mas la muerte ya se asoma	but already death was looming
y la quiere arrebatar.	eager to snatch it.
Al despuntar de la aurora	When morning dawned
en el puro azul del cielo,	in the pure blue of the heavens,
por último desconsuelo	in its final affliction
se estremece con dolor ...	it trembled with pain ...
Y bamboleando su cuerpo	Its body reeled
cae ya desfallecida,	and faintly it fell to the ground,
y al morir enternecida	and as it died, it uttered
¡suspira llena de amor!	a tender sigh of love!)

(José Sebastián Barranca, in Ugarte Chamorro)

After the Conquest the Spanish presence was concentrated mainly in the coastal capital of Lima and a few provincial urban centres, and, despite domination, the Quechua-speaking peoples of the Andean regions retained a culture of their own which continued to flourish throughout the colonial and republican periods down into modern times, although modified by contact with European culture and the process of miscegenation. This takes the form of a vigorous folklore in which, alongside traditional fables and tales, love lyrics and agricultural songs, we find songs and stories which convey the vision of a subject people.[10] Some songs express the so-called "soledad cósmica" (cosmic solitude) of the Indian, a despairing sense of utter abandonment on a now alien world:

> Nací cual planta en el desierto
> brota sin savia y sin calor,
> y en cuyo tallo, cadáver yerto,
> brota ese germen que no da flor.
>
> Pues fue mi estrella como ninguna
> porque ni en sombras las vi lucir.
> Amargo llanto regó mi cuna;
> sólo he nacido para sufrir.

[10] For a collection of songs and stories in English translation, see Ruth Stephan, ed., *The Singing Mountaineers. Songs and Tales of the Quechua People* (Austin: Univ. of Texas Press, 1957).

Junto conmigo mi triste historia
en el olvido terminará,
y ni mi nombre, ni mi memoria
nadie en el mundo recordará.   (Razzeto)

(I was born like a plant in the desert
that sprouts without sap and without warmth,
and in whose inert corpse of a stem
buds the germ that yields no flower.

For my star was like no other
since not even in darkness did I see them shine.
Bitter tears watered my cradle;
I have been born only to suffer.

Together with me my sad story
will end in oblivion,
and no one in this world will recall
my name or my memory.)

Others, like "El gamonal", denounce the exploitation the Indian has suffered at the hands of the white man:

¡Qué pobre la llama!	(How wretched the llama!
con ser tan humilde	Being so humble,
ni de comer le dan;	they don't even feed him
y siempre la cargan.	and they always burden him down.
Al puma le tiemblan,	The puma makes them tremble,
siendo orgulloso y ladrón	and being arrogant and thieving,
donde quiere come,	he eats where he wants
y nadie lo molesta [. . .]	and no one interferes with him [. . .]
Cuando el amo vino	When the master came
nada, nada trajo,	he brought nothing, absolutely nothing,
y en nuestras tierras	and on our lands
para siempre se acomodó.	he settled himself down for ever.)
(Razzeto)	

However, the very fact that Quechua culture has endured and continues to flourish indicates that the downtrodden Indians have retained a strong sense of their own separate identity and a belief in themselves as a race. Not all of their oral literature is sombre and defeatist in tone. "El sueño del pongo", for example, wields humour as a weapon to strike back at the hated oppressor.[11] This tale relates the dream of a humiliated Indian serf in which he and his master die at the same time and are transported to heaven to stand naked before

---

[11] For the most accessible version of this story see José María Arguedas, *Relatos completos* (Buenos Aires: Losada, 1974). For an English version, see "The *Pongo*'s Dream", trans. Luis Harss, *Review* (New York), 25/26 (1980), 50-52.

the Lord. There, in apparent keeping with their respective stations, the master is smeared in honey and the serf in excrement, but in a surprise climax the tables are turned when the pair are ordered to lick each other clean. By looking forward to a day of judgement when the white oppressor will receive his come-uppance, albeit in the after-life, the story points to a major theme of Quechua folk literature which is most clearly expressed in the myth of Inkarrí.[12] Though there are various versions of this myth, they have certain common features which embody the Indians' vision of the history and destiny of their race. Inkarrí (the name is a contraction of the Quechua word "Inka" and the Spanish "rey") is the historical figure of the last Inca, recalled not merely as a ruler but as a divine being representing the principle of order. He was defeated by his Spanish enemy and, as in the *Tragedia del fin de Atawallpa*, decapitated in symbolic representation of the cataclysm which destroyed the order of the world and introduced an era of chaos, but in the underworld where he lies buried he is reconstructing himself and will one day re-emerge on the face of the earth to restore order. Underlying the world-view of the Quechua people, it would seem, is a millenarian outlook which regards white domination as a temporary disruption of the order of the world and looks forward to the time when they will come into their own again.

In the contemporary period attempts to create a written Quechua literature have been made by cultivated artists like Andrés Alencastre (Kilku Waraka) and José María Arguedas, both of whom have published poetry in that language.[13] Their verses give expression to Andean man's traditional values — his community spirit, his identification with the earth, his reverent sense of the magic of the natural world —, but they contain, too, a strong socio-political ingredient, reflecting not only the views and hopes of the authors but also a growing political awareness on the part of the Indian. Both aspects come together in Alencastre's poem "Illimani", where the ancient mountain god is invoked to arouse his people and to inspire them to create a new future by imposing their traditional values on the world:

---

[12] See *Ideología mesiánica del mundo andino*, ed. Juan M. Ossio A. (Ignacio Prado Pastor, 1973).

[13] See Andrés Alencastre (Kilku Waraka), *Taki Parwa* (Cuzco: Garcilaso, 1955); *Taki Ruru* (Cuzco: Univ. Nac. de San Antonio Abad, 1964)/José María Arguedas, *Katatay* (INC, 1972). See also Antonio Cornejo Polar, "On Arguedas' Poetry", *Review* (New York), 25/26 (1980), 32-35.

Illimani, poderoso dios, señor de todos los dioses montañas,
que tu nieve brille
en nuestras cabezas pensantes,
que tu nieve descienda
de nuestro corazón a lo profundo
para que podamos ser hombres unidos
de vidas hermosas que no ofendan [...]
Illimani, poderoso dios,
fortaleza de nieve de huesos de piedra,
en tu cumbre ha de erguirse
el hombre elegido, el excelso, que renovará el mundo.

(Illimani, powerful god, lord of all the mountain gods,
let your snow shine
on our thinking heads,
let your snow descend
to the depths of our hearts
that we may be men united
leading fine lives that do not offend [...]
Illimani, powerful god,
stronghold of snow of bones of stone,
on your peak there will rise up
the exalted one, the man chosen to renovate the world.)

Arguedas' "A nuestro padre creador Tupac Amaru" evokes a whole people on the march and envisages mass migration from the sierra to Lima as leading not so much to the break-up of traditional Andean culture as to a transformation of Peruvian society under the impact of the influx of Quechua-speaking migrants and their values:

Al inmenso pueblo de los señores hemos llegado y lo estamos removiendo [...] Somos miles de millares, aquí, ahora. Estamos juntos; nos hemos congregado pueblo por pueblo, nombre por nombre, y estamos apretando a esta inmensa ciudad que nos odiaba, que nos despreciaba como a excremento de caballos. Hemos de convertirla en pueblo de hombres que entonen los himnos de las cuatro regiones de nuestro mundo, en ciudad feliz, donde cada hombre trabaje, en inmenso pueblo que no odie y sea limpio, como la nieve de los dioses montañas donde la pestilencia del mal no llega jamás ...

(To the immense village of the lords and masters we have come and we are stirring it up [...] We are thousands upon thousands, here, now. We are together; we have congregated, village by village, individual by individual, and we are pressing down on this enormous city that hated us, despising us as if we were the dung of horses. We shall change it into a village of men who chant the hymns of the four regions of our world, into a happy city where every man labours, into a huge village free of hate, clean as the snow of the mountain gods which the pestilence of evil never reaches ...)

The work of these poets not only illustrates the potential of the Quechua language as a medium of literary expression, but can be interpreted as a vindication of a traditional rural culture and an assertion of its continuing validity in the modern world. Yet one can hardly speak of a Quechua literary renaissance, for writers in that language are few and the dilemma facing them is highlighted by the case of Arguedas, who chose to write the vast bulk of his work in Spanish. The sad fact is that, given widespread illiteracy among Quechua-speakers and ignorance of Quechua in cultivated circles, the artist who opts to express himself in Quechua is condemned to be an author virtually without a public.

Since the Conquest, then, Quechua literature has been marginal in that it has existed only in oral form as folklore or in written form in works accessible only to a limited few. Clearly, though, it is important in its own right as a manifestation of one of Peru's two main cultural traditions. It is relevant, too, to a study of Peruvian literature in Spanish. For not only do the Indian and his world constitute a central theme of that literature, but Quechua literary forms, such as the *harawi*, have passed into Spanish and Quechua values and attitudes have left their mark on Spanish-speaking writers such as Vallejo. Just as Quechua culture has been modified by contact with Spanish culture, so it in its turn has exercised a significant influence on the latter, and, indeed, given the social changes which have taken place in Peru in recent years and particularly the massive influx of Quechua-speakers into the capital, it may well be that in the future that influence will increase rather than diminish.

CHAPTER 2

THE COLONIAL EXPERIENCE

Part I
Prose and Drama in the Colonial Period

The earliest literature produced by the Spaniards in the New World were log-books and reports chronicling the epic of the Discovery and Conquest. In Peru eye-witness accounts of Pizarro's campaigns were compiled by his secretaries for despatch to the King. Francisco de Jerez recorded events up to the execution of Atahualpa in his *Verdadera relación de la conquista del Perú*, published in Seville in 1534,[1] while Pedro Sancho de Hoz continued the story up to the capture of Cuzco and the pacification of the surrounding provinces in his *Relación de la conquista del Perú*, completed in 1534 and published in Italian translation around 1550.[2] Both works are written in the plain, succinct, unvarnished style of official reports. While Sancho does include an interesting description of Cuzco and information about the country and the natives, the writers' main concern is to render account of the military events. Written under Pizarro's orders, the reports are clearly intended to present him in a favourable light to the King and to forestall any criticism of his

[1] See *Crónicas de la conquista del Perú*, ed. Julio Le Riverend (Mexico City: Editorial Nueva España, 1946), pp. 29-124; *Reports on the Discovery of Peru*, trans. Sir Clements Markham (London: Hakluyt Soc., 1872; reprinted Chur [Switzerland] Plata Publishing, 197?), pp. 1-109.

[2] Pedro Sancho de Hoz, *Relación de la conquista del Perú* (Madrid: Porrúa Turanzas, 1962); *An Account of the Conquest of Peru*, trans. Philip Ainsworth Means (New York: Cortés Soc., 1917; reprinted New York: Kraus, 1969).

actions. Thus the execution of Atahualpa is represented as a just punishment for the Inca's treachery and as being welcomed by the natives, who hated him for his oppression. The Spaniards' right to dominion over the Indians is taken for granted, justified by the conversion of the heathens to Christianity and by the wealth and glory won for Spain. Above all, both writers exude pride in the achievements of the conquistadores. For them no other people in history ever realised exploits to match those of the Spaniards in America.

The first writer to undertake a comprehensive history of Spain's new colony was Pedro Cieza de León (c. 1520-54), who campaigned in Colombia for some twelve years before moving to Peru in 1547 to join the loyalist forces in the struggle to suppress the rebellion of Gonzalo Pizarro. There Pedro de la Gasca, the King's representative, appointed him official chronicler of the civil wars and he was afforded facilities which enabled him to pursue the history which he had begun writing in 1541. His *Crónica del Perú* was planned in four parts: a geographical description of the country; a description of Inca civilisation; an account of the Conquest; and an account of the civil wars comprising five books. Remarkably, given his premature death, he succeeded in completing all but the last two books of the fourth part. The first part was published in 1553, the remainder remaining unpublished until modern times.[3] What distinguishes the *Crónica del Perú* from the earlier reports is not only its comprehensiveness, but also the fact that, in keeping with the contemporary concept that history was a branch of letters, Cieza demonstrates a literary awareness, employing an austere, precise style that is aimed, above all, at clarity, order and propriety of expression.

Of greatest interest are the first two parts in that they represent the literary revelation of a new world. The first part, which has come to be known by the title of the whole, is based largely on Cieza's own observations on his travels in South America. Starting with a description of Panama, it moves southwards through the various

[3] Pedro Cieza de León, *Crónica del Perú. Primera Parte* (La Católica, 1984); translated as *Travels* by Sir Clements Markham (London: Hakluyt Soc., 1864); *El Señorío de los Incas* (Instituto de Estudios Peruanos, 1967); *Second Part of the Chronicle of Peru*, trans. Sir Clements Markham (London: Hakluyt Soc., 1883). For an abridged English version of the first two parts, see *The Incas of Pedro de Cieza de León*, trans. Harriet de Onís (Norman: Univ. of Oklahoma Press, 1959). The other texts are less accessible; for details see Francisco Esteve Barba, *Historiografía indiana* (Madrid: Gredos, 1964), pp. 417-19. On Cieza see Waldemar Espinoza Soriano, *Pedro Cieza de León* (BHP XII, 1964); Pedro R. León, *Algunas observaciones sobre Pedro Cieza de León y la "Crónica del Perú"* (Madrid: Gredos, 1973).

provinces and settlements to Peru and covers the whole of that country as far as Chile and Tucumán, giving detailed descriptions of the towns founded by the Spaniards, the customs of the various Indian peoples, and the landscape, climate, flora and fauna and economic resources of each region. The second part, *El Señorío de los Incas*, consists of a survey of the pre-Inca period, a description of Inca institutions, and a reign-by-reign political history of the Empire ending with Atahualpa's defeat of Huascar. The book is the product of on-the-spot research. On his travels Cieza questioned the local Indians for information, he conducted a series of interviews with the Inca nobility of Cuzco, and he consulted veteran conquistadores for corroborating evidence. This information is sifted and assessed critically and when faced with conflicting versions of the facts he either declines to commit himself or opts for the one that seems the most likely. Yet on the whole he seems to have been convinced that the essential truth of the past was contained in the version preserved by the Inca nobility. Hence what he transmits to us is to all intents and purposes the official Inca version of the imperial past, a selective and doctored history designed to enhance the power and prestige of the ruling élite. Thus, while he seems to intuit the existence of developed civilisations prior to the Incas, he repeats the legend which presents the latter as enlightened civilisers of barbaric savages and attributes to them all cultural achievements.

Like his predecessors Cieza takes pride in the exploits of the Spaniards in the New World and does not question their right to dominion over it. Holding a typically providentialist view of history, he sees the hand of God behind the Conquest, whose object was to rescue the natives from the clutches of the Devil and to bring them to knowledge of the true faith. What distinguishes him is that he was not merely a soldier or a fortune-seeker, but a man with a lively intellectual curiosity and a genuine interest in the country and its people, whom he treats with sympathy and understanding. He recognises and is unstinting in his praise of the Incas' cultural and political achievements. He applauds their social organisation and the order and stability of their political system; he does not hesitate to rank them above the Romans for their skill at road building; he confesses that he has seen nothing in Spain to rival their architectural feats and he censures his compatriots for thoughtlessly destroying Inca buildings or allowing them to fall into disrepair. Sharing the religious attitudes of the times, he is intolerant of the religion of the natives and dismisses it as heathen idolatry, but he is free of many of the prejudices of his contemporaries and defends the Indians against unjust criticism. Thus, while he admits that human sacrifice was practised, he argues that it was much less common than was claimed by the Spaniards, who used it as a pretext to justify and cover up their own abuses.

Indeed, despite his pride in the Conquest, he is highly critical of the conduct of his fellow countrymen in Peru and recognises that the imperial record of the Incas was superior to that of the Spaniards. He laments the violence and cruelty with which the latter oppressed the natives and devastated a once well-ordered kingdom, and he argues that the civil wars and the violent deaths which befell many of the conquistadores were a divine punishment for their betrayal of their mission in the New World. Here Cieza's Christian humanitarianism and his admiration for the Incas coincide with the political ideals he shared with La Gasca. For in depicting the wise imperialism of the Incas, he is holding up a model for his ideal of a stable, efficient, well-run Christian colony which would repair the disorder and chaos of the immediate post-Conquest period.

Other Spanish writers, too numerous to mention here, were to make their contribution to the historiography of Peru.[4] Not all were as sympathetic and open-minded as Cieza in their treatment of native civilisation. Indeed, during the administration of Francisco de Toledo (1569-81) the Viceroy, as part of his policy to consolidate the authority of the Spanish Crown, initiated an ideological revision of the pre-Columbian past designed to discredit the Incas, and several historians dutifully trotted out the official line. Thus, for example, Pedro Sarmiento de Gamboa (c. 1530-c. 1592) was commissioned to write a history which would conclusively prove Spain's right to dominion in Peru and in 1572 he produced his *Historia Indica* depicting the Incas as cruel tyrants and usurpers who could not be regarded as the legitimate rulers of the country.[5]

It was to counter such ideas that a native Peruvian, the self-styled Inca Garcilaso de la Vega (1539-1616), undertook to write the history of his country.[6] The son of an Inca princess and a conquistador of

---

[4] For a fuller survey see Esteve Barba, *Historiografía indiana*, pp. 385-515; Philip Ainsworth Means, *Biblioteca Andina* (Detroit: Blaine Ethridge, 1973).

[5] As it turned out, that particular work remained unpublished until modern times. See Pedro Sarmiento de Gamboa, *Historia de los Incas*, 3rd ed. (Buenos Aires: Emecé, 1947); *History of the Incas*, trans. Sir Clements Markham (London: Hakluyt Soc., 1907).

[6] El Inca Garcilaso de la Vega, *La Florida del Inca* (Mexico City: Fondo de Cultura Económica, 1956); *The Florida of the Inca*, trans. John Grier Varner and Jeanette

noble lineage, he spent his childhood and adolescence in his native Cuzco, but in 1560 he went to Spain never to return. In many ways he was a typical Renaissance man of letters and his first work, published in 1590, was a translation into Spanish of the *Dialoghi d'amore* of the neo-Platonist León Hebreo. This was followed in 1605 by *La Florida del Inca*, an account of Hernando de Soto's expedition to Florida. His major work, the *Comentarios reales*, sets out to give an account of the birth, growth and fall of the Inca empire. The first part, published in 1609, deals with the history of the Incas and their civilisation from their legendary origins to the arrival of the white man. The second part, which appeared posthumously in 1617 under the title *Historia general del Perú*, is the story of Spanish domination, ending with the accomplishments of Toledo, who effectively put an end to dreams of an Inca restoration with the execution of Tupac Amaru, the last pretender to the Inca throne.

The *Comentarios reales* draws heavily on earlier historical writings, but Garcilaso's stated purpose is to amplify the accounts of Spanish historians and to correct their errors of interpretation. He could claim to be in a particularly favoured position to do so, for in his early years he had absorbed information about the Inca past from his maternal relatives and he was able to make use of his contacts in Cuzco to gather further material. However, what makes the *Comentarios* different from previous histories is not just its more intimate knowledge of the Inca world, but that it is also an artistic creation. The new humanist historiography of the Renaissance period rejected the medieval chronicles' mechanical exposition of

---

Johnson Varner (Austin: Univ. of Texas Press, 1951); *Comentarios reales*, 2 vols. (Caracas: Biblioteca Ayacucho, 1976); *Historia general del Perú*, 3 vols. (Buenos Aires: Emecé, 1944); *Royal Commentaries of the Incas and General History of Peru*, trans. Harold V. Livermore, 2 vols. (Austin and London: Univ. of Texas Press, 1966). On Garcilaso see Luis A. Arocena, *El Inca Garcilaso y el humanismo renacentista* (Buenos Aires: Centro de Profesores Diplomados de Enseñanza Secundaria, 1949); Juan Bautista Avalle Arce, *El Inca Garcilaso en sus "Comentarios"* (Madrid: Gredos, 1964); Donald G. Castanien, *El Inca Garcilaso de la Vega* (New York: Twayne, 1969); José Durand, *El Inca Garcilaso, clásico de América* (Mexico City: SepSetentas, 1976); Susana Jákfalvi-Leiva, *Traducción, escritura y violencia colonizadora: un estudio de la obra del Inca Garcilaso* (New York: Maxwell School of Citizenship and Public Affairs, Syracuse Univ., 1984); Aurelio Miró Quesada, *El Inca Garcilaso* (Madrid: Instituto de Cultura Hispánica, 1948); id., *Nuevos estudios sobre el Inca Garcilaso de la Vega* (Banco de Crédito del Perú, 1955); Raúl Porras Barrenechea, *El Inca Garcilaso en Montilla, 1561-1614* (San Marcos, 1955); Enrique Pupo-Walker, *Historia, creación y profecía en los textos del Inca Garcilaso de la Vega* (Madrid: Porrúa Turanzas, 1982); Luis Alberto Ratto, *Garcilaso de la Vega* (BHP IV, 1964); Luis Alberto Sánchez, *Garcilaso Inca de la Vega. Primer criollo* (Santiago de Chile: Ercilla, 1939); Luis E. Valcárcel, *Garcilaso el Inca* (Imprenta del Museo Nacional, 1939); John Grier Varner, *El Inca: The Life and Times of Garcilaso de la Vega* (Austin: Univ. of Texas Press, 1968).

information in favour of an imaginative interpretation of the past and required that the historical discourse should have the same qualities as prose fiction. An all-round man of letters, Garcilaso was greatly concerned with questions of style and it would seem that his earlier writings, meritorious though they are in their own right, were a kind of literary apprenticeship in which he prepared himself for what he regarded as his life's work. Written in a simple but polished prose, the *Comentarios* employs a wide range of literary devices, notably intercalated passages of imaginative narrative, which serve to enliven the text and to communicate on levels other than the merely documentary. Moreover, over and above the history it relates, the *Comentarios* creates its own reality. Few historians have been as personally involved with their subject-matter as Garcilaso, but it is not simply a question of his mingling history and autobiography. For the Inca writing was a kind of ontological endeavour, an attempt to define and establish his cultural identity both as an individual and, since he perceived himself in symbolic terms, as a representative of American man, and the literary text is the space where that drama is worked out. Hence, on the one hand, Garcilaso's work is obsessively self-referential, continually reflecting on and questioning itself, while, on the other, it maintains an intertextual dialogue with a corpus of texts representing a cultural tradition with which it lives in conflictive dependence as it struggles to assert a distinct identity.

Despite the fact that he was of noble blood on both sides and a cultivated man of letters, Garcilaso approaches his task with a diffidence of manner which is perhaps symptomatic of the sense of inferiority he experienced as a mestizo in Spanish society. He humbly presents himself as a modest Indian with no claims to learning, the title defines his book as a mere commentary on the work of others as if a history or a chronicle were too pretentious for such as him, and he seems compelled constantly to apologise for and to justify his forwardness in differing with established Spanish historians. None-theless, the book exudes pride in his Indian ancestry and is clearly intended as a vindication of him and his kind. It has to be seen against a background of personal humiliations and the political climate of the times. His parents' union was never legalised and his father subsequently married a Spanish woman, leaving him bastardised, and in Spain he never received the official or social recognition which he felt to be his due. Meanwhile, in Peru Viceroy Toledo had embarked on a policy of breaking down the last vestiges of Inca power and of eradicating the prestige and influence of the surviving Inca caste. In describing the glories of a great empire destroyed by the Spaniards, Garcilaso is not rejecting his Spanish heritage, for he himself was brought up as the son of a Spanish nobleman and he writes from the point of view of a man who has adopted the superior values of Western Christendom. Rather his concern is to break down the prejudices of the Spanish public and to dispel the image of the Indians as a barbaric race, to demonstrate the merits of native Americans in the hope of improving the status and fortunes of his mother's people and of the new breed of mestizos to which he himself belonged. Nor can he really be seen as a spokesman for the Indian masses, for his bias is essentially aristocratic and it is above all his own caste that he is vindicating. Nonetheless, by implication he is speaking for his compatriots as a whole, and the *Comentarios* has come to be regarded by Peruvians as the first expression of their national literature.

Far from being an objective historian, Garcilaso offers a highly idealised account of the Inca past which helped to create in Europe the legend of the noble savage. The splendours of the Inca empire are repeatedly compared to those of Greece and Rome. The conquests of the Incas are represented as a benevolent imperialism which brought the blessings of civilisation to primitive savages, and their paternal government is seen to have established social harmony, provided for the material well-being of all their subjects and accomplished remarkable achievements in the arts and sciences. The one serious flaw in their culture, in fact, was their religious beliefs but even these were evolving towards a monotheism which made them ripe for conversion to the Christian faith. Garcilaso, in short, depicts a near-perfect society which links his work to the utopian literature of the period. Such idealisation can be explained partly by the fact that, like Cieza, he is repeating in essence the official history of the Incas, a version which, as has already been observed, reshaped events to enhance the prestige of the ruling élite. That version came to him, too, in the form of an oral tradition refined by retelling from generation to generation, and it had been transmitted to him in the main by people whose memories would have been coloured by nostalgia for a lost past. Moreover, since Garcilaso's aim was the justification of his mother's race, he was obviously concerned to present the Incas in as favourable a light as possible. Furthermore, it is important to bear in mind that he was writing in accordance with Renaissance concepts which viewed history as a creative art concerned with essential truths rather than scientific fact and seeking to extract from the study of the past guiding principles applicable to the present. The value of the *Comentarios*, therefore, lies not so much in its strict historical accuracy as in its account of how the Incas saw themselves and in the way it uses history.

The *Comentarios*, in fact, may be interpreted not only as a vindication of the Incas, but also as a commentary on the society of the Spanish conquerors. Garcilaso does not condemn the Conquest. Its justification being the gift of the Gospel, he sees it as the culmination of a long process whereby the Indians were brought to salvation, and he recognises, too, that the Spaniards bestowed other benefits on the New World. Nonetheless, the dominant tone of nostalgia for vanished glories suggests the underlying view that the Conquest has left the Indians in a sorry state and that, paradoxically, it has ruined Peru while saving it. Typically, there is relatively little direct criticism of the Spaniards, except as regards acts of vandalism and failure to fulfil the obligation to teach the word of God. However, as in all utopian literature, the description of an ideal society implies an imperfect society with which it is being contrasted and the depiction of Inca civilisation tacitly invites the reader to draw comparisons with the Spanish system of government. It would seem, indeed, that Garcilaso's real intentions in the *Comentarios* went far beyond his stated aim of correcting the errors of Spanish historians, for in effect he is holding up the Inca state as a model of a successfully run empire and implying that the Spanish regime leaves much to be desired.

It is the *Historia general* which reveals what Garcilaso found most distasteful in the Spanish regime. His version of the early decades of the colony is less reliable than other accounts, but it has the particular interest that he lived through the troubled years that followed the Conquest and knew many of the leading characters of the period. In contrast to the picture of order and stability that characterises the *Comentarios*, this is a story of conflict, recounting the struggle of the Spaniards against the Indians, the power-struggles amongst the conquistadores themselves and the struggle of the Crown's representatives to impose its authority on the rebellious settlers. Though in many ways it is an unedifying tale of greed, disloyalty and violence, Garcilaso takes great pride in the exploits of his father's people and he is full of extravagant admiration for Pizarro and the other early conquistadores. His antipathy, in fact, is reserved for a later generation of reformers and bureaucrats. He sided with the settlers in their opposition to the New Laws which provided for the gradual extinction of the *encomienda*[7] and was unremittingly hostile to Toledo for his policy of removing Inca influence from the life of the colony. It appears, therefore, that his real ideal was a colonial system ruled by an aristocratic élite who would continue the paternalism of the Inca period.

If Garcilaso shows us Peru's history through the eyes of a mestizo, the viewpoint of the indigenous population finds its best expression in his contemporary, Felipe Guaman Poma de Ayala (c. 1535-c. 1615). Guaman Poma was one of a trio of native chroniclers who adopted the doubly alien medium of written Spanish to communicate to their conquerors the vision of the vanquished.[8] A minor provincial chief, he compiled his *El primer nueva corónica y buen gobierno* over a period of about thirty years, completing it around 1613 and adding some amendments in 1615.[9] The manuscript was subsequently sent to Philip III, only to languish in oblivion until modern times.

[7] The *encomienda* was a system whereby settlers were given control of and responsibility for groups of Indians.

[8] See Rolena Adorno, ed., *From Oral to Written Expression: Native Andean Chronicles of the Early Colonial Period* (New York: Maxwell School of Citizenship and Public Affairs, Syracuse Univ., 1982); Raquel Chang-Rodríguez, "Sobre los cronistas indígenas del Perú y los comienzos de una escritura hispanoamericana", *RevIb*, 120/121 (1982),533-48.

[9] Felipe Guaman Poma de Ayala, *El primer nueva corónica y buen gobierno*, edición crítica de John V. Murra y Rolena Adorno, 3 vols. (Mexico City: Siglo XXI, 1980); *Nueva coronica y buen gobierno*, modernised and punctuated, ed. Franklin Pease, 2 vols. (Caracas: Biblioteca Ayacucho, 1980); *La nueva crónica y buen gobierno*, trans. into modern Spanish by Luis Bustíos Gálvez, 3 vols. (Editorial Cultura, 1956-66); *Letter to a King*, arranged, edited and trans. Christopher Dilke (London: George Allen & Unwin, 1978). See also Rolena Adorno, "The Language of History in Guaman Poma's *Nueva corónica y buen gobierno*", in *From Oral to Written Expression*, pp. 109-73; id., "Bartolomé de las Casas y Domingo de Santo Tomás en la obra de Felipe Waman Puma", *RevIb*, 120/121 (1982), 673-79; id., "The *Nueva corónica y buen gobierno* of Don Felipe Guamán Poma de Ayala: A Lost Chapter in the History of Latin-American Letters", Diss. Cornell 1974 (Univ. Microfilms, 1983); Federico Kauffmann, *Guaman Poma de Ayala* (BHP IV, 1964); Mercedes López-Baralt, "La crónica de Indias como texto cultural: articulación de los códigos icónico y lingüístico en los dibujos de la *Nueva coronica* de Guaman Poma", *RevIb*, 120/121 (1982), 461-531; Guillermo Ludeña de la Vega, *La obra del cronista indio Felipe Guamán Poma de Ayala* (Nueva Educación, 1975); id., *Vocabulario y quechua utilizado por el cronista indio Felipe Guamán Poma de Ayala* (Perúgraph, 1982); Richard N. Luxton, "The Inca *quipus* and Guaman Poma de Ayala's *First New Chronicle and Good Government*", *Iberoamerikanisches Archiv*, 5 (1979), 315-41; Juan M. Ossio, "Guaman Poma: *Nueva corónica* o carta al rey. Un intento de aproximación a las categorías del pensamiento andino", in *Ideología mesiánica del mundo andino* (Ignacio Prado Pastor, 1973), pp. 153-213; id., "Guaman Poma y la historiografía indianista de los siglos XVI y XVII", *Historia y Cultura*, 10 (1976-77), 181-206; Abraham Padilla Bendezú, *Huaman Poma: el indio cronista dibujante* (Mexico City: Fondo de Cultura Económica, 1979); Raúl Porras Barrenechea, *El cronista indio Guaman Poma de Ayala* (Edición auspiciada por Grace y Cía, 1948); José Varallanos, *Guaman Poma de Ayala* (G. Herrera, 1979); George L. Urioste, "The Spanish and Quechua Voices of Waman Puma", *Review* (New York), 28 (1981), 16-19.

To some extent Guaman Poma follows a chronological scheme tracing the history of the early Indian peoples, the reigns of the various Incas, the events of the Conquest and the rule of the Spanish viceroys. However, his main method is to build up piece by piece an overall picture of pre-Columbian and colonial societies by describing the various sections of the social order and the principal features of social, political and economic organisation. By so doing, he has produced a work which is an invaluable source of information about both periods and particularly about indigenous culture and folklore and about the abuses suffered by the natives under Spanish rule.

The *Nueva corónica* represents an attempt by the Andean mind to come to terms with the trauma of the Conquest. While Guaman Poma adopts the medium of European historiography, his own cultural tradition was one which viewed history in cyclical terms and emphasised the enduring and archetypal character of human experience, and the perspective from which he writes is an essentially mythical one. Pre-Columbian Peru, as he depicts it, was a stable, ordered world in which everyone had his place in the social hierarchy and life followed the same unchanging pattern. Though he pays lip service to the principle of historical chronology by presenting biographical accounts of a long succession of Incas, what he is really giving us is a synchronic description of Andean society, for the historical individuals come across mainly as archetypal figures overseeing the continuation of the social order and embodying the enduring values of Andean civilisation. From that perspective the Conquest is a cosmic catastrophe which turned the world upside down and Guaman Poma's long catalogue of the evils of Spanish colonial rule shows order reduced to chaos. This new state of affairs is one which had no precedent in Andean experience and to make sense of it Guaman Poma rewrites history to fit it into a pattern he can reconcile with his Andean world-view. In effect he gives an apocryphal version of the Conquest in which he insists that the Indians peacefully accepted the Spanish invasion and not only never offered resistance but even helped to quell the conquistadores' rebellions against the Crown. By this means he converts the Conquest into a peaceful transfer of power, so that it merely repeats a pattern already traced in his account of ancient Andean experience. This reconstruction of events did not alter the real situation, of course, but it did afford him a recognisable framework within which to operate and it enabled him to direct himself to the new "Inca" to intercede with him to restore order to the Andean world.

Guaman Poma writes as a spokesman for the Andean people, though it should be emphasised that his allegiance is to the Indian race as a whole rather than to the Inca caste, for, as a descendant of the Yarovilcas, he does not hesitate to categorise the Incas as usurpers nor to portray them at times in an unflattering light. The *Nueva corónica*, in fact, is conceived not only as history but also as a letter to the King and, to lend weight to his advocacy, Guaman Poma inflates his own genealogy, attributing to himself the hereditary status of Viceroy of the Inca. Towards the end of the book its purpose is made clear in an imagined dialogue in which he answers the monarch's questions about the state of Peru and offers advice for its good government, calling for reform through stricter supervision of clergy and royal administrators. He addresses himself, too, to the Spanish settlers themselves, urging them in moralising tones to mend their ways and to conduct themselves like true Christians. However, he appears to have had little faith in a change of heart on the part of the Spaniards or that partial reforms would assure the welfare of the Indians, and he also proposes a much more radical solution. This is nothing less than a total segregation of the two races, with the Spaniards withdrawing from Indian territories and the natives being ruled by their "natural" leaders, the local chieftains. Such a solution would have restored the traditional Andean order under the Spanish Crown, and in his attempt to convince the monarch Guaman Poma appeals to his self-interest as well as to his sense of justice, justifying it on the grounds of greater efficiency and profitability.

Guaman Poma's political ideal, then, was to restore hegemony in the Andes to the indigenous population and he is less concerned with strict historical accuracy than with using history as a vehicle of persuasion. Though his thought patterns are Andean, he was obviously familiar with the work of Spanish historians and to advance his case he exploits the liberal philosophy of conquest expounded by Bartolomé de las Casas and others. Indeed, his rewriting of Andean history is to be understood partly in the light of that philosophy's definition of a just war. Not only does his version of the Conquest show the Indians offering no resistance but he claims that Christianity had reached Peru long before the arrival of the Spaniards. In this way he is able to argue that the conquistadores had no just cause to wage war on the Indians and to deny their right to authority over the lands they have occupied and the natives they have subjugated, and so to demonstrate that it is the Indians who are the legitimate owners of the country under the Crown.

The *Nueva corónica* is not an easy book to read, for by normal literary standards it is very poorly written. It is a long, unwieldy work, tediously repetitious both in its individual sections and in its overall structure, and not only is the Spanish defective in grammar and spelling but it often fails to make sense and it is liberally sprinkled with phrases in Quechua. What has to be understood, of course, is that Guaman Poma was writing from within his own cultural tradition and expressing himself in a language that was not his own. Internal evidence in the form of interpolated Quechua texts suggests that he wrote competently in his own language and most of the anomalies of grammar and spelling found in his Spanish can be attributed to interference by his mother tongue. Likewise he uses Quechua when he can find no Spanish equivalent and many of his apparently incomprehensible statements are due to the fact that he has plumped for the wrong equivalent in Spanish. Similarly, the book's repetitiveness stems partly from its being constructed on an Andean organising principle of recurrent symmetrical patterns and partly from the fact that it transfers to the written page the indigenous tradition of prolix oral narration. However, be that as it may, the *Nueva corónica* presents difficulties for the reader and, while Guaman Poma had recourse as a weapon of self-defence to what he perceived to be the Europeans' instrument of civilisation and domination, he seems to have distrusted his own ability to communicate through writing. For the text is accompanied by some 456 pictorial illustrations which constitute a visual history of Peru from pre-Inca times to the author's own day. Though modelled to some extent on European evangelising literature, this visual art is, above all, part of Guaman Poma's own cultural heritage and, rather than serve as a mere adjunct to the text, the pictures constitute the core of his work, for they communicate more eloquently than his 800-odd pages of prose and it is through them that he imposes his views on the reader. Moreover, the pictures function not only on a mimetic level but convey a symbolic meaning through an Andean spatial code. Guaman Poma creates a perfect model of the Andean universe in a symbolic map of the world and his pictures of pre-Columbian times reflect its positional values while those of the colonial period contradict them, so that through fragmentation and subversion of the original design he shows how colonisation turns order into chaos.[10] In the end, therefore, Guaman Poma communicates his

[10] See Adorno, "The Language of History ...".

message largely through the medium of his own cultural tradition. That message fell on deaf ears, of course, and in any case Spanish settlement was too far advanced by 1615 for it to be feasible to turn the clock back as he proposed. Nonetheless, the *Nueva corónica* is more than a rich source of information about the Peruvian past and an invaluable insight into the indigenous mentality. Though a record of defeat, it shows that native resistance did not end on the battlefield. Guaman Poma not only uses history to speak up for his people and to demand redress of their grievances but he reformulates their traditional values in a new vehicle of communication and interprets new experiences in traditional modes. In that sense the *Nueva corónica* is a monument of native resistance to domination by an alien culture.

While the colonial period was marked by a proliferation of histories and chronicles, prose fiction was a genre that never got off the ground, and it was not until the publication of Fernández de Lizardi's *El Periquillo Sarniento* in Mexico in 1816 that Spanish America could claim its first novel. Conditions in the colonies, in fact, discouraged the development of the genre. Because of the scantiness of the population aspiring local writers had no prospect of reaching the kind of public accessible to their peninsular counterparts; among the colonies' small cultural élite fiction lacked the prestige of poetry; and they could not hope to compete with fashionable Spanish authors in a society that looked towards the mother country. Moreover, though printing was introduced into the New World at a fairly early stage — in Peru in 1584 —, the presses tended to restrict themselves largely to the production of devotional tracts and government publications. Furthermore, the Church exercised literary censorship and from 1531 onwards various royal edicts prohibited the printing and circulation of fictional histories and books of romances which dealt with profane and fabulous subjects as being harmful to the moral health and well-being of the natives. This did not prevent a considerable number of peninsular novels from finding their way into the colonies, but the denial of an outlet to local writers effectively stifled the production of imaginative fiction in the New World.

However, from the early chronicles onwards many non-fiction prose works contained imaginative elements and it has become commonplace in literary histories to regard certain later books of this type as embryonic novels. One such work is *El lazarillo de ciegos caminantes*, published in Lima in 1775 or 1776.[11] Its author was Alonso Carrió de la Vandera (c. 1715-83), a Spaniard who came to the New World as a young man and settled in Lima after a few years in Mexico. The book is an account of a journey he made between Buenos Aires and Lima in 1771 with the official mission of inspecting the postal stations on the route. Its narrator, however, is not Carrió himself but Calixto Bustamante Carlos Inca, alias Concolorcorvo, a Peruvian mestizo who accompanied him as secretary on part of the journey. Indeed, the original edition attributes the composition to Concolorcorvo and also assigns to the book an apocryphal place and date of publication (Gijón, 1773). It is believed that this subterfuge was employed by the author to shield himself against attacks which his criticisms of colonial government and society might have provoked. If such is the case, his caution seems excessive. For such criticisms as he makes are minor in character and mild in tone and a large part of the book is taken up by a lengthy justification of the Spaniards' treatment of the Indians in reply to accusations from abroad. Carrió appears in this book very much as the government functionary that he was, anxious to see improvement and progress within the colonial system which he staunchly upheld.

The title of the work, its journey form, the inclusion of a number of humorous anecdotes, and the roguish tone of the prologue in which the narrator alludes to his dubious origins in a manner reminiscent of Lazarillo de Tormes, have led many critics to see in it an affinity with the Spanish picaresque novel and to attribute to it novelistic features it is far from possessing. *El lazarillo de ciegos caminantes* is in fact very much the travel guide it purports to be, written in a practical and utilitarian spirit by a representative of the Enlightenment with the aim of improving his countrymen's knowledge of the world in which they lived. Judged as such, it is an outstanding work of its kind. Carrió was an acute observer and, in addition to offering the prospective traveller useful tips and warnings and descriptions of the towns and geography of the route, he provides such a wealth of information about social organisation and local trades, customs and

[11] Alonso Carrió de la Vandera (Concolorcorvo), *El lazarillo de ciegos caminantes*, ed. Emilio Carilla (Barcelona: Labor, 1973); *El Lazarillo: A Guide for Inexperienced Travellers between Buenos Aires and Lima*, trans. Walter D. Kline (Bloomington: Indiana Univ. Press, 1965). See also Emilio Carilla, *El libro de los misterios: El lazarillo de ciegos caminantes* (Madrid: Gredos, 1976); Enrique Pupo-Walker, "Notas para una caracterización formal de *El lazarillo de ciegos caminantes*", *RevIb*, 120/121 (1982), 647-70; Alan Soons, "An Idearium and its Literary Presentation in *El lazarillo de ciegos caminantes*", *Romanische Forschungen*, 91 (1979), 92-95.

human types that it has remained an important source book for twentieth-century scholars. Moreover, though it can be heavy going at times, it is written in a lively style which saves it from being a dry catalogue of information.

If *El lazarillo de ciegos caminantes* cannot properly be considered a forerunner of the novel, recent research has turned up finds which necessitate a revision of the long-held view that no works of fiction were produced in the colonial period. One such discovery is a manuscript which must now be regarded as the first piece of prose fiction composed in Peru, Juan de Mogrovejo de la Cerda's *La endiablada*, believed to have been written around 1626.[12] This short narrative reports a conversation between two demons overheard one night in the streets of Lima. One, Asmodeo, recently arrived from Spain, relates his adventures on the voyage to the New World. Among the people whose body he has inhabited are a hypocritical *beata* (pious woman) and a penniless nobleman with all the vices of his class. The second devil, Amonio, then answers questions put to him by the newcomer and on the basis of his own long experience informs him of the conditions he can expect to find in Lima. The society described by him is characterised by materialism, hypocrisy, vanity and bad faith: property is acquired by dishonest manoeuvres; merchants are greedy and crooked; priests traffic in religion; lawyers are a plague; doctors kill off the sick with their advice and prescriptions; backbiters and gossip-mongers abound, as do ostentatious and grasping women; the men-about-town sport extravagant fashions; everyone is out to get rich quick; and writers of talent are despised by the public. In such an environment, Amonio assures his new colleague, he will quickly reap an abundant harvest of souls for Satan. A rich vein of satirical humour runs through the work. Marriages of convenience are likened to slavery worse than that of the galleys, and the prohibition of the *tapada* (semi-veiled dress) is described as ushering in an age of disillusionment since women can no longer conceal their defects. In its social satire the book is reminiscent of much Spanish literature, but there is, too, an affinity with the verse satire that was a tradition in colonial Peru and the setting and social types and customs are distinctively American. Because of its shortness it can hardly be classified as a novel and a

---

[12] For the text and an introductory study see Raquel Chang-Rodríguez, "*La endiablada*, relato peruano inédito del siglo XVII", *RevIb*, 91 (1975), 273-85; also in id., ed., *Prosa hispanoamericana virreinal* (Barcelona: Borrás, 1978), pp. 43-76. See also Stasys Gostautas, "Un escritor picaresco del Perú virreinal: Juan Mogrovejo de la Cerda", *CIILI*, I, 327-41.

major weakness is that it lacks a sustained narrative, degenerating into a mere catalogue of social evils. Nonetheless, it remains an important work, demonstrating that prose fiction in Peru had much earlier origins than was hitherto believed and initiating a tradition of social criticism that was to be a feature of the later Peruvian novel.

Also recently come to light are a number of short novels of Pablo de Olavide (1725-1803).[13] Olavide presents the unusual case of a Peruvian who lived the greater part of his life in Europe. In the Spain of Charles III he held important offices and was a prominent member of the mother country's intellectual élite, but his liberal ideas brought him into conflict with the Inquisition and he was forced into exile, spending twenty years in France and Switzerland before being restored to favour in 1798. A representative figure of the Enlightenment, he wrote on political and philosophical matters and translated a number of French neo-classical dramas, but towards the end of his life he wrote works in prose and poetry in which he abjured many of his earlier ideas and embraced the Christian religion. Thanks to the investigative labours of Estuardo Núñez, it is now known that in his latter years he also penned seven novels which were published posthumously in New York in 1828, though one still remains to be located.

Olavide's novels are all set in Spain and the uniformity of style suggests that they were all written at the same period. They are exemplary novels in the tradition of Cervantes but written in the manner of the sentimental novel initiated by Richardson. Thus, *El incógnito o el fruto de la ambición*, the longest and most accomplished of them, narrates the idyllic existence of two peasant families whose happiness is made complete by the pure and innocent love of their respective offspring, Albano and Rufina. On the eve of the marriage Rufina's father fortuitously makes the acquaintance of a rich nobleman, who falls in love with her. To secure her hand the nobleman invites the father to Madrid, where he introduces him to a life of luxury, and the father, dazzled by the prospects promised by such an alliance, breaks off the marriage with Albano. Unfortunately his unhealthy ambition only succeeds in bringing tragedy on the two families, for Albano commits suicide in despair and Rufina dies of a broken heart.

---

[13] Pablo de Olavide, *Obras narrativas desconocidas*, ed. Estuardo Núñez (Biblioteca Nacional del Perú, 1971). See also Marcelin Defourneaux, *Pablo de Olavide ou l'Afrancesado* (Paris: Presses Universitaires de France, 1959); Guillermo Lohmann Villena, *Pablo de Olavide* (BHP XV, 1964); Estuardo Núñez, *El nuevo Olavide* (Villanueva, 1970).

Olavide's preoccupation in these novels is didactic rather than aesthetic, his concern being evident in the double titles — *Paulina o el amor desinteresado* (*Paulina or Disinterested Love*), *Marcelo o los peligros de la corte* (*Marcelo or the Dangers of the Capital*) etc. — and in the prologues, where the moral is underlined. After the fashion of Rousseau he preaches the virtues of the simple life, associated with the countryside, and denounces the vices of an urban society which corrupts man's natural goodness. Following the literary canons of the period, which saw the object of art as being to expound universal and exemplary truths, he attaches little importance to realism. The pastoral settings are stylised and idealised, the characters are archetypes of virtues or vices, and the narratives are full of fortuitous and improbable occurrences which heap disaster upon disaster or bring a chain of good fortune. Regrettably, though it is perhaps unfair to judge a writer by criteria other than his own, this all-pervading lack of realism constitutes a major artistic defect in these novels and condemns them to be merely works of historical interest as typical products of their age. In the end their main significance lies less in their intrinsic worth than in their uniqueness, since Olavide appears to have been the only writer in the Spanish language to cultivate the sentimental-didactic novel.

Mogrovejo and Olavide wrote their works long before the publication of *El Periquillo Sarniento*, yet it would be difficult to assign to either of them the honour of being the first Spanish American novelist. In the case of Mogrovejo, it is doubtful whether *La endiablada* is long enough to constitute a novel, and in that of Olavide, his long residence in Europe and the setting and subject-matter of his works call into question the validity of regarding him as a Peruvian rather than a Spanish writer. More important, the works of both men remained unpublished during the colonial period and if, as seems likely, they did not circulate in manuscript form, they cannot be said to have exercised an influence on the development of the genre. They are interesting in their own right and as reflections of their age and because they suggest a greater fictional activity than was formerly believed, but in terms of the literary history of Peru and Spanish America they must be considered marginal.

In contrast to the novel the theatre soon established itself in Peru as elsewhere in the New World.[14] Missionaries transplanted the

[14] See José Juan Arrom, *Historia del teatro hispanoamericano (Epoca colonial)* (Mexico City: Andrea, 1967); Guillermo Lohmann Villena, *El arte dramático en Lima durante el virreinato* (Madrid: Escuela de Estudios Hispanoamericanos de la Univ. de

theatrical traditions of medieval Spain to spread the Catholic faith among the natives and plays based on themes from the Bible and the lives of the saints were performed in the open air in the Indian languages. As in the mother country religious occasions such as the feast of Corpus Christi were celebrated with performances in Latin or Spanish of eucharistic plays (*autos sacramentales*) which took the form of allegories of aspects of dogma. It became the custom, too, to stage public performances of plays to celebrate major public occasions, such as the accession of the King or Viceroy, and to welcome visiting dignitaries of Church and State. As the sixteenth century advanced secular influences increasingly asserted themselves and the theatre became a popular form of entertainment. The works of the major Spanish dramatists of the Golden Age soon reached the colonies and were enthusiastically received. By the end of the century Lima had its first permanent playhouse and thereafter the capital always had at least one theatre.

In practice, though, Peru's colonial theatre produced very little in the way of home-grown drama and virtually nothing of any quality. Not surprisingly, the tendency of colonial society to look to Spain for its cultural standards was particularly evident in a public genre like the theatre and it was the imported drama of peninsular playwrights like Lope de Vega and Calderón which predominated. Constrained by the lack of a tradition of their own, by public taste and by the authorities' distrust of the theatre, local writers who ventured into drama took the Spanish masters as their models and, without the latter's talent or expertise, created only works that were at best second-rate. Moreover, in the course of the colonial period there was a growing tendency for theatre to become mere entertainment. In part this was a result of the decline of Spanish drama with the passing of the Golden Age, but it reflects, too, the conventional taste of colonial society and the courtly environment of the viceregal capital where plays were often the centre-piece of public festivities. Thus the most popular types of plays tended to be cloak-and-dagger intrigues (*comedias de capa y espada*) and later, from the end of the seventeenth century onwards, musical comedies (*zarzuelas*). The outcome was a theatre which was purely conventional, with stereotyped plots and stock characters, and which aimed at the spectacular through the use

---

Sevilla, 1945); Carlos Miguel Suárez Radillo, *El virreinato del Perú*, vol. II of *El teatro barroco hispanoamericano* (Madrid: Porrúa Turanzas, 1981); Rubén Vargas Ugarte, ed., *De nuestro antiguo teatro* (Compañía de Impresiones y Publicidad, 1943; Milla Batres, 1974).

of grandiloquent versification, elaborate stage effects, music and song.

This overall trend is illustrated by the major works of the one Peruvian colonial dramatist of any consequence, Pedro de Peralta Barnuevo (1664-1743).[15] A versatile artist as well as a scholar of encyclopaedic learning, Peralta was often pressed into service to provide entertainment for major public events. Thus, *Triunfos de amor y poder* (1711), a Greek mythological fable with musical accompaniment, was commissioned to celebrate the Spanish victory at Villaviciosa, while *Afectos vencen finezas* (1720), an involved intrigue of love and honour in the manner of Calderón, was staged to honour the birthday of the Viceroy. Apart from some skilful handling of verse, both plays have little to commend them, being entirely conventional in setting, theme, plot and characterisation. Of greater interest is *La Rodoguna*, whose dates of composition and first performance are unknown. An adaptation of Corneille's *Rodogune*, it is significant as an early example of French neo-classical influence and Peralta demonstrates considerable ingenuity in welding together French tragedy, traditional ingredients of the Spanish *comedia* and Italian operatic elements. Nonetheless, it remains, above all, a work of adaptation combining material from three different sources, and as such it exemplifies the essential conventionality of the theatre of the period.

The one area of the theatre affording an opportunity for local self-expression were the short pieces which accompanied the main performance. *Criollo* writers often supplied the skits which served to amuse the audience between acts or were preludes or after-pieces to the plays, and these brought a local flavour to the colonial theatre by their realistic and satirical portrayal of local types, customs and situations.[16] It was precisely in that area that Peralta produced his best work and it is on the basis of the short pieces which accompanied

---

[15] Pedro de Peralta Barnuevo, *Obras dramáticas*, ed. Irving A. Leonard (Santiago de Chile: Imprenta Universitaria, 1937); *Obras dramáticas cortas* (Biblioteca Universitaria, 1964). See also Raúl H. Castagnino, "El teatro menor de Pedro de Peralta Barnuevo", in *Escritores hispanoamericanos desde otros ángulos de simpatía* (Buenos Aires: Nova, 1971), pp. 103-15; Irving A. Leonard, "Pedro de Peralta: Peruvian Polygraph (1664-1743)", *Revista Hispánica Moderna*, 34 (1968), 690-99; Guillermo Lohmann Villena, *Pedro de Peralta* (BHP XV, 1964); Augusto Tamayo Vargas, "Obras menores en el teatro de Peralta", *Letras*, 72/73 (1964), 70-85.

[16] Among those who produced such skits was the poet Juan del Valle Caviedes (c. 1650-97). See *Obras de Don Juan del Valle y Caviedes*, ed. Rubén Vargas Ugarte (Studium, 1947), pp. 323-35. See also Julie Greer Johnson, "Three Dramatic Works by Juan del Valle y Caviedes", *Hispanic Journal*, III, 1 (1981), 59-69.

his longer plays that he may be regarded as the precursor, if not the founder, of Peru's national theatre. These pieces are still derivative in that they show European influence, notably that of Molière. However, Peralta successfully adapts foreign models to his own environment to depict local types with convincing realism and authentic colloquial speech. In them he reveals, too, an unsuspected side to his personality, satirising customs, fashions and institutions with which his other work seems to identify him, and employing a light-hearted, and at times even popular, tone which contrasts strongly with the ponderousness of his other writings.

Costumbrism is particularly evident in the skit (*baile*) accompanying *Afectos vencen finezas*, a piece reminiscent of the *comédie-ballet* cultivated by Molière. Mercury, the ambassador of Jove, celebrates a "festival of love" in which five beaux and five ladies participate and when each of the suitors has identified himself and expressed his preferences, Mercury forms five couples who sing the triumph of love. In the figures of the lovers Peralta presents types of the period with picaresque realism: a Quito man who prides himself on his astuteness as a deceiver; a wealthy miner for whom love is something to be bought; a blue-blooded gentleman from Pisco who goes wooing with patents of nobility; a narcissistic Limeñan who spends his life looking at himself in the mirror; and a cocky Don Juan from Madrid who boasts that he has no need of money to make amorous conquests. A similar piece is the interlude (*entremés*) of *La Rodoguna*, which has the added linguistic interest of reproducing colloquial pronunciation. More satirical are the after-pieces (*fines de fiesta*) of *Triunfos de amor y poder* and *Afectos vencen finezas*. Modelled on one of the *intermèdes* of Molière's *Le malade imaginaire*, the first is a parody of a medical student's qualifying examination conducted in jumbled Latin and represents a satire of the medical profession in the tradition of Caviedes[17] and of the method of university examination. The second, inspired by Molière's *Les femmes savantes*, is a satire of the vacuous extravagances which constituted the "good taste" of the period and of which his own poetry is a glaring example. Set in a literary salon, it parodies the pedantic discussions on fatuous topics which were the fashion of the age, the affected language in which they were conducted and the ornate contorsions of contemporary poetic style. These short pieces reveal a talent which circumstances unfortunately did not encourage

[17] See pp. 50-52.

Peralta to develop fully. Nonetheless, they broke ground which was later to be cultivated with some success and to be the basis of the national theatre created by Manuel Ascensio Segura.

Part II
Poetry in the Colonial Period

The earliest poetry in the Spanish language composed in Peru was essentially popular in character.[1] The conquistadores, for the most part men of humble background and unsophisticated literary tastes, brought with them from the mother country the popular culture of the times — ballads, *coplas* (short, witty pieces of verse), *villancicos* (carols), etc. It is recorded, for example, that on the occasion of a meeting between the feuding Almagro and Pizarro in 1537, a soldier warned the former of treachery planned against him by quoting the opening lines of a well-known ballad:

> Tiempo es, el caballero,
> tiempo es de andar de aquí ...

> ('Tis time, good sir knight,
> time to be gone from here ...)

From the outset the familiar form of the *copla* was adopted as a medium for passing comment on the events and personalities of the Conquest and the civil wars which followed.[2] The first, in fact, preceded the Spaniards' actual arrival on the mainland. This is the quatrain sent to the Governor of Panama in 1527 by the handful of unwilling conquistadores who remained with Pizarro on Gallo

---

[1] For a survey of colonial poetry see Luis Alberto Sánchez, *Los poetas de la Colonia y de la Revolución* (P.T.C.M., 1947; CAP, 1974). For selections of colonial poetry see Alejandro Romualdo and Sebastián Salazar Bondy, eds., *Antología general de la poesía peruana* (Librería Internacional del Perú, 1957); Raquel Chang-Rodríguez, ed., *Cancionero peruano del siglo XVII* (La Católica, 1983); Rubén Vargas Ugarte, ed., *Rosas de Oquendo y otros clásicos* (Clásicos peruanos vol. V, 1955).

[2] See Horacio H. Urteaga, "Los copleros de la Conquista", *Mercurio Peruano*, 31/37 (1921), 120-42.

Island while Almagro returned north for supplies and reinforcements. Urging the Governor to call off what seemed to them a hopeless enterprise, it expresses the soldiers' resentment against the two leaders of the expedition by stigmatising Almagro as a drover seeking fresh cattle for his partner to butcher:

> Pues, señor Gobernador,
> miradlo bien por entero,
> que allá va el Recogedor
> y acá queda el Carnicero.

> (Beware, Sir Governor, beware,
> look at the matter close and clear,
> for while the Drover journeys there,
> the cruel Butcher sits waiting here.)

A later example are the lines sung by royalist soldiers mocking the Archbishop of Lima and the judge Hernando de Santillán for the less than energetic manner in which they pursued the campaign against the rebel Francisco Hernández Girón in 1553-54:

> El uno jugar y el otro dormir,
> ¡Oh qué gentil!
> No comer y apercibir,
> ¡Oh qué gentil!
> El uno duerme y el otro juega.
> Así va la guerra.

> (The one plays and the other sleeps,
> Oh how genteel!
> To go unfed and not get paid,
> Oh how genteel!
> The one plays and the other sleeps.
> So goes the war.)

Likewise the major events of the age — the execution of Almagro, the rebellions of Francisco Hernández Girón and Lope de Aguirre — inspired ballads written from a partisan point of view, though only a mere handful has survived.[3] As in Spain these popular forms continued to thrive in later centuries alongside a more sophisticated poetry,[4] but in the early decades of the colonial period they were — understandably — the only type of verse produced in Peru, at a time

---

[3] See Emilia Romero, *El romance tradicional en el Perú* (Mexico City: Fondo de Cultura Económica, 1952).

[4] See Nicomedes Santa Cruz, ed., *La décima en el Perú* (INC, 1982); Rubén Vargas Ugarte, ed., *Nuestro romancero*, 2 vols. (Clásicos peruanos vol. IV, 1951; vol. VI, 1958).

when in the metropolis they had been superseded, in courtly circles at least, by an Italianate poetry. The conquistadores, in short, brought to Peru a poetry that was Spanish and, in terms of literary history, already outmoded. From the first days of the Conquest, therefore, Peruvian letters were colonial, not only in that they were an extension of Spanish culture, but also in that they lagged behind developments in the mother country. At the same time, however, this popular poetry could legitimately be regarded as marking the beginning of a local tradition in that the *coplas* initiated a current of satirical verse that was to be one of the main features of Peruvian poetry down through the centuries, reflecting discontent with the prevailing order in a rigidly stratified society.

Understandably, in view of the unsettled conditions of the times and the cultural limitations of the men involved, the Spanish conquest of the Inca Empire gave birth to no epic poem worthy of comparison with Alonso de Ercilla's *La Araucana*, which deals with the later pacification of Chile. However, some mention must be made of Juan de Miramontes y Zuázola's *Armas Antárticas*, one of a series of Spanish American historical epics in the Renaissance mould inspired by Ercilla's example and believed to have been written between 1608 and 1615.[5] As the title indicates, the poem celebrates Spanish feats of arms in the southern hemisphere in accomplishment of Spain's mission to spread and defend the true faith. The opening cantos narrate the events of the Conquest and the civil wars that followed, but the main body of the work is concerned with the defence of Spain's overseas empire against the attacks of English pirates led by Drake and Oxenham, campaigns in which Miramontes personally participated. As a story the poem is a "good read", conveying a sense of excitement and adventure and enlivened by love interest. It also panders to the European taste for the exotic, with a long seven-canto digression taking us back to Inca times and recounting an idyllic love affair with a tragic outcome. Unfortunately, the work suffers from most of the defects of its kind. Apart from some fine lyrical passages, it is for the most part little more than a rhymed chronicle-cum-adventure-story. It is also structurally weak. Miramontes seems to run out of steam at the end of the tenth canto and when, after the aforementioned digression, he returns to the theme of the struggle against English piracy, the remaining three

---

[5] Juan de Miramontes y Zuázola, *Armas Antárticas*, ed. Rodrigo Miró (Caracas: Biblioteca Ayacucho, 1972). Miramontes was a Basque who served as a soldier in Panama and later moved to Peru. His poem was not published until modern times.

cantos are lame and end the poem inconclusively.[6] Judged by the standard set by Ercilla's masterpiece, *Armas Antárticas* has to be deemed a very mediocre work.

As the colony settled down after the upheavals of the Conquest and the civil wars and Lima became established as the viceregal capital of South America, there emerged a small intellectual élite who cultivated a more sophisticated poetry.[7] Though the names of many colonial poets have come down to us, little of their verse has survived, but it is clear that poetry was held in high esteem as the obligatory pastime of the educated man, a trend that has remained characteristic of Peruvian letters even in modern times. Some of the poetry of the period is of remarkably high standard and even if the bulk of it was made up of a mass of mediocre verse composed by cultivated amateurs, that too has its positive side, for the main importance of these early colonial writers lies in the mere fact that they wrote at all and by so doing laid the foundations of the country's literature. What has to be admired in them is their devotion to the arts in what, after all, was still a frontier society, an attitude epitomised by two of the most accomplished poems of the early seventeenth century, both of them penned by anonymous poetesses. The "Discurso en loor de la poesía", published in 1608, is intellectual in character, being a long didactic poem in the Renaissance style elaborating a theory and history of the poetic genre.[8] By contrast, lyricism is the hallmark of the "Epístola a Belardo", published in 1621, a poetic epistle addressed to Lope de Vega by one of his Peruvian admirers under the name of Amarilis, in which, employing a style reminiscent of much of Lope's own verse, she expresses her admiration for the genius of the great Spanish poet and dramatist and declares herself platonically in love with him.[9] What the two poems share is a common love of poetry. The "Discurso", as the title indicates, is a eulogy of poetry, considered as the supreme gift of God, while the "Epístola" is an

[6] It is possible, of course, that the work was never completed or that the final cantos have been lost.

[7] By the early years of the seventeenth century there flourished in Lima a circle of poets known as the Academia Antártica. See Alberto Tauro, *Esquividad y gloria de la Academia Antártica* (Huascarán, 1948).

[8] The poem was published in the first part of Diego Mexía's *Parnaso Antártico* (see below, pp. 45-46). For the text and a critical study, see Antonio Cornejo Polar, *Discurso en loor de la poesía* (San Marcos, 1964); also in *Letras*, 68/69 (1962), 81-251.

[9] The "Epístola" was published in Lope's *La Filomena*. See Dora Bazán, "Algunas observaciones acerca de la 'Epístola a Belardo'", *Letras*, 66/67 (1961), 154-61; Irving A. Leonard, "More conjectures regarding the identity of Lope de Vega's 'Amarilis Indiana'", *Hispania*, 20 (1937), 113-20; Alberto Tauro, *Amarilis Indiana* (Ediciones Palabra, 1945).

expression of passionate enthusiasm for poetry in the form of a fan-letter to one of its foremost exponents.

As one would expect, in the early days most of these poets were Spaniards, but whatever the origins of the poets, colonial poetry developed as an offshoot of Spanish literature and evolved in its wake. This cultural identification with Spain is highlighted by the Indian polygraph, Juan de Espinosa Medrano (1632-88), who is known primarily for a prose work published in Lima in 1662, *Apologético en favor de D. Luis de Góngora y Argote, príncipe de los poetas líricos de España* ....[10] Here he reveals himself to be a stylist of the highest order and the book is rightly regarded as the best example of *culterano* prose-writing in Spanish America. Yet what is most striking is that, instead of speaking with a distinctively Peruvian voice, Espinosa Medrano seems to have felt impelled to prove to the world that a humble Indian was capable of matching the Europeans on their own ground, and his main claim to fame is an elegant and impassioned defence of the master of Spanish *culteranismo* written some thirty-odd years after the latter's death. His case demonstrates that colonial writers, even the most talented of the native-born, were operating within the cultural orbit of the mother country and took as their models the great Spanish writers of the age.

An initial phase of classical verse in the Renaissance manner, spanning roughly the period 1550-1630, produced at least two estimable minor poets in Diego Dávalos y Figueroa and Diego Mexía de Fernangil, both native Andalusians who settled in Peru. In 1602-03 Dávalos published in Lima his *Miscelánea Austral*, a collection of forty-four colloquies in prose and verse discoursing on a wide range of general topics such as love, poetry, fortune, death, as well as relating episodes of the poet's own life and describing the new world encountered by him in Peru.[11] Included in the *Miscelánea* are a number of fine poems in the Petrarchan style and it was accompanied by *Defensa de Damas*, a poetic vindication of women defending them against the charges conventionally levelled against them. For his part, Mexía was the author of *Parnaso Antártico*, of which the first

[10] See Juan de Espinosa Medrano, *Apologético*, ed. Augusto Tamayo Vargas (Caracas: Biblioteca Ayacucho, 1982), a volume that includes selections of his other work. See also Robert Jammes, "Juan de Espinosa Medrano et la poésie de Góngora", *Caravelle*, 7 (1966), 127-40; J. Agustín Tamayo Rodríguez, *Estudios sobre Juan de Espinosa Medrano (El Lunarejo)* (Studium, 1971).

[11] See Luis Jaime Cisneros, "Sobre literatura virreinal peruana (Asedios a Dávalos y Figueroa)", *Anuario de Estudios Americanos*, 12 (1955), 219-52; Alicia de Colombí-Monguió, *Petrarquismo peruano: Diego Dávalos y Figueroa y la poesía de la "Miscelánea Austral"* (London: Tamesis, 1985).

part, published in Seville in 1608, consists of translations of Ovid and the second, still unpublished, is made up mainly of two hundred sonnets on religious themes.[12]

That period also produced the first colonial poet of stature in Diego de Hojeda (c.1571-1615), whose *La Cristiada*, published in Seville in 1611, is considered to be the best sacred epic in the Spanish language.[13] Born in Seville, Hojeda went to Peru as a young man, joined the Dominican Order in 1591, and spent the remainder of his life in monasteries in Lima and the provinces. The poem, it seems, was begun in his youth and its composition stretched over many years. It is an account, in twelve cantos, of the Passion of Christ, from the Last Supper to the Crucifixion, but by the use of characteristic epic devices such as scenes of divine intervention and infernal interferences, prophecies and flashbacks, allegory, lengthy descriptions, speeches and lyrical passages, the familiar New Testament story is expanded and given fresh life and colour. Writing in an age when the imitation of established models was a prerequisite of every work of art, Hojeda draws heavily from the twin traditions of contemporary European culture: the literature of the classics, particularly Virgil's *Aeneid*, and the corpus of Christian religious literature, including works, like Vida's *Christias*, which adapted the example of Virgil to the life of Christ. This double source of inspiration is apparent in the presentation of Christ, who in a sense appears as a new Aeneas, the hero who transcends his humanity by overcoming the trials and tribulations imposed on him in accordance with the divine plan, but who is also God, imposing on himself the trial of playing out the role of propitiatory victim. But behind the poem is a preoccupation with spiritual renovation typical of the Counter-Reformation period and Hojeda is concerned, above all, to remind us of the significance of the Passion. The divine presence is manifest throughout, as when the Archangel Gabriel comforts Christ in the Garden of Olives, while Satan and his host also intervene in their attempts to thwart Christ's mission. Likewise, flashbacks to the miracles of Christ and the deeds of the heroes of the Old Testament and prophecies concerning the future founders of the

[12] See José de la Riva Agüero, "Diego de Mexía Fernangil y la Segunda Parte de su *Parnaso Antártico*", *Revista Histórica*, 21 (1954), 37-75.

[13] See Diego de Hojeda, *La Cristiada*, ed. Rafael Aguayo Spencer (P.T.C.M., 1947). See also Frank Pierce, "Diego de Hojeda", in *Historia de la literatura hispano-americana. Tomo 1: Epoca colonial*, ed. Luis Iñigo Madrigal (Madrid: Cátedra, 1982), pp. 225-34.

Church set the immediate events in a wider context. Unfortunately, at times Hojeda has a tendency to preach and the poem is marred by diffuse theological disquisitions and lapses into the prosaic. However, on the whole his vigorous style holds the reader's interest and the lapses are often offset by passages of impressively realistic description or lyrical beauty. Indeed, it is in his lyrical moments that Hojeda is seen at his best, as in the following passage from the seventh canto expressing his anguished reaction to the cruelty of Christ's suffering:

> Mas ¡ay, que baja por el aire apriesa
> Sobre el cuerpo de Cristo el fiero azote!
> ¡Ay, Dios, que llueven, cual de nube espesa,
> Golpes en el supremo Sacerdote!
> ¡Ay, Dios, que de sacar sangre no cesa,
> Para que toda en el dolor se agote
> La cruel disciplina! ¡Ay, Dios amado!
> ¡Ay, Jesús, por mis culpas azotado!
>
> Yo pequé, mi Señor, y tú padeces;
> Yo los delitos hice, y tú los pagas;
> Si yo los cometí, tú ¿qué mereces,
> Que así te ofenden con sangrientas llagas?
> Mas voluntario, tú, mi Dios, te ofreces;
> Tú del amor del hombre te embriagas;
> Y así, porque le sirva de disculpa,
> Quieres llevar la pena de su culpa.
>
> (But, oh, the fearful scourge whistles through the air
> To beat without mercy on Christ's holy body!
> Oh, dear God, like rain from a lowering cloud,
> Blows pour and pour on the Priest of priests!
> Oh, dear God, the cruel whip draws blood without cease,
> As though to drain it dry in the awful pain!
> Oh, God, my God, my beloved God!
> Oh, Jesus, scourged for my faults!
>
> I sinned, Lord, and it is you who suffers;
> The offences are mine, and it is you who pays;
> If I committed them, how do you deserve
> That they should offend you thus with bloody wounds?
> But you, my God, willingly offer yourself,
> Enraptured by your selfless love of man;
> And so, in order to exonerate him,
> You choose to bear the punishment for his guilt.)

After 1630 poetry was to become more and more conventional and formalistic, for, on the one hand, there was an increasing tendency to churn out occasional verse effusively commemorating births, marriages and deaths in the royal and viceroyal families, the arrival of a new viceroy to take office, and religious and secular festivals, while, on the other, the pervasive influence of the *culteranismo* of Luis de Góngora inspired a host of untalented imitators to pour forth a torrent of verse characterised by its extravagant conceits, distorted syntax and affected style.[14] Despite the nascent influence of French neo-classicism, this trend was to persist well into the eighteenth century in the poetry of Pedro José Bermúdez de la Torre and Pedro de Peralta Barnuevo.[15] This general pattern can be explained by the fact that this culture was not only that of a colonial ruling minority which looked to the metropolis for its standards, but one which was based mainly in Lima, where the viceregal court institutionalised the Spanish presence and encouraged a spirit of conformity. Thus, Raimundo Lazo aptly defines the literature of the period in the following terms: "La literatura peruana colonial es una versión académica o cortesana limeña, temáticamente peruana, de la literatura española, cuyo contenido ideológico y tipos estilísticos de expresión se empeña en remedar" (Peruvian colonial literature is a Limeñan academic or courtly version, thematically Peruvian, of Spanish literature, whose ideological content and stylistic modes of expression it strives to copy).[16]

Without doubt, the foremost and most attractive poet of colonial times was Juan del Valle Caviedes (c.1650-97). Very little is known of his life. Born in Andalusia, he emigrated to Peru at an early age. He appears to have had little formal education, but was obviously well versed in the Spanish literature of his day. It seems, too, that he tried his hand at mining, apparently without success, and that for much of his life he lived in humble circumstances, keeping a little shop in

[14] Typical of the period are the works of the Franciscan friar Juan de Ayllón and the Jesuit Rodrigo de Valdés. The former's *Poema*, published in Lima in 1630, deals with the festivities celebrating the canonisation of twenty-three Franciscan martyrs. The latter was the author of a *Poema heroyco hispano-latino panegírico de la fundación y grandezas ... de Lima*, published in Madrid in 1687.

[15] Pedro José Bermúdez de la Torre y Solier (1661-1746) and Pedro de Peralta Barnuevo (1664-1743) were among the great erudites of the age. As poets they were prolific writers of occasional and panegyric verse. In addition Bermúdez was the author of *Telémaco en la isla de Calipso*, an unpublished poem written in 1728 and which he himself described as an "amorous epic". See José M. Navarro Pascual, "Un poema narrativo de la Colonia: *Telémaco en la isla de Calipso*", *Humanidades*, 4 (1970-71), 213-39; Luis Alberto Sánchez, "*Telémaco en la isla de Calipso*. Poema inédito por el limeño D. Pedro José Bermúdez de la Torre", *Revista Histórica*, 8 (1925), 243-84. Peralta wrote religious poetry and a ponderous epic, *Lima Fundada o la Conquista del Perú*, which was published in Lima in 1732. See Gerardo Diego, "Poética y poesía de Don Pedro de Peralta Barnuevo", *Revista Histórica*, 27 (1964), 42-62.

[16] Raimundo Lazo, *Historia de la literatura hispanoamericana. El período colonial* (Mexico City: Porrúa, 1965), p. 78.

Lima. Manuscripts of his work circulated in his lifetime, but no editions were published until more than a hundred and fifty years after his death.[17]

A substantial part of Caviedes' output is made up of love lyrics and religious and philosophical poems. The former apparently belong to the early stage of his career and consist largely of fairly conventional laments, but the latter include compositions which compare favourably with the best Spanish poetry of the Golden Age. He seems to have undergone an evolution typical of many Hispanic poets of the period and philosophical poems like the sonnets "Lo que son riquezas del Perú" and "No hay cosa cierta en la vida" manifest a baroque disillusionment with the world, while in his religious verse he turns away from the world to God and expresses repentance for the sins of his life.

However, it is, above all, in his satirical verse that Caviedes reveals the best of his talent. The globe-trotting Mateo Rosas de Oquendo had already satirised Lima after a brief residence there at the end of the sixteenth century,[18] but Caviedes was the first poet systematically to hold up to ridicule a society more accustomed to poets who sang panegyrics in its praise. In this, of course, he is in a sense merely carrying on a Spanish tradition of verse satire and he has often been labelled, somewhat unfairly, as a Peruvian Quevedo. What makes him different is not just that the society being satirised is Peruvian instead of Spanish, but that Caviedes was in some respects intellectually in advance of his times. In spite of being largely self-educated — or perhaps because of it — he had a faith in reason which sets him apart from the vast majority of his contemporaries in the Hispanic world. That faith is asserted in the sonnet "Que no hay más felicidad en esta vida que el entendimiento" and is implicit in a poetic

[17] See Juan del Valle Caviedes, *Obras*, ed. Rubén Vargas Ugarte (Studium, 1947); *Obras completas*, ed. Daniel R. Reedy (Caracas: Biblioteca Ayacucho, 1984). See also Guiseppe Bellini, "Actualidad de Juan del Valle y Caviedes", *Caravelle*, 7 (1966), 153-64; Raúl Bueno Chávez, "Algunas formas del lenguaje satírico de Juan del Valle Caviedes", *Literatura de la Emancipación*, 349-55; María Leticia Cáceres, *La personalidad y obra de D. Juan del Valle y Caviedes* (Arequipa: El Sol, 1975); Luis Jaime Cisneros, *Juan del Valle Caviedes* (BHP XXXI, 1966); Eduardo Hopkins Rodríguez, "El desengaño en la poesía de Juan del Valle Caviedes", *RevCrit*, 2 (1975), 7-29; Glen L. Kolb, *Juan del Valle y Caviedes. A Study of the Life, Times and Poetry of a Spanish Colonial Satirist* (New London: Connecticut College Monographs No. 7, 1959); Daniel R. Reedy, *The Poetic Art of Juan del Valle Caviedes* (Chapel Hill: Univ. of North Carolina Press, 1964); Luis Fabio Xammar, "La poesía de Juan del Valle Caviedes en el Perú colonial", *RevIb*, 12 (1947), 75-91.

[18] Mateo Rosas de Oquendo was a Spanish poet and adventurer who travelled extensively in Spanish America in the last decades of the sixteenth century. His best known poem is a long "Sátira a las cosas que pasan en el Perú, año de 1598". See p. 41, n.1.

epistle addressed to the Mexican poetess Sor Juana Inés de la Cruz, where, confessing his lack of education, he claims with some pride that his knowledge of life has been derived from his use of his reason and his observation of the world and his fellow men:

> Sólo la razón ha sido
> doctísima Salamanca
> que entró dentro de mi ingenio,
> ya que él no ha entrado en sus aulas [...]
> en cada hombre tengo un libro
> en quien reparo enseñanza ...

> (Reason alone has been
> the scholarly university
> that came to lodge in my mind,
> since it ne'er entered lecture halls [...]
> in every man I have a book
> in which to study lessons ...)

A rational approach to life is evident, too, in poems like the sonnet "Que los temblores no son castigo de Dios" and the *romance* "Juicio del cometa". The first, inspired by the earthquake which devastated Lima in 1687, challenges the popular belief that the catastrophe was a manifestation of the wrath of God for the sins of men and explains it from a rational point of view. The second, inspired by the appearance of a comet in the Peruvian sky in 1681, refutes the view that it was sent by God to warn man of imminent misfortune and satirises the astrologers for their absurd efforts to predict the comet's effects. Caviedes' standpoint in his satirical verse, therefore, is that of a man of common sense appalled by the empty myths and false values of the society in which he lived. Reason, he complains elsewhere, is a quality held in little regard in Peru:

> ... anda en esta tierra
> lo racional muy perdido,
> muy ajado lo discreto.

> (... in this land of ours
> reason goes about lost
> and sense in a sorry state)

The principal object of his satire was the medical profession. The *Diente del Parnaso*, his only titled book,[19] is a collection of forty-

---

[19] María Leticia Cáceres ("El manuscrito de Ayacucho como fuente documental para el estudio de la obra literaria de Don Juan del Valle y Caviedes", *Literatura de la Emancipación*, 356-60) argues that the title is apocryphal.

seven poems directed against the doctors of Lima and is described by
the poet as a revelation of "deeds of ignorance brought to light by a
patient who miraculously escaped from the errors of the physicians".
Many of the poems single out well-known doctors of Lima by name
and subject them to virulent personal attacks, holding them up to
ridicule not only for their quackery but also for their physical
peculiarities:

> Ramírez con su rellena
> cara y potente cogote,
> siendo un pobre matalote
> presume que es Avicena.
> Y cuando me tiene llena
> la bóveda de despojos
> con sus prudentes arrojos,
> el vulgo sin experiencia
> dice que es pozo de ciencia,
> porque es gordo y trae anteojos.

> (Ramírez, with his bulging face
> and powerful neck of a bull,
> is only a miserable butcher
> who puts on airs of Avicenna.
> And when he has filled the house
> to the roof with scraps and leavings
> of his deeds of judicious dash,
> the common herd in their ignorance
> say that he's a fount of learning
> because he's fat and wears spectacles.)

Others are built around fictitious situations. Thus, in "Coloquio que
tuvo con la muerte un médico moribundo", a dying doctor
complains to Death that it is unfair of her to kill him since he brings
her a lot of business. It is in her interest to keep him alive, he argues,
for he will supply her with a steady supply of corpses:

> El mundo todo es testigo,
> Muerte de mi corazón,
> que no has tenido razón
> de portarte así conmigo.
> Repara que soy tu amigo,
> y que de tus tiros tuertos
> en mí tienes los aciertos;
> excúsame la partida,
> que por cada mes de la vida
> te daré treinta y un muertos.

> (All the world will bear me witness,

> beloved Death dear to my heart,
> that you are wrong and sadly mistaken
> to behave this cruel way with me.
> Consider that I am your friend,
> and that your shots that run astray
> are guided to the bull by me;
> spare me departure from this world,
> for for every month of life
> I will give you thirty-one corpses.)

In such poems Caviedes is out to make the reader laugh and he himself obviously relishes lambasting his victims, but, above all, he is concerned to expose pretentious quackery parading itself as science. For he had more confidence in the self-healing powers of the body than in the primitive medical science of his day and he saw that so-called science as a mystification employed by doctors for their own social advancement. Behind an appearance of knowledge his doctors are shown to be dangerous incompetents and parasites on the social body.

However, Caviedes' satire does not limit itself to doctors but embraces a whole range of social types. The tone of the society depicted in his verses would seem to be set by the viceregal court around which it revolves. For it is a society characterised by its pretensions to nobility and grandeur, epitomised by the "caballeros chanflones" (counterfeit nobles) who pass themselves off as aristocrats. In the series of poems entitled "Remedios para ser lo que quisieres" (Prescriptions for being whatever you wish), a kind of guide to social climbers, it is presented as a society based on appearances, where men and women put on masks of saintliness, learning or nobility in order to acquire status, offices and wealth. The prostitutes who are a frequent object of his satire exemplify the mercenary character of this essentially parasitical society, where success is achieved by pandering to those in positions of wealth and power. At bottom there is little difference between them and the social climbers, as is shown in the sonnet "Para labrarse fortuna en los palacios", which lists the qualifications necessary to gain favour in the palaces of government:

> Para hallar en Palacio estimaciones
> se ha de tener un poco de embustero,
> poco y medio de infame lisonjero,
> y dos pocos cabales de bufones.
>
> Tres pocos y un poquito de soplones
> y cuatro de alcahuetes recaderos,

cinco pocos y un mucho de parleros,
las obras censurando y las acciones.

Será un amén continuo a cuanto hablare
el Señor o el Virrey a quien sirviere
y cuanto más el tal disparatare

aplaudir con más fuerza se requiere,
y si con esta ganga continuare
en Palacio tendrá cuanto quisiere.

(To find grace and favour at Court
what's needed is a spoonful of the liar,
a spoonful and a half of vile flatterer,
and two generous spoonfuls of clown.

Add three spoonfuls and a smidgen of tattle-tale
and four more of pimping go-between,
then heap five big ones of gossip,
belittling others for their works and their actions.

You must be one continuous amen to every word
spoken by the Lord or Viceroy whom you serve
and the more nonsensically he prattles and prates

the more loudly should ring your applause,
and if you persist with this charade
you'll have at Court everything you'll ever wish.)

In such a society merit counts for nothing. Instead success depends on looking and acting the part and on having influential connections, as is made clear by the following lines addressed to the university professors of Lima:

me digan si el ascenso que han tenido
por sus méritos sólo han alcanzado,
porque el mérito a nadie ha graduado [...]
porque es ciencia el saber introducciones,
y el que mejor hiciere estas lecciones,
haciendo a la virtud notable agravio
es docto-necio e ignorante-sabio.

(tell me if the promotion you've had
was achieved by merit alone,
for merit never advanced anyone [...]
for learning is to know about introductions,
and the man who learns that lesson best,
offending virtue in the process,
is learned fool and ignorant sage.)

As for the poor, Caviedes was well aware of the humiliations to which they were subject and lists them in a short *romance* ironically entitled "Privilegios del pobre" (Privileges of the Poor). He appears, therefore, as a man of independent mind exposing the corruption behind the splendid façade of viceregal society.

A feature of Caviedes' satirical verse are mocking caricatures of his victims' physical deformities, which not only reflect the baroque preoccupation with the grotesque, but portray external ugliness as a manifestation of inner corruption. His poetry abounds, too, in witty plays on words conveying several levels of meaning with a single word or phrase in the manner of Spanish *conceptismo*. However, as one would expect of a writer who was the enemy of affectation, the style of these poems has none of the inflated and bombastic manner of his contemporaries. The form most commonly used is that of the popular *romance* (poem in the traditional ballad metre), the language is generally free of erudite vocabulary and characterised by the frequent use of Americanisms, and an earthy humour flouts the conventions of so-called good taste. Above all, his satirical writing has a freshness and vigour which contrast strongly with the artificiality of most literature of the day.

This satirical tradition was carried on in the following century by Esteban de Terralla Landa's *Lima por dentro y fuera* (1797),[20] one of the few formal verse satires in Spanish in the tradition of Juvenal. Terralla was an Andalusian who sought his fortune in Lima, apparently without success, and the poem expresses his disenchantment with the viceregal capital. It presents an interesting contrast with Bernardo de Balbuena's *Grandeza Mexicana* (1604). Like the latter, it is a poetic epistle, but while Balbuena extols the excellences of Mexico City, Terralla warns his correspondent of the woes that lie in store for him should he be foolish enough to set foot in Peru. Colonial Lima he depicts as a city of appearances without a solid mercantile base, where ostentatious splendour conceals an underlying reality of squalor and vice and the inhabitants are characterised by their vanity, presumption and parasitism. At first sight this view is close to that of Caviedes, but the key difference is that while the latter adapted to his new country and criticises it from the inside, Terralla is very much the unassimilated Spanish immigrant looking on from the outside, and though his comments on the economic order tempt one to classify him as a man of the Enlightenment, his response to

---

[20] See Esteban de Terralla Landa, *Lima por dentro y fuera*, ed. Alan Soons (Exeter: Univ. of Exeter Hispanic Texts XIX, 1978). See also Thomas C. Meehan and John T. Cull, "'El poeta de las adivinanzas': Esteban de Terralla y Landa", *RevCrit*, 19 (1984), 127-57.

colonial society is essentially an expression of personal disappointment and a tribal gut-reaction to a changing social situation. It is perhaps significant that stylistically the poem is a late Baroque work which relies heavily on puns and other conceptual conceits, for this outdated poetic manner is the vehicle for attitudes which are equally outdated. In effect, the contempt which Terralla voices for *criollos*, mestizos and Negroes betrays the prejudices, resentment and insecurity of a Spaniard who has come to the New World too late to enjoy the position of economic and social privilege which he regards as due to him because of his Peninsular origins, and who instead finds himself confronted by a colonial system on the verge of breaking up and by natives who are increasingly getting above themselves:

> verás pues cómo reputan
> por simples los forasteros
> porque no guardan sus usos
> y sus modos indiscretos [...]
> Verás con qué gran zurrapa
> hablan por detrás de ellos,
> pero en siendo cara a cara,
> ¡qué famosos lisonjeros! [...]
> verás pues cómo censuran
> cuando les dan los empleos,
> quejándose amargamente
> porque ven su desempeño,
> sin querer hacerse cargo
> que los obtienen por premio
> de su misma habilidad
> por ser inútiles ellos.

> (you'll see the way they deem strangers
> to be poor fools and simpletons
> because they don't share their customs
> nor their indiscreet behaviour [...]
> You'll see them speak behind their backs,
> smearing them with great piles of dirt,
> but how notoriously they flatter
> when they're together face to face! [...]
> you'll see them voice disapproval
> when it's they who are given posts,
> complaining loud and bitterly
> when they discharge their duties well,
> for they refuse to understand
> that they gain those posts on merit
> as due reward for their talent,
> while they are utterly useless.)

Lima por dentro y fuera is far from being a great poem and, indeed, it is rather loosely and carelessly written. Its main interest lies precisely in the light it throws on the tensions of a colonial society entering into crisis. Reflecting a changing climate in Peruvian society in the last decade of the eighteenth century, it indicates that the colonial period was drawing to a close and with it Peru's cultural identification with Spain.

Throughout the colonial period and particularly in the eighteenth century popular discontent frequently manifested itself in lampoons satirising the authorities, and a growing nationalist feeling was given literary expression in the neo-classical verse that proliferated in the years leading up to Independence and during the Independence period itself.[21] That nationalist spirit also pervades the work of the last major colonial poet, the Arequipeñan Mariano Melgar (1790-1815), whose social and political views are expressed directly in his civic poetry and allegorically in his fables.[22] Underlying Melgar's poetry is the discontent of the enlightened *criollo* at the exclusion of his class from participation in government and at Europe's economic exploitation of the New World:

> Oíd, patriotas sabios,
> Cuyas luces doblaban el tormento
> De mirar al talento
> Lleno siempre de agravios,
> Cuando debiera ser director justo
> Y apoyo y esplendor del trono augusto.
>
> Oye, mundo ilustrado,
> Que viste con escándalo a este mundo
> En tesores fecundo
> A ti sacrificado,
> Y recogiendo el oro americano,
> Te burlaste del preso y del tirano.
>
> (Hear me, learned patriots,
> Whose wisdom intensified the torment

---

[21] See Xavier Bacacorzo, "El pasquín y su trascendencia en la lucha libertaria nacional", *Literatura de la Emancipación*, 16-26; Luis Monguió, "La poesía y la Independencia, Perú 1808-1825", *Literatura de la Emancipación*, 7-15. For a collection of poetry of the Independence period, see Aurelio Miró Quesada, ed., *La poesía de la Emancipación*, vol. XXIV of *Colección Documental de la Independencia del Perú* (Comisión Nac. del Sesquicentenario de la Independencia del Perú, 1971).

[22] See Mariano Melgar, *Poesías completas* (Academia Peruana de la Lengua, 1971); *Antología poética* (CAP, 1975). On Melgar see Antonio Cornejo Polar's prologue to the above-mentioned anthology; Luis Jaime Cisneros, *Mariano Melgar* (BHP XXVII, 1965); Jorge Cornejo Polar, "Melgar y la Emancipación", *Literatura de la Emancipación*, 56-59.

Of beholding talent
Ever slighted and wronged,
When it should have been just director
And support and splendour of the august throne.

Hear me, enlightened world,
Who beheld the scandal of this world of ours,
Abundant in rich treasures,
Made sacrifice to you,
And as you harvested American gold,
Scoffed alike at tyrant and oppressed.)

At the same time, however, Melgar was one of the first to speak out
on behalf of the downtrodden Indian population of Peru. The fable
"El cantero y el asno" argues that if the Indians appear brutish it is a
consequence of the treatment meted out to them, for, as he says
elsewhere, they are no more than serfs in their own land:

Oíd: cese ya el llanto;
Levantad esos rostros abatidos,
Esclavos oprimidos,
Indios que con espanto
Del cielo y de la tierra sin consuelo
Cautivos habéis sido en vuestro suelo.

(Hear me: cease now your weeping;
Lift up with manly pride those downcast faces,
Slaves crushed and oppressed,
Indians who in fear and terror,
Without consolation in heaven or earth,
Have lived in bondage in this your own land.)

These poems reveal, too, a progressive radicalisation of outlook.
Initially his hope was for a liberalisation of the colonial regime, a
hope which seemed to be fulfilled with the promulgation of the
Spanish Constitution of 1812, and his ode to the Count of Vista
Florida celebrates the appointment of the liberal José Baquíjano y
Carrillo as Councillor of State and forecasts a bright new future for
Peru. This process of liberalisation he saw confirmed by the election
of Arequipa's first constitutional town council in December 1812, an
event which the "Oda a la Libertad" euphorically greets as the end of
tyranny:

Por fin libre y seguro
Puedo cantar. Rompióse el duro freno,
Descubriré mi seno
Y con lenguaje puro
Mostraré la verdad que en él se anida,
Mi libertad civil bien entendida.

(At long last I can sing
Freely and safely. Broken is the rough bridle,
I may open up my breast
And in language virgin pure
Reveal the truth sheltered there within,
My civil liberty truly understood.)

Yet while this poem continues to express loyalty to Spain, these reforms are seen as being merely "el primer paso al bien tan suspirado" (the first step towards the blessing so long sighed for), and Melgar was later to come round to the view that the only solution to his country's aspirations was a total break with Spain. And in "Marcha patriótica", written on the occasion of the entry of the revolutionary forces of Pumacahua into Arequipa in late 1814, he sings the dawn of national liberty and calls on his compatriots to join the struggle:

> Ya llegó el dulce momento
> En que es feliz Arequipa,
> Ya en mi suelo se disipa
> El Despotismo feroz [...]
> Levantad, pues, hijos bellos
> Del Perú siempre oprimido,
> Incrementad el partido
> De esta grande Redención.

> (Come now is the moment of sweetness
> In which Arequipa waxes happy,
> Vanished now is fierce Despotism
> From this my native soil [...]
> Rise up, therefore, you fine strapping sons
> Of Peru as ever oppressed,
> Swell the ranks of the party
> Of this great and glorious Redemption.)

The significance of Melgar's civic verse, therefore, is that it reflects the ideological evolution of liberal *criollos* in the years leading up to Independence.

More than just a poet, Melgar is a figure of legend in Peru. His participation in Mateo Pumacahua's abortive revolution and his execution by the Spaniards earned him the crown of martyr of Independence and the thwarting of his love affair with the adolescent María Santos Corrales — the "Silvia" of his poetry — that of tragic lover, and at first sight he would appear to be the archetypal Romantic. In practice his work is much less innovatory than the legend would suggest. Melgar was formed in the liberal classical tradition of the eighteenth century at the Seminary of San Jerónimo, where he trained for the priesthood and himself taught Philosophy, Mathematics and Physics as well as Grammar and Latin, and the bulk of his poetry is very much neo-classical in style, though written with an austere simplicity free of the rhetorical excesses of earlier Peruvian neo-classicists like Peralta. His neo-classicism is particularly evident in his philosophical poems such as the odes "A la Soledad", which is reminiscent of Luis de León's "Vida retirada", and "Al Autor del Mar", where exclamations of awe at the sea's might and immensity give way to reflections on the ocean's place in the divine scheme and the practical benefits mankind derives from it. Likewise, his civic verse is neo-classical in style and though it voices libertarian and nationalistic sentiments, it betrays a continued cultural dependency in that its language and form still conform to the literary models of the mother country. As such, it highlights the basic contradiction and limitation of virtually all Spanish American literature of the Emancipation period.[23]

In his love poetry, too, Melgar must be regarded as a pre-romantic, for if compositions like the long "Carta a Silvia" seem to herald a new sensibility in their frank outpouring of personal emotion, his best poems, his elegies, express a restrained melancholy reminiscent in manner and tone of the sentimentalism of the late Spanish neo-classicist Meléndez Valdés:

> Mustio ciprés que viste
> Crecer mi amor seguro
> Y en cuyo viejo tronco
> Escribí: "Silvia, ya mi pecho es tuyo";
>
> Y tú claro arroyuelo,
> Cuyo dulce murmullo
> Acompañó sus voces
> Al ofrecerme su corazón puro:
>
> Oídme, ya no puedo
> Callar el mal que sufro;
> Ya Silvia en ira ardiendo,
> Apagar quiere cuanto amor me tuvo.
>
> (Sear cypress who witnessed
> The sure thriving of my love
> And on whose venerable trunk
> I carved: "Silvia, my heart is now yours";

---

[23] See Antonio Cornejo Polar, "Sobre la literatura de la emancipación en el Perú", *RevIb*, 114/115 (1981), 83-93.

> And you, oh clear-flowing brook,
> Whose murmur so soft and sweet
> Accompanied her gentle voice
> When her pure heart to me she offered:
>
> Hear me, no longer can I
> Silence the pain I suffer;
> For such is Silvia's anger
> That she would extinguish her love for me.)

However, it was in another area of his love poetry that Melgar was to make his most significant contribution to Peruvian letters. For one of the forms he cultivated was the *yaraví*, a popular love song whose origins go back to the pre-Columbian *harawi* which had passed into Spanish and had been modified by Hispanic influence. In his adaptations of the form he sings the desolate sense of abandonment which is the basic theme of the genre, sometimes by means of one of the classic motifs of Quechua lyric poetry, that of the dove flown from the nest:

> Vuelve, que ya no puedo
> Vivir sin tus cariños;
> Vuelve, mi palomita,
> Vuelve a tu dulce nido [...]
>
> Ninguno ha de quererte
> Como yo te he querido;
> Te engañas si pretendes
> Hallar amor más fino.
> Habrá otros nidos de oro,
> Pero no como el mío:
> Por quien vertió tu pecho
> Sus primeros gemidos.
> Vuelve, mi palomita,
> Vuelve a tu dulce nido.
>
>
> (Come back, for no more can I
> Live without your caresses:
> Come back, my darling little dove,
> Come back to your nest so sweet [...]
>
> No one will ever love you
> As well as I loved you;
> You're deceived if you hope
> To meet with a love more fine.
> Other nests there may be of gold,
> But none to compare with mine:
> For it was there that your heart
> First sobbed tears of lament.

Come back, my darling little dove,
Come back to your nest so sweet.)

In the sad and melancholy *yaraví* Melgar found a form which was not only well suited to his own emotional state, but which is generally regarded as expressing a peculiarly Peruvian sensibility, and his elevation of it to the dignity of a literary genre represents a move away from a literature that was Spanish and essentially aristocratic in character towards a national literature drawing its inspiration from a popular native tradition. Thus, if his civic verse merely preaches emancipation, his *yaravíes* mark an important step towards a genuinely emancipated literature.

CHAPTER 3

INDEPENDENCE AND THE SEARCH FOR LITERARY EXPRESSION (1821-c. 1925)

Part I
Fiction in the Republican Era

Given, on the one hand, the political and psychological uncertainty experienced by a young republic still finding its feet and unsure of where it was going, and, on the other, the wish to create a national literature, it is hardly to be wondered at that Peruvian fiction in the nineteenth century should be concerned almost exclusively with its own local reality. Nor, in view of the absence of a sizeable book-buying public and a flourishing book industry,[1] is it any more surprising that the genre which enjoyed the greatest vogue in the decades after Independence should be the essentially journalistic form of the costumbrist sketch.[2] Imported from Europe, the genre assured local writers a wider readership and provided a vehicle both for depicting the distinctive life-style of their own society and for opening the eyes of the public to their national shortcomings.

The form was first introduced by Felipe Pardo y Aliaga (1806-68)

[1] It is significant that Fuentes' *Aletazos del Murciélago*, Cisneros' two novels and the first two editions of Clemente Palma's *Cuentos malévolos* were all published in Europe, while *Aves sin nido* was brought out in simultaneous editions in Lima and Buenos Aires. Equally the success of Ricardo Palma was due in no small measure to prestigious foreign editions of his *Tradiciones*.

[2] For a general study of the costumbrists see Maida Isabel Watson, *El cuadro de costumbres en el Perú decimonónico* (La Católica, 1980).

in his short-lived satirical journal *El Espejo de mi tierra* (1840),[3] and though his output was scant — a mere two sketches — it makes up in quality what it lacks in quantity and is undoubtedly the best that the genre produced in Peru. Of the early costumbrists it is Pardo who adopts the most radically critical attitude towards the society of his day. By birth a member of the country's upper echelons and a conservative by political conviction, he had a jaundiced view of democracy and he satirises the disorder of the new republic in "El paseo de Amancaes", a light-hearted account of a shambles of a picnic whose political symbolism he underlines at the end by comparing the returning picnickers to a congress about to go into recess. Yet far from wishing to turn the clock back, Pardo attributes the prevailing instability to the traditional Hispanic lack of discipline and criticises the new regime for its failure to reform basic attitudes. In particular his satire is directed against the *criollo* upper classes whose hereditary shortcomings disqualify them from furnishing the enlightened élite he believed necessary to guide the destinies of the new republic. Thus, in the same sketch, the persistence of a colonial life-style and attitudes is symbolised by the household of Don Pantaleón, a little kingdom made up of a numerous family and a horde of servants and hangers-on and whose traditional character is stressed by an ironic reference to it as a colony. The indolence and ineffectualness of the upper-class male is personified by the master of the household, who is utterly dependent on his wife to run his affairs, while Doña Escolástica, linked by name with the philosophy which dominated the colonial past, embodies the narrow-minded conservatism of the old-fashioned Hispanic matron totally prejudiced against anything that smacks of intellectualism and liberal thought. Likewise, "El viaje" satirises the narrow provincialism and feckless indecisiveness of the *criollo* upper classes. The sketch revolves around Don Goyito's proposed business trip to Chile, a relatively easy journey which, nonetheless, causes a major upheaval in his household, where it is regarded as an expedition to the furthest ends of the earth. Don Goyito himself is one of the most memorable figures in Peruvian literature. Pampered by a crowd of doting sisters and still known as "niño Goyito" (master Goyito) despite the fact

---

[3] See Felipe Pardo y Aliaga, *El Espejo de mi tierra* (CAP, 1971). See also Jorge Cornejo Polar, *Dos ensayos sobre Pardo y Aliaga* (Arequipa: Univ. Nac. de San Agustín, 1967); Raúl Porras Barrenechea, "Don Felipe Pardo y Aliaga, satírico limeño", *Revista Histórica*, 19 (1952), 41-60; Alberto Tauro, "*El Espejo de mi tierra*", *RevIb*, 8 (1942), 333-44; Alberto Varillas Montenegro, *Felipe Pardo y Aliaga* (BHP XIX, 1964).

that he is in his fifties, he is a man who has never grown up and learned to take decisions or to assume responsibility, so that, though his business is urgent, he spends three years procrastinating before he can bring himself to undertake the trip and then only after lengthy consultations with his confessor, his doctor and friends. In these sketches, particularly in "El paseo de Amancaes", which bears a certain similarity to "El castellano viejo", the conservative Pardo coincides with the liberal Mariano José de Larra, the master of Spanish costumbrism, in his criticism of traditional Hispanic failings. They reveal him, therefore, to be far from the reactionary he is usually held to be.

If it is the *criollo* establishment that is portrayed in Pardo's sketches, the forties and fifties were to see the genre focus on and adopt the perspective of the capital's emergent middle classes in the hands of such writers as Manuel Ascensio Segura (1805-71), Ramón Rojas y Cañas (1830-81) and Manuel Atanasio Fuentes (1820-89).[4] All three give expression to that class's disenchantment with a republican regime that had failed to fulfil its hopes and aspirations. Thus Segura's "Los viejos" contrasts the stability of the colonial period with the turbulence and inefficient government of republican times, while Fuentes' "Catecismo para el pueblo" is a biting satire of every aspect of the country's political organisation. Such criticism tends to be couched in moral terms, condemning Peruvians' lack of a proper sense of patriotism and civic duty, but easily detectable behind it is the disgruntlement of a class whose marginal and insecure social and economic status did not match its expectations. Favourite targets of abuse are foreign capitalists who prosper at the expense of local businessmen and the military and the well-connected who monopolise posts in the civil service. Typical of this tendency is Rojas y Cañas' "Lima es madrastra de los limeños", where he complains about the preferential treatment foreigners receive over natives and about not being given the governmental post to which he feels entitled. Perhaps the most striking feature of the social criticism of the costumbrists of the forties and fifties is that, in stark contrast to that of Pardo, it lacks an ideological base and, apart from the call for greater public morality, seems to advocate reforms no more sweeping than protection from foreign competition and a more equitable distribution of government patronage. Indeed, rather than

---

[4] See Manuel Ascensio Segura, *Artículos de costumbres* (CAP, 1968); Ramón Rojas y Cañas, *Museo de limeñadas* (J. Montoya, 1853); Manuel Atanasio Fuentes, *Aletazos del Murciélago* (Paris: Laine et Havard, 1866).

voice discontentment with the social order as such, it expresses the bewildered dissatisfaction of a class excluded from the economic and political power it had expected the Republic to bring it.

While Fuentes' costumbrist articles are predominantly political in character, Segura and Rojas y Cañas are mainly concerned to improve standards of social behaviour through the humorous portrayal of their fellow countrymen's failings and foibles. In "Los apodos" the latter categorises Lima as a large provincial town ruled by a petty provincial mentality, and both writers satirise such vices as the love of gossip and scandal, the preoccupation with appearances, lack of propriety on public occasions, religious superstition, a philistine attitude towards culture and the mindless aping of foreign fashion. However, their sketches tend to consecrate the life-style of the middle classes as much as they criticise it. An obvious rapport between writer and public is evident in their familiar, relaxed style and in their abundant use of local expressions. Segura, particularly, adopts a tone of amused complicity towards some of the customs he is supposedly censuring, so that in "Los Carnavales", for example, he appears to enjoy the excesses of the pre-Lenten celebrations as much as anyone, though his object in writing is to condemn them. Rojas y Cañas, for his part, anticipates Palma in the delight he takes in explaining the significance of popular turns of speech in articles like "Los disfuerzos", and in "Una verdad como un templo" he laments the passing of typical *criollo* traditions. Ultimately, therefore, the costumbrist sketch became a mirror in which the capital's middle classes saw themselves portrayed with their virtues and defects and in which they found expressed their aspirations and grievances. By giving that class a sense of its own identity it contributed to the creation of a national self-awareness. It also helped to foster the complacent assumption that *criollo* Lima constituted Peru.

Akin to the costumbrist sketch are the *Tradiciones peruanas* of Ricardo Palma (1833-1919), the foremost and most renowned Peruvian writer of the age.[5] Palma began his literary career as a

[5] See Ricardo Palma, *Tradiciones peruanas completas*, ed. Edith Palma (Madrid: Aguilar, 1964); *Tradiciones en salsa verde* (Biblioteca Universitaria, 1973); *Cien tradiciones peruanas*, ed. José Miguel Oviedo (Caracas: Biblioteca Ayacucho, 1977); *Tradiciones peruanas*, ed. Pamela Francis (Oxford: Pergamon, 1969); *Epistolario*, 2 vols. (Cultura Antártica, 1949); *Cartas inéditas* (Milla Batres, 1964); *Cartas indiscretas* (Moncloa, 1969). See also Shirley L. Arora, *Proverbial Comparisons in Ricardo Palma's "Tradiciones peruanas"* (Berkeley and Los Angeles: Univ. of California Press, 1966); Dora Bazán Montenegro, *Los nombres en Palma* (Biblioteca Universitaria, 1969); Robert Bazin, "Les trois crises de la vie de Ricardo Palma", *Bulletin Hispanique*, 56 (1954), 49-82; Merlin D. Compton, *Ricardo Palma* (Boston: Twayne, 1982); Alberto

second-rate Romantic poet and dramatist, but later, through an interest in historical research which produced scholarly works such as his *Anales de la Inquisición de Lima* (1863), he was to hit on a medium for his own particular talent in a genre of his own creation. His earliest prose writings were run-of-the-mill Romantic legends following the vogue inspired by Sir Walter Scott, but by the mid-sixties they had already evolved into the distinctive form of the *tradición*, a chatty anecdote recounting episodes from the nation's history with a roguish, down-to-earth humour that has little in common with melodramatic Romantic idealisations of the past. A first series, published in 1872, was followed in the next few decades by a succession of volumes, a total production of over five hundred *tradiciones* embracing every period of Peru's history from Inca times to the mid-nineteenth century and covering the regions of the interior as well as the cities of the coast. Nonetheless, the title of the *Tradiciones peruanas* is somewhat misleading, for, since the vast majority are set in eighteenth-century Lima, they tend to constitute a chronicle of the capital's days of viceregal splendour rather than of the past of the nation as a whole.

In a sense Palma is a historian *manqué*. His *tradiciones* are the fruit of research born of a curiosity aroused by a popular saying or an incident recalled from his youth or some interesting scrap of information come across in a book or manuscript or picked up orally, and in many of them he makes a habit of interrupting the narrative to fill in background information, much of which has no direct relevance to the story being told. But the *tradiciones* are not history in the accepted sense. In the first place, they are concerned not so much with the great events of the past as with the minutiae of history. Many are simply pleasant exercises in lexicography explaining the origin of an amusing phrase or proverb, while most of the rest

Escobar, *Ricardo Palma* (BHP X, 1964); id., "Tensión, lenguaje y estructura: *Las tradiciones peruanas*", in *Patio de Letras*, pp. 68-140; Paul A. Georgescu, "Lectura moderna de Ricardo Palma", *Studi di Letteratura Ispano-Americana*, 12 (1982), 5-21; Jean Lamore, "Sur quelques procédés de l'ironie et de l'humour dans les *Tradiciones peruanas*", *Bulletin Hispanique*, 70 (1968), 106-15; Luis Loayza, *El sol de Lima*, pp. 83-115; César Miró, *Don Ricardo Palma: el patriarca de las Tradiciones* (Buenos Aires: Losada, 1953); José Miguel Oviedo, *Genio y figura de Ricardo Palma* (Buenos Aires: Eudeba, 1965); Raúl Porras Barrenechea, *Tres ensayos sobre Ricardo Palma* (Mejía Baca, 1954); Luis Hernán Ramírez, "El estilo de las primeras tradiciones de Palma", *Sphinx*, 14 (1961), 126-55; Daniel R. Reedy, "Las *Tradiciones en salsa verde* de Ricardo Palma", *RevIb*, 61 (1966), 69-75; Noël Salomon, "'Las orejas del alcalde' de Ricardo Palma: un exemple de fabrication littéraire", *Bulletin Hispanique*, 69 (1967), 441-53; Roy L. Tanner, "The Art of Characterization in Representative Selections of Ricardo Palma's *Tradiciones peruanas*", Diss. Illinois 1976 (Univ. Microfilms, 1979).

revolve around the gossip of the past — scandals such as the secret sexual adventures of those in high places or unseemly public squabbles between prominent figures; sensational stories of great crimes, illicit love affairs, violent feuds and bloody revenge; amazing accounts of unusual or miraculous happenings and of the curious doings of society's eccentrics. Moreover, the *tradición* is above all a literary genre. Real characters and events are merely the starting-point for artistic creation and ultimately Palma's version of the past owes as much to his own imagination as to his historical investigations.

It would seem that in part the past represented for Palma a form of escapism. "Prefiero vivir en los siglos que fueron," he wrote in one of his letters. "En el ayer hay poesía, y el hoy es prosaico ..., muy prosaico" (I prefer to live in the centuries that are gone. In our yesterday there is poetry and our today is prosaic ..., very prosaic). In history and literature he found refuge from personal disappointments and from the depressing reality of contemporary politics, with which he had become progressively disillusioned after years of active involvement. Yet it is equally clear that at the same time he believed that his literary work constituted a service to the nation. In the opening paragraphs of "Un virrey y un arzobispo" he laments America's ignorance and disregard of its own past and sees it as his mission to preserve a national heritage that is in danger of being lost forever, making it palatable by presenting it in a form attractive to the ordinary man-in-the-street: "Entre tanto, toca a la juventud hacer algo para evitar que la tradición se pierda completamente. Por eso, en ella se fija de preferencia nuestra atención, y para atraer la del pueblo creemos útil adornar con las galas del romance toda narración histórica" (In the meantime, it is up to the younger generation to do something to prevent tradition from disappearing completely. For that reason I have fixed my attention on it, and in order to gain the attention of the people, I believe it useful to adorn all my historical narratives with the trappings of romance). The justification and significance of the *tradiciones*, in other words, is that they represent an attempt to give the citizens of a new and unstable republic a sense of national identity by making them aware of their roots.

Palma's disenchantment with the politics of the day manifests itself in frequent jibes at politicians, not only in contemporary *tradiciones* like "Historia de un cañoncito", whose theme is the accepted custom of buying and selling political favours, but in ones set in the colonial period, such as "Los caballeros de la capa" where the civil wars beween the conquistadores are seen as foreshadowing the power struggles of the nineteenth-century military caudillos. That in itself is sufficient to indicate that his view of the past is not unrealistic. Rather it is ambivalent. For if, on the one hand, he regards the past with affection as his national heritage and with the nostalgia that each new age feels for the supposedly more romantic one that preceded it, on the other his perspective is essentially that of a nineteenth-century liberal democrat. His anti-clericalism reveals itself in his ironical treatment of worldly churchmen and religious superstitions, but in *tradiciones* like "El alacrán de Fray Gómez" and "Los ratones de Fray Martín" this does not prevent him from celebrating the humanity of saintly men while deriding the miracles attributed to them. Equally he does not begrudge admiration for the political and human virtues of distinguished colonial officials, but at the same time he shows a healthy disrespect for hierarchy and authority by poking irreverent fun at overbearing or dishonest public figures and by delighting in their discomfiture, as in "Las orejas del alcalde". The accusation frequently levelled against him that he helped create a nostalgic myth of a colonial arcadia hardly seems justified, therefore, on the evidence of the *tradiciones* themselves. What he does do is to reinforce the egocentric misconception that confuses Lima with Peru and to offer the capital's middle classes a flattering, ego-boosting image of themselves by celebrating the feminine gracefulness, the male gallantry and, above all, the humour and sharp wit which are traditionally held to be the characteristic traits of the *criollo*. Furthermore, his view of Peru's history is essentially superficial. Serious issues are avoided, human suffering is glossed over or diluted by humour, and the social criticism, hidden behind a smiling irony, is never openly offensive and rarely goes beyond the level of street-corner murmuring. It is that, in the view of many critics, which makes the *tradiciones* a genuine expression of the *criollo* mentality.

Yet Palma was perhaps the most widely read Spanish American writer of his day and his success was due not merely to the charm of his stories but to the manner in which they were presented. In contrast to the costumbrists, of whom only Pardo could claim to be a stylist and most of whose sketches are carelessly written, Palma demonstrates the artistic craftsmanship of a man with a true literary vocation. A correspondent of the Spanish Academy, he produced scholarly linguistic studies like *Neologismos y americanismos* (1896) and *Papeletas lexicográficas* (1903), and this concern with language is evident in the style of the *tradiciones*, which graft Americanisms on to a pure classical Spanish to convey the flavour of colloquial Peruvian speech. He was also a perfectionist who patiently and painstakingly reworked and polished his writings. By so doing he mastered the art of contriving to give an impression of naturalness and spontaneity, making the reader feel that he is listening to a popular story-teller spinning amusing anecdotes in an off-the-cuff manner. He also succeeded in inventing a literary reality which conveys a feel of the past, bringing it alive in such a way that his creation becomes "más historia que la historia misma" (more history than history itself).[6] Though very much a minor art form, the *tradiciones* are nonetheless masterpieces of prose writing, and whatever reservations one may have about his interpretation of the past, there can be no doubt that Palma set a standard of sheer literary professionalism which, unfortunately, no other writer of the age was able to match.

A stark contrast with Palma's consummate artistry is provided by the amateurish efforts of the country's earliest novelists. Significantly, the first novel — *El Padre Horán* of Narciso Aréstegui (1826-69) — did not appear until 1848 and then in serialised form in a Lima newspaper.[7] Apart from initiating the genre, it is an important work in that it marks a break away from the prevailing literary preoccupation with Lima and establishes a trend of social and political criticism that was long to characterise the Peruvian novel. Set in Cuzco, it depicts the social and economic backwardness in which the region languished in the decades following Independence and indicts the Republican regime for its failure to improve the quality of life in the provinces. The central theme, narrating the murder of a young girl by her confessor when she resists his attempts to seduce her, anticipates Clorinda Matto de Turner in its condemnation of the excessive influence of the Church in provincial life and in its exposure of clerical hypocrisy and corruption and of the evils of narrow-minded religiosity. Aréstegui also denounces the authorities' failure to stimulate local agriculture and industry and several sub-plots, such as that describing the hardships of a woman who was left

---

[6] Raúl Porras Barrenechea, *El sentido tradicional en la literatura peruana* (Porras, 1969), p. 58.

[7] See Narciso Aréstegui, *El Padre Horán*, 2 vols. (CAP, 1969). See also Nello Marco Sánchez Dextre, *Aréstegui y la novela peruana* (Cuzco: Prelatura de Sicuani, 1982); Silvana Serafin, "*El Padre Horán* e la società peruviana del secolo XIX", *Studi di Letteratura Ispano-Americana*, 11 (1981), 125-48; Augusto Tamayo Vargas, "El indigenismo peruano y *El Padre Horán* de Narciso Aréstegui", *Letras*, 70/71 (1963), 70-83.

destitute when her conscript husband was killed in the Wars of Independence and who dies in misery unassisted by an uncaring officialdom, build up a picture of the widespread poverty and squalor of the region. Another sub-plot takes up the cause of the downtrodden Indian peasantry by exposing the plight of a family struggling to survive under the burden of iniquitous impositions, and to Aréstegui, therefore, belongs the credit of preparing the ground for *Aves sin nido* and subsequent *indigenista* fiction. Unfortunately the novel is as deficient artistically as it is thematically important. The characters are exaggerated stereotypes of good and evil; dialogue is artificial; the omniscient narrator intervenes obtrusively to pass judgement on his characters and on the state of society; emotions and situations are over-dramatised; and plots are contrived, with strangers being revealed at the end to be long-lost relatives. In short, it bears the mark of a clumsy inexpertise that was to remain a feature of the Peruvian novel for the rest of the century.

Lagging in the wake of cultural developments in Europe, Peru did not produce a generation of Romantic writers until the middle of the century and among them only one novelist of any consequence in Luis Benjamín Cisneros (1837-1904).[8] Cisneros' fiction combines a Romantic glorification of love with criticism of the social order, but both are attenuated by his mild and moderate temperament and by his belief in order and peaceful progress. Hence amorous fulfilment is conceived in terms of tranquil domesticity rather than of rapturous passion, and social criticism takes the form not of violent denunciations but of gentle moral sermons. *Julia* (1861) is set in middle-class Lima against a background of growing prosperity generated by the guano boom. Here the idyllic romance of the lovers Andrés and Julia is cut short not by Romantic fate but by the unhealthy atmosphere of a *nouveau-riche* society preoccupied with luxury and ostentation. In her inexperience Julia succumbs to corrupting influences and forsakes her unpretentious fiancé to marry a dashing young man-about-town, only to come to grief when her husband squanders his fortune on gambling and deserts her after absconding with his company's funds. In the end, however, his fortuitous death frees her to marry the faithful Andrés and to share with him the true happiness of quiet family life. The second of Cisneros' two novels, *Edgardo o un joven de mi generación* (1864), is another tale of Romantic love which by contrast ends tragically when the hero, a

[8] See Luis Benjamín Cisneros, *Julia* (CAP, 1971); *Edgardo o un joven de mi generación* (El Lucero, 1906).

young army officer, dies futilely in one of the many civil wars of the fifties. Edgardo is clearly intended to stand as a symbol of a whole generation of young Peruvians whose patriotic idealism and dreams of personal happiness are destroyed by the sterility of the political upheavals of the period. Thus, just as *Julia* advocates the virtues of orderly family life, *Edgardo* implicitly appeals for political order and stability and a more rational approach to the nation's problems. Essentially, therefore, Cisneros speaks with the voice of moderation and common sense protesting against the senseless excesses he sees in the society around him. Technically his novels have the merits of well-constructed plots and an elegantly simple prose. They suffer, however, from the Romantic tendency to over-dramatise, particularly noticeable in the prolonged death scene in *Edgardo*. Nor do his characters ever really come alive because, though they are described at length both physically and psychologically, the author seems more concerned with defining them than with letting them speak and act for themselves. Moreover, events are never allowed to follow their course but serve rather as pegs on which to hang long moral disquisitions. Ultimately Cisneros fails as a novelist because, like Aréstegui before him, he regarded the novel primarily as a vehicle for expressing ideas and neglected to master the fundamental skills of the trade.

However, the essentially lightweight character of Palma's *Tradiciones peruanas* becomes obvious when they are compared with the fiction of the latter decades of the century. The humiliating disaster of the War of the Pacific (1879-83), which saw the occupation of Lima by Chilean troops and the loss of the nitrate-rich provinces of the south, induced a crisis of national morale similar to that which was later to afflict the Spanish Generation of 1898 and prompted the country's intellectuals to embark on an agonised reappraisal of every aspect of Peruvian life. Foremost in this process was Manuel González Prada (1844-1918), who exposed the bankruptcy of the nation's leaders and institutions in a series of speeches and essays which were reprinted in *Páginas libres* (1894).[9] Spain had bequeathed

[9] See Manuel González Prada, *Páginas libres/Horas de lucha* (Caracas: Biblioteca Ayacucho, 1976). See also Adriana de González Prada, *Mi Manuel* (Cultura Antártica, 1947); Luis Felipe Guerra, *González Prada* (BHP XX, 1964); Robert G. Mead, Jr., "González Prada, el prosista y el pensador", in *Temas hispanoamericanos* (Mexico City: Andrea, 1959), pp. 13-40; Bruno Podestá, *Pensamiento político de González Prada* (INC, 1975); Luis Alberto Sánchez, *Don Manuel* (San Marcos, 1964); id., *Mito y realidad de González Prada* (Villanueva, 1976); id., "Un incidente que definió el pensamiento peruano, Ricardo Palma versus Manuel González Prada", *Cuadernos Americanos*, 125 (1974), 145-59.

a sorry legacy of venality, corruption and intellectual obscurantism which had turned Peru into a sick organism, he argued, and the nation would never be made healthy till the oligarchy, the Church, the military and all the other institutions of the past were destroyed, till Lima's stranglehold on the country was broken, and till the mestizo proletariat and the Indian peasantry were freed from their servitude and servility. With the exhortation "¡Los viejos a la tumba, los jóvenes a la obra!" (Old men to the tomb, young men to work!), he urged Peruvian youth to undertake a radical transformation of their country and to that end he called for a literature which, breaking with the traditionalism he identified with Ricardo Palma, would develop new forms of expression to confront the realities of the modern age. Though an iconoclast rather than the creator of a coherent political ideology — his later philosophy, contained in *Horas de lucha* (1908), evolved in the direction of anarchism —, González Prada nonetheless initiated a new phase in Peru's political and intellectual history and his diagnosis of the country's ills was to be both the inspiration and the basis of twentieth-century radicalism. In the field of prose fiction the new and more radical spirit which he championed was to be reflected in the work of Abelardo Gamarra, Clorinda Matto de Turner and Mercedes Cabello de Carbonera.

The costumbrist sketch underwent a major evolution with Abelardo Gamarra (1852-1924), who, under the pseudonym of El Tunante, published a steady stream of articles in Lima newspapers over a period of fifty years, reprinting the best of them in several collections, of which the most notable was *Rasgos de pluma* (1889).[10] A *serrano*, though he lived most of his life in Lima, he was the first costumbrist writer to extend his vision beyond the capital. Many of his sketches are indeed set in Lima, such as the highly entertaining "El tranvía de Pelagatos", an affectionate view of the capital's dilapidated tramway system, but Gamarra had an ardent belief in the oneness of Peru and lovingly describes typical highland scenes in articles like "La trilla" and "Una corrida de toros en la sierra" and in others portrays customs and scenes of virtually every region of the country. He was a great lover of folk culture, which he saw as an expression of national character. Many of his articles are devoted to popular music, dances, dishes etc., and in "El pianito ambulante"

---

[10] See Abelardo Gamarra, *Rasgos de pluma* (Renovación, 1923); *Cien años de vida perdularia* (Comisión Nacional de Cultura, 1963); *En la ciudad de Pelagatos* (Peisa, 1975). See also Justo Fernández C., *Abelardo Gamarra, "El Tunante", su vida y obra* (Cuzco: H.G. Rozas, 1954).

and "Una serenata" he laments the passing of many of the old traditions with the advent of modern fashions. Yet Gamarra is far from being a backward-looking conservative. In the articles referred to his aim is to foster a pride in the Peru he himself loved and that was essentially a Peru of the people. Politically he was a man of progressive and radical views and most of his costumbrist articles — over three hundred of them — are, in fact, of a political nature. In some he speaks out for the oppressed, denouncing trafficking in Indian children in "Los cholitos" and hypocritical exploitation of servants and vendors by the middle classes in "La regatona". More commonly he adopts a mischievously ironic tone to expose Peruvian politics as a farce disguising a harsh and bitter reality of venality and nepotism, particularly in *Cien años de vida perdularia*, a collection of sketches published in 1921 on the occasion of the first centenary of Independence. Here we are given a global view of the Peruvian political scene, in the capital and in the provinces, with descriptions of all the main institutions and practices and pen portraits of typical figures like the boot-licking provincial deputy and the prefect who milks his department. Underlying the volume is the message that Peru's first hundred years of Independence have been marked by the dissipation of the country's resources, talents and aspirations. This Gamarra attributes in part to sheer cynical opportunism, but above all to the fact that Peruvians have never learned to subordinate personal and group interests to a collective ideal and that he shows to be the greatest obstacle to national progress. Aimed at a popular audience and written in popular language, Gamarra's sketches have no great literary pretensions. They are, however, lively and entertaining, and, above all, their importance lies in the assertion of a new nationalism embracing the provinces and in the revelation of the need for a new public morality and new ideologies to replace a political system shown to be totally bankrupt.

The *tradición*, too, was to undergo a change in the hands of Clorinda Matto de Turner (1852-1909), whose *Tradiciones cuzqueñas*, written in the 1870s and early 1880s, were published in two collections in 1884 and 1886.[11] Her *tradiciones*, it has to be admitted,

---

[11] See Clorinda Matto de Turner, *Tradiciones cuzqueñas completas*, ed. Estuardo Núñez (Peisa, 1976); *Aves sin nido*, ed. Luis Mario Schneider (New York: Las Américas, 1968); *Indole*, ed. Antonio Cornejo Polar (INC, 1974); *Herencia*, ed. Antonio Cornejo Polar (INC, 1974). See also Margaret V. Campbell, "The *Tradiciones cuzqueñas* of Clorinda Matto de Turner", *Hispania*, 42 (1959), 492-97; Francisco Carrillo, *Clorinda Matto de Turner y el indigenismo literario* (Biblioteca Universitaria, 1967); Antonio Cornejo Polar, "*Aves sin nido*: indios, notables y forasteros", in *La*

are somewhat dull and lifeless in comparison with those of Palma, on which they are modelled, but, dealing as they do with the local traditions of her native Cuzco, they break with her master's predominantly Limeñan perspective and vindicate the role of the provinces in the nation's history. Moreover, in contrast to Palma, she is forthright in her criticism of the country's social and political situation, using episodes from the past as a vehicle for condemning the evils of the present, and in anecdotes like "Vaya un decreto" and "El santo y la limosna" she exposes the injustices perpetrated against the downtrodden Indian masses. Her *tradiciones* thus represent a movement towards a literature of greater social commitment.

However, the *Tradiciones cuzqueñas* constituted no more than Clorinda Matto's literary apprenticeship and it was as a novelist of the realist school that she was to achieve fame and notoriety, with *Aves sin nido* (1889), the first novel of any merit to confront directly the social problems of the sierra and to protest against the oppression and exploitation of the Indian masses.[12] Set in Killac, a fictional community representative of the feudal backwardness of all small Andean towns, it depicts the systematic extortion to which the Indian peasantry are subjected at the hands of the local notables headed by the governor and parish priest. When Fernando and Lucía Marín, a cultured and humanitarian couple from Lima, intervene on behalf of the Yupanqui, a hard-pressed Indian family, the notables interpret their action as a subversion of the traditional social order and stage an assault on their home to drive them out, and when their plan backfires they shift blame from themselves by "framing" another unfortunate Indian. Deciding that they cannot go on living in such an environment, the Marín subsequently return to Lima, but not before using their influence to have the innocent Indian cleared and the real culprits brought to justice. A second plot traces the growing love between the governor's stepson Manuel, an enlightened young man educated in Lima, and Margarita Yupanqui, whom the Marín adopt on the death of her parents. Manuel follows them to Lima and asks for her hand in marriage, only for it to be revealed that they have the

---

novela peruana: siete estudios, pp. 7-32; Manuel E. Cuadros Escobedo, *Paisaje y obra, mujer e historia: Clorinda Matto de Turner* (Cuzco: H.G. Rozas, 1949); Julio Rodríguez-Luis, *Hermenéutica y praxis del indigenismo* (Mexico City: Fondo de Cultura Económica, 1980), pp. 17-55; Alberto Tauro, *Clorinda Matto de Turner y la novela indigenista* (San Marcos, 1976).

[12] It was not, however, the first novel to do so. For its literary antecedents, see A. Tauro, *op. cit.*

same natural father, the former parish priest of Killac, now an eminent bishop. Their tragically thwarted love affair, however, is more than simply a rehash of one of the stock themes of Romantic fiction, for it is intended to expose the sexual depredations of a corrupt clergy and to support the author's thesis that priests should be married.

There are certain obvious limitations in Matto's presentation of the social order of the sierra. In the first place she concentrates on the political superstructure of Andean society and almost completely overlooks the economic reality underpinning it. The land-owning class is noticeably absent from the novel, whose villains are the local authorities — governor, judge, parish priest etc. — who use their positions to exploit the Indian peasantry. The novel, in short, focuses attention on the abuse of authority without taking account of the powerful economic interests which authority serves, and at times it seems almost to suggest that the appointment of enlightened and humanitarian officials would be enough to resolve the problems of the sierra and the pitiful condition of the Indian masses. Furthermore, the vision we are given of the Indians is essentially an external one. On the one hand, they are romantically conceived as being possessed of a natural innocence and goodness and, on the other, they are presented as passive victims, despairing yet resigned and submissive under the weight of oppression. They appear, in fact, merely as stereotypes of a downtrodden people and there is nothing to indicate that they are a distinct race with their own distinct culture. More than that, despite the author's sympathy for the Indians, the assumption of their cultural inferiority is implicit throughout the novel. Behind her moral indignation lies the ideology of the liberal, progressive middle classes which advocates the modernisation of the sierra and universal education as the main means of achieving it. Lima is constantly evoked in opposition to Killac as a Mecca of civilisation and progress, while the Marín embody the spirit of progressive liberalism — he, significantly, is a working capitalist, manager and part-owner of a mine — in conflict with the traditionalism of the local notables. And the love affair which brings Manuel and Margarita together under the auspices of the Marín and eventually takes them to Lima is clearly symbolic, representing the bridging of the social and racial gulf between notables and Indians by their joint assimilation into modern civilisation. Ultimately, therefore, Matto sees the solution of the region's problems and the salvation of the Indians in a process of modernisation, a process which would have the inevitable effect of destroying the Indians' cultural identity. Yet if it was left to later writers to place the Indian problem in economic perspective and to assert the validity and viability of Quechua culture in the modern world, the importance of *Aves sin nido* cannot be overestimated as the first work to break through the nation's complacency and to rouse consciences to the appalling plight of the Indian peasantry.[13]

The other leading exponent of realism in Peru was Mercedes Cabello de Carbonera (1845-1909), who, in *Blanca Sol* (1889), wrote what is perhaps the best Peruvian novel of the nineteenth century.[14] Set in Lima, the novel depicts the moral corruption that González Prada had denounced in that society. Taking up the theme treated rather insipidly by Cisneros in *Julia*, that of the moral and economic downfall of a woman blinded by the false glamour of a life of opulent ostentation, Cabello develops her social criticism through the medium of a central character shaped and corrupted by the society of which she is a product. Spoiled from birth, Blanca Sol has been brought up to expect to be indulged, pampered and admired, and she regards it as her destiny to occupy a dazzling position in high society and to bask in its adulation. This ambition she achieves by cynically marrying for money, for she is coldly calculating and totally amoral where her wishes are concerned. She is also wilful and domineering. Completely subjugating her weak spouse, she squanders his fortune on expensive clothes and lavish entertainments till she becomes the leading light in the social firmament, and not content with being the consort of a vulgar businessman, she employs her charms to have him elevated to the rank of government minister. Towards her husband she is strikingly lacking in gratitude. She soon comes to regard him as unworthy of her, despising him for his unattractive

---

[13] Neither of Matto's two later novels has the importance of *Aves sin nido*. In *Indole* (1891), also set in the sierra, she switches her attention from the plight of the Indian to renew her attack on the corruption of the clergy and on priestly celibacy. *Herencia* (1895) is a sequel to her first novel in that it follows the fortunes of the Marín in Lima, seen now as a society ruled by false values. As the titles indicate, both novels also set out to demonstrate the naturalist thesis that moral conduct is determined by inherited character and upbringing.

[14] See Mercedes Cabello de Carbonera, *Blanca Sol* (Carlos Prince, 1893). For her ideas on the novel, see her essay *La novela moderna* (Hora del Hombre, 1948). Cabello's most ambitious work is *El conspirador* (E. Sequi, 1892), a first-person narrative recounting the career of a typical caudillo of the period. The novel is clearly intended to expose the bankruptcy of contemporary politics, but it fails to realise its aim because, rather than re-create the political world, it consists merely of a series of commentaries on it, and because the protagonist's moral awareness makes him totally unconvincing as the prototype of the power-hungry opportunist he purports to be.

appearance, his intellectual limitations and his lack of social graces, and she subjects him to all manner of humiliations. She indulges, too, in a series of flirtations, partly to fill the romantic void in her life but mainly to glory in the homage paid to her by society's most desirable males and in the notoriety that it brings her, and if none of these affairs actually reaches the stage of adultery, it is not because of moral scruples — for she is utterly indifferent to the pain she causes others — but because she derives her satisfaction from toying with men's affections and savouring her power over them. In the end, when her extravagance brings her husband to bankruptcy and her seeming infidelity drives him out of his mind with jealousy, she finds herself ostracised by the society that had formerly paid court to her. Even then she is incapable of recognising her faults or of mending her ways. Consumed by a desire to avenge herself on the society that has cast her out and knowing no way of earning a living other than by her charms, she resolves to foster its perdition with her own and, recruiting women from neighbouring apartments, turns her modest home into a squalid den for the entertainment of men. Though the theme is a stock one of nineteenth-century fiction, the novel nonetheless has a distinctively Peruvian flavour in that its protagonist is a characteristic type of Limeñan womanhood, and despite certain obvious artistic deficiencies, notably the obtrusive moralising of the omniscient narrator, it is redeemed by its convincing portrayal of Blanca Sol, in whom Cabello has created the first major rounded character to appear in the pages of a Peruvian novel. For that reason and because of the vision it offers of Limeñan society, it ranks as a work of considerable merit.

Unfortunately, if the writers mentioned responded to González Prada's exhortations by attempting to create a literature which would be a more authentic reflection of national reality, they failed to emulate Palma's artistic mastery and to give adequate literary expression to that enterprise. A glaring illustration of that failure is provided by *Aves sin nido*, the most famous novel of the period. To a large extent the novel's shortcomings are a direct consequence of Matto's didactic concern. Animated by a strong sense of social commitment, the author intervenes constantly and obtrusively to pass judgement on people and events. The characters, too, have a tiresome tendency to moralise at every opportunity, and rather than as individuals, they come across as embodiments of attitudes and social positions and divide simplistically into good and evil, with their moral natures identified by external appearance. Equally, certain episodes, such as the priest's public confession of his sins, do not arise naturally out of the action and have no other justification than that of illustrating an argument. Moreover, the novel's realism is undermined by a residual romanticism, so that realistic accounts of the social order are offset by sentimental treatment of nature and love and the language switches back and forth incongruously between extremes of lyrical evocation and the scientific terminology of positivism. Other defects, such as grammatical errors, over-use of adjectives and lapses into the trite, are attributable quite simply to a lack of artistic rigour. *Aves sin nido*, unhappily, is not an exception, for its faults are shared to a greater or lesser extent by all novels of the period, *Blanca Sol* not excluded. Indeed, it highlights the major flaw of Peruvian fiction in the nineteenth century in that it demonstrates that a good subject, moral indignation and a message are not in themselves enough to produce a good novel.

It was not, in fact, until the Modernist period that Palma's stylistic awareness came to be shared by other writers, and it is symptomatic of the country's backwardness in relation to the outside world that, like Romanticism, Modernism arrived late in Peru. Peruvian Modernism produced only one novel, the very brief *Cartas de una turista* (1905) by Enrique A. Carrillo (1877-1938), but slight though it is, it is vastly superior in literary craftsmanship to any of the novels previously discussed.[15] It takes the form of a series of letters written to a friend by a young Englishwoman holidaying in Chorrillos, the fashionable resort for Lima's upper classes. In them she conveys her impressions of the landscape and local society and describes her flirtations with the local beaux and an incipient love affair which she prudently cuts short. Having lived in contact with the more sophisticated societies of Europe, where he spent several years in the diplomatic service, Carrillo, like his fellow Modernists and like Felipe Pardo before him, was dismayed by the cultural backwardness of his own country and derides it, with an irony that is none the less pointed for being gentle, through his heroine Gladys who, accustomed to the brilliant society of Brighton, Trouville and the Côte d'Azur, finds Chorrillos dull and provincial. At the same time the novel breaks with the prevailing preoccupation with the national scene and takes up a more universal theme, the typically Modernist one of the gulf between the ideal world of the imagination and the prosaic world

---

[15] See Enrique A. Carrillo, *Cartas de una turista* (Asociación Peruana por la Libertad de la Cultura, 1959).

of everyday reality. Gladys, assailed by a vague dissatisfaction and a longing for a fulfilment she has never known, experiences a few hours of ecstasy with one of her suitors one evening when her own mood and the exotic romantic atmosphere combine to transform the world, but realising that such happiness can never survive the reality of marriage, she sensibly but regretfully decides to return to England to her solid, practical and totally unimaginative fiancé. As befits a Modernist, Carrillo writes with a concern for style that manifests itself in his polished and masterly manipulation of language, and he reveals a genuine novelistic talent in his impressionistic descriptions of landscape and in conveying the psychology and changing moods of his heroine, with her engaging habit of mocking her own lapses into sentimentality. It is regrettable that, like many Peruvian writers, he seems to have lacked the creative stamina to sustain that talent and it exhausted itself in one slim volume.

It is another Modernist writer, Clemente Palma (1872-1946),[16] to whom the credit belongs for establishing the short-story form in Peru. The genre had already been used sporadically by the Romantics, but Palma was the first writer to cultivate it systematically, with narratives that appeared in Lima periodicals from the late nineties onwards, and his *Cuentos malévolos* (1904), a collection of twelve tales, was the first published book of Peruvian short stories. Palma is one of the most underrated figures in Peruvian letters, and though his stories show the influence of Maupassant and Poe among others, they nonetheless reveal an original talent and a mastery of short-story technique and he ranks, after his father Ricardo, as the most accomplished Peruvian prose-writer of the Republican era.

Palma's work is marked by the cosmopolitan outlook that is characteristic of Spanish American Modernism, and characters of different nationalities play out their roles in a wide variety of settings, as though to demonstrate that his tales could unfold anywhere in the world. His writings thus represent a movement away from national themes and problems towards a literature concerned with the human condition, and an attempt to lift Peruvian letters out of their provincialism into the mainstream of Western culture.

---

[16] See Clemente Palma, *Cuentos malévolos* (Peisa, 1974); *Cuentos malévolos*, 2nd ed. (Paris: Paul Ollendorf, 1923); *Historietas malignas* (Garcilaso, 1925); *XYZ (Novela Grotesca)* (Perú Actual, 1934). See also Earl M. Aldrich, Jr., *The Modern Short Story in Peru*, pp. 5-25; Alberto Escobar, "Incisiones en el arte del 'cuento modernista'", in *Patio de Letras*, pp. 141-79; Donald A. Yates, "Clemente Palma: *XYZ* y otras letras fantásticas", *Literatura de la Emancipación*, 194-99; Virgil A. Warren, "La obra de Clemente Palma", *RevIb*, 3 (1940), 161-71.

His stories are also impregnated by the spirit of the *fin de siècle*. An essentially anguished view of man and his place in the cosmos disguises itself behind a mask of ironic cynicism and black humour. As the title of the volume forewarns us, the stories set out to mock conventional values. Some are blasphemous in that they deride the fundamental tenets of Christianity and put forward the thesis that evil is what makes the world go round. In "El quinto evangelio" Satan gloats over Christ as he hangs on the cross and tells him that he has died in vain since the salvation he offers is the denial of all that man holds most dear. In "El hijo pródigo" God finally forgives Satan and allows him to reoccupy his original place in heaven, but with the removal of his influence the universe returns to the void, since it is the presence of evil which inspires man to strive for higher things. Other stories belittle conventional morality in a manner reminiscent of the French decadents. Thus, in order to liberate his mistress from his perverse tyranny the protagonist of "Idealismos" kills her by instilling a death-wish in her. Marcof, the Russian protagonist of "Los canastos", advances the cynical proposition that it is better to be remembered for a cruel deed than to be forgotten for some act of kindness. A prey to the ennui of the typical decadent hero, he takes a perverse pleasure in the misfortune of a poor carter whose load falls into the river unnoticed, and then, having deliberately refrained from warning him, he completes his enjoyment by informing him of his loss so that he can observe his despairing reaction.

Yet the cynicism of the stories cannot conceal a sense of anguish at the horror of life in a world whose traditional values are collapsing. Thus the protagonist of "El Príncipe Alacrán" suffers a nightmare in which he is assailed by an army of scorpions. Similarly, "Leyendas de haschichs", which describes the hallucinations of a man under the influence of drugs, leads the protagonist through a horrific world of pestilence and corruption in the midst of which he is abandoned by his female guide, the symbol of unattainable fulfilment.

The most novel story in the collection is "La granja blanca", where, anticipating the fictions of the Argentinian Jorge Luis Borges, Palma expresses his existential uncertainty and his scepticism with regard to accepted philosophical assumptions in a disconcerting metaphysical fantasy. The protagonist is a philosopher preoccupied with the notion that life is an illusion and men fictitious entities acting out the dreams of a higher being. After two years of marital bliss on an isolated country estate his wife vanishes and he learns from his old mentor that his marriage has been a figment of his imagination since she died of an illness on the eve of their wedding. Yet he is able to bring forward evidence of her existence in the form of an infant daughter who is her living image, proof that illusion is more real than reality and that it perpetuates itself. The tale ends in horror when the mentor, outraged at the protagonist's intention of reliving his relationship with his wife through his daughter, destroys the child, symbol of a reality and a morality his conventional world-view is unable to accept.

Unlike Carrillo, Palma went on to increase his fictional output. A second edition of *Cuentos malévolos* (1923) included eight new stories and was followed by *Historietas malignas* (1925), another collection in the same vein. He also pursued his interest in the fantastic with the novel *XYZ* (1934), one of Peru's few contributions to the science-fiction genre. Sadly, however, Palma's writing declined rather than improved and his later work is markedly inferior to his first volume. Nonetheless, on the strength of that volume he remains one of the major figures of the period, not only as the initiator of the short-story genre but, above all, because of his stylistic concern and his attempt to write a literature of universal significance.

Despite the cultural backwardness reflected in Peru's slowness to catch up with international trends and in the lack of professionalism of most of the writers here discussed, the picture presented by Peruvian fiction in the Republican era is far from being as bleak as it might seem at first sight. Indeed, given Peru's position as a small, underdeveloped, newly independent nation, with a tiny reading public and virtually no book industry to speak of, it is remarkable that so much was achieved. Attempts were made to express a national identity and to come to grips with the major realities of national life and, towards the turn of the century, to lift the nation's literature into the mainstream of Western culture. The period gave rise, too, to works of great thematic importance and, if most fiction was artistically deficient, it also produced a number of highly accomplished works, such as Pardo's costumbrist sketches, the *Tradiciones peruanas* and *Cuentos malévolos*. It is true that no author succeeded in finding a major literary expression, but collectively the writers of the period prepared the way for later generations and, above all, Ricardo Palma set an example of literary craftsmanship which twentieth-century writers were to assimilate as they learned to treat major national themes in an artistically satisfying manner and in the process to produce literature of universal significance.

Part II
Drama and Poetry in the Republican Era

In Peru, as in other Spanish American countries, Neo-classicism remained the dominant literary mode in the years after Independence, a phenomenon reflecting the continuing cultural dependency of the former colony, where political independence had merely transferred power to the *criollo* élite and left the social structure basically unaltered. Significantly, its main exponent, Felipe Pardo y Aliaga (1806-68), was a member of the country's upper echelons.[1] When Peru became independent in 1821 he was taken to Spain with his family, and there, as a pupil of Alberto Lista, he received a classical formation in the tradition of the Enlightenment. On his return to Lima in 1828 he involved himself in politics as a prominent member of the Conservative Party and soon established himself as the foremost literary figure of the age, cultivating journalism, the costumbrist sketch, poetry and drama. In keeping with his classical formation, all of his work is based on the utilitarian belief that literature should serve a social function by instructing the public, and he is an accomplished craftsman who stands apart from his contemporaries primarily because of his expertise in the handling of language and form.

On his return from Europe Pardo was also appalled by the low level of culture he saw all around him. In particular he was dismayed by the deplorable state of the Peruvian theatre, and as theatre critic of local newspapers he attacked the poor standard of acting and production and his compatriots' provincialism and lack of taste and praised the productions of touring European companies as models to be emulated. Animated by the desire to improve the literary taste of the Lima public, he himself wrote three plays, but failed to make the

---

[1] See Felipe Pardo y Aliaga, *Teatro* (CAP, 1969); *Poesías*, ed. Luis Monguió (Berkeley: Univ. of California Press, 1973).

impact he hoped for. The best of the three is *Frutos de la educación* (1830), a comedy of manners in the tradition of Moratín, the Spanish Neo-classicist.[2] His intention of educating the public and raising its cultural standards is evident in the underlying theme that Peru will enter the ranks of civilised societies only when it sheds its provincial lack of refinement and the traditional Hispanic shortcomings of indolence and indiscipline and acquires the decorous habits and European virtues of discipline and industry represented by the English businessman Don Eduardo. More specifically, he censures laxity in the upbringing of the young. As a result of the deficient manner in which Don Feliciano and Doña Juana bring up their daughter and their ward, the future of both young people is blighted, for Bernardo leads a life of dissipation and eventually runs off to marry a mulatto girl, while Pepita's engagement to Don Eduardo is broken off when he is shocked by her lack of decorum at a dance. Pardo's great weakness as a playwright is that he is concerned primarily with the expression of abstract ideas, and characterisation and plot construction suffer as a consequence of their subordination to moral intent. Don Eduardo comes across merely as an insufferable prude and his unexpected change of heart over his proposed marriage is too abrupt and flimsily justified to be convincing. Lacking the dramatic craftsmanship to match his ambition, Pardo illustrates that it was not enough to adapt Spanish models to the Peruvian scene to produce good theatre.

While Pardo sought unsuccessfully to bring the Peruvian theatre into line with that of Europe, his contemporary Manuel Ascensio Segura (1805-71) demonstrated that it was possible to create a genuinely national theatre of quality.[3] Segura frequently protested against the lack of encouragement and appreciation given to local artists and was highly critical of the cultural inferiority complex which led Peruvians to overvalue everything foreign and to deride the works of their own countrymen. He himself was the author of thirteen plays depicting the middle-class world to which he belonged. A popular successs, these gave a much needed boost to the capital's languishing theatre.

---

[2] Pardo's other two plays are *Una huérfana en Chorrillos* (1833) and *Don Leocadio y el aniversario de Ayacucho* (1834), the first of which remained unstaged.

[3] See Manuel Ascensio Segura, *El Sargento Canuto. Las tres viudas* (CAP, 1970); *Ña Catita. La saya y manto* (CAP, 1972). See also Luis Alberto Sánchez, *El señor Segura, hombre de teatro* (San Marcos, 1976); Alberto Varillas Montenegro, *Manuel A. Segura* (BHP XIX, 1964).

Segura's dramatic principles are expounded in *La saya y manto* (1841) where, through a mouthpiece, he defines himself as a moralist whose aim it is to "corregir las costumbres, los abusos, los excesos/de que plagado se encuentra/por desgracia nuestro suelo" (correct the customs, abuses, excesses with which our land is unfortunately plagued). The main target of his criticism is his countrymen's lack of a proper sense of patriotism and civic virtue, exemplified in this play by the scramble for lucrative jobs in the administration by people seeking only security, enrichment and privilege. Don Mariano is the epitome of the legendary *viveza criolla*. Completely devoid of moral sense or political principles, he makes love to three women simultaneously, is willing to serve any government that will give him a job, and cynically uses one of his women to intercede with the minister to obtain a post for him. And in the course of the play we are given a damning view both of the frivolity of Limeñan womanhood and of the machinery of government by the fact that in love and employment the unprincipled Mariano is preferred over the solid, honest Don Bonifacio.

Segura's most biting criticism is to be found in the one-act *El Sargento Canuto* (1839), his first staged play and one of his best. The arrogant Canuto, eager to advance himself through marriage, succeeds in impressing Don Sempronio with his talents and prospects, and gaining his backing, lays imperious claim to the hand of his daughter Jacoba, only to be thwarted in the end by the resolute opposition of Jacoba herself and her lover Pulido. In Canuto Segura has portrayed a type thrown up by the civil wars of the turbulent years following Independence. Swollen up with self-importance, he struts and swaggers and rides roughshod over all those who do not wear a uniform, and full of ambition, he believes that the nation owes him a living and expects the world to bend to his will, though in the end his much vaunted courage is revealed to be mere bluster. Canuto in fact embodies the militarism of an age dominated by a succession of caudillos like Bolívar, Santa Cruz and Gamarra. Strongly anti-militarist, Segura here exposes the self-seeking and absolutist mentality of the military and shows, too, that the threat must and can be forestalled by resolute civilian opposition.

However, though social criticism is present in most of his works, Segura was not primarily a thinker or a man of radical views like Pardo. His talent was above all that of a perceptive observer of the social scene and his plays are memorable mainly for their lively and entertaining depiction of Limeñan customs and types. A particularly rich range of typical characters is to be found in perhaps his best work, *Ña Catita*, first presented in three acts in 1845 but later revised and staged as a four-act play in 1856. Here the fatuous aping of foreign manners is satirised in the figure of Don Alejo, a rich man-about-town who shows off his superior taste by sporting foreign fashions and putting on foreign airs. Dazzled by his fine manners, the socially pretentious Doña Rufina welcomes him as a prospective son-in-law and tries to foist him as a husband on her daughter Juliana, despite the opposition of her husband and the unwillingness of the girl herself. The family conflict is exacerbated by the meddling of Ña Catita. A widow in straitened circumstances, the latter sponges off others by ingratiating herself into their homes with a show of sympathy and kindly interest in their affairs, but behind her façade of religious piety and neighbourly concern, she is in fact an interfering busybody and scandalmonger and through her habit of siding with and encouraging all parties to their face and talking about them behind their back, she aggravates the tensions in the household.

As a versifier Segura lacks Pardo's polished style and his not infrequent lapses into the prosaic include some of the most execrable lines ever perpetrated in Spanish, but on the whole he writes with flowing facility and mastery of dialogue and his language, abounding in colloquial expressions, captures the flavour of popular speech. His plots are often weak, particularly in the much overrated *Las tres viudas* (1862), which is based on an implausible web of intrigue and misunderstandings, and even the splendid *Ña Catita* is rather spoiled by a contrived denouement which resolves the conflict artificially, with Doña Rufina being brought to her senses by the revelation that Don Alejo is already married. Nonetheless, despite his flaws, Segura displays an innate mastery of dramatic technique which sets his plays apart from the rather amateurish efforts of his contemporaries. If it would be difficult to rank him as one of the world's great playwrights, he is to be respected and admired for his not inconsiderable achievements and well merits the often applied label of "father of the Peruvian theatre". Apart from his role in establishing a national theatre, his significance lies perhaps in the fact that, like the *Tradiciones* of Ricardo Palma and the water-colours of the painter Pancho Fierro, his plays, by portraying the Peruvian middle classes to themselves, contributed to the creation of a sense of identity and national awareness so essential to a young country. Unfortunately, Peru was unable to produce other leading dramatists to succeed him and after his death the national theatre went into a long decline from which it did not emerge until the 1940s.[4]

Meanwhile, the poetic scene was dominated by Pardo, who was, above all, a civic poet. Satire was his favourite medium and the bulk of his production consists, in fact, of satirical poems ridiculing social customs, the literary scene, political opponents and, above all, the political state of the country. Inevitably much of it is circumstantial, but his best poems, particularly those written in the latter stages of his career, offer penetrating analyses of the social and political reality of the new Republic and elevate the genre by their formal proficiency.

At times, it must be said, Pardo comes across as a snobbish reactionary filled with the prejudices of his class and hostile to changes which threaten its interests. This is particularly so in poems such as "El Rey Nuestro Señor", which derides the sovereignty of the people as rule by an ignorant and unruly mob, "A mi hijo en sus días", where he ironically congratulates his son on attaining his majority and thus becoming the equal of his Negro servants, and "La lavandera", which presents the surly unreliability of Lima's laundresses as a symptom of a breakdown of the social order occasioned by the advent of democracy. In fact, the impression conveyed by such poems is misleading, for Pardo was a conservative in the best sense of the term, speaking out for a concept of orderly progress based on discipline, industry, civic virtue and respect for culture. This ideology is most clearly expressed in "El Perú", a long poem reminiscent of "La agricultura de la zona tórrida" of Andrés Bello, the major Spanish American Neo-classicist. Here Pardo contrasts Peru's unhappy state of political turmoil with the fabulous natural resources with which she has been blessed, and calls on her leaders to set the people an example of industry and public duty and so to guide the still immature nation along the path of progress. Another long poem, the satire "Constitución política", draws an ironic contrast between the fine ideals enshrined in the constitution and the sad reality of the national situation. Attributing Peru's ills to doctrinaire Liberalism which has foisted a misconceived democracy on a nation unprepared for it, the poet bitingly observes that it requires more than the

---

[4] The only other dramatist of any consequence during the period covered in this chapter was Leonidas Yerovi (1881-1917), who in the early years of the twentieth century achieved considerable box-office success with a series of light comedies, of which perhaps the best is *La de cuatro mil* (1903). Though writing in the costumbrist tradition of Segura, Yerovi makes no pretension to social comment and his plays are designed purely and simply as popular entertainment. On that level they are effective and at least have the merit of having kept the national theatre alive. See Leonidas Yerovi, *Poesía y teatro* (CAP, 1969).

adoption of European political models to convert a colony into a republic:

> ... fiesta de máscaras exóticas
> Es adaptar con afanosa táctica
> Trajes franceses a costumbres góticas
> Y así ponerlas a danzar en práctica;
> Como si empalmaduras estrambóticas
> De temas de política didáctica
> Bastaran a curar dolencias públicas
> Y a convertir colonias en repúblicas.

> (... a festival of exotic masks
> Is this feverish tactic of adapting
> French costumes to Gothic customs
> And setting them to dance in practice;
> As if outlandish couplings
> Of exercises in political theory
> Were enough to cure public ills
> And to convert colonies into republics.)

The liberty and equality proclaimed by the constitution are empty phrases, he argues, when the state fails to guarantee the rights of its citizens and to provide education to enable the uncultured masses to better themselves, and democracy is doomed to remain a farce as long as the nation's leaders continue to lack the culture and sense of civic responsibility to promote the general welfare. For Pardo the failure of democracy as practised in Peru was evident for all to see in the constant oscillations between anarchy and dictatorship, and to break out of that vicious circle and achieve progress he believed that the country needed the discipline of a strong but enlightened and responsible government which would eschew hollow slogans and apply itself to the task of raising the general quality of life:

> Yo a un buen Ejecutivo le diría
> Por toda atribución: "Coje un garrote,
> Y cuidando sin vil hipocresía
> Que tu celo ejemplar el mundo note,
> Tu justicia, honradez y economía,
> Y que nadie esté ocioso, ni alborote,
> Haz al pueblo el mejor de los regalos:
> Dale cultura y bienestar a palos."

> (To a good executive I would give
> Only one brief: "Take a cudgel,
> And eschewing vile hypocrisy, make sure
> That the world notes your exemplary zeal,

Your justice, your honesty and economy,
And that no one is idle or riotous.
Make the people the best of gifts:
Give them culture and well-being with the stick.")

Unfortunately, his was a voice crying in the wilderness and the values which he preached were ones which were to remain conspicuously unpractised throughout the nineteenth century.

It is a reflection on the unhappy social and political situation of the young Republic that for most of the nineteenth century the dominant poetic mode continued to be satire, of which, as has been seen, there was a tradition going back to the colonial period and which is regarded by some critics as the form most distinctive of Peruvian, or more exactly *criollo*, literature. Virtually every poet practised it, including Segura, who penned *La Peli-Muertada* (1851), a mock-epic poem satirising the political state of the country.[5] However, none did so more systematically or savagely than Pedro Paz Soldán y Unánue (1839-95),who wrote under the pseudonym of Juan de Arona.[6] Arona satirised the literary and intellectual milieu of Lima, and, above all, the social and moral climate of the capital. A typical poem is "Pierde el Perú la pereza", where he ridicules the atmosphere of torpor and stagnation that permeates the whole country:

¡Ocio, abandono, estancamiento, incuria,
pregonan los talleres y oficinas,
y casas, campos, tiendas y cocinas,
todo llora de brazos la penuria!

En vano día y noche hecho una furia
recorro del Perú las cuatro esquinas,
y del hombre las huellas peregrinas
afanoso busqué media centuria.

¿Qué es del Progreso? ¿Su impulsiva rueda
paralizada está? ¿No hay un mal asno,
un mal belitre que moverla pueda?

¿No hay aquí pueblo? —¿Pueblo? Sí, a la fe mía.
—¿Pues dónde se halla? —Es pueblo *Sober-asno*
y está ejercitando la *sober-asnía*.

---

[5] See Manuel Ascensio Segura, *La Peli-Muertada*, ed. Alberto Tauro (San Marcos, 1957).

[6] See Pedro Paz Soldán y Unánue (Juan de Arona), *Poesías completas*, 2 vols. (Academia Peruana de la Lengua, 1975); Julio Ortega, *Juan de Arona* (BHP XXXV, 1966). Arona was one of the country's leading intellectuals, famous for his dictionary of Peruvianisms.

(Idleness, dereliction, stagnation, neglect,
proclaim workshops and offices,
and houses, fields, shops and kitchens,
all of them weeping the dearth of hands!

In vain I furiously scour
the four corners of Peru day and night,
and for half a century I feverishly
sought the trail of man's passage.

What's become of Progress? Is its dynamic wheel
paralysed? Isn't there some poor donkey,
some wiseacre who can move it?

"Isn't there a people here?" "A people? Yes, upon my word."
"Where is it, then?" "It's a sover-asinine people
and it's busy exercising its sover-asininity.")

Arona differs from Pardo in that whereas the latter might be said to
have cultivated satire as an art form in that his work had an
ideological base and a didactic intent and he brought to it his
considerable poetic skills, for the former satire tends to be a
testimony of personal frustration expressed directly, with a minimum
of literary elaboration. Indeed, the significance of Arona's verse lies
not in its literary quality but in that sense of frustration with a stifling
environment unfavourable to creative activity. In part, at least, that
would seem to provide an explanation for the poverty of Peruvian
poetry of the period.

For, satire apart, the nineteenth century was in the main a lean
time for poetry. Romanticism came late to Peru and when it did
arrive it was something of a non-event. In the Lima of the 1850s there
emerged a group of young writers who enthusiastically and uncriti-
cally adopted the poses and repertoire of the European Romantics in
what may be regarded as an attempt to assert the status of the artist in
an uncultured society and to integrate national literature into the
mainstream of the modern literature of the period.[7] In this attempt
they failed dismally, largely because they were operating in a cultural
void. These young rebels had nothing to rebel against because Peru
had produced virtually no Neo-classical literature to speak of and its
one figure of stature — Felipe Pardo — was admired and respected
by them precisely because he was the only writer of the Republican

---

[7] See Ricardo Palma, *La bohemia de mi tiempo*, in *Tradiciones peruanas completas*
(Madrid: Aguilar, 1964), pp. 1293-1321. See also Raimundo Lazo, *Historia de la
literatura hispanoamericana. El Romanticismo* (Mexico City: Porrúa, 1971), pp. 56-60;
José Miguel Oviedo, "El romanticismo peruano, una impostura", *Letras Peruanas*, 14
(1963), 15-17.

period who had established literary credentials. Nor had they anything in common with their European counterparts, for their Romanticism had reached them second-hand and had been embraced for mainly emblematic reasons and they lacked a genuine appreciation of the movement, so that their work was almost wholly derivative and artificial. Moreover, in a society where there was little public interest in literature standards tended to be undemanding, for if it was relatively easy to make a name for oneself, there was no tradition or critical pressure to encourage the artist to hone his work and Peruvian writers had still not acquired the habit of self-criticism and a proper sense of vocation. Hence for the most part the Romantic generation succeeded only in producing a mass of mediocre verse that was sloppily written, shallow in content and ridden with the worst clichés of the epoch.

The one exception in this dismal panorama is Carlos Augusto Salaverry (1830-91), who penned what little of quality Peruvian Romanticism produced.[8] Alone among his generation, Salaverry possessed a genuinely Romantic sensibility and underlying his work is a philosophy of sorts which he elaborated in *Misterios de la tumba* (1883), a series of metaphysical meditations on death and the immortality of the soul. Salaverry believed that that would be his definitive work but aesthetically it is less than successful and it is in some of his earlier, less pretentious sonnets that he best expresses his Romantic conception of life. Thus, in "A la esperanza" he sadly recognises the illusory nature of human dreams and aspirations but refuses to give way to disenchantment and stubbornly persists in living life with illusion:

> Yo sé que eres una ave fugitiva,
> Un pez dorado que en las ondas juega,
> Una nube del alba que desplega
> Su miraje de rosa y me cautiva.
>
> Sé que eres flor que la niñez cultiva
> Y el hombre con sus lágrimas la riega,
> Sombra del porvenir que nunca llega,
> Bella a los ojos, y a la mano esquiva!

[8] Salaverry was the author of four collections of poetry: *Cartas a un ángel* (originally published in a Lima journal from 1858 onwards); *Diamantes y perlas* (1869); *Albores y destellos* (1871); *Misterios de la tumba* (1883). See Carlos Augusto Salaverry, *Poesía*, ed. Alberto Escobar (San Marcos, 1958). See also Alberto Escobar, *Carlos A. Salaverry* (BHP XXXV, 1966); id., "'Acuérdate de mí': tres variantes y una reflexión", in *Patio de Letras*, pp. 41-67; Augusto Tamayo Vargas, "El romanticismo peruano y Carlos Augusto Salaverry", *RevIb*, 40 (1955), 243-61.

Yo sé que eres la estrella de la tarde
Que ve el anciano entre celajes de oro,
Cual postrera ilusión de su alma, bella;

Y aunque tu luz para mis ojos no arde,
Engáñame ¡oh mentira! Yo te adoro,
Ave o pez, sombra o flor, nube o estrella.

(I know that you are a fugitive bird,
A golden fish sporting in the waves,
A cloud of the dawn unfurling
Its rosy mirage to captivate me.

I know that you are a flower cultivated in childhood
And watered by adult tears,
A shadow of the future which never arrives,
Beautiful to the eye and elusive to the hand!

I know that you are the evening star
Which the old man sees among golden skyscapes,
Like his soul's last beautiful illusion;

And though your light does not burn before my eyes,
Deceive me, o falsehood! I adore you,
Be you bird or fish, shadow or flower, cloud or star.)

However, what mainly distinguishes Salaverry is that he was the finest lyricist of his generation. Most of his work, notably his civic poetry, reveals the same defects as that of his contemporaries, but in his better moments, particularly in some of the love poems of *Cartas a un ángel*, he succeeds in combining intensity of feeling with a restrained delicacy of expression and has a handful of not inestimable poems to his credit. Of these perhaps the finest is the elegy "¡Acuérdate de mí!", where the rhythm and musical cadence create an atmosphere of melancholy in which the abandoned poet laments the barren desolation of his life yet salvages something of his lost happiness by clinging to the belief that his love transcends separation:

Parece ayer! ... De nuestros labios mudos
El suspiro de "¡Adiós!" volaba al cielo,
Y escondías la faz en tu pañuelo
        Para mejor llorar!
Hoy! ... nos apartan los profundos senos
De dos inmensidades que has querido,
Y es más triste y más hondo el de tu olvido
        Que el abismo del mar!

Pero ¿qué es este mar? ¿qué es el espacio?
¿Qué la distancia, ni los altos montes?
¿Ni qué son esos turbios horizontes
        Que miro desde aquí;

Si al través del espacio y de las cumbres,
De ese ancho mar y de este firmamento
Vuela por el azul mi pensamiento
    Y vive junto a ti?

(It seems only yesterday! . . . From our silent lips
The sigh of "Farewell!" ascended heavenwards,
And you hid your face in your handkerchief
    To weep more freely!
Today! . . . we are separated by the deep gulfs
Of two vastnesses of your choosing,
And sadder and deeper than the sea
    Is the abyss of your forgetfulness!

But what is this sea? What is space?
What is distance or the high mountains?
What are those blurred horizons
    I gaze on from here,
If across space and summits,
Across the wide sea and the firmament
My thoughts fly through the azure
    To live by your side?)

If Romanticism arrived late in Peru and the Romantic generation produced virtually nothing of note, Romantic attitudes persisted into the twentieth century in the work of Manuel González Prada (1848-1918), who began writing in the 1870s but whose two major volumes, *Minúsculas* and *Exóticas*, did not appear until 1901 and 1911 respectively.[9] Indeed, it could be argued that it was only with González Prada that the Romantic sensibility truly established itself in Peru, for part of his significance lies in the fact that he was the first Peruvian poet to give full and authentic expression to the Romantic *mal du siècle*. The dominant note of his poetry is existential anguish, a sense of the meaningless futility of life in a world where everyone and everything are but birds of passage flitting briefly across the earth on a journey to oblivion:

[9] See Manuel González Prada, *Antología poética*, ed. Carlos García Prada (Mexico City: Cultura, 1940); *Minúsculas*, 4th ed. (P.T.C.M., 1947); *Exóticas. Trozos de vida* (P.T.C.M., 1948); *Baladas peruanas* (Biblioteca Universitaria, 1966); *Presbiterianas*, 2nd ed. (El Inca, 1928); *Grafitos* (Paris: L. Bellenand, 1937); *Libertarias* (Paris: L. Bellenand, 1938); *Letrillas* (Milla Batres, 1975); *Cantos del otro siglo* (San Marcos, 1979); *Poemas desconocidos* (La Clepsidra, 1973). See also José Ferrer Canales, "González Prada y Darío", *Hispania*, 41 (1958), 465-70; Robert G. Mead, Jr., "Panorama poético de Manuel González Prada", *RevIb*, 39 (1955), 47-64; Estuardo Núñez, "La poesía de Manuel González Prada", *RevIb*, 10 (1942), 295-99; Francisco E. Porrata and Jorge A. Santana, eds., *Antología comentada del modernismo* (Sacramento: Dept. of Spanish and Portuguese, California State Univ., 1974), pp. 1-22; Irving B. Rothberg, "The dominant themes of González Prada's *Minúsculas*", *Hispania*, 38 (1955), 465-71.

Aves de paso que en flotante hilera
recorren el azul del firmamento,
exhalan a los aires un lamento
y se disipan en veloz carrera,
son el amor, la gloria y el contento.

¿Qué son las mil y mil generaciones
que brillan y descienden al ocaso,
que nacen y sucumben a millones?
   Aves de paso.

Inútil es, oh pechos infelices,
al mundo encadenarse con raíces.
Impulsos misteriosos y pujantes
nos llevan entre sombras, al acaso,
que somos ¡ay! eternos caminantes,
   aves de paso.

(Love, happiness and contentment
are birds of passage that in floating line
traverse the blue of the firmament,
breathe a lament to the air
and vanish in swift flight.

What are the thousands upon thousands of generations
that shine and sink at sunset,
that are born and succumb in millions?
   Birds of passage.

Oh unhappy souls, it is useless
to bind oneself to the world with roots.
Powerful and mysterious impulses
carry us among shadows, aimlessly,
for, alas, we are eternal travellers,
   birds of passage.)

However, González Prada is also very much a poet of his times in
that in him this Romantic anguish is exacerbated by the philosophical
theories of the late nineteenth century, which lead him, in poems like
"Determinismo", to view man as being but a helpless instrument of
the forces of creation. In face of the futility of existence his most
common response is a forced stoicism and a desperate grasping after
such happiness as life affords. Elevating love and poetry as the only
things of worth in a senseless world, he anticipates, or at least
coincides with, the Spanish American Modernist movement in his
pursuit of fulfilment through art and the senses:

El rítmico vuelo de la estrofa alada
Y el rayo de ardiente, pasional mirada,
Encierran lo bello, lo mejor del mundo.
¡Amor! ¡Poesía! ... Lo restante ¡nada!

(The rhythmic flight of the winged verse
and the lightning of passion's ardent gaze
Encapsulate the beautiful, the best of the world.
Love! Poetry! ... All the rest is nothing!)

González Prada was also the first writer to come to terms with the fact that in a country like Peru poetry was destined to be a lonely vocation pursued on the margin of and at odds with society. Poems like "Por la rosa" satirise the philistinism of a society which despises poetry as being of no practical use, yet he recognises that the bourgeoisie is too insensitive to be affected by satire. Nonetheless, he insists that the poet must not compromise his ideals and adopts a stance of Olympian isolation that was to become characteristic of the Modernist movement. The poet must combat the philistinism around him by cultivating his art in spite of it, embracing his vocation as an alternative life-style devoted to the pursuit of beauty:

Si sois brutal mayoría
¿Qué haremos hoy los amantes
De la hermosa Poesía?

[...] en verso combatamos
Por la azucena y la rosa.

(If you are the brutal majority,
What are we to do,
The lovers of fair Poetry?

[...] let us fight in verse
For the lily and the rose.)

It would be easy but unfair to dismiss such a statement as one of the clichés of the Modernist era, for in the Peruvian context the situation highlighted by González Prada was a very real one and his plea to poets to be true to their vocation was particularly opportune.

Yet González Prada was far from being a poet of the Ivory Tower, for, as has been seen, he was a man very much involved in the political life of his country and the combative radicalism which animates his prose writings is carried over into much of his poetry. In the 1870s he composed his *Baladas peruanas*, an attempt to create a national ballad revolving around the Indian. Some of these pieces are based on Inca legends and episodes from the Conquest and others, such as "El mitayo" which movingly conveys the plight of the peasant uprooted from his home for enforced labour in the mines, deal with the social injustice perpetrated against the indigenous population. Likewise, he renews his attack on all that is outworn and

rotten in Spanish American life in *Presbiterianas*, a collection of anti-
clerical verse which appeared anonymously in 1909, and in the
mordant epigrams of *Grafitos* and the social and political pieces of
Libertarias, both of which were published posthumously. The disgust
and alienation inspired in him by the political, social and cultural
environment of his native country are nowhere expressed more
forcefully than in "El Perú":

> ¡Abyección y podredumbre!
> Bajo el peso de la infamia,
> viene y va la muchedumbre.
>
> ¿Dónde aquí la noble idea?
> En el fango de la charca
> todo se hunde o chapotea [...]
>
> Y si aquí rodó mi cuna,
> soy aquí tan extranjero
> como en Londres o en la Luna.
>
> A mi pueblo y a mis gentes,
> ¿qué me liga, qué me enlaza?
> Yo me siento de otro mundo,
> yo me siento de otra raza.
>
> (Abjectness and rottenness!
> Under the burden of infamy
> the herd comes and goes.
>
> Where here is the noble idea?
> In the muddy pool
> everything sinks or gets splattered [...]
>
> And if it was here my cradle rocked,
> here I'm as much a foreigner
> as in London or on the Moon.
>
> What links me, what binds me
> to my people and to my folk?
> I feel I belong to another world,
> I feel I belong to another race.)

González Prada's anti-traditionalism also manifests itself in his
attitude to form. He had a low opinion of Spanish poetry and not
only dismissed most contemporary poetry as cliché-ridden bombast
but regarded Spanish verse as being inherently limited by its formal
poverty and its slavish adherence to academic precepts. He himself
sought to enrich and revitalise the genre and developed the
foundations of a new theory of versification, advocating in particular
a poetry based on rhythm rather than on rhyme:

Sueño con ritmos domados al yugo
de rígido acento,
libres del rudo carcán de la rima.
Ritmos sedosos que efloren la idea,
cual plumas de un cisne
rozan el agua tranquila de un lago.

(I dream of rhythms tamed and yoked
to rigid stress,
free of rhyme's rough slave-collar.
Silky rhythms which will stroke the idea
as a swan's feathers
skim the tranquil waters of a lake.)

He also interested himself in non-Hispanic literatures and imitated and adapted into Spanish forms and metres from France, England, Italy, Germany and the East. Of these the most notable were the *rondel* and its variations, the *rispetto, balata, estornelo, gacela, laude,* the Malayan *pantum* and Persian quatrains. Among his own poetic inventions the most interesting was the *polirritmo sin rima,* free verse with varying accents and rhythms. Unfortunately he was not always able to harmonise formal experiment and meaning. Often his poems are little more than intellectual exercises demonstrating his theories, and on other occasions he veers to the opposite extreme and lapses into prosaic over-explicitness in his concern to convey his message. Nonetheless, his formal innovations represent a major contribution to the development of Peruvian and Spanish American verse and his best work makes effective use of a simple, concentrated style which marks a welcome departure from the bombastic verbosity of most poetry of the period.

Though his influence as a poet was diminished somewhat by the fact that relatively little of his poetry was published during his lifetime and that his major volumes — *Minúsculas* (1901) and *Exóticas* (1911) — appeared in book form only after Spanish American Modernism was already well established, González Prada was one of the main precursors of that movement because of certain attitudes expressed in his work — his view of the role of the poet, his exaltation of beauty and the senses, his cosmopolitan outlook — and, above all, because of his formal innovations. Yet it is another indication of the poverty of Peruvian letters at that time in relation even to the rest of Spanish America that, like Romanticism before it, Modernism flowered late in that country. However, when it did arrive its leading representative was to emerge as one of the movement's major figures and to bring to it a distinctive voice.

José Santos Chocano (1875-1934) is a unique phenomenon in the history of Peruvian letters.[10] Driven by a hunger for fame and glamour, he led a colourful life and was the first — and only — Peruvian poet to reach a wide audience and to become a public celebrity in his own lifetime. He first came to prominence in 1894-95 when he was imprisoned by General Cáceres and castigated the dictator in the manner of Victor Hugo in a volume entitled *Iras santas*. In 1900 he was sent to Central America on a diplomatic mission and spent most of the next twenty years abroad. In the course of his career he churned out a vast body of poetry, his most important works being *Alma América* (1906) and *¡Fiat Lux!* (1908), and such was the reputation he made for himself throughout the Spanish-speaking world that he became an international celebrity and the friend of prominent political figures and after his return to Lima in late 1921 he was triumphantly crowned his country's Poet Laureate. To the end of his days he remained in the public eye, spending a year in prison after killing a young man in a brawl and eventually meeting his own death in Chile at the hands of a madman.

Like his fellow Modernists, Chocano saw the poet as a noble spirit at odds with the egalitarian mediocrity of the modern world. In "Anacronismo" he complains that he has been born out of his time, in an inglorious age, and in "El palacio de los virreyes" likens democracy to an elephant's foot crushing a flower. In the course of his life this attitude led Chocano to identify with dictatorial regimes in Peru and other Spanish American countries. In his poetry it expresses itself in nostalgia for the more glorious times of the past. Thus poems like "El palacio de los virreyes" harp back to the aristocratic elegance and grace of the colonial period. However, Chocano stands out among the Modernists in that he remained a Romantic at heart and his muse is essentially heroic. In "La musa fuerte" he confesses that he prefers the metal of the trumpet to the chords of the violin and it is the heroic age of the Conquest that attracts him above all. He himself felt that he had been born to perform some great role in life and in "Blasón" he proclaims that his heritage is that of the Inca emperors and the Spanish conquistadores and implies that to be a poet is to be a modern-day hero:

[10] See José Santos Chocano, *Obras completas*, ed. Luis Alberto Sánchez (Mexico City: Aguilar, 1954); *Antología poética*, ed. Alfonso Escudero (Buenos Aires: Espasa Calpe, 1947). See also Porrata and Santana, *Antología comentada del modernismo*, pp. 521-45; Phyllis Rodríguez-Peralta, *José Santos Chocano* (New York: Twayne, 1970); Luis Alberto Sánchez, *Aladino o Vida y obra de José Santos Chocano*, 2nd ed. (Universo, 1975); id., *José Santos Chocano* (BHP XXX, 1965).

Soy el cantor de América autóctono y salvaje:
mi lira tiene un alma, mi canto un ideal.
Mi verso no se mece colgado de un ramaje
con un vaivén pausado de hamaca tropical ...

Cuando me siento inca, le rindo vasallaje
al Sol, que me da el cetro de su poder real;
cuando me siento hispano y evoco el coloniaje,
parecen mis estrofas trompetas de cristal.

Mi fantasía viene de un abolengo moro:
los Andes son de plata, pero el león, de oro;
y las dos castas fundo con épico fragor.

La sangre es española e incaico es el latido,
y de no ser poeta, quizás yo hubiera sido
un blanco aventurero o un indio emperador.

(I am the singer of America, autochthonous and savage:
my lyre has a soul, my song an ideal.
My verse does not rock with the leisurely oscillation
of a hammock hanging from tropical branches ...

When I feel myself Inca, I render homage
to the Sun and receive from him the sceptre of his royal
          power;
when I feel myself Spanish and sing of colonial times,
my verses are like crystal trumpets.

My rich imagination comes from old Moorish stock:
the Andes are of silver, but the lion is of gold;
and I fuse the two races in myself with epic din.

My blood is Spanish and Incaic its pulsation,
and were I not a poet, I might have been
a white adventurer or an Indian Emperor.)

In keeping with this heroic self-image Chocano cast himself in the role of a champion waging a poetic crusade on behalf of Spanish America. He took Rubén Darío, the major Modernist poet, to task for cultivating a cosmopolitan poetry dominated by French influences and gave a new direction to the movement by singing of American themes and settings. An early epic, *La epopeya del Morro* (1899), seeks to salvage national pride from the disaster of the War of the Pacific by celebrating the heroic resistance of Bolognesi and his troops in the battle of Arica. Later he was to see himself as the voice of the whole continent and as his international reputation grew he came to be known as the Poet of America. His famous claim that "Walt Whitman tiene el Norte; pero yo tengo el Sur" (Walt Whitman has the North; but I have the South) is typically self-glorifying, but it is also a statement of the mission he set himself: that of affirming Hispanic America's pride in itself and asserting its greatness and values in face of those of the encroaching Anglo-Saxon colossus.

The vision of America presented by Chocano's poetry is, above all, one of nobility and grandeur. "Ciudad colonial" is only one of several compositions recalling the graceful elegance of Lima's days of glory as the viceregal capital of South America, and others, such as the opening section of "La tierra del Sol", go back still further to evoke the sumptuous splendour and majesty of the Inca empire. More commonly Chocano adopts an epic tone to re-create scenes from the Conquest, celebrating the courage and exploits of the conquistadores or recounting the equally heroic deeds of famous indigenous warriors such as Cuacthemoc, Caupolicán or Cahuide. A stirring sense of the adventure and excitement of that period is particularly well caught in "Los caballos de los conquistadores", where the insistent rhythm evokes the clatter of the horses' hoofs as they traverse mountains and valleys in conquest of a New World. A similar sense of the noble and grandiose is present in a host of poems glorifying the natural beauty of the continent. The sonnets "La magnolia" and "Las orquídeas" display a surprisingly delicate touch to capture the fragile grace of exotic tropical flora. More characteristically poem after poem depicts the awesome immensity of the American landscape, the imposing majesty of the Andes, the brooding silence of the high plateaux, thundering cataracts, luxurious tropical jungles. In that magnificent setting other poems portray equally magnificent creatures — alligators, boas, tigers, pumas, condors. The latter, indeed, could be regarded as an emblem of Chocano's work in contrast to the delicate swan that is Darío's symbol. Perched above the world in the solitary splendour of a snow-capped peak, the majestic bird of "El sueño del condor" seems to embody the poet's grandiose conception of himself and his continent:

Al despuntar el estrellado coro,
pósase en una cúspide nevada:
lo envuelve el día en la postrer mirada;
y revienta a sus pies trueno sonoro.

Su blanca gola es imperial decoro;
su ceño varonil, pomo de espada;
sus garfios siempre en actitud airada,
curvos puñales de marfil con oro.

Solitario en la cúspide se siente:
en las pálidas nieblas se confunde;
desvanece el fulgor de su aureola;

y esfumándose, entonces, lentamente,
se hunde en la noche, como el alma se hunde
en la meditación cuando está sola ...

(As the starry choir makes its appearance,
he perches on a snow-capped peak:
day envelops him in its last gaze;
and echoing thunder explodes at his feet.

His white ruff is an imperial decoration;
his manly frown, a sword pommel;
his claws, in attitude ever fierce,
curved daggers of marble with gold.

Solitary on the peak he feels:
in the pale mists his outline is blurred;
the brilliance of his aureole disappears;

and then, fading slowly away,
he sinks into the night, as the soul
sinks into meditation when it is alone ...)

Chocano brought a fresh vigour to Modernism by veering away
from the preciosity of his contemporaries and he gave the movement
a new direction by breaking with the cult of France, neo-Hellenism
and Oriental exoticism to focus on American themes and settings.
Yet it is not surprising that the exalted reputation he enjoyed at the
height of his career should have declined in his later years and after
his death. For that success can be attributed largely to the superficial
appeal of the exotic America he presents to his readers and to the
equally superficial glitter of his verse and imagery. Chocano was an
important historical phenomenon in that his work inspired a new
pride in his compatriots and fellow Spanish Americans at a time
when Peru was still recovering from the traumatic defeat at the hands
of Chile and the Hispanic nations were nursing an inferiority
complex in the face of North American expansion. However, his
grandiose vision of America is one which is essentially superficial. It
is obviously so in his treatment of the Indian, which dwells only on
the romanticised grandeur of a legendary past or, in later poems,
presents the contemporary Indian as the stereotyped impassive
enigma, but it is also true of his equally romanticised versions of the
Conquest and the colonial period and of his descriptions of nature,
which fix on the striking and communicate no real feel of the
landscape. At his best Chocano was a competent poet whose main
strength lay in his imaginative re-creations of nature and who
exploited Modernist advances in versification to good effect, particularly in the areas of rhythm and onomatopoeia. However, his

poetry is also superficial in that its impact is direct and immediate, leaving little to the imagination of the reader. Furthermore, he tends to make excessive and often extravagant use of visual imagery and to declaim at the top of his voice and his arrogant, self-glorifying personality keeps obtruding on the reader. At his worst he comes across as a throw-back to the shallow grandiloquence of the Romantic era, and if his public success did much to raise the status of the poet in Peru, that success is itself a damning comment on the literary taste of the public.

The best poets of the period, in fact, were men who shunned the public gaze and unobtrusively went about their business in quiet isolation. Modernism persisted late and produced at least one fine minor poet in Alberto Ureta (1885-1966), whose work is characterised by a tone of quiet intimacy, a resigned melancholy at the fleetingness of time and a bitter-sweet nostalgia for moments of lost happiness.[11] However, the first major figure of modern times was José María Eguren (1874-1942).[12] It is another manifestation of Peru's cultural backwardness that although Eguren belongs chronologically to the post-Modernist period — the first of his three volumes was published in 1911 and the last in 1929 — and is usually classified as a post-Modernist, he is still operating within the Modernist sensibility. Yet if that makes him something of an anachronism in international terms, it does not detract from the intrinsic quality of his work and in the national context he represents the starting-point of the remarkable flourishing of Peruvian poetry in the twentieth century.

[11] See Alberto Ureta, *Antología poética* (Buenos Aires: Losada, 1946); *Rumor de almas* ("La Revista", 1911); *El dolor pensativo* (Sanmartí, 1917); *Las tiendas del desierto* (Gil, 1933); *Elegías de la cabeza loca* (Paris: L. Bellenand, 1937). See also Julio Ortega, *Figuración de la persona*, pp. 147-50.

[12] Eguren published three volumes of poetry: *Simbólicas* (1911), *La canción de las figuras* (1916) and *Poesías* (1929); the latter book includes the collections *Sombra* and *Rondinelas*. He also wrote essays in prose which were first published in 1959 under the title *Motivos estéticos*. See José María Eguren, *Obras completas* (Mosca Azul, 1974). See also Xavier Abril, *Eguren el obscuro* (Córdoba, Arg.: Univ. Nac. de Córdoba, 1970); Emilio Armaza, *Eguren* (Mejía Baca, 1959); César A. Debarbieri, *Los personajes en la poética de José María Eguren* (Univ. del Pacífico, 1975); Jorge Díaz Herrera, "Contra el Eguren que no es", *RevCrit*, 13 (1981), 83-91; Américo Ferrari, "La función del símbolo. Notas sobre José María Eguren", *Insula*, 332/333 (1974), 4; James Higgins, *The Poet in Peru*, pp. 1-23, 91-108; Estuardo Núñez, *José María Eguren. Vida y obra* (Villanueva, 1964); Julio Ortega, *José María Eguren* (BHP XXX, 1965); id., *Figuración de la persona*, pp. 89-116; Roberto Paoli, "Eguren, tenor de las brumas", *RevCrit*, 3 (1976), 25-53; id., "Las raíces literarias de Eguren", in *Estudios sobre literatura peruana contemporánea*, pp. 7-53; Phyllis Rodríguez-Peralta, *Tres poetas cumbres en la poesía peruana* (Madrid: Playor, 1983), pp. 61-95; José Luis Rouillon Arróspide, *Las formas fugaces de José María Eguren* (Imágenes y Letras, 1974); Ricardo Silva-Santisteban, ed., *José María Eguren. Aproximaciones y perspectivas* (Univ. del Pacífico, 1977).

In contrast to Chocano, Eguren was a gentle, timid man who led an uneventful life in the tranquil seclusion of the little seaside resort of Barranco just outside Lima. His vital attitude is defined in "Peregrín cazador de figuras", a kind of "portrait of the artist" where he presents himself in the guise of Peregrín who, from a lonely belvedere, peers into the night and explores a dark, mysterious landscape symbolic of the world of the imagination:

> En el mirador de la fantasía,
> al brillar del perfume
> tembloroso de armonía;
> en la noche que llamas consume;
> cuando duerme el ánade implume,
> los órficos insectos se abruman
> y luciérnagas fuman;
> cuando lucen los silfos galones, entorcho,
> y vuelan mariposas de corcho
> o los rubios vampiros cecean,
> o las firmes jorobas campean;
> por la noche de los matices,
> de ojos muertos y largas narices;
> en el mirador distante,
> por las llanuras;
> Peregrín cazador de figuras,
> con ojos de diamante
> mira desde las ciegas alturas.

> (In fantasy's belvedere,
> amid the sparkle of perfume
> tremulous with harmony;
> in the flame-consuming night;
> while the unfledged duckling sleeps,
> the Orphic insects swamp one another
> and glow-worms smoke;
> when the sylphs sport stripes and braid
> and moths of cork flit through the air
> or the grizzled vampires lisp
> ·   or the resolute hunchbacks patrol;
> through the night of nuances,
> dead eyes and long noses;
> in the distant belvedere,
> across the plains;
> with eyes of diamond
> Peregrine the hunter of images
> gazes from the dark heights.)

Peregrín appears as a completely isolated figure engaged in an essentially solitary activity, and through him Eguren expresses his repudiation of an alienating social environment and his withdrawal into his own private world to devote himself to his artistic pursuits. Part of the significance of Eguren, indeed, is that he was the first Peruvian poet to commit himself totally to his vocation and to embrace poetry as a way of life.

"Peregrín cazador de figuras" also delineates Eguren's version of the Symbolist aesthetic, of which he was perhaps the only genuine representative in Spanish America. Its basis is formed by a myriad host of strange characters — the figures hunted by Peregrín — and his most distinctive poems are built around them. The poems often take the form of anecdotes or dramatic vignettes and are frequently placed in remote settings — exotic lands such as the Orient or the Nordic countries, or an indeterminate past that is vaguely medieval — which detach them from reality as the reader knows it. The best of them are characterised by their concision and objectivity: the poet limits himself to presenting the characters to us and rarely intervenes to comment or to give us clues as to how we should interpret the poems. The poems, in other words, operate firstly on an immediate level as versified tales or character sketches with no apparent reference to anything but themselves. At the same time, however, the characters embody in synthesised form the emotions which Eguren sought to exteriorise in his verse, and by the suggestive manner of their presentation point to another reality hidden beneath the surface of the poem. Hinting rather than stating, Eguren endows his work with a suggestive power which gives his superficially simple and transparent verse a rich density of meaning that is only gradually discovered after several readings.

Eguren's repudiation of the society of his day is expressed in a series of poems which make a veiled criticism of the values of contemporary civilisation. He was appalled by the aggressiveness of the Western way of life, which seemed to him to be ushering in a new Dark Age, and "El caballo" and "La ronda de espadas" evoke respectively the horrors of modern warfare and the oppressive atmosphere of the modern police state. He also regarded the modern age as one in which life had been fossilised by bourgeois convention and the protagonist of "El dominó" personifies the spiritual bankruptcy of a social order that has been sapped of its vitality and lost the capacity to approach life with illusion and enthusiasm. In his view the sickness of our civilisation had its roots, above all, in modern man's want of a religious sense, as is suggested by "El dios cansado", a poem which introduces the figure of an exhausted deity no longer able to cope and ignored by a world unaware of his existence:

Plomizo, carminado	(Leaden, banished
y con la barba verde,	and with beard of green,
el ritmo pierde	the weary god
el dios cansado.	loses his rhythm.
Y va con tristes ojos,	And he travels sad-eyed
por los desiertos rojos	across the red deserts
de los beduinos	of the Bedouins
y peregrinos.	and pilgrims.
Sigue por las obscuras	He presses on through the dark,
y ciegas capitales	blind capitals
de negros males	of black evils
y desventuras.	and misfortunes.
Reinante el día estuoso,	In the heat of the day
camina sin reposo	he journeys without rest
tras los inventos	on the track of inventions
y pensamientos.	and ideas.
Continúa, ignorado,	Unnoticed, he continues on his way
por la región atea;	through the atheistic region;
y nada crea	and the weary god
el dios cansado.	creates nothing.)

The weary god may be interpreted firstly as a symbol of the old god in whom men can no longer believe, of the old religion which has worn itself out and become fossilised in ritual and dogma. Yet the poem also hints that God has changed his nature, that, in an attempt to win men back to faith in him, he has made himself a god of progress, scouring the world for ideas and inventions which would restore him to favour in men's eyes. But not only does he fail to win men's allegiance, but by his inability to create he demonstrates that he has been dispossessed of his divinity. The impotent god, therefore, is also a symbol of the new faith that has replaced the old religion, the positivistic cult of scientific and material progress which denies the power of God and the very existence of spiritual forces in the universe. Needless to say, the weary god is also the image of modern man who, having lost faith in traditional religious creeds, has cast around him for a new centre for his existence and has turned to science. In so doing he has gone astray, for, since the new faith takes no account of spiritual realities, he has lost his "rhythm", his sense of spiritual harmony with his world. Eguren, in fact, attributed contemporary man's alienation to the loss of his primitive innocence, believing that he had developed his reason at the cost of stunting his

other faculties and that in dominating the world he had lost all sense
of its magic and wonder. Significantly, several poems introduce us
into the realms of Nordic mythology ("Los gigantones") and
children's fantasy ("El Duque", "Juan Volatín"). For underlying all
of his work is the conviction that man must recover the spiritual
innocence of children and primitive peoples if he is to overcome his
alienation and live once more in harmony with the world.

If Eguren was a man out of tune with the society of his day, it was
above all a positive impulse that determined his withdrawal from
that society. For he originated in Peru the visionary or neo-mystical
poetics that was virtually a religion among the French Symbolists
and which was to become a major current in twentieth-century
Peruvian poetry. That poetics elevates poetry into an alternative life-
style devoted to the passionate pursuit of self-fulfilment, an activity
akin to that of the mystic in which the poet withdraws into solitary
contemplation in an attempt to apprehend an ineffable cosmic
harmony. Eguren, therefore, turns his back on the world, not merely
because he is at odds with society, but because his concern is not with
the things of the world but with a greater spiritual reality. His poetics
is most clearly expressed in the afore-cited "Peregrín cazador de
figuras", where the isolated protagonist explores a dark, mysterious
landscape and hunts the weird and fantastic creatures who inhabit it.
That landscape may be taken as a symbol of the other side of life,
those dark areas of reality which lie outside our rational experience
and which cannot be illuminated or explained by the light of reason.
It is, firstly, the natural world, or, more exactly, the spiritual universe
which Eguren, in defiance of the mechanistic vision of a scientific
age, believed lay concealed behind the material world, but at the
same time it is also the poet's own inner world, the realm of the
subconscious, fantasy, memory and dreams. Like Peregrín, Eguren
was an explorer of a mysterious universe whose secrets he sought to
apprehend intuitively and to capture in symbolic figures who would
embody his perceptions of life's underlying harmony.

The moment of epiphany that is the goal of this poetics is
celebrated in "La niña de la lámpara azul":

En el pasadizo nebuloso
cual mágico sueño de Estambul,
su perfil presenta destelloso
la niña de la lámpara azul.

(In the shadowy passageway,
like a magical dream of Stambul,
she presents her sparkling profile,
the girl with the blue lamp.

Agil y risueña se insinúa,	Lithe and smiling she glides,
y su llama seductora brilla,	and her enticing flame burns bright;
tiembla en su cabello la garúa	on her hair trembles the spray
de la playa de la maravilla.	from the shores of wonder.
Con voz infantil y melodiosa	With childlike melodious voice
en fresco aroma de abedul,	in fresh aroma of birch,
habla de una vida milagrosa	she speaks of a miraculous life,
la niña de la lámpara azul.	the girl with the blue lamp.
Con cálidos ojos de dulzura	With eyes warm with sweetness
y besos de amor matutino,	and kisses of morning love,
me ofrece la bella criatura	the fair creature shows me
un mágico y celeste camino.	a magical, heavenly road.
De encantación en un derroche,	Lavishing enchantment,
hiende leda, vaporoso tul;	she gaily rends the misty veil;
y me guía a través de la noche	and she guides me through the night,
la niña de la lámpara azul.	the girl with the blue lamp.)

The protagonist is both a manifestation of another reality and a symbol of the spiritual qualities necessary to perceive it. A young girl poised on the brink of adolescence and characterised by her gaiety, her freshness, her ingenuous love of all things, she represents the capacity to approach life with childlike illusion and to feel the wonder and magic of the world. Bearing the guiding light of illusion, she manifests herself to the poet as an apparition from a marvellous universe where life is "miraculous" and towards which she leads him by a "magical and heavenly path". Such moments of ecstatic transportation, the poem suggests, are the privilege of those who, unatrophied by life-sapping reason, are able to approach life with the sense of illusion which she embodies.

In general, however, the tone of Eguren's poetry is not one of ecstatic transportation but rather one of serene contemplation as the poet glimpses a cosmic order amid the beauties of the natural world. Among the best examples are "Los reyes rojos", where the elemental struggle for life embodied by two endlessly-warring birds of prey is seen as fitting into a wider pattern of universal harmony, and "Los ángeles tranquilos", which captures the spirit of the magical moment of early dawn when the miracle of creation is daily repeated. In the latter poem the peaceful calm of the first moment of day is announced and highlighted by the abrupt dying down of a storm:

Pasó el vendaval; ahora,	(The storm has passed; now,
con perlas y berilos,	with pearls and beryls,
cantan la soledad aurora	the tranquil angels
los ángeles tranquilos.	sing the dawn solitude.

Modulan canciones santas	They modulate holy songs
en dulces bandolines;	on sweet mandolins
viendo caídas las hojosas plantas	as they see fallen the leafy plants
de campos y jardines.	of fields and gardens.
Mientras sol en la neblina	While in the mist the sun
vibra sus oropeles,	vibrates its tinsel,
besan la muerte blanquecina	they kiss whitened death
en los Saharas crueles.	in the cruel Saharas.
Se alejan de madrugada,	The tranquil angels
con perlas y berilos,	depart in the early morn,
y con la luz del cielo en la mirada	with pearls and beryls
los ángeles tranquilos.	and the light of heaven in their
	eyes.)

That calm is then embodied in the persons of the tranquil angels, symbolic figures who imply a spiritual presence behind the material universe. Their joyful hymns of praise amidst a scene of storm-wrought devastation celebrate the new life which dawn will bring forth, and then, in a temporal progression typical of much of Eguren's poetry, they fade away as the sun forces its way through the morning mist and bathes a reborn world in dazzling light. The whole poem is thus informed by a sense of continuity and order, of an unending cycle in which day is continually reborn out of night and life out of death. Indeed, the final stanzas open the poem out, with the tranquil angels who lovingly embrace death and depart with the light of heaven in their eyes becoming a symbol of spirit for which death in this world is the prelude to rebirth on another plane of existence. It is thus suggested that the order of the natural world mirrors a supernatural order.

Unfortunately, such visions of harmony tend to be short-lived and much of Eguren's work is dominated by nostalgia for the lost idylls of the past and by a sense of the fleeting nature of life and of the tragic inevitability of death. However, his visionary poetics assumes the existence of an ideal world beyond the grave, of which the beauties glimpsed in this world are a confirmation, and ultimately, in poems like "El bote viejo" and "La canción del regreso", he is able to view death with serene optimism as a kind of homecoming, since it is only by passing through the portals of death that man can gain access to his true spiritual home, that ideal world where the soul will bask in the bliss of perfect beauty.

It would be difficult to overestimate Eguren's significance in the development of Peruvian poetry. It is not just that, by giving expression to the modern artist's experience of alienation and by raising poetry into a medium for apprehending a greater reality, he initiated two of the main currents of his country's poetry in the twentieth century. Above all, he was the first Peruvian to pursue his vocation with total commitment on the margin of society and the first with the aesthetic consciousness to develop a poetic language capable of creating an imaginative universe rich in suggestion and dense in meaning. As such, he set an example for later generations to follow. Indeed, it could be asserted with only slight exaggeration that Peruvian poetry effectively begins with Eguren.

CHAPTER 4

THE BIRTH OF A LITERATURE (c. 1915-c.1941)

Part I
Regionalist Fiction and the Establishment of a Novelistic Tradition

Throughout Spanish America the second decade of the twentieth century saw a movement away from Modernist cosmopolitanism to a fiction concerning itself with local reality and in particular with life in the rural areas, a tendency that reflects a growing nationalist feeling and a disenchantment with a seemingly spiritually-bankrupt Europe.[1] In Peru the initiator of this regionalist trend was Abraham Valdelomar (1888-1919), whose best fiction is contained in two collections of short stories, *El caballero Carmelo* (1918) and the posthumous *Los hijos del sol* (1921).[2] The bulk of his work is, in fact, still Modernist in

[1] For a study of the development of the short story, see Earl M. Aldrich, Jr., *The Modern Short Story in Peru* (Madison: Univ. of Wisconsin Press, 1966).

[2] See Abraham Valdelomar, *Obras* (Pizarro, 1979); *Cuentos*, ed. Armando Zubizarreta (CAP, 1969); *Cuento y poesía*, ed. Augusto Tamayo Vargas (San Marcos, 1959); *Our Children of the Sun*, trans. M.M. Thompson (Carbondale: Southern Illinois Univ. Press, 1968). See also Maureen Ahern, "Mar, magia y misterio en Valdelomar", *Sphinx*, 13 (1960), 9-29; César A. Angeles Caballero, *Valdelomar, conferenciante* (Ica: Univ. Nac. San Luis Gonzaga, 1962); id., *Valdelomar, vida y obra* (Ica: Univ. Nac. San Luis Gonzaga, 1964); Myrna Goldman, "Impressionism in Abraham Valdelomar's Prose Fiction", Diss. Wisconsin 1978 (Univ. Microfilms, 1979); Luis Loayza, "El joven Valdelomar", in *El sol de Lima*, pp. 147-66; Phyllis Rodríguez-Peralta, "Abraham Valdelomar, a Transitional Modernist", *Hispania*, 52 (1969), 26-32; Luis Alberto Sánchez, *Valdelomar o La belle époque* (Mexico City: Fondo de Cultura Económica, 1969); Augusto Tamayo Vargas, *Abraham Valdelomar* (BHP XXXVII, 1966); id., *Cuento y poesía*, pp. 11-92; Luis Fabio Xammar, *Valdelomar: signo* (Sphinx, 1940); Armando Zubizarreta, *Perfil y entraña de "El caballero Carmelo"* (Universo, 1968); id., "La angustiada intimidad de Abraham Valdelomar", *Literatura de la Emancipación*, 138-47.

content and style, particularly notable being his reworking of Inca legends in *Los hijos del sol*, where he re-creates the sumptuous magnificence of the pre-Columbian past in a manner reminiscent of Flaubert's *Salammbô*. It is, however, another group of national stories which was to prove Valdelomar's most significant contribution to his country's literature. Behind the sophisticated bohemian image which he liked to project, there lurked a sensitive and sentimental provincial filled with nostalgia for the simple rural world in which he grew up, and it was that side of his personality and his realisation of the literary potential of that unsung world which were to lead him to diverge from the prevailing fashions of Modernism. Emblematic of this change of direction is the story "El caballero Carmelo". For whereas the Modernists turned their backs on the vulgarity of ordinary everyday life to go in search of a nobler, more refined reality, Valdelomar here employs an archaic vocabulary and the rhetoric of the novels of chivalry to raise the eponymous fighting cock into a symbol of the natural dignity and nobility of the humble folk of rural Peru. The story thus marks the beginning of a revaluation of regional values and ways of life.

Valdelomar's so-called "cuentos criollos" (Creole tales) are recollections of episodes from his childhood in the little port of Pisco. They evoke the landscape of the Peruvian coast, the tranquil yet hazardous existence of its fishing communities and, above all, the warmth of the family home. Yet costumbrist elements are never gratuitous but are skilfully interwoven into the narrative and contribute to its development. This is particularly so in "El caballero Carmelo", where the aged fighting cock, whose prowess leads the narrator to identify him with the paladins of old and who over the years has virtually become a member of the family, stands as an effective symbol of the Golden Age of childhood. Furthermore, the stories are enriched by the ambivalence of the childhood world, which is evoked not just as a carefree idyll but as a period often fraught with sadness and uncertainty. For these are stories of initiation in which the narrator evolves from childish innocence to knowledge of evil and human frailty. Thus when the hero of "El caballero Carmelo" is brought out of retirement in response to a challenge and dies of the wounds incurred in his final triumph, the animal's death marks the end of the narrator's childhood with his discovery of the harsh cruelty of life. A much more sombre story is "Los ojos de Judas", where a sense of foreboding dominates the young boy's friendship with a mysterious lady whom he meets on the beach during Holy Week. Though he does not realise it, she is the same woman who, he heard previously, had been intimidated by the authorities into denouncing her husband as a murderer and in reprisal had her son snatched from her. As they watch the preparations for the burning of the effigy of Judas, the woman, in an indirect plea for forgiveness, asks the boy if he could find it in his heart to pardon Christ's betrayer but receives a negative reply. Subsequently the burning of the effigy coincides with the discovery of the woman's corpse in the sea and the boy is seized by guilt as he senses that his childish intolerance has unwittingly driven the desperate woman to suicide.

The best of these coastal narratives are minor masterpieces, expertly structured, written with great stylistic economy, evoking atmosphere by the use of various impressionistic techniques and always insinuating rather than stating overtly. Valdelomar's significance, therefore, resides not only in that he initiated a move towards regionalism, but also in that he brought to the treatment of national reality the formal preoccupations and skills that were the legacy of Modernism.

An equally impressive mastery of language and technique characterises the work of his contemporary, Ventura García Calderón (1886-1959), most of whose life was spent in Europe, where he combined a diplomatic career with journalism and writing.[3] His first volume of short stories, *Dolorosa y desnuda realidad* (1914), was a typically Modernist work of little originality, with cosmopolitan characters and settings and reflecting the cynical disenchantment of the *fin de siècle*. However, with *La venganza del cóndor* (1924), he turned towards Peruvian settings and characters, and Peru was again to be the setting for later collections written in French, of which the most important were *Danger de mort* (1926) and *Couleur de sang* (1931).[4] Embracing the three main regions of the country, these tales can be seen in part as an attempt by a rootless cosmopolitan to define his origins and affirm his own national identity. At the same time

---

[3] See Ventura García Calderón, *La venganza del cóndor* (Madrid: Sucs. de J. Sánchez Ocaña y Cía., 1948); *Cuentos peruanos* (Madrid: Aguilar, 1952); *Dolorosa y desnuda realidad* (Paris: Garnier, 1914); *Danger de mort* (Paris: Excelsior, 1927); *Couleur de sang* (Paris: Excelsior, 1931); *Virages* (Paris: Bernard Grasset, 1933); *Le sang plus vite* (Paris: Gallimard, 1936); *Le serpent couvert de regards* (Paris: Ed. Oceanes, 1947). See also Alberto Escobar, "Incisiones en el arte del cuento modernista", in *Patio de Letras*, pp. 141-79; Lydia de León Hazera, *La novela de la selva hispanoamericana* (Bogotá: Instituto Caro y Cuervo, 1971), pp. 104-20.

[4] Most of these were subsequently translated into Spanish, many by the author himself.

they are directed essentially towards a European public and represent an attempt to make his country and its people better known in the outside world.

All García Calderón's stories exude a pride in his country, a pride he wishes his compatriots to share. Implicit in them is a recognition of Peruvians' ignorance of their own country, particularly evident in stories like "El hombre de los cuarenta y ocho hijos" and "Un soñador" where a well-educated young Limeñan entering the strange world of the Peruvian highlands for the first time has to adjust to an entirely new reality and a different set of values. Somewhat unfairly, he has often been criticised for a lack of social awareness, when in fact condemnation of the white man's treatment of other races is present in many stories, notably in "Fue en el Perú", while others, such as "Historias de caníbales", question the white man's assumptions of cultural superiority. More valid are criticisms of the shallowness of his portrayal of national reality. Partly because he is writing for foreign readers and partly because his first-hand experience of the interior was limited, the Peru he depicts is an exotic and mysterious land of picturesque customs and colourful characters where the marvellous is commonplace. "El despenador", for example, introduces a curious Andean figure whose job it is to put dying people out of their misery and relates a strange case in which one such character himself dies at the hands of an old chief who recovers at the last moment. Likewise the characters tend to be mere literary archetypes. Thus the Indians of the Andean tales are either submissive like the young girl of "Amor indígena", who attaches herself as a docile mistress to the man who rapes her, or inscrutable like the guide of "La venganza del cóndor", who is mysteriously avenged when the white man who ill-treats him is swept over a cliff by a condor. Similarly, the protagonists of his coastal narratives, like the landowner of "Murió en su ley" who on his death-bed attempts to murder his life-long enemy, are latter-day versions of the conquistadores, arrogant of manner, fierce fighters, implacable enemies and punctilious in the defence of their honour.

In terms of literary craftsmanship García Calderón, like other writers of the Modernist generation, did much to raise the standard of Peruvian prose. Unfortunately, the obvious superficiality of his stories condemns him to be no more than a minor figure in the history of his country's letters and, in fact, by the time *La venganza del cóndor* appeared its vision of regional life had already been superseded by the greater realism of Enrique López Albújar (1872-

1966).[5] López Albújar's *Cuentos andinos* (1920) was the fruit of his experiences in Huánuco, where he served as a judge for several years.[6] In the main the Indian is treated sympathetically and there are frequent references to the oppression and exploitation of which he has been a victim, but López Albújar's concern is not to make social criticism but to portray in a realistic light the Indian as he knew him.[7] The main impression conveyed is of the lawlessness existing at the time in remote rural districts, where banditry was often rife, and the stories frequently revolve around some brutal crime which attests to the atavistic violence of which the Indian was capable. In such an environment the Indian peasantry administer their own brand of justice on the margin, and often in contravention, of the Law of the State. Thus, in "El campeón de la muerte" an old couple hire a professional gunman to wreak vengeance on their daughter's murderer, and community justice is shown in operation in "Ushanan-jampi", where a *comunero* expelled for persistent theft is put to death for daring to return. Set mainly in the village of Chupán, the stories give the first convincing account of life in an Indian community. One of the most interesting is "La mula de taita Ramun", which, against the background of the January feast, describes the Indians' social organisation, their religious beliefs and customs, their exploitation by a mercenary parish priest, and the violent clashes arising out of age-old rivalry between neighbouring communities. The encroachment of the outside world on this traditional way of life is the theme of "El licenciado Aponte", which highlights the problem of re-adjustment of the conscript who returns home full of new ideas and ambitions at the end of his military service. In this case, in keeping with the underlying determinism of much of López Albújar's work,

---

[5] It is one of the less edifying episodes of Peruvian literary history that García Calderón apparently attempted to usurp historical precedence over López Albújar by claiming that *La venganza del condor* was originally published in 1919. To my knowledge no one has ever been able to track down that mysterious 1919 edition.

[6] See Enrique López Albújar, *Cuentos andinos* (Mejía Baca, 1965); *Nuevos cuentos andinos* (Santiago de Chile: Ercilla, 1937); *Matalaché* (Mejía Baca, 1966); *El hechizo de Tomaiquichua* (Peruanidad, 1943); *Las caridades de la señora de Tordoya* (Mejía Baca/Villanueva, 1955); *La diestra de don Juan* (INC, 1973). Also of interest are his autobiographical works: *Memorias* (Villanueva, 1963); *De mi casona* (Mejía Baca, 1966). See also Tito Cáceres Cuadros, *Indigenismo y estructuralismo en López Albújar* (Arequipa: Univ. Nac. de San Agustín, 1981); Raúl-Estuardo Cornejo, *López Albújar, narrador de América* (Madrid: Anaya, 1961); Antonio Cornjeo Polar, "*Matalaché*: las varias formas de la esclavitud", in *La novela peruana: siete estudios*, pp. 33-47; Tomás G. Escajadillo, *La narrativa de López Albújar* (CONUP, 1972).

[7] The later *Nuevos cuentos andinos* (1937) was to adopt a more critical attitude to social injustice. With the exception of "El brindis de los ayas", which is perhaps his best story, this second volume of Andean tales is markedly inferior to the first.

the young man ends up by following in the footsteps of his criminal father, for, ostracised by the villagers, he is led by his ambitions to embark on a career as a smuggler.

A keen observer, López Albújar offers perceptive insights into the Indian character. Indeed, his main achievement was to break away from the shallow stereotypes of Clorinda Matto and to portray the Indian convincingly as a human being for the first time. Far from conforming to the traditional image of the servile native, his Indian has a proud and independent spirit which he disguises behind a mask of submissiveness in his dealings with the white man, and he is characterised by his sense of justice, his love of the earth and his community, and his attachment to his magical-religious beliefs and to ancestral laws and customs. Nonetheless, López Albújar's vision of the Indian is limited by the fact that it is essentially an outside view which does not take us inside the native psyche and which, furthermore, is coloured by his experiences as a judge. Above all, it is distorted by his sociological preconceptions. In contrast to later writers he tends to condemn the Indian's magical-religious beliefs as mere superstition, manifesting a paternalistic attitude which assumes the superiority of Western culture and the necessity of integrating the native into it, and his observations on the Indian, made in obtrusive interventions by the narrator, are often arbitrary and questionable and sometimes contradicted by the characters portrayed in the narratives. Artistically, too, the stories are uneven in quality. Some, like "El campeón de la muerte" and "Ushanan-jampi", are well constructed and developed with vigour and economy, but others, notably "El licenciado Aponte" and "La mula de taita Ramun", fail to live up to their initial promise because they change direction in mid-course. Yet, for all its limitations, *Cuentos andinos* marks a major step forward in the literary representation of the Indian and his world and it paved the way for later writers like Alegría and Arguedas.

By the early twenties, then, not only had regionalism established itself in the short story but, despite its relatively recent origins in Peru, the genre had been brought to a considerable degree of artistic excellence. There was, however, no parallel development in the novel.[8] Disappointingly, too, no new short-story writers emerged in

---

[8] One member of the post-Modernist generation who might have made a significant contribution to the development of the novel was José Félix de la Puente (1882-1959). La Puente published his first novel in 1917 but his early works were at best mediocre and he did not realise his literary potential until late in his career with *Evaristo Buendía,*

the twenties to build on the achievements of Valdelomar, García Calderón and López Albújar and most of the decade was characterised by a dearth of quality fiction of any kind.[9]

It was, however, a period of political and intellectual ferment. In particular, the success of the Russian and Mexican Revolutions encouraged the spread of radical thought and the twenties saw the emergence of organised left-wing political movements with the founding of Víctor Raúl Haya de la Torre's Apra (Alianza Popular Revolucionaria Americana) in 1924 and the breakaway Socialist party in 1928.[10] Apra was subsequently to develop into the largest single political party in Peru, but it was José Carlos Mariátegui (1895-1930), the founder of the Socialist party, who was the leading intellectual figure of the age.[11] In his *Siete ensayos de interpretación de la realidad peruana*, a collection of previously published articles issued in book form in 1928, he provides the first Marxist analysis of Peru's history. Attributing the country's social, political and economic backwardness to the persistence of feudalism in the shape of the land-owning oligarchy, he argues that national progress and the

---

candidato (1945). Set in 1919, the novel takes up one of the standard themes of nineteenth-century realism, that of the impoverished but ambitious young man struggling to climb in society. One of the most memorable characters in Peruvian literature, Evaristo Buendía is very much a *criollo* version of Julien Sorel, the mediocre opportunist who, if he never scales the heights of success, nevertheless manages to land on his feet and to avoid heroic failure. The novel also links up with regionalist fiction in that a large part of it is devoted to Evaristo's trip to the sierra to conduct an electoral campaign and we are provided with a devastating insight into the Peruvian political system of the period. Despite certain obvious artistic defects, it is a fine example of realist fiction and, had it been written in the twenties, it would almost certainly have ranked as one of Peru's most important novels. As it is, it appeared too late to make an impact and remains a curious anachronism marginal to the development of the novel as a genre. See *Evaristo Buendía, candidato* (Populibros Peruanos, 1964).

[9] The only works worthy of note to appear in the early twenties were César Vallejo's *Escalas* and *Fabla salvaje*, both published in 1923. The first is a collection of short stories, some of them pieces of poetic prose based on his prison experiences, the others mainly studies of abnormal psychological states. The second is a novelette again dealing with a case of psychological abnormality. They are interesting largely for the light they throw on Vallejo's poetry rather than for their intrinsic merit. See César Vallejo, *Novelas y cuentos completos* (Moncloa, 1967).

[10] The Socialist party subsequently split and a separate Communist party was formed.

[11] See José Carlos Mariátegui, *Siete ensayos de interpretación de la realidad peruana* (Caracas: Biblioteca Ayacucho, 1979); *Seven Interpretative Essays on Peruvian Reality*, trans. M. Urquidi (Austin: Univ. of Texas Press, 1971). See also John M. Baines, *Revolution in Peru: Mariátegui and the Myth* (Alabama: Univ. of Alabama Press, 1972); Armando Bazán, *Mariátegui y su tiempo* (Amauta, 1969); Eugenio Chang Rodríguez, *La literatura política de González Prada, Mariátegui y Haya de la Torre* (Mexico City: Andrea, 1957); Jorge Falcón, *Anatomía de los siete ensayos de Mariátegui* (Amauta, 1978); Various, *Mariátegui y la literatura* (Amauta, 1980); María Wiesse, *José Carlos Mariátegui. Etapas de su vida* (Amauta, 1959).

emancipation of the indigenous peasantry can be achieved simultaneously by a programme of agrarian reform which would break the power of the oligarchy and restore land to the Indian communities, which he sees as a viable social and economic institution. As a political thinker Mariátegui exercised an enormous influence, but he was equally important as a stimulator of intellectual activity. From 1926 until 1930 he edited *Amauta*, a journal of socialist orientation aimed at promoting both a deeper understanding of Peru and a widening of its cultural horizons. It published poetry and fiction as well as articles on science, geography, politics, art and history, and not only included contributions from prominent foreign intellectuals but provided an outlet for young Peruvian writers, whatever their political affiliations. As such it gave a great boost to the intellectual life of the country.

By the end of the twenties this intellectual ferment had begun to bear literary fruit. For in 1928 the Peruvian novel came of age with the publication of two works which in their different ways reflect a new spirit and which mark the real origins of the genre in Peru.

In many respects Enrique López Albújar's *Matalaché* is something of an anachronism.[12] A historical novel set in Piura in the last days of the colonial period, it is a denunciation of the evils of the long abolished institution of slavery. Its plot, dealing as it does with the ill-fated love affair of a slave-owner's daughter and a mulatto slave, is conventionally romantic, though couched in deterministic terms. In form it is traditional, with a linear plot and an omniscient narrator whose presence becomes obtrusive, particularly in the interior monologues of the protagonists. Yet within its limitations it is a well written work and by labelling it a "novela retaguardista" (rearguard novel) López Albújar makes it clear that he consciously and deliberately chose to write his novel in the old-fashioned manner. That decision appears to have been born of the view that avant-garde experimentation and innovation were neither desirable nor feasible in Peru until a solid novelistic tradition had been established. The fact that it was the traditional type of novel that was to predominate in Peru until the fifties would seem to justify him in that view.

What makes *Matalaché* a novel of its times is its theme, which is more complex and richer in significance than would appear at first sight. In practice López Albújar is using history as a medium for commenting on the contemporary state of his country. Like

---

[12] For bibliography see note 6 above.

Mariátegui in his *Siete ensayos,* he is reappraising the past in order to question the very basis of modern Peru. He is asking what political independence has brought in social and human terms and the implied answer is that it has produced very little real change. Thus the novel reflects a new and more radical political sensibility.

The background to the action is the tension in colonial society occasioned by the struggle for independence being waged in other parts of the continent. Against this background the protagonists are represented as being engaged in their own rebellion against the established order. Ironically, white slave-owning society is seen as being itself enslaved by its own social and sexual taboos, whose distortion of nature is reflected in the all too common pattern of marriages of convenience followed by adultery on the part of the husband. María Luz, however, embodies a longing for personal freedom and emotional fulfilment sparked off by the discovery of her own sexuality. The apparently conventional romantic love theme is presented in essentially deterministic terms, and in describing her sexual awakening López Albújar gives us what must be the first portrait of female sensuality in Peruvian literature. Her sexuality is aroused by the torrid climate of Piura and by the realisation that she is an object of male lust, and what draws her to the sexually attractive mulatto slave is the irresistible mating urge of the species. Her growing physical and emotional desire leads her to question the values of her class and to assert the right of every individual to shape his own life, and when eventually she surrenders to her passion, she repudiates those false values in what is, above all, an act of personal emancipation. As for Matalaché, his condition inevitably condemns him to play a somewhat passive role in the novel, so that though he nurses a dream of freedom and equality, he is limited to the articulation of those ideals. However, he stands apart from his fellow slaves because of his independence of spirit, and by daring to love his master's daughter he challenges the very basis of the social order, asserting his humanity and equality with the whites in defiance of inflexible social and racial codes.

Needless to say, the rebellion of the lovers is doomed as soon as the affair is discovered and ends with Matalaché's horrendous death at the hands of his master. Ironically, Don Juan Francisco is presented as one of the more liberal of the slave-owners and an advocate of independence from Spain. Don Juan Francisco, in fact, embodies a fundamental contradiction pointed out by Mariátegui with regard to the independence movement in Peru: the embracing of fashionable liberal ideology by a class bent on preserving and strengthening its social and economic privileges. Despite their high-sounding clichés about liberty, equality and justice for all, he and his kind envisage no change in the internal structure of Peru, least of all the emancipation of the slaves on whom their wealth and power are built, as is demonstrated clearly at the end of the novel when he is revealed in his true colours. The novel thus points forward to a future independent Peru ruled by liberals such as him, a Peru where the status quo will remain fundamentally unaltered, where the oppression and exploitation represented by slavery will persist in one form or another, where social and racial prejudice will perpetuate class divisions, where rigid conventions and taboos will stifle the freedom of the individual. Like Mariátegui, López Albújar seems to be implying that even after independence Peru has remained an essentially feudal society with all the basic evils of the colonial past.

Yet there is a decidedly optimistic note running throughout the book. Matalaché's mulatto condition is repeatedly emphasised — he is a synthesis of the best features of both white and black races, combining physical strength and grace, intellectual ability and natural creative talent — and he seems to stand as a symbol of a new breed of man with whom the future lies. And although he dies at the end, his line does not die with him, for as well as the child carried by María Luz, he has fathered numerous other offspring on the Negresses he has serviced. In fact, his seed has presumably been spread throughout the region, so that he lives on despite his death. An advocate of miscegenation, López Albújar seems to be suggesting that the way to a genuinely free and egalitarian Peru lies in the breaking down of racial barriers through the intermingling of the races. However, there is a serious weakness in the novel which to some extent undermines its central thesis. Partly for reasons of verisimilitude — to make the unlikely love affair more plausible for the reader — and partly to highlight the idea of racial intermingling, López Albújar is at pains to stress that Matalaché is not a Negro but a mulatto. And in his concern to exalt his merits, he tends to portray the Negro slaves in somewhat derogatory terms, as either totally abject and submissive or as brutalised subhumans. Thus, while there is no doubt as to his sympathy for the plight of the Negroes, he gives the impression at times that he himself was not entirely free from the prejudices he condemns. Nonetheless, despite its weaknesses, *Matalaché* is an important work in the Peruvian context, for apart from helping to lay the foundations of a novelistic tradition, it was the first novel to examine the "state of the nation" by questioning a key event in the country's history.

A very different kind of novel is Martín Adán's *La casa de cartón*, an avant-garde work clearly influenced by Proust, Joyce and the surrealists.[13] Written when he was still a teenager and before he went on to become one of Peru's major poets, it is a kind of "portrait of the artist as a young man" in which the narrator looks back on his adolescence in Barranco, a once-fashionable seaside resort in the process of being converted into another suburb of Lima. There is no narrative in the accepted sense. There is a central plot of sorts revolving around the narrator's relationship with his friend Ramón, their amorous experiences with the promiscuous Catita and Ramón's death, but it is not developed at any length and, indeed, is limited to a few episodes and allusions. The novel consists, in fact, of a series of brief and seemingly disconnected vignettes evoking scenes, people and events from the past in jumbled chronological sequence. Furthermore, the vignettes tend not to be developed logically but to follow the abrupt twists and turns of the narrator's train of thought. What gives the novel its unity is his consciousness, and the various sections piece together like a jigsaw to build up a picture of him and his relationship with the world. Needless to say, the novel represents a departure from the tradition of realist fiction which aspires objectively to reproduce the outside world. External reality is presented subjectively, through the eyes of the narrator whose sensibility filters and transforms the world around him. Moreover, he is a narrator who, because of his poetic bent, tends to see and think in images rather than to describe and analyse rationally. Indeed, sections of the novel are constructed on rhythmic patterns similar to those found in verse and could be regarded as prose poems, and the final result is a work of aesthetic impressionism, sometimes lyrical and other times surrealist, rather than a photographic reproduction of the world. *La casa de cartón* is not an easy novel to read, but it is a

---

[13] See Martín Adán, *Obras en prosa*, ed. Ricardo Silva-Santisteban (Edubanco, 1982). See also Mario Castro Arenas, "Cimientos estéticos de *La casa de cartón*", in *De Palma a Vallejo* (Populibros Peruanos, 1964), pp. 125-35; John M. Kinsella, "The Artist as Subject: a Study of Martín Adán's *La casa de cartón*", in *Belfast Spanish and Portuguese Papers*, ed. P.S.N. Russell-Gebbett et al. (Belfast: Queen's Univ., 1979), pp. 69-77; id. "Realism, Surrealism, and *La casa de cartón*", in *Before the Boom: Four Essays in Latin American Literature before 1940*, Centre for Latin American Studies Monographs 10, ed. Steven Boldy (Liverpool: Univ. of Liverpool, 1981), pp. 31-39; Luis Loayza, "Martín Adán en su casa de cartón", in *El sol de Lima*, pp. 127-41; Hubert P. Weller, "*La casa de cartón* de Martín Adán y el mar como elemento metafórico", *Letras*, 66/67 (1961), 142-53.

rewarding experience because it achieves an overall effect of poetic ambiguity offering multiple insights rather than a clearly defined vision of reality.

One of the most interesting aspects of the novel is its highlighting of the predicament of the aspiring writer in Peru. A bookish boy with artistic leanings, the narrator inhabits a country still culturally underdeveloped and belongs to a society that is essentially bourgeois. The middle classes of Barranco have no interest in art and the only cultural event capable of arousing their enthusiasm is a sentimental love film starring Valentino. The young boys of the narrator's circle who do read have been brought up on Spanish writers and have only superficial and quaint notions of world literature acquired second-hand. The narrator, who is familiar with foreign writers and pedantically keeps dropping names to prove it, feels spiritually and intellectually superior to his environment, but he is conscious of the limitations of his own frantically-acquired and ill-digested culture. However, though he frequently dreams of travel, he ironically dismisses the customary trip to Paris as a solution, for experience has taught him that visiting Peruvian intellectuals do no more than sample the bright lights of Europe and then return with a phony veneer of cosmopolitan sophistication.

However, his predicament is not just that he is conscious of living in a cultural desert. It is that he must resist social pressure to renounce his literary aspirations and turn into the practical and respectable bourgeois his middle-class origins destined him to be. This pressure is felt particularly acutely by Ramón, who in one of his poems states that he would be arrested by the police if he were to let it be known that he is a poet, and who at one stage suffers a crisis of despair at the prospect of the comfortable, affluent life mapped out for him. The narrator's rejection of the shallowness and sterility of the bourgeois life-style is expressed in a series of ironic and extremely funny pen-portraits of the inhabitants of Barranco. On a symbolic level the temptation offered by the man-hungry Catita appears to represent pressure to conform, to become a man in the conventional sense, and occurring as it does in the wake of his sexual coming-of-age with her, Ramón's death would seem to be a metaphor of the extinction of an artistic vocation by the force of social pressures. After his death the narrator, in a moment of sentimental weakness, allows himself to be emotionally blackmailed into taking on himself the obligation of consoling Catita, but when she writes him a tearful letter he is too absorbed in his solitary contemplation to be lured into her web. Thus he survives Ramón not only literally but also metaphorically in that he remains true to his literary calling.

Throughout the novel the countryside and the sea are presented as symbols of freedom in opposition to the restrictions of the town, and the narrator lives most intensely when he is away from human company, alone in silent contemplation of the landscape, which his imagination, given free rein, transforms and creates into a reality of his own. His artistic credo is expressed through an image which likens him to a pool over which faces pass and are reflected back in distorted form, and in pursuit of his vocation he withdraws from active involvement in life to live instead in his own created universe forged imaginatively out of the raw material contemplated in the real world. The only world in which he is truly at home, in other words, is the world of literature, the reality contained within book covers, the cardboard house of the title, and the novel is a profession of faith in which he pledges his allegiance to literary creation.

Though in many respects a work of brilliance, *La casa de cartón* is not without its faults. The poetic monologues tend at times to be complacently self-indulgent and narcissistic, and in spite of the author's gift with words, one cannot fail to notice a certain lack of critical self-judgement in some of his prose. Thus, the novel is dated by his predilection for the vocabulary of modern technology which was trendy in the twenties, and in self-consciously trying to be clever by creating daring images after the fashion of the surrealists, he sometimes succeeds only in being ridiculous, as when the moon is described as a lump of sugar in the coffee-cup of the sky.

Nonetheless, allowance must be made for the author's extreme youth and *La casa de cartón* remains a landmark in Peruvian letters. Unfortunately, because of the backwardness of the literary environment, it was doomed to remain a curiosity, much admired but exercising very little influence on the development of the genre.[14] Adán himself was to abandon prose to devote himself to poetry and in the following decades it was the traditional realist novel of the type favoured by López Albújar that was to predominate. It was not, in fact, until the advent of the new fiction in the fifties and sixties that the process of renovation of narrative technique initiated by *La casa de cartón* got properly under way.

While *Matalaché* and *La casa de cartón* both mark a departure

---

[14] The one exception is José Diez-Canseco's novelette *Suzy* (1930), an evocation of childhood in Barranco. Clearly modelled on *La casa de cartón*, it is a very feeble work by comparison.

from regionalism, José Diez-Canseco (1904-49), the outstanding prose-writer of the early thirties, could be classified as a regionalist in that about half the narratives of his *Estampas mulatas* (1929-40) are set in the provinces — some on the coast, others in the lower sierra — and abound in costumbrist detail.[15] Diez-Canseco's concern, however, is not so much with a particular region as with a national culture spanning city and countryside, sierra and coast. His protagonists have in common that they are all mestizos, whether *cholos* or *zambos*, and through them he seeks to capture the distinctive identity and way of life of the Peruvian *criollo*. As the title indicates, he had a special sympathy for the *zambos* of the coast and it is mainly on them that his stories concentrate. A sense of identification with their world is achieved by the fact that the narrator employs the same informal, uninhibited tone and popular speech as his characters. External features of the *criollo* life-style are presented with loving detail, but more importantly the stories capture the personality and psychology of the *zambos*: their uninhibited vitality and love of fun; their mischievous humour and gift for verbal repartee; their highly developed sense of machismo. It is this last element which lends unity to the book. Diez-Canseco seems to see the *criollo* way of life as being ruled by a *machista* code of honour and in virtually every story the characters, both *cholos* and *zambos*, live in accordance with that code. Thus, the protagonist of "El velorio" murders his best friend for making advances to his wife, while in "Chicha, mar y bonito" a cuckolded fisherman, unable to face life without honour, scuttles his boat and drowns together with the man who has dishonoured him.

However, Diez-Canseco's main significance lies not in these stories but in his role as precursor of the urban fiction of the fifties. Not only was he the first Peruvian writer to portray characters belonging to the urban proletariat but he is one of the few to have done so convincingly. The protagonists of the novelettes "El gaviota" and "El kilómetro 83" are the dispossessed of the poorer districts of Lima and Callao, young men of the street eking out a hand-to-mouth existence as newspaper and lottery-ticket vendors and shoe-shine boys. Surprisingly, perhaps, in view of the political climate of the age, Diez-Canseco steers clear of social criticism. He

[15] See José Diez-Canseco, *Suzy* (Perugraph, 1979); *Estampas mulatas*, ed. Tomás G. Escajadillo (CAP, 1973); *Duque*, ed. Tomás G. Escajadillo (Peisa, 1973). The first edition of *Estampas mulatas*, published in 1930, consisted of the two novelettes "El gaviota" and "El kilómetro 83". The second edition of 1938 included four short stories and in 1951 a posthumous edition added three more. The various narratives date from 1929 to 1940.

shows us the precariousness of his characters' existence and the toughness of the world they inhabit, but he is interested in them primarily as human types and as picaresque embodiments of the *criollo* way of life rather than as victims of the social order, and it is on that level that he identifies with them. In these novelettes Diez-Canseco betrays an unsureness of the technique of longer fiction and their impact is diluted and their artistic unity undermined by somewhat extraneous second parts. By contrast "El trompo", the last story he wrote, is a minor masterpiece in which he reaches a peak of artistic maturity. Unfolding in an atmosphere of melancholy, the narrative develops two parallel stories. In the one, Chupitos' father, deceived by his wife, punishes her and throws her out of the house. In the other, the son loses his favourite spinning-top in a game and, regarding it as sullied by belonging to another, he avenges the dishonour, not by winning it back, but by using another top to destroy it. The episode thus marks the boy's initiation into manhood as he learns to live by the same imperious *machista* code as his father, and the end of the story shown Chupitos silently abandoning the game, his toys and his gang of friends. For in learning to be a man he has left childhood behind him and has come to experience the painful hardness of life.

The other extreme of the social scale is depicted in *Duque*, a novel written in 1929 but not published until 1934. The narrative centres around the introduction into Lima's high society of Teddy Crown-chield Soto Menor, a rich young Peruvian educated in Europe, and traces his love life, which comes to an unfortunate climax when his fiancée breaks off their engagement after discovering that he has had a homosexual affair with her father. The plot, however, is little more than a peg on which to hang minutely detailed scenes of the world of the capital's upper classes and the reader is taken on a tour of mansions, country clubs, golf-courses, tea-rooms, night-clubs, bro-thels and opium dens. As in the *Estampas mulatas* the author has no political axe to grind. Rather his concern is to show the utter shallowness of the frivolous life-style of Lima's idle rich, the vulgarity underlying their snobbish pretentiousness and the moral decadence of a class drifting into vice out of ennui and inertia. Himself a member of the class he portrays, Diez-Canseco apparently based his novel on real people and places. Unfortunately, the realism that is its main virtue also constitutes its principal weakness, for though enlivened by a crisp, slick avant-garde narrative style, it lacks the literary qualities to raise it above a mere documentary of a particular society and time. Nonetheless, it is significant as a forerunner of the work of later writers like Vargas Llosa and Bryce Echenique who were to make literary capital out of the depiction of that same social class.

Meanwhile, the political and intellectual ferment of the twenties had given rise to a growing *indigenista* campaign on behalf of the Indian, a movement which sought to vindicate native culture and to improve the social lot of the indigenous population.[16] *Indigenismo* produced important works of non-fiction, such as Luis E. Valcárcel's *Tempestad en los Andes* (1927), but its fictional expression tended to limit itself to a crude social realism denouncing the exploitation and oppression of the Indian, typical examples of which are the stories published by María Wiesse and Gamaliel Churata (Arturo Peralta) in the pages of *Amauta*.[17] One of the earliest writers of this type was César Falcón (1892-1970),[18] whose "Los buenos hijos de Dios", a story from the collection *Plantel de inválidos* (1921), exposes the cynical peddling of religion and alcohol to the Indians to maintain them in a state of degradation and subservience. Similarly, his novel *El pueblo sin Dios*, written in 1923 and published in 1928, depicts the sordid political intrigues of the leading citizens of a small Andean town and, as a secondary theme, the abuses suffered by the Indians at their hands. However, the foremost example of this tendency is César Vallejo's *El tungsteno* (1931),[19] a novel set in an Andean mining community and portraying the exploitation of the Peruvian proletariat, the Indian in particular, by foreign capital and the national middle classes. Significantly, the Indian occupies a secondary

---

[16] *Indigenismo* was not limited to Peru, of course, but embraced the neighbouring Andean republics of Bolivia and Ecuador. For an overview of *indigenista* fiction, see Antonio Cornejo Polar, *La novela indigenista* (Lasontay, 1980); Raimundo Lazo, *La novela andina* (Mexico City: Porrúa, 1971); Julio Rodríguez-Luis, *Hermenéutica y praxis del indigenismo* (Mexico City: Fondo de Cultura Económica, 1980).

[17] See María Wiesse, "El forastero" (*Amauta*, April 1928) and "El veneno" (*Amauta*, Sept.-Oct. 1929); Gamaliel Churata, "El gamonal" (*Amauta*, Jan.-Feb. 1927). Wiesse's stories were subsequently included in her *Nueve relatos* (E. Bustamante y Ballivián, 1933). Churata subsequently settled in Bolivia and went on to write *El pez de oro*, which remained unpublished till 1957 and is still virtually unknown in Peru, but which some critics regard as a work of major importance. A long, hermetic book, it employs a surrealist technique, a mixture of genres (narration, poetry, essay) and a hybrid language combining Spanish with Quechua and Aymara, in what seems to be an attempt to portray the spiritual world of Andean man. See *El pez de oro* (La Paz: Canata, 1957).

[18] See César Falcón, *Plantel de inválidos* (Madrid: Historia Nueva, 1928); *El pueblo sin Dios* (Madrid: Historia Nueva, 1928). See also Roland Forgues, "Alienación y emancipación en 'Los buenos hijos de Dios' de César Falcón", in *La sangre en llamas* (Studium, 1979), pp. 99-109.

[19] See César Vallejo, *Novelas y cuentos completos* (Moncloa, 1967).

position in both novels, for both were written in Europe by adherents of international Marxism and, rather than focus the Indian question as a unique problem involving a distinct race and culture and requiring particular solutions, they situate it within the wider context of the class struggle. Though much more radical in their treatment of social injustice, such works betray the same artistic defects as *Aves sin nido*. Characterisation is superficial and simplistic, stereotyped to suit the thesis expounded, and the Indians in particular are presented in purely external terms, by Falcón as brutalised victims of oppression and by Vallejo as idealised examples of primitive communalism. Nonetheless, by their uncompromising denunciation of oppression and economic exploitation such writers brought another dimension to the fictional treatment of the Indian.

The thirties saw the emergence of a different regionalist current with works aimed, not at offering a political interpretation of regional life, but at promoting among Peruvians a knowledge of their own country. It is perhaps significant that the leading representatives of this trend were not primarily literary men. Thus, Emilio Romero (b. 1899) was an economist and historian who first made his name as the author of scholarly articles on his native region of Puno and the short stories of *Balseros del Titicaca* (1934) are clearly intended to complement those by portraying the characteristics of the area and its people.[20] Thus, the title-story is an account of a typical day in the life of the fishermen of Lake Titicaca, who after toiling to make their catch get only a few cents for it in Puno and then go back to repeat the process in order to eke out a meagre living. Other tales deal with the tragically hard existence and the superstitions of the sierra Indians or with the tedium and narrowness of small-town life. The plots tend to be thin and the characters little more than representative types, but the stories are written in a precise, austere language and with a detached objectivity which make them artistically satisfying despite their limitations.

A more interesting author is his namesake Fernando Romero (b. 1905),[21] a naval officer whose *Doce novelas de la selva* (1934) — later revised and retitled *Doce relatos de la selva* — was born of his experiences as a member of an expedition which carried out an exploratory study of the nation's jungle waterways. The book bears a

---

[20] See Emilio Romero, *Balseros del Titicaca* (Perú Actual, 1934).
[21] See Fernando Romero, *Doce relatos de la selva* (Mejía Baca, 1958); *Mar y playa* (Nuevos Rumbos, 1959).

certain similarity to the earlier jungle fiction of the Uruguayan Horacio Quiroga and the Colombian José Eustasio Rivera. The protagonists are mostly pioneer settlers engaged in a struggle to tame and wrest a living from the jungle and the stories convey a sense of the puniness of man and the precariousness of existence in an inhospitable natural environment. The jungle is presented as a violent, aggressive foe, a place fraught with physical dangers and dreaded diseases which can strike a man down suddenly and unexpectedly. In stories like "Las tangaranas" it is also seen as exercising an insidious malignant influence on the human spirit, so that men are infected by the sensuality and brutality of their natural surroundings. However, the struggle against an inhospitable environment is also shown to bring out the best in man, and tales like "La creciente" exalt the qualities of courage, tenacity and resourcefulness of which human beings are capable in face of adversity. More originally, a sympathetic attitude towards the indigenous inhabitants of the jungle and their culture is manifested in narratives based on native legends and folklore and particularly in "Yaimanco", a story which recounts the white man's insensitive, rapacious and brutal invasion of the jungle from the viewpoint of the Indians. Moreover, in "De regreso", which narrates the disillusionment of a planter when he finally realises his life-long ambition of returning to Lima in style, Romero challenges one of the great clichés of Latin American literature, the traditional dichotomy between the civilisation of the cities and the barbarism of the countryside. Questioning the assumption that civilisation is limited to the urban centres of the continent, he suggests that the inhabitants of the jungle have evolved their own form of civilisation which, primitive though it might appear, has its own virtues and, above all, is adapted to the peculiar nature of the environment.

In comparison to his jungle narratives Romero's second book of fiction is something of a disappointment. *Mar y playa* (1940) is a collection of tales set on the coast and portraying characters who in one way or another make their living from the sea. Like Diez-Canseco Romero conveys the machismo and outward-going life-style of the coastal *zambo* and the sadness of lonely, marginal figures engaged in the hard struggle for life, but story after story is spoiled by the melodramatic sensationalism of the endings. Nonetheless, the volume contains what is perhaps Romero's best story in "Santos Tarqui", where the feud between two shipmates highlights the confrontation of the mutually incomprehensible cultures of the coastal mulatto and the sierra *cholo*.[22] In that story, as in his jungle narratives, Romero reveals himself to be a fine minor writer.

However, it was only with the emergence of Ciro Alegría and José María Arguedas in the mid-thirties that regionalism and *indigenismo* were to find major literary expression. Ciro Alegría (1909-67)[23] took up writing in exile, into which he was forced by political persecution as a result of his militancy in the ranks of the Apra party. His first two novels, *La serpiente de oro* (1935) and *Los perros hambrientos* (1938), established his literary credentials and in 1941 he achieved international celebrity with the prize-winning *El mundo es ancho y ajeno*, the *indigenista* novel *par excellence*. After that his career went into decline and his subsequent production was limited to short stories and two uncompleted novels.

All three novels set out to give a sympathetic account of the way of life of the rural peoples of the remote regions of northern Peru where Alegría grew up. Thus *La serpiente de oro* is set in the valley of the Marañon, in the little settlement of Calemar, whose *cholo* inhabitants make a living by raising crops and ferrying passengers, cattle and goods across the river. Because of its geographical isolation the area

---

[22] It is interesting to note that whereas Diez-Canseco envisages a common *criollo* culture shared by *zambos* and *cholos*, Romero sees the two racial groups as being separated by their very different cultures.

[23] See Ciro Alegría, *Novelas completas*, 2nd ed. (Madrid: Aguilar, 1963); *El mundo es ancho y ajeno* (Madrid: Alianza, 1983); *El mundo es ancho y ajeno*, ed. Antonio Cornejo Polar (Caracas: Biblioteca Ayacucho, 1978); *Broad and Alien is the World*, trans. Harriet de Onís (London: Merlin, 1973); *The Golden Serpent*, trans. Harriet de Onís (New York: Farrar and Rhinehart, 1943); *Lázaro* (Buenos Aires: Losada, 1973); *El dilema de Krause* (Varona, 1979); *Duelo de caballeros* (Buenos Aires: Losada, 1965); *La ofrenda de piedra* (CAP, 1969); *Siete cuentos quirománticos* (Varona, 1978); *El sol de los jaguares* (Varona, 1979); *Mucha suerte con harto palo. Memorias*, ed. Dora Varona (Buenos Aires: Losada, 1976). See also Xavier Bacacorzo et al., *La obra de Ciro Alegría* (Arequipa: Univ. Nac. de San Agustín, 1976); Henry Bonneville, "L'indigenisme littéraire andin", *Les Langues Néo-Latines*, 200/201 (1972), 1-58; id., "El mestizaje y Ciro Alegría", *Literatura de la Emancipación*, 206-10; Hans Bunte, *Ciro Alegría y su obra* (Mejía Baca, 1961); Antonio Cornejo Polar, "La imagen del mundo en *La serpiente de oro*", in *La novela peruana: siete estudios*, pp. 49-64; Mario Leonardo D'Onofrio, "La construcción de la narrativa indigenista andina: Ciro Alegría", Diss. Case Western Reserve 1978 (Univ. Microfilms, 1979); Eileen Early, *Joy in Exile. Ciro Alegría's Narrative Art* (Washington: Univ. Press of America, 1980); Tomás G. Escajadillo, *Alegría y "El mundo es ancho y ajeno"* (San Marcos, 1983); Alberto Escobar, *"La serpiente de oro* o el río de la vida", in *Patio de Letras*, pp. 180-257; Jorge J. Rodríguez-Florido, *El lenguaje en la obra literaria* (Sacramento: Dept. of Spanish and Portuguese, California State Univ., 1977); Lewis Taylor, "Literature as History: Ciro Alegría's View of Rural Society in the Northern Peruvian Andes", *Ibero-Amerikanisches Archiv*, 10 (1984), 349-78; Goran Tocilovac, *La comunidad indígena y Ciro Alegría* (Biblioteca Universitaria, 1975); Eduardo Urdanivia Bertarelli, "Para una nueva lectura de Ciro Alegría", *RevCrit*, 7/8 (1978), 183-91; Dora Varona, ed., *Ciro Alegría, trayectoria y mensaje* (Varona, 1972); Matilde Vilariño de Olivieri, *La novelística de Ciro Alegría* (Río Piedras: Univ. de Puerto Rico, 1980); Carlos E. Zavaleta, *Retrato de Ciro Alegría* (Lluvia, 1984).

is very much a world apart and the *vallinos* (valley-dwellers) take pride in being different from the people of other regions. The government of Lima is utterly remote from their lives and their sporadic contact with its representatives has led them to associate authority with corruption and high-handedness and to resent it as an intrusion on their independence. Life in Calemar, in fact, seems to unfold on the margin of the state and of history. The narrative emphasises the importance of traditions and customs handed down from generation to generation, and it creates a sense of an existence which is a daily re-enactment of man's struggle with the environment and which year after year follows the cyclical rhythm of nature. Hence the river itself stands as a symbol of a way of life which has remained basically unaltered as far back as anyone can remember.

Repeating the stock Spanish American theme of the confrontation between man and nature, Alegría emphasises the awesome immensity of the Peruvian landscape and the dangers which threaten its inhabitants — rapids, landslides, wild beasts, tropical diseases, etc. But at the same time he breaks with the literary tradition which depicts man as a puny victim of nature. On the one hand, nature is seen as being generous as well as cruel and the *vallinos* make a good living from the river and the fertile land on its banks. On the other, if the novel presents tragic episodes like the drowning of Rogelio Romero, it also exalts the heroism of men engaged in a daily struggle with their environment, from which on the whole they emerge triumphant. The distribution of chapters is so arranged as to alternate scenes of tension and expansiveness to convey the dual nature of the *vallinos'* existence, and if the river on which that existence depends appears as a symbol of destiny, it is an ambivalent symbol, for the river Marañon is a golden serpent which both enriches life and destroys it.

Alegría also reappraises the great Latin American cliché of civilisation and barbarism. The ability of the *vallinos* to run their own affairs is highlighted by Calemar's governor, a local man elected by popular acclaim and who, though illiterate, performs his duties with a common sense, a knowledge of the region and a scrupulous fairness which contrast with the corruption and bureaucratic mentality of the government-appointed officials in other villages in the region. The civilising mentality is represented in the novel by Osvaldo Martínez, a Limeñan engineer who visits the area with grandiose schemes for exploiting its natural resources and who is possessed of all the city-dweller's prejudices about the backwardness of the locals. But the *vallinos* are shown to have developed a way of life perfectly adapted to their environment, and in the course of his stay with them he learns to adopt customs he had previously despised and his ambitious projects come to naught precisely because, for all his book-learning, he lacks the practical experience necessary to survive in jungle conditions. Thus the novel calls into question the superiority of so-called civilisation and vindicates the validity of regional rural culture.

Technically the novel highlights the major problem confronting the regionalist writer, that of communicating to the urban reader a reality very different from his own. As in all his work, Alegría adopts the manner and tone, though not the language, of the popular story-tellers of his childhood on whom he modelled his narrative style, and there is no doubt that his main asset as a novelist is his ability to involve the reader in the narrative as if he were listening to a tale recounted orally. Again as in his other works, the narrative is interspersed with anecdotes and folk-tales recounted directly by the characters themselves in their own popular speech and serving to create atmosphere; costumbrist scenes depicting different aspects of the day-to-day life of the region; and descriptive passages, essentially lyrical in character and employing a sensual imagery to convey the feel of river and jungle, which testify to the author's gift for evoking landscape. Structurally the novel has no central plot and does not follow a linear sequence, consisting instead of a series of more or less independent chapters and scenes, fragments linked by the unifying presence of the river and which cumulatively build up an overall picture of the Marañon region. The narrative perspective is that of the *vallinos* themselves in that we are given what purports to be an inside view by one of the group, who introduces the reader into his world as if he were a visitor from outside. Unfortunately, the impression of authenticity that this approach achieves is offset somewhat by the incongruity it leads to. Not only does the narrator recount events he could not possibly have witnessed, but, more importantly, the demands of comprehensibility oblige him to narrate in a literary Spanish which jars with the popular speech reproduced in the dialogues. Ultimately what the novel reveals, therefore, is the impossibility of achieving an authentic inner expression of one culture in a literature aimed at a public belonging to another culture.

Alegría himself seems to recognise this in *Los perros hambrientos*, where he turns his attention to the Indian and mestizo *colonos* of the northern sierra. For here he opts for a narrative perspective that is consciously external, with an omniscient narrator who clearly does not belong to the world he is describing, as is evidenced by the different language spoken by him and his characters, and whose role is that of intermediary revealing and explaining to the reader a world that is foreign to him. His second novel is also different from the first in that it is built around a central linear plot tracing the progress and ravages of a terrible drought. At the same time, however, the narrative continues to be interspersed with descriptive passages, costumbrist scenes and intercalated anecdotes and folk-tales, and it also includes sub-plots which serve to widen our vision of the life of the region and to act as interludes creating suspense.

As in the previous novel we are introduced into a stable, unchanging world where life is lived in close relationship with the earth and follows the cycles of nature. A series of colourful scenes evokes the various activities that make up the day-to-day life of the peasant, the imposing presence of the environment is brought out by visual and auditive descriptions which make the Andean landscape stand out from the page, and the relationship between man and the earth is underlined by Alegría's characteristic technique of describing human beings in terms of images drawn from nature. The life of the *colonos* is shown to be frugal and fraught with hardship. The land they work never belongs to them, since it is the property of the *hacendado*, and it is generally poor, since he retains the best lands on the estate for his own use. They have to contend with the rigours of a harsh physical environment and the vagaries of the elements. They have to suffer, too, the unjust and often brutal impositions of the white man, as when Mateo Tampo is forcibly separated from his wife and son and pressed into military service or when the unreasonable exactions of the *hacendado* drive the Celedonios to banditry. But at the same time the peasants are shown to be possessed of a stubborn resilience which enables them to shrug off both the inclemency of nature and the abuses of the white man and to persevere in the struggle to wrest a living from the land, and by virtue of hard work and their intimate knowledge of the earth men like Simón Robles manage to prosper and on the whole to live contented with their lot.

The nucleus of the novel is the cataclysm which threatens to destroy that stable world. Alegría graphically conveys the horrors of drought and famine and with great narrative skill traces their gradual impact on the peasants till even their basic humanity begins to crumble as men turn against one another in the struggle to survive. But even at the height of their privations human values are kept alive by Simón Robles' gesture in spontaneously offering hospitality to the destitute Jacinta and ultimately the peasants' tenacity enables them to withstand their long ordeal and to emerge unbowed to resume the normal pattern of their lives. The final chapter, evoking the coming of rain, points backwards to the first, which had described the prosperity of the Robles family, conveying by this circular structure an impression of a recommencing cycle. What emerges from the novel, therefore, is a sense of human life endlessly following the eternal rhythm of nature and tenaciously enduring in spite of adversity.

As the title indicates, dogs play a prominent role in the novel and are one of the principal vehicles whereby its major themes are expressed. The peasants' constant companions, the dogs share their masters' work, their food and their joys and sorrows. On one level, the intimate association between men and animals underlines the peasants' close relationship with the natural world. On another, the story of the dogs parallels that of the peasants. Like their masters these mongrels are perfectly adapted to their surroundings and skilled in the work of the countryside. They, too, must contend with the rigours and dangers of a harsh environment and suffer the violence of men. For them also life is good when the earth is generous, but when the famine sets in they are driven to savagery by hunger and cast out as the bonds of affection and loyalty are broken by the demands of self-preservation. Finally, however, the return of Wanka to the home of Simón Robles on the last page highlights the endurance of dogs and men and signals their common resumption of the normal round of life.

The major weakness of Alegría's first two novels is that, in his concern to celebrate the virtues of the rural peoples of northern Peru and to vindicate their traditional ways of life, he tends to ignore the march of history and to underplay the impact of outside forces on their remote, isolated worlds. In *El mundo es ancho y ajeno*, on the other hand, he broadens his canvas to take account of those outside forces. Here his subject is another isolated rural people, the Indian *comuneros*, but they are involved in a struggle not only with nature but also with an expansive land-owning oligarchy with the backing of white society and the state apparatus behind it. Alegría again uses the same basic techniques — omniscient narrator acting as intermediary, vivid descriptive passages, costumbrist scenes and interpolated folk-tales — to introduce the reader into the world of the Indian, but the central plot brings that world into confrontation with an alien social order represented by the *hacendado* and the several sub-plots which take various characters to different parts of Peru situate the local within a national context.

By choosing to write about an enclosed community isolated from the outside world by its geographical remoteness and the central government's neglect of the interior, Alegría is able to depict the traditional Indian way of life as it has existed down through the centuries, virtually unaffected by contact with the white man. That is not to say that Rumi has been totally isolated from the outside world or that it has been immune to outside influences. Aspects of its culture, such as its administrative structure with its *cabildo* (town council), *alcalde* (mayor) and *regidores* (aldermen), are Spanish in origin, and these northern Indians, unlike those of the south, no longer speak Quechua but Spanish. Nonetheless, their own culture has been strong enough to assimilate outside influences without losing its own distinctive identity and for that reason Rumi may legitimately be regarded as a symbol of the traditional Indian way of life.

The fundamental values of that way of life are incarnated in the patriarchal figure of Rosendo Maqui, the mayor of Rumi, a man respected, on the one hand, for his experience and knowledge of agricultural matters and, on the other, for his unflagging labours on behalf of the community and his wisdom in handling its affairs. For the twin bases of Indian society are shown to be the community and the land, which not merely provides the Indian with a livelihood but gives his existence its meaning. In the opening section of the novel Rumi is depicted as a flourishing community, prospering thanks to the wise guidance of Rosendo Maqui and the hard work and agricultural skills of the *comuneros* themselves. The picture we are given of it is somewhat idealised in that, while Alegría does not gloss over the Indians' human failings or the hardships of rural life, he does tend to portray it in rather too idyllic terms. Such idealisation is comprehensible, of course, given that the author's aim is to convince the reader of the merits of Indian culture, and despite it, it would seem that his account of community life is substantially accurate. What emerges is an image of a remarkably self-sufficient society perfectly adapted to its environment, a society whose traditional values and wisdom have enabled it to thrive in remote isolation down through the centuries.

Unfortunately, the community cannot remain forever on the margin of history and it suffers the encroachment of the outside world when, by intimidation, bribery and legal chicanery, the *hacendado* Don Alvaro Amenábar seizes possession of its lands and then repeats the process when the *comuneros* remove to another site in the barren uplands. The novel shows that to dispossess the *comuneros* of their land and break up their communities is to destroy the Indians as a people by depriving them of the very basis of their existence, an idea conveyed graphically by an image which compares the dispossessed community to a tree uprooted from the earth. The *comuneros* who are driven to seek a livelihood in other areas of the country are unable to adapt to life away from their beloved land, and without the protection of the community they become a series of defenceless individuals reduced to serfdom on estates, plantations and mines where they are exploited, oppressed and degraded till they are unrecognisable as the people they once were.

The despoilation of Rumi is not presented as an isolated injustice but is placed in the context of a process that has been going on for centuries throughout the whole country. Rosendo's recollections of the history of his race as handed down to him by his elders hark back to a time when all the land belonged to the communities, a golden age that came to an end with the arrival of the Europeans, since when the communities have been disappearing year by year. Likewise, the various sub-plots reveal that everywhere in Peru the Indians have been reduced to the level of landless serfs toiling for the new masters. As the title suggests, wherever the Indian goes in this wide world he finds that it belongs to others and that it is inhospitable to him. On the final page Rumi's last survivors despairingly ask themselves, "¿Adónde iremos?" (Where are we to go?), words which voice the plight of the whole indigenous population, a race of landless, defenceless orphans without a place in a world that once belonged to them.

Justification of the destruction of traditional indigenous culture on the grounds of progress is exposed by Alegría as utterly spurious. The state is shown to have done nothing to help the Indian to improve his lot, ignoring him completely except to exact taxes, military service and labour for public works, and the deliberate thwarting of the community's attempts to establish a school suggests that the oligarchy has striven to keep the Indian in a state of ignorance in order to maintain its dominance over him. The novel's several plots, in fact, demonstrate cumulatively that European civilisation has brought the Indian only exploitation and oppression, and a contrast between the *comuneros* of Rumi and Don Alvaro's *colonos* reveals that, far from civilising the Indian, the white man has degraded a once proud and happy people to apathetic, cowering abjection.

Indeed, in depicting the confrontation of Peru's two cultures, represented by Rumi and Don Alvaro respectively, Alegría again inverts the conventional dichotomy between civilisation and barbarism. In virtually every respect the traditional Indian way of life is shown to be superior to the so-called civilisation imposed by the white man. Indian culture is based on a cooperative ethic whose goal is the communal well-being. In contrast, the white man's motivating force is personal ambition which has led to the creation of a feudal order where the masses are exploited and downtrodden by an oligarchy in whose hands land, wealth and power are concentrated. Corrupt public officials misuse their positions to line their own pockets and, like the Law and every other institution, are instruments of the powerful. Nor is the superiority of Indian culture only moral. The *comuneros* are shown to make more effective use of the land than the *hacendado*, whose vast estates remain largely uncultivated and whose only interest in expropriating the community's lands is in securing the services of the *comuneros* as a labour-force for his mines. Furthermore, Don Alvaro's refusal to cooperate with the *comuneros* in the construction of a road indicates that the Indian community is more progressive than the feudal oligarch. Like Mariátegui, therefore, Alegría vindicates the traditional Indian community both as a social organisation and as an economic unit, while exposing the feudal *latifundio* as the fount of social injustice and economic backwardness.[24]

Sadly, the traditional virtues which enabled the community to flourish in isolation do not equip it to cope with the encroachment of the outside world and its wise old mayor finds himself out of his depth when confronted by the machinations of Don Alvaro. But the novel shows the community capable of adapting to change and after Rosendo's death he is replaced by Benito Castro, a *cholo* whose travels through Peru have made him familiar with the ways of the white man, and whose prominence in the latter part of the novel seems to reflect the author's belief that native culture would evolve naturally in the direction of *mestizaje*. Under his leadership the *comuneros* learn to overcome ancient superstitions and to take advantage of technological progress, as we see when they drain a

[24] In his above-cited article Lewis Taylor questions Alegría's portrayal of the community and the *latifundio* and, by implication, the whole *indigenista* thesis.

sacred lake. They also cease to be passive as they acquire a new awareness and stand their ground when threatened with expulsion for a second time. Their tragedy is that as a small, isolated group they face hopeless odds in their attempt to defend their land and way of life against the aggression of an oligarch with the resources to whip up public opinion in his favour and able to call on government backing, and the novel ends with the extermination of the community, wiped out by army machine-guns.

El mundo es ancho y ajeno is thus primarily a protest against the systematic destruction over the centuries of the Indian people and their culture by a white civilisation essentially feudal in character. It is also a vindication of Indian culture as a way of life which has proved itself down through the ages and demonstrated its continuing viability by its ability to adapt to change, and a denunciation of the *latifundio* system as the major obstacle to the nation's social and economic progress. Its most striking weakness is an unfortunate side-effect of the author's main aim. For in his concern to arouse the conscience of the world to the plight of the Indians and to the injustices perpetrated by the land-owning oligarchy, Alegría has tended to paint too negative a picture of the Indians' ability to resist oppression, leaving the reader with the impression that they are a race without a future, a people doomed to extinction. Artistically, too, the novel is less than satisfying because of the narrator's tendency to over-explain and the simplistic presentation of characters as black and white stereotypes, and the various subordinate narrative elements do not always cohere well with the central plot. Nonetheless, Alegría's significance in the history of Peruvian letters cannot be underestimated. Not only was he the first novelist to create a substantial body of work, but in *El mundo es ancho y ajeno*, a work comparable in scope to the great European social novels of the nineteenth century, he produced the first novel on a grand scale and the first to encapsulate the major reality of national life, the clash of its two cultures. For that reason it ranks as Peru's first fictional classic.

If *El mundo es ancho y ajeno* represents the culmination of *indigenista* fiction, a much more profound interpretation of the Indian and his world was to be provided by Alegría's contemporary, José María Arguedas (1911-69).[25] All Arguedas' work is marked by

[25] See José María Arguedas, *Relatos completos* (Buenos Aires: Losada, 1974); *Yawar Fiesta* (Buenos Aires: Losada, 1974); *Yawar Fiesta*, trans. Frances Horning Barraclough (Austin: Univ. of Texas Press, 1985; London: Quartet Books, 1985). For main bibliography, see p. 211.

an intimate understanding of the Indian mind and a personal identification with Indian culture. Born in the southern Andean town of Andahuaylas, he lived the formative years of his childhood among the Indians of the region and grew up speaking Quechua as his first language, and as a result of early experiences of ill-treatment at the hands of his own relatives he always felt emotionally identified with the world of the Indian rather than with that of the whites. His whole career was devoted to vindicating and promoting an understanding of Indian culture. As a scholar he made collections and translations of Quechua literature and folklore and published important literary and anthropological studies. As a writer he set out to correct the distorted, stereotyped image of the Indian which earlier fiction had presented to the world. His own literary portrayal of the Indian, it should be emphasised, is still an outside view in that it is the work of a non-Indian writing for other non-Indians. Nonetheless, it gives us a deeper insight into the Indian mentality than the work of any other writer before or since. The basis of Indian culture, we are shown, is a magical-religious view of the universe which regards the earth not merely as something to be conquered and exploited, but rather looks on nature as a single cosmic order animated by supernatural forces and linking man, animals, plants and even objects in a universal harmony. What enables Arguedas to convey that world-view so convincingly is not merely his knowledge of the Indian mind but his emotional attachment to the world he is describing and his skilful use of language. In contrast to previous writers Arguedas writes of Indian culture with the personal conviction and involvement of one who identifies with it. Artistically he was faced with the problem of translating into the alien medium of Spanish the sensibility of a people who express themselves in Quechua. In his early works he attempted to resolve this problem by modifying Spanish in such a way as to incorporate the basic features of Quechua syntax and thus reproduce in Spanish something of the special character of Indian speech. This artificial language had the merit of effectively expressing Indian attitudes and thought patterns, but it was not an unqualified success since many of its forms jarred in Spanish and it was not until his later work that he evolved a language which fully satisfied the twin demands of authenticity and universality.

Like Alegría, Arguedas began his literary career in 1935, with *Agua*, a collection of three short stories recounted by a child narrator. Set in a small Andean village, they portray sierra life as a conflict between two classes and cultures, the one represented by the oppressive land-owning oligarchy and the other by the downtrodden Indian peasantry. In each of the stories the region is ruled by a tyrannical landowner whose word is law and who rides roughshod over the rights of the neighbouring Indian communities. In the title-story, for example, Don Braulio has appropriated control of the local water supply and denies the *comuneros* their quota, so that they are unable to irrigate their plots. The Indians are depicted as having been completely cowed by centuries of injustice and are totally lacking in any capacity for rebellion. Yet they find a source of strength in their own culture and, despite their abjection, are seen as possessing inner riches lacking in the whites. They share a sense of brotherhood, expressed in their collective songs and dances, and they live in communion with the magical forces of nature. Indeed, the order imposed by the whites, characterised by a violence that is foreign to the Indian, is seen not only as socially unjust but as a desecration of the natural order. This is highlighted by "Los escoleros", which hinges on the ownership of the best cow in the village. The animal belongs to a widow and the friendly, fraternal way in which the Indians treat it symbolises their relationship with nature. But for the landowner it is an offence to his status that such a beast should be the property of a mere Indian widow and when he fails to gain possession of it he chooses to kill it, for the most valuable objects must belong to the feudal lord or to no one. Thus the established order reasserts its dominance over the natural order.

The clash of cultures is also depicted on an internal level, in the predicament of a boy caught between the two. Though white by birth, the child narrator rejects the white world whose violence and injustice make it uninhabitable for him, and he wishes to belong to that of the Indians among whom he has been brought up. He is drawn to the Indians because he and they are brothers in orphanhood and suffering, sharing a common condition of ill-treatment and humiliation, and he identifies himself with them by rebelling against the oppression of the *mistis*, the white ruling class. Moreover, he finds in their spiritual world the comfort he is denied in the society of his own kind. Not only do the Indians treat him with a kindness he never receives from the whites, but he finds fleeting happiness and human warmth in their songs and dances and spiritual comfort in constant dialogues with animals and nature. Yet though he is drawn towards the Indians, he cannot escape the fact that he is different. He is frequently tormented by a sense of being a "mak'tillo falsificado", a counterfeit Indian as much an outsider in their world as in that of the whites, and in the last paragraph of the book we see him in Lima, dreaming nostalgically of that beloved world from which he is now twice removed. These stories, of course, have a strong autobiographical basis and reflect the predicament that beset Arguedas all his life. They also express his own personal adhesion to the Indian world and its values.

While *Agua* undoubtedly offers a deeper insight into the Indian sensibility than previous fiction, its interpretation of the social reality of the sierra continues to present it in terms of a simple confrontation between oppressive landowners and downtrodden Indians and to express a pessimistic view of the latter's capacity to resist the former. However, in his first novel, *Yawar Fiesta* (1941), published in the same year as *El mundo es ancho y ajeno*, Arguedas sets out to highlight the complexity of Andean society and to situate the Indian within the context of a complicated network of relationships. In describing the little sierra town of Puquio not only does he establish a distinction between *comuneros* and *colonos*, but the *mistis* are seen to be divided among themselves and the mestizos caught betweeen the two racial groups and divided in their allegiance. Furthermore, though the *comuneros* of Puquio have been despoiled of their best lands and have had to accommodate themselves to social and economic oppression, they are far from being crushed, and indeed oppression has served to strengthen their culture, for it is by clinging to their traditional ways and refusing to be absorbed into the white order that they have retained their pride and sense of identity. Moreover, Arguedas demonstrates that coexistence between white and Indian has led to a process of acculturation whereby each has assimilated something of the culture of the other, but while it is the whites who dominate socially and economically, culturally it is the Indian influence which is seen to be predominant, pervading the outlook of the *mistis* despite their assumptions of cultural superiority.

The festival which gives the novel its title and around which it revolves serves to highlight this paradoxical unity in Andean society achieved through the predominance of Quechua culture. If the bullfight is a Spanish tradition which the Indians have adopted, it is one which they have absorbed into their own culture and transformed into the *turupukllay*. And that festival binds the whole town together in a common enthusiasm, so that the *mistis* take as much pride in it as the Indians and boast of it as an emblem of their distinctive identity as *serranos*. Yet since it means different things to the two races, it also reflects the divisions between them. Indeed, representing as it does a symbolic confrontation between the Indian (the bullfighter) and the Spanish (the bull), the festival is seen to be a ritual cathartic re-enactment of the hostilities and tensions of Andean society.

Not only does Arguedas reveal the complexity of traditional Andean society as had never been done before, but he was the first writer to explore the impact of change on that society. For the events of *El mundo es ancho y ajeno*, which span the second and third decades of this century, do not constitute change but merely reflect the anachronistic persistence of the old feudal order. *Yawar Fiesta*, on the other hand, is set in the years immediately following, at a time when the sierra's centuries-old isolation was being broken down by improved communications with the coast. That period saw the start of an increasingly massive migration of Indians and mestizos to the coast in search of work and education, and for the first time the Lima government began actively to concern itself with the affairs of the sierra. In the novel change is symbolised by a government decree banning the Indian festival. Just as the festival itself was used by the author as a vehicle to convey the complex reality of Andean society, so too the ban serves to reveal the ramifications and implications of change.

On the face of it the ban appears to be a progressive measure, but through the attitudes of the *costeño* Sub-Prefect it is shown to represent the imposition on the sierra of an alien concept of progress, in an arbitrary and insensitive manner and without understanding of or consideration for local feeling and conditions. Nonetheless, it is actively supported by the politicised mestizos of the emigrants' association in Lima, who, regarding the festival as a symbol of the *mistis'* exploitation of the Indians, welcome the ban as an opportunity to free the Indians of their superstitions and to enlighten them politically. To that end a commission travels to Puquio only to run up against the resistance of the Indians themselves, and in their attempt to ensure the enforcement of the ban they end up in the contradictory position of allying themselves with the Indians' traditional enemies. This tragic gulf between the Indians and their political sympathisers highlights the latter's failure to understand the Indian. The fundamental weakness of the left-wing political parties, Arguedas believed, was that they, too, interpreted the Andean situation in terms of alien ideologies which presupposed the backwardness of Indian culture.

Among the *mistis* of Puquio the main opponent of the ban is Don

Julián, the most powerful landowner in the region, who fears change as a threat to his feudal status and seeks to forestall it by siding with the very Indians he oppresses, so that paradoxically the two extremes of Andean society join forces in defence of tradition. However, as so often happens in cases where the oppressor woos the oppressed for self-preservation, the effect is that it leads to a further weakening of his position. Don Julián surreptitiously encourages the Indians to resist by making them a present of his bull Misitu, but he is brought to heel by the Sub-Prefect, and when the Indians capture and slay in the arena the hitherto indomitable creature that was the emblem of his status, it is a sign that his days of limitless power have gone forever. In contrast the "progressive" Don Demetrio and Don Antenor favour change because, as allies of the authorities against the conservative feudal landowner, they hope to increase their own power and status and gain control of the town. With the downfall of Don Julián they achieve their aim, but they are shocked and alarmed when he is imprisoned at the instigation of the emigrants' delegates, for the emergence of a new self-confident class of mestizos who can treat them on a level of equality, insult their betters with impunity and even exert influence on the authorities, represents a threat to them also. Change, they discover, entails consequences they had not bargained for.

The main opponents of the ban are, of course, the Indians themselves, who cling to their traditional culture as the bulwark of their own separate universe and their defence against centuries of domination. Behind their rejection of the Spanish bullfighter brought in from Lima to replace the traditional festival lies a refusal to consider themselves a part of the white order, and in defence of their own culture they demonstrate their strength by celebrating their festival in defiance of the government and the *mistis*. Yet if the novel ends with a victory for the Indians that victory is largely illusory, and in a sense the socialist student Escobar is right when he describes them as the victims of their own superstitions. For while they show themselves willing and able to fight to defend their culture, they remain seemingly incapable of channelling their strength into political action. In the arena they display their valour and express their defiance of the *mistis*, but the festival merely ritualises their antagonism and so not only leaves the social order intact but actually reaffirms it. The novel thus presents the situation of the Indians as a seemingly insoluble dilemma. Their traditional culture which has enabled them to survive and flourish despite centuries of oppression is also shown to be their principal weakness, since their religious outlook prevents them from viewing their situation in political terms and taking effective action to remedy it. Conversely, while progress in the form of social, political and economic change offers them liberation from their feudal servitude, it also threatens to destroy their culture and thereby their existence as a separate people. The novel thus leaves a great question-mark hanging over the future.

Undoubtedly *Yawar Fiesta* has its flaws — in particular, its artistic unity is undermined by the lengthy and somewhat old-fashioned introduction which postpones the narrative till the third chapter, and its characterisation of Don Demetrio and Don Antenor tends to degenerate into caricature — and, indeed, Arguedas did not produce his best work until the fifties and sixties when his career took off again after a prolonged silence.[26] Nor is it really surprising that in the years following its publication it should have been overshadowed by the success of *El mundo es ancho y ajeno*, for not only did editorial good fortune enable the latter novel to reach an international readership but its dramatic impact brought home the plight of the Indian to a wide public for the first time. Yet in its profound portrayal of the Indian sensibility and its re-evaluation of the bewildering complexities of Andean society, *Yawar Fiesta* is perhaps the better novel. Be that as it may, with the publication of both books in the same year, 1941 represents a high point in the history of Peruvian fiction, marking not only the emergence of major literary interpretations of the Indian and the sierra but the establishment of a solid novelistic tradition.

---

[26] Arguedas' later work will be dealt with in chapter 5.

Part II
The Poetic Avant-Garde

While Modernism remained in vogue in Peru into the 1920s, the second decade of the century saw the emergence of a number of poets who initiated a move away from the dominant aesthetic.[1] An important transitional figure was Abraham Valdelomar (1888-1919), the founder of *Colónida* (1916), a literary magazine which, though it lasted for only four issues, served as a rallying point for a group of young writers dedicated to revitalising their country's literature.[2] A provincial of humble origins, Valdelomar achieved notoriety in the capital by assuming the title of El Conde de Lemos and adopting the extravagant aristocratic dress and air of a dandy in the manner of Oscar Wilde. There was more to his exhibitionism, however, than a desire to make a name for himself. His public persona was both an assertion of the spiritual superiority of the artist and a mockery of a society whose snobbish pretentiousness was belied by its bourgeois vulgarity of taste, and it implied, too, the embracing of art as a way of life. Unfortunately, Valdelomar's career was tragically brief, but his poetic output, though slight, includes a number of compositions which mark a new direction in Peruvian poetry.

The *Colónida* group, it should be emphasised, was not primarily in rebellion against the Modernist aesthetic but against the conservatism and philistinism of the socio-cultural environment and it is a reflection of Peru's position as a cultural backwater that at the time of the First World War Valdelomar should adopt as an emblem of innovation a persona fashionable in Europe at the end of the previous century. Yet though much of his work is Modernist in manner, particularly in the early period, from 1913 onwards Valdelomar began to discover a voice of his own. Beneath his arrogant public persona he remained a sensitive provincial who was never at home in the city and to express his inner world he began to

---

[1] For a survey of the poetry of the period see Luis Monguió, *La poesía postmodernista peruana* (Berkeley and Los Angeles: Univ. of California Press, 1954); Ricardo González Vigil, "La poesía peruana en los años 20", *Revista de la Universidad Católica*, 5 (1979), 109-19; Mirko Lauer, "La poesía vanguardista en el Perú", *RevCrit*, 15 (1982), 77-86; Estuardo Núñez, "La recepción del surrealismo en el Perú", in *Surrealismo/Surrealismos. Latinoamérica y España*, ed. Peter G. Earle and Germán Gullón (Philadelphia: Dept. of Romance Languages, Univ. of Pennsylvania, 1977), pp. 40-48.

[2] See Abraham Valdelomar, *Obra poética* (Asociación Peruana por la Libertad de la Cultura, 1958); *Poesía y estética* (CAP, 1971). For further bibliography see p.111.

cultivate a simple, plain style shorn of Modernist rhetoric. At the same time, like several of his contemporaries in other Spanish American countries, notably the Mexican López Velarde, he forsook exotic Modernist themes and settings to write about the everyday world of the provinces. That world is evoked with nostalgia. Only in its tranquil atmosphere, amidst the unaffected warmth of simple, homely folk, has he found refuge from the cares and pains of life:

> En mi Dolor pusisteis vuestro cordial consuelo;
> en vuestro hogar mis penas encontraron un nido;
> para mi soledad, vuestras almas han sido
> como dos alas blancas bajo la paz del cielo.

> (On my Pain you put your cordial comfort;
> in your home my troubles found a nest;
> for my loneliness your souls have been
> like two white wings beneath the peace of the sky.)

Many of his poems are recollections of his family home in the little port of Pisco. Now abandoned, the house becomes a symbol of lost happiness and innocence, of the empty desolation that has invaded his life:

> Ya la casa está muerta. ¡Ya no es la misma casa!
> El jardín florecido se extinguió ... A la desierta
> alcoba ya no sube, escaladora experta,
> la vida en frescos pámpanos en racimos escasa.

> (The house is dead now. It's no longer the same house!
> The flowering garden has withered ... And meagre
> in clustering fresh tendrils, life, that expert climber,
> no longer scales the wall to the deserted bedroom.)

Yet in the main childhood is not recalled as an idyll of unalloyed happiness, for Valdelomar's recollections are marked by their ambivalence. If the rural landscape gave him an appreciation of the beauties of nature, it also instilled in him an awareness of man's loneliness in the world, and the atmosphere of emotional security that reigned in his home was clouded by the hardships encountered by his parents as they struggled to raise a large family in straitened financial circumstances. His childhood experience, he tells us in the sonnet "Tristitia", left him with a predisposition towards melancholy that was to remain with him all his life:

> Mi infancia que fue dulce, serena, triste y sola
> se deslizó en la paz de una aldea lejana,
> entre el manso rumor con que muere una ola
> y el tañer doloroso de una vieja campana.

Dábame el mar la nota de su melancolía,
el cielo la serena quietud de su belleza,
los besos de mi madre una dulce alegría
y la muerte del sol una vaga tristeza.

En la mañana azul, al despertar, sentía
el canto de las olas como una melodía
y luego el soplo denso, perfumado del mar,

y lo que él me dijera aún en mi alma persiste;
mi padre era callado y mi madre era triste
y la alegría nadie me la supo enseñar ...

(My childhood which was sweet, serene, sad and lonely
slipped past in the peace of a distant village,
among the gentle murmur of a dying wave
and the pained tolling of an ancient bell.

The sea gave me the note of its melancholy,
the sky the serene quietude of its beauty,
my mother's kisses a sweet happiness
and the death of the sun a vague sadness.

In the blue of the morning, when I awoke,
I heard like a melody the song of the waves
and then the thick, perfumed whisper of the sea,

and what it said to me still persists in my soul;
my father was silent and my mother was sad
and joy was something no one was ever able to teach me ...)

Away from the security of the home, that sense of melancholy
developed into an anguished pessimism and an obsession with death
which are often expressed in symbols drawn from everyday provincial
life. Thus, in the sonnet "Cobardía" the futility of struggling against
the inevitability of death is symbolised by a turtle's half-hearted
attempt to escape from the fisherman's net.

Standing in stark contrast to Valdelomar's provincial poems are
two compositions expressing his vision of the urban world. "Nocturno" takes the reader on a tour of Lima in the small hours to
convey a sense of the ugly squalor of the urban environment and of
the loneliness and emptiness of city life. "Luna Park", a long
description of a Parisian amusement park, shows decadent Western
society seeking escape from its tedium and loss of faith in life. The
grotesque carnival witnessed by the poet is like a dance of death as a
moribund civilisation drifts to its eclipse:

Vi rostros cadavéricos, exhaustos, huesudas manos,
como en funambulesca danza diabólica pasar,
bocas descoloridas de metálicos dientes

sonriendo entre las luces como en un triste carnaval.
Cutis marchitos, toses hondas y huecas, flores deshojadas,
cuentas, garzones, cansancio, malestar,
atmósfera pesada, colillas de cigarros;
las luces se comenzaban a apagar ...

(I saw cadaverous, exhausted faces, bony hands,
pass by as in a diabolical, funambulesque dance,
colourless mouths with metallic teeth
smiling among the lights as in a sad carnival.
Withered complexions, deep, echoing coughs, leafless flowers,
beads, handsome youths, weariness, malaise,
a heavy atmosphere, cigarette ends;
the lights began to go out ...)

In these two compositions Valdelomar seems to be moving tentatively
in the direction of avant-garde poetry. "Luna Park" is written in free
verse, "Nocturno" has the occasional "modern" image, and both are
"anti-poetic" in their caustic irony and emphasis on the ugly. It is
possible that had he lived longer, he might have gone further in that
direction. As it is, his main contribution to the development of post-
Modernist poetry in Peru lies in his abandonment of rarefied themes
and settings for a poetry dealing with everyday reality and, above all,
in that by freeing himself from artificial literary language and
imagery and adopting a simple, direct style, he initiated a much
needed process of purification of poetic language. Thus, though his
career was too short and his production too slight for him to be a
major poet or more than a transitional figure, he performed an
important role in helping to clear the ground for later artists.

Another important transitional figure was the expatriate Juan
Parra del Riego (1894-1925), a native of Huancayo who left Peru in
1917 and subsequently settled in Uruguay.[3] Though he also wrote
poetry of an intimate nature, the most characteristic note of his work
is the celebration of the marvel of life in all its manifestations. Much
of his work is fairly traditional, but a number of poems exploit
modern imagery and free verse with varying rhythms to convey the
excitement and vitality of twentieth-century life. The best of these are
his *polirritmos*, which date from the early twenties though they were
not published in book form till 1937. "Polirritmo dinámico de la
motocicleta" communicates the thrilling sense of speed and power
experienced by a motor-cyclist:

---

[3] See Juan Parra del Riego, *Poesía* (Montevideo: Biblioteca de la Cultura Uruguaya,
1943).

Y corro ... corro ... corro ...
hasta que ebrio y todo pálido
de peligro y cielo y vértigo en mi audaz velocidad,
ya mi alma no es mi alma:
es un émbolo con música,
un salvaje trompo cálido,
todo el sueño de la vida que en mi pecho incendio y lloro,
la feliz carrera de oro
de la luz desnuda y libre que jamás nos dejará.

(And I race ... race ... race ...
till drunk and completely pale
with danger and sky and vertigo in my daring speed,
my soul is no longer my soul:
it's a piston with music,
a wild, hot spinning-top,
the whole dream of life which in my breast I set on fire and
      weep,
the happy golden race
of naked, free light which will never leave us.)

"Polirritmo dinámico a Gradín, jugador de football" captures the
football-crazy atmosphere of Montevideo in the early twenties as it
celebrates the graceful skills of one of the stars of the Uruguayan
national team. The rhythm of the poem follows the movements of the
player and the pattern of the play:

¡Flecha, víbora, campana, banderola!
¡Gradín, bala azul y verde! ¡Gradín, globo que se va!
Billarista de esa súbita y vibrante carambola
que se rompe en las cabezas y se enfila más allá ...
y discóbolo volante,
pasas uno ...
dos ...
tres ... cuatro ...
siete jugadores ...

La pelota hierve en ruido seco y sordo de metralla,
se revuelca una epilepsia de colores
y ya estás frente a la valla
con el pecho ... el alma ... el pie ...
y es el tiro que en la tarde azul estalla
como un cálido balazo que se lleva la pelota hasta la red.
¡Palomares! ¡Palomares!
de los cálidos aplausos populares ...

(Arrow, viper, bell, pennant!
Gradín, a blue and green bullet! Gradín, a disappearing
      sphere!
Billiards-player making that sudden, vibrant cannon

that breaks against heads and carries beyond ...
and like a flying discus-thrower,
you pass one ...
two ...
three ... four ...
seven players ...

The ball surges amid the dry, dull sound of shrapnel,
colours thrash in an epileptic fit
and now you're in front of the goal
with your breast ... your soul ... your foot ...
and the drive that explodes in the blue afternoon
is like a hot gunshot carrying the ball towards the net.
Dovecots, dovecots
of warm popular applause!)

These poems are undoubtedly the most successful example of futurist
poetry produced by a Peruvian, but unfortunately Parra was too
remote from his native country and the poems themselves too late in
circulating for him to exercise any significant influence there.

The standard-bearer of the avant-garde was another provincial,
Alberto Hidalgo (1897-1967), who burst on to the scene with
aggressive rebelliousness to do battle against the conservatism of the
social and literary environment.[4] He first made a name for himself in
his native Arequipa with his *Arenga lírica al Emperador de Alemania*
(1916), in which he identifies himself with Kaiser Wilhelm in his war
against France, implying that they are allies in the common cause of
exterminating a decadent civilisation:

> I Emperador i Bardo —tú i yo— de bracero
> iremos vencedores al vicioso París.
>
> (And Emperor and Bard — you and I — arm in arm
> we'll march as conquerors on depraved Paris.)

Subsequently he moved to Lima where he published *Panoplia lírica*
(1917), a book which included a number of poems influenced by
Marinetti, and futurism continued to be a feature of his next two

---

[4] See Alberto Hidalgo, *Panoplia lírica* (Víctor Fajardo, 1917); *Las voces de colores*
(Arequipa: A. Quiroz, 1918); *Joyería* (Buenos Aires: Virtus, 1919); *Química del espíritu*
(Buenos Aires: Mercatali, 1923); *Simplismo* (Buenos Aires: El Inca, 1925); *Descripción
del cielo, poemas de varios lados* (Buenos Aires: El Inca, 1928). Hidalgo's principal later
works are *Actitud de los años* (Buenos Aires: M. Gleizer, 1933); *Dimensión del hombre*
(Buenos Aires: F.A. Colombo, 1938); *Edad del corazón* (Buenos Aires: Teatro del
Pueblo, 1940); *Oda a Stalin* (Buenos Aires: El Martillo, 1945); *Anivegral* (Buenos
Aires: Mía, 1952); *Biografía de yo mismo* (Mejía Baca, 1959); *Arbol genealógico* (Mejía
Baca, 1963). See also Octavio R. Armand, "El yo en la poesía de Alberto Hidalgo",
Diss. Rutgers 1974 (Univ. Microfilms, 1980); Frederick S. Stimson, *The New Schools of
Spanish American Poetry* (Chapel Hill: Univ. of North Carolina, 1970), pp. 111-31.

collections, *Las voces de colores* (1918) and *Joyería* (1919). Here he celebrates the beauty of cars, aeroplanes, motor cycles, sport and war, manifestations of a new creative spirit which is destroying the old world to build a new, a process in which the poet collaborates in his own particular sphere. Thus "La nueva poesía" calls for a poetry exalting the energy and vigour which will enable humanity to leave the past behind and to forge a brave new future:

> Dejemos ya los viejos motivos trasnochados
> i cantemos al Músculo, a la Fuerza, al Vigor.
>
> (Let's now leave behind the old, obsolete motifs
> and sing to Muscle, to Strength, to Vigour.)

Lima was apparently too conservative for his taste and in 1919 he established himself in Buenos Aires, where he remained resident for the rest of his life. However, in contrast to the case of Parra del Riego, his works circulated in Peru and had a considerable impact.

In practice Hidalgo's early books are much less innovative than the content of some of the poems would seem to suggest, for stylistically they are very conservative and Modernist influence is still present. However, in the course of the twenties and particularly in *Química del espíritu* (1923), *Simplismo* (1925) and *Descripción del cielo* (1928), he immersed himself more deeply in the avant-garde currents and invented a poetics of his own which he called "simplismo". His theories, expounded in the prologue to *Simplismo*, are not particularly original but reflect his awareness of and ability to absorb the ideas that were in the air at the time. Effectively "simplismo" means the reduction of poetry to its essentials: rhyme, music, narration and description should be shunned, the poem should be constructed on the basis of metaphors, the hallmark of the poem should be brevity and condensation. Above all, he argued that each poet should develop his own personal language and he aspired to write not in Spanish but in "Hidalgo". Where he is at his most daring is perhaps in his experiments in typographical arrangement. Thus "Sabiduría" consists of five vertical lines, the three centre ones being straight and the outside ones crooked; "Jaqueca" consists of lower-case and capital letters scattered over the page; "El destino" is printed in a circle with a dot in the centre. This experimentation reaches its culmination in *Descripción del cielo*, whose twelve poems are printed in large type on poster-size pages, each of which is folded to fit within the book's cover. The texts themselves are "poems with several sides" in which the lines, though linked to a central idea or emotion, constitute independent units and can be read in any order the reader chooses.

From the very beginning of his career a feature of Hidalgo's work was the exaltation of self. A section of *Panoplia lírica* is entitled "La religión del yo"(The Religion of the Self) and in one poem he declares:

> Me siento inmensamente superior a los hombres
> i pongo de los genios junto a sus grandes nombres
> mi nombre que resuena como un noble tambor.

> (I feel myself immensely superior to men
> and alongside the names of the world's great geniuses
> I place my name which resounds like a noble drum.)

Exercised by this aspect of his work, critics have often tended to equate it with Chocano's enormous self-conceit and to dismiss it as megalomania. However, there is more to his obsessive preoccupation with himself than mere narcissism. Many of his more extravagant claims are uttered tongue in cheek with the purpose of scandalising a bourgeois public. Moreover, behind the public image lurked a sensitive soul familiar with suffering — he was orphaned at an early age and had an unhappy childhood — and it would seem that to a considerable extent the aggressive, self-promoting persona he created for himself was a defensive wall erected around him for protection from a world he felt to be hostile. Furthermore, for Hidalgo the self is the starting-point of all knowledge. Living through an age of crisis, he sought in himself the certainty he could not see in the crumbling world outside him and his self-centred poetry represents an attempt to discover in himself the ultimate reality which he believed was contained within the individual. His experimentation with avant-garde techniques is part of that search, the disarticulation of language being designed to break down accepted ways of looking at reality and the reduction of the poem to essentials reflecting his quest for the authentic. "Viaje alrededor de mí mismo" describes this process of self-exploration in which he strives to liberate the universal being within him, to transcend self by discovering his true self:

> como los suspicaces políticos
> salen a recorrer aldeas
> hacia las vísperas de las elecciones,
> me he puesto a caminar por los caminos
> de mi YO.

¡cómo tardo en volver
al punto de que partí!
¡oh!
¡cómo tardo!

(just as canny politicians
go out and tour villages
on the eve of elections,
I've set to travelling the roads
of my EGO.

how long I am in returning
to the point from which I parted!
oh!
how long I am!)

Descripción del cielo brings that quest to a successful conclusion with the discovery of heaven within himself as the barriers separating him from the world are abolished and self and cosmos merge into a harmonious whole. In "Poema del saltador", for example, the self arrives at a state of absolute consubstantiation with everything that exists:

Luego de haber recorrido el día la noche y el mundo el
        saltador vio que estaba otra vez en su punto de
        partida.
Era su frente el cielo
La tierra era su carne
En su pulso golpeaba frenética el agua de los ríos
No había nada más allá del hombre

(After traversing the day the night and the world the
        springer saw that he was back at his starting-point.
His face was the sky
The earth was his flesh
In his pulse beat frantically the water of the rivers
There was nothing beyond man)

One of the most prolific of Peruvian poets, Hidalgo went on writing poetry into the sixties, producing in all over twenty volumes, but if he merits a place in the history of his country's literature it is largely on the strength of his early work. Not that he was ever more than a mediocre poet, for his artistic talent never matched his ambition or his theoretical grasp of the avant-garde aesthetic and all too often his poetry is merely a parade of clever metaphors or a versified exposition of his philosophical thought. Nonetheless, as champion and theorist of a new kind of literature, he is a figure of considerable historical importance.

If Hidalgo rarely managed to translate his avant-garde theories into effective poetry, his fellow provincial, César Vallejo (1892-1938), was meanwhile in the process of producing a work of genius radically different from anything previously written in Spanish.[5] A creator rather than a theorist, Vallejo did not engage in polemics but

[5] See César Vallejo, *Obra poética completa* (Moncloa, 1968); *Obra poética completa*, ed. Enrique Ballón Aguirre (Caracas: Biblioteca Ayacucho, 1979); *César Vallejo: An Anthology of his Poetry*, ed. James Higgins (Oxford: Pergamon, 1970); *Selected Poems*, trans. Ed. Dorn and Gordon Brotherston (Harmondsworth: Penguin, 1976); *Trilce*, trans. David Smith (New York: Grossman, 1973); *The Complete Posthumous Poetry*, trans. Clayton Eshelman and José Rubia Barcia (Berkeley: Univ. of California Press, 1982). Other works by Vallejo include *Novelas y cuentos completos* (Moncloa, 1967); *Teatro completo*, 2 vols. (La Católica, 1979); *Rusia en 1931: Reflexiones al pie del Kremlin* (Labor, 1965); *Rusia ante el Segundo Plan Quinquenal* (Labor, 1965); *Artículos olvidados* (Asociación Peruana por la Libertad de la Cultura, 1960); *Contra el secreto profesional* (Mosca Azul, 1973); *El arte y la revolución* (Mosca Azul, 1973); *Epistolario general* (Valencia: Pre-Textos, 1982). On Vallejo see Xavier Abril, *Ensayo de aproximación crítica* (Buenos Aires: Front, 1958); id., *César Vallejo o la teoría poética* (Madrid: Taurus, 1962); id., *Exégesis trílcica* (Labor, 1980); Enrique Ballón Aguirre, *Vallejo como paradigma (un caso especial de escritura)* (INC, 1974); André Coyné, *César Vallejo* (Buenos Aires: Nueva Visión, 1968); Alberto Escobar, *Cómo leer a Vallejo* (Villanueva, 1973); Juan Espejo Asturrizaga, *César Vallejo. Itinerario del hombre* (Mejía Baca, 1965); York S. Febres, "Peruanismos y otros orígenes y aspectos del vocabulario poético de César Vallejo", Diss. Minnesota 1975 (Univ. Microfilms, 1977); Américo Ferrari, *El universo poético de César Vallejo* (Caracas: Monte Avila, 1972); Angel Flores, ed., *Aproximaciones a César Vallejo*, 2 vols. (New York: Las Américas, 1971); Jean Franco, *César Vallejo: The Dialectics of Poetry and Silence* (Cambridge: Cambridge Univ. Press, 1976); Víctor Fuentes, *El cántico material y espiritual de César Vallejo* (Barcelona: Anthropos Editorial del Hombre, 1981); James Higgins, *Visión del hombre y de la vida en las últimas obras poéticas de César Vallejo* (Mexico City: Siglo XXI, 1970); id., *César Vallejo: An Anthology of his Poetry*, pp. 1-82; id., *The Poet in Peru*, pp. 24-45, 109-22; Juan Larrea, *César Vallejo o Hispanoamérica en la cruz de su razón* (Córdoba, Argentina: Univ. Nac. de Córdoba, 1958); id., *César Vallejo y el surrealismo* (Madrid: Visor, 1976); id., *Al amor de Vallejo* (Valencia: Pre-Textos, 1980); Francisco Martínez García, *César Vallejo; acercamiento al hombre y al poeta* (León: Colegio Universitario de León, 1976); Giovanni Meo Zilio, *Stile e poesia in César Vallejo* (Padua: Liviana, 1960); id. et al., "Neologismos en la poesía de César Vallejo", in *Lavori della Sezione Fiorentina del Gruppo Ispanistico C.N.R.*, Serie I (Florence: D'Anna, 1967), pp. 11-98; Luis Monguió, *César Vallejo. Vida y Obra* (New York: Hispanic Institute in the United States, 1952; Lima: Perú Nuevo, 1960); Eduardo Neale-Silva, *César Vallejo en su fase trílcica* (Madison: Univ. of Wisconsin Press, 1975); Julio Ortega, *Figuración de la persona*, pp. 15-86; id., ed., *César Vallejo* (Madrid: Taurus, 1974); Yolanda Osuna, *Vallejo, el poema, la idea* (Caracas: Univ. Central de Venezuela, 1979); Roberto Paoli, *Poesie di César Vallejo* (Milan: Lerici, 1964); id., *Mapas anatómicos de César Vallejo* (Messina-Florence: D'Anna, 1981); Willy F. Pinto Gamboa, *César Vallejo: en torno a España* (Cibeles, 1981); Iván Rodríguez Chávez, *La ortografía poética de Vallejo* (Compañía de Impresiones y Publicidad, 1974); Georgette de Vallejo, *Apuntes biográficos sobre "Poemas en prosa" y "Poemas humanos"* (Moncloa, 1968); id., *Vallejo: allá ellos, allá ellos, allá ellos!* (Zalvac, 1980); José Luis Vega, *César Vallejo en "Trilce"* (Río Piedras: Univ. de Puerto Rico, 1983); María Irene Vegas-García, "Sobre la estructura del lenguaje poético de César Vallejo en *Trilce*", Diss. Berkeley 1978 (Univ. Microfilms, 1981); Saúl Yurkievich, *Fundadores de la nueva poesía latinoamericana* (Barcelona: Barral, 1971), pp. 11-51. See also *Aula Vallejo* (Univ. Nac. de Córdoba, Arg.), 1 (1961), 2/4 (1963), 5/7 (1967), 8/10 (1971), 11/13 (1974); *César Vallejo: actas del coloquio internacional, Freie Universität Berlin, junio 1979*, ed. G. Beutler and A. Losada (Tübingen: Max Niemayer, 1981); *Revista Iberoamericana*, 71 (1970); *Visión del Perú*, 4 (1969).

quietly and unobtrusively went about the business of developing a new poetic language attuned to his own sensibility and to that of the age, and in time he was to be recognised as an artist of world stature, the greatest poet not only of Peru but of all Spanish America. A mestizo born and brought up in the little rural township of Santiago de Chuco in the heart of the northern sierra, he studied and taught in Trujillo before moving to Lima in early 1918. His first volume, *Los heraldos negros* (1919), is essentially a book of transition. Much of it is derivative, betraying the marked influence of Modernism in both themes and idiom, but it also reveals an evolution which parallels that already noted in the case of Valdelomar. The cycle of five poems which make up the section "Canciones del hogar" evokes the humble, everyday world of his provincial home, and these and other compositions employ a simple, direct, almost colloquial idiom as he frees himself from literary influences and moves towards a style that is a genuine expression of personal experience and emotions. In some poems, too, there are the first tentative signs of the new poetic language which he was to develop in his later work.

Mirroring the general spiritual crisis of modern times, *Los heraldos negros* expresses the metaphysical anguish of a young man who is no longer able to accept the religious beliefs in which he was brought up. Not surprisingly, given the somewhat limited cultural formation Vallejo received in the provinces, the poems sometimes have an old-fashioned ring to them as he casts himself in the role of the alienated Romantic. Thus, in "Los dados eternos" he points an accusing finger at God, charging him with being insensitive to the suffering of the creatures he has irresponsibly brought into being, while "Espergesia" presents him as an outsider suffering a spiritual emptiness which no one else can share or understand:

Hay un vacío	(There's a vacuum
en mi aire metafísico	in my metaphysical atmosphere
que nadie ha de palpar.	that no one will ever probe.)

However, Vallejo's poetry is given a very personal tone by a sense of almost childish inadequacy in face of the world which colours his view of the human condition. Thus, in "La cena miserable" unfulfilled humanity, stranded in a world not made to its measure, is likened to a child who has woken up in the night crying with hunger and sits alone in the darkness, endlessly waiting for a meal that is never served:

> Ya nos hemos sentado
> mucho a la mesa, con la amargura de un niño
> que a media noche, llora de hambre, desvelado . . .

> (We've been sitting
> a long time now at table, with the bitterness of a child
> who at midnight sobs with hunger, unable to sleep . . .)

God, too, is often depicted as being equally impotent, defrauding man's expectations by his inability to convert his good intentions into reality, as in "La de a mil" where he is compared to the ragged lottery-ticket vendor whose title of "suertero" (bringer of luck) is a purely nominal one:

> Pasa el suertero que atesora, acaso
> nominal, como Dios,
> entre panes tantálicos, humana
> impotencia de amor.

> (The lottery vendor/bringer of luck goes past, perhaps
> nominal, like God,
> hoarding, amongst tantalising loaves,
> human impotence of love.)

The full extent of the crisis Vallejo comes face to face with in *Los heraldos negros* is revealed, above all, in the title-poem, where we see him reacting with confused bewilderment to the gratuitous cruelty of life, shaking his head disbelievingly at the hardness of its blows, unable to understand or explain why they should befall him:

> Hay golpes en la vida, tan fuertes . . . Yo no sé!
> Golpes como del odio de Dios; como si ante ellos,
> la resaca de todo lo sufrido
> se empozara en al alma . . . Yo no sé!

> Son pocos; pero son . . . Abren zanjas oscuras
> en el rostro más fiero y en el lomo más fuerte.
> Serán tal vez los potros de bárbaros atilas;
> o los heraldos negros que nos manda la Muerte.

> Son las caídas hondas de los Cristos del alma,
> de alguna fe adorable que el Destino blasfema.
> Esos golpes sangrientos son las crepitaciones
> de algún pan que en la puerta del horno se nos quema.

> Y el hombre . . . Pobre . . . pobre! Vuelve los ojos, como
> cuando por sobre el hombro nos llama una palmada;
> vuelve los ojos locos, y todo lo vivido
> se empoza, como charco de culpa, en la mirada.

> Hay golpes en la vida, tan fuertes . . . Yo no sé!

(There are blows in life, so hard ... I don't know!
Blows as if from the hatred of God; as if in the face of them
the backwash of everything we'd suffered
had welled up in the soul ... I don't know!

They're rare; but they're real enough ... They open dark weals
on the toughest face and on the stoutest back.
They're maybe the steeds of barbarous attilas;
or the black heralds sent by Death.

They are the falling low of the Christs of the soul,
of some adorable faith blasphemed by Destiny.
Those bloody blows are the crackling
of a loaf that burns on us in the oven's door.

And man ... Poor soul! He looks round, as when
over the shoulder we are summoned by a clapping hand;
he looks round in panic, and the whole of life
wells up in his eyes like a pool of guilt.

There are blows in life, so hard ... I don't know!)

Here the poet is confronted by a reality with which his mind is unable
to cope. The traditional doctrines in which he has been brought up,
with their assumptions of an ordered universe and a benevolent God,
simply do not correspond to his experience of life. Nor does reason,
the tool on which Western civilisation has traditionally relied to
understand the world, enable him to explain that experience. But,
more than that, the language he has inherited does not equip him to
define that experience, for he is unable to find words capable of
expressing the pain inflicted by the blows and his attempts to describe
it taper off in an expression of hopeless inadequacy. All of Vallejo's
later poetry could be said to stem from this opening poem of his first
volume. For the books which followed represent an attempt to
develop a personal language which will faithfully express his
experience of the world, a language which will enable him to define
that experience and thereby come to terms with it. Ultimately it is
through poetry that Vallejo strives to come to terms with a reality
which is otherwise beyond his grasp.

Trilce (1922) is one of the great landmarks in modern literature, for
it is a book which revolutionised poetry in the Spanish language.
Remarkably, it is the work of a young Peruvian provincial operating
in remote isolation from the centres of Western culture and with only
a limited knowledge of contemporary literature. This is not to say
that Trilce emerged from a vacuum. Vallejo did have a certain
familiarity with contemporary trends acquired from anthologies of
French poetry in Spanish translation and from Spanish reviews like

Cervantes, which published European avant-garde texts, and there is no doubt that he was influenced by literary developments in Europe. However, he was mature enough to assimilate that influence and, above all, he was encouraged and stimulated by the example of the European avant-garde to pursue his own experimentation and to develop his own poetic style, and to a large extent *Trilce* was written independently of what was happening elsewhere. In fact, it could even be argued that precisely because Vallejo did not feel himself to be at the centre of the Western literary tradition and, indeed, felt that tradition to be alien, he was unhampered by conservative attitudes and more inclined to experiment. Be that as it may, he represents a new phenomenon, that of a Spanish American writer who no longer follows in the wake of the great European writers but stands on equal footing with them at the forefront of world literature.

The most immediately obvious avant-garde technique to be found in *Trilce* is the employment of graphic devices such as the use of capitals to highlight words or parts of words or the adoption of a new disposition of words on the page to reinforce their meaning plastically. However, such devices are used sparingly and the core of Vallejo's new poetic style lies elsewhere. This is, firstly, a poetry that is remarkably concise and elliptic, with the result that the relationship between the different parts of a sentence is often only implicit. It is, too, a poetry which abandons traditional metres and verse forms in favour of free verse, developing its own internal rhythm reinforced by alliteration, reiteration, enumeration and binary and parallel lines. Above all, it is a poetry whose logic is internal, with the relationship between apparently disconnected images functioning on the level of the poetic emotion. Described thus in general terms, *Trilce* merely appears to share characteristics common to most modern poetry. What is distinctive about it is its extraordinarily original use of language. Vallejo confounds the reader's expectations by his daring exploitation of the line pause, which often leaves articles, conjunctions and even particles of words dangling at the end of a line, by his frequent resort to harsh sounds to break the rhythm, by employing alliterations so awkward as to be tongue-twisters. He distorts syntactic structures, changes the grammatical function of words, plays with spelling. His poetic vocabulary is frequently unfamiliar and "unliterary", he creates new words of his own, he often conflates two words into one, he tampers with clichés to give them new meaning, he plays on the multiple meaning of words and on the similarity of sound between words. He repeatedly makes use of oxymoron and paradox and, above all, catachresis, defamiliarising objects by attributing to them qualities not normally associated with them. Vallejo, in short, deconstructs the Spanish language in an unprecedented manner, and by so doing he breaks down accepted habits of thought and forces the reader to view reality in a new light.

Like *Los heraldos negros*, *Trilce* expresses Vallejo's alienation in a world that has lost its meaning. That alienation is intensely felt, for not only is it born of an intellectual view of the world but it has its roots in his personal experience. Accustomed to the sheltered security of his rural home, Vallejo felt out of his depth as a lonely *serrano* immigrant in Lima. Not surprisingly, therefore, his poetry is dominated by a sense of inadequacy and insecurity, by a feeling that he is a boy in a world too big for him to cope with, and the poetic persona which he most consistently adopts is that of a child left to fend for himself in a dark, incomprehensible and menacing universe.

Various poems record Vallejo's experience of Lima. Poem XIV, for example, summarises the reaction of the recently arrived provincial overawed and intimidated by the strange new world of the capital, by

> Esa manera de caminar por los trapecios.
> Esos corajosos brutos como postizos.
> Esa goma que pega el azogue al adentro.
> Esas posaderas sentadas para arriba.
> Ese no puede ser, sido.
> Absurdo.
> Demencia.
>
> (That manner of getting about on trapezes.
> Those toughs as brutish as they're phony.
> That rubber which sticks the quicksilver to the inside.
> Those buttocks seated upwards.
> That can't be, been.
> Absurd.
> Madness.)

Totally unprepared for the reality he encounters there, he is bewildered and overwhelmed by a city where the natural order as he knows it seems to have been turned on its head. His arrival in Lima thus marks his initiation into an apparently absurd and senseless world.

In 1920 Vallejo suffered another traumatic experience when, on a visit to Santiago, he became the innocent victim of local political squabbles and was jailed for three and a half months. The subject of a number of poems, that experience reinforced his belief in the world's arbitrary cruelty and his sense of inadequacy in face of it. Thus, in poem XVIII the four white walls of the prison cell become a symbol of the cold, implacable laws of the heartless, sterile world in which he now finds himself trapped:

> Oh las cuatro paredes de la celda.
> Ah las cuatro paredes albicantes
> que sin remedio dan al mismo número.
>
> (Oh the four walls of the cell.
> Ah the four dazzling white walls
> which without fail come out at the same number.)

To a large extent, therefore, *Trilce* is a lament for the passing of the childhood which the poet left behind him when he left the family home and which was brought to a definitive end by the death of his mother in 1918. In a personal version of the myth of paradise lost his provincial home, seen from the perspective of distance, becomes an idyll to be evoked with nostalgia, a norm for measuring the world of the present and underlining its deficiencies. The axis of that happy, integrated world, where his childhood unfolded in an atmosphere of peace, love and security, was the archetypal figure of the mother, the purveyor of life, love and nourishment. Poem XXIII recalls her distributing biscuits to her children, nourishing them emotionally with her love at the same time as she gave sustenance to their bodies. In the timeless mythical world of childhood life was regulated by that twice-daily ritual which had all the solemnity and significance of the Christian communion:

> En la sala de arriba nos repartías
> de mañana, de tarde, de dual estiba,
> aquellas ricas hostias de tiempo, para
> que ahora nos sobrasen
> cáscaras de relojes en flexión de las 24
> en punto parados.
>
> (In the room upstairs you shared out among us,
> morning and afternoon, from dual store,
> those rich hosts of time, only for
> us now to have left over
> husks of clocks with hands stopped
> on the dot of midnight.)

But now the clocks of the historical world of adulthood mark the end of true time as they measure out the minutes and seconds that are but indigestible left-overs from that eternal, fulfilling past. Cast out of the childhood paradise, the orphaned poet must now fend for himself, struggling for survival in a competitive world where nothing is given freely out of love and everything must be fought and paid for:

> Tal la tierra oirá en tu silenciar,
> cómo nos van cobrando todos
> el alquiler del mundo donde nos dejas
> y el valor de aquel pan inacabable.
>
> (And so the earth will hear in your silence
> how they all keep charging us
> the rent of this world where you're leaving us
> and the price of that never-ending bread.)

Vallejo's nostalgia for childhood is, of course, also a nostalgia for lost innocence, for his view of the world in *Trilce* is the disillusioned one of a man who can see no meaningful pattern to existence. The oracle that once explained the enigma of life has fallen silent in modern times, we are told in poem LVI, and all man can perceive are disjointed fragments of a confusing reality whose overall coherence escapes him:

> Flecos de invisible trama
> dientes que huronean desde la neutra emoción,
>   pilares
> libres de base y coronación,
> en la gran boca que ha perdido el habla.
>
> (Fringes of an invisible weave,
> teeth which ferret from neutral emotion,
>   pillars
> free of base and crown,
> in the great mouth which has lost its speech.)

Therein lies the general significance of the disconcerting poetic techniques employed in *Trilce*, for their purpose is to sabotage assumptions of order and harmony and to convey a sense of apparently meaningless chaos. The volume abounds, too, in scientific and technical terms ironically emptied of their usual connotations of logic and certainty. Thus, instead of measuring reality, numbers, like the coin in poem XLVIII, seem to take on a life of their own and multiply to infinity, mirroring a reality that cannot be pinned down:

> Ella, siendo 69, dase contra 70;
> luego escala 71, rebota en 72.
> Y así se multiplica y espejea impertérrita
> en todos los demás piñones.

(Being 69, it collides with 70;
then it scales 71, and bounces into 72.
And so it multiplies and glitters undaunted
on all the other pinions.)

What numbers designate, above all, is the empty repetitiveness of existence, for, greatly influenced by evolutionist theory, Vallejo saw the sole purpose of life as being its perpetuation and the sole purpose of the individual as being to serve the species. In poem V he protests against the senseless process of reproduction, symbolised by numbers which are also a visual pun on the mating urge of the sexes:

Pues no deis 1, que resonará al infinito.
Y no deis O, que callará tanto,
hasta despertar y poner de pie al 1.

(So don't utter 1, for it will echo to infinity.
And don't utter O, for it will keep so silent
that it will wake up the 1 and make it rise.)

In *Trilce*, therefore, there is a constant conflict between the poet's aspirations as an individual and his subjection to biological laws, and again and again his longing for freedom and transcendence is thwarted as he keeps banging his head against the existential limitations imposed by his human condition:

Cabezazo brutal. Asoman
las coronas a oír,
pero sin traspasar los eternos
trescientos sesenta grados.

(Brutal bang of the head. The crowns
peep out to listen,
but without going beyond the eternal
three hundred and sixty degrees.)

Trilce, then, shows man trapped in an absurd world which makes a nonsense of his assumptions of meaning and order. However, Vallejo's concept of the absurd is an ambivalent one, for he is convinced that the apparently senseless chaos of life conceals some unifying principle which harmonises all the conflicting and contradictory elements of existence. That unifying principle, which seems an absurdity from a rational viewpoint since it confounds our logic and our conventional notions of order, is for Vallejo the only true reality, since it is only in the contemplation of its authentic harmony that he can go beyond the limitations and imperfections of everyday life and satisfy his spiritual hunger in an ecstatic state of plenitude:

> Absurdo, sólo tú eres puro.
> Absurdo, este exceso sólo ante ti se
> suda de dorado placer.

> (Absurd, only you are pure.
> Absurd, only in your presence does one sweat
> this excess of golden pleasure.)

Trilce, in fact, continues and renovates the Symbolist visionary poetics represented in Peru by Eguren, in that it posits the existence of a super-reality which is part and parcel of the terrestrial everyday world and from which man is separated by the habit of logical, rational thinking which has conditioned him to accept too readily the limitations imposed by so-called natural laws. Vallejo coincides with, and even anticipates, the Surrealists in their attempt to develop a new mode of perception which would reconcile life's apparent heterogeneity and contradictions in a great, all-embracing synthesis. And like the Surrealists, he conceives poetry as a subversive activity aimed at sabotaging established values and liberating the human spirit from the fetters of conventional thought. Thus, in a personal declaration of independence, he asserts his right to be dangerously anarchic in his pursuit of self-fulfilment:

> Tengo pues derecho
> a estar verde y contento y peligroso, y a ser
> el cincel, miedo del bloque basto y vasto:
> a meter la pata y a la risa.

> (I have the right, then,
> to be green and content and dangerous, and to be
> the chisel, the terror of the rough, vast block;
> and to put my foot in it and to laugh.)

The new poetic language of *Trilce* is at the heart of that enterprise, for it is intended both to undermine traditional concepts of order and to convey the notion of an "absurd" super-reality. Thus, in poem XXXVIII that absurd harmony is symbolised by an everyday object, the glass, to which are attributed qualities which are absurd in logical terms:

> Este cristal aguarda ser sorbido
> en bruto por boca venidera
> sin dientes. No desdentada.
> Este cristal es pan no venido todavía.

> (This glass is waiting to be swallowed
> whole by a future mouth
> without teeth. Not one that has lost them.
> This glass is bread yet to come.)

The glass is potential food capable of satisfying our spiritual hunger when we learn to recognise it as such and to approach it in the proper fashion. It is implied that we are unable to perceive the harmony of the absurd because we are conditioned to look at the world in rational terms and to dismiss everything that does not conform to a logical pattern. Moreover, as the symbol of the teeth indicates, reason is incapable of grasping that harmony because, since it proceeds analytically, it fragments life's essential unity. The glass which must be swallowed whole by a toothless mouth thus symbolises an absurd harmony which can only be apprehended intuitively by a mind that has become liberated from the tyranny of convention and reason.

In 1923 Vallejo travelled to Europe never to return to Peru. He settled in Paris, where he experienced considerable financial hardship and suffered bouts of illness, and in the late twenties he underwent a personal crisis, as a result of which he became a militant communist. Nonetheless, he continued writing poetry, which was published posthumously in 1939 as *Poemas humanos* and *España, aparta de mí este cáliz*.[6] The poetic language of Vallejo's later work is essentially the same as that of *Trilce*, with, if anything, an even greater cultivation of techniques such as oxymoron, paradox and catachresis. There are, however, two new developments which in a sense are contradictory. On the one hand, in many of the shorter poems and even within longer pieces there is a noticeable return to more regular forms and patterns, which up to a point represent a "return to order" after the avant-garde experimentation of the previous book. On the other hand, the poems often tend to be longer, being for the most part rambling, inconclusive monologues marked by an increased use of reiteration and chaotic enumeration and in which the formulae of rational discourse are undermined by the abrupt twistings and turnings of the text.

Vallejo's fundamental inability to cope with life persists into *Poemas humanos*, for as a South American exile in Paris he experienced the same loneliness and insecurity as in Lima, aggravated now by the rigours of the European climate, his precarious economic situation and illness. Thus, in "Piedra negra sobre una piedra blanca" he feels that the whole world is ganging up on him to beat

---

[6] *Poemas humanos* included a number of prose poems, composed between 1923 and 1929, and which Vallejo apparently intended to be published as a separate book entitled *Poemas en prosa*.

him to death and all he can do about it is to protest like a defenceless
child unjustly punished:

> César Vallejo ha muerto, le pegaban
> todos sin que él les haga nada;
> le daban duro con un palo y duro
>
> también con una soga ...
>
> (César Vallejo is dead, they all beat him
> when he'd done nothing to them;
> they hit him hard with a stick and hard
>
> too with a rope ...)

In *Trilce* Vallejo found in the walls of his prison cell a concrete
symbol for the limitations imposed on him by a world which
thwarted his aspirations to a full and satisfying life. In *Poemas
humanos* those limitations assume dingy material form in the trivia of
the dull day-to-day routine with which his straitened circumstances
made him all too familiar. Now his prison is the house where he is
trapped by the domestic routine, repeating the same inconsequential
acts day after day in an endless cycle of futility:

> Ello es que el lugar donde me pongo
> el pantalón, es una casa donde
> me quito la camisa en alta voz ...
>
> (The fact of it is that the place where I put on
> my trousers is a house where
> I take off my shirt at the top of my voice ...)

With a weary sense of frustration which is often disguised by a self-
deprecating irony, Vallejo observes the absurdity of life in his own
being. For while his spirit holds up to him a vision of a higher life, his
experience of hunger and illness confirms evolutionist theory by
bringing home to him the extent to which his existence is lived on an
elemental level, through that frail, decaying body of his which
constantly demands satisfaction of its appetites and repeatedly
breaks down under the effects of illness and age. "Epístola a los
transeúntes" describes his daily life as the elemental routine of an
animal. Each morning he goes out fearfully to engage in the daily
struggle for survival, cowering before the world like a hunted rabbit,
and at night he returns to the safety of his burrow to relax with the
bloated contentment of a sleeping elephant:

> Reanudo mi día de conejo,
> mi noche de elefante en descanso.

(I resume by rabbit's day,
my night of elephant in repose.)

Again and again *Poemas humanos* insists on the frustration of the
poet's spiritual aspirations by the limitations of the flesh. Though his
imagination is able to roam freely beyond all earthly bounds, he can
never reach the realms it so tantalisingly reveals to him, for he is held
prisoner by a body too strong for him to subjugate, living

> ... cautivo en tu enorme libertad,
> arrastrado por tu hércules autónomo ...
>
> (... captive in your enormous freedom,
> dragged along by your autonomous hercules ...)

At the same time Vallejo's later poetry reflects another collective
crisis, for in the uncertain political and economic climate of Europe
in the 1920s and 1930s he witnessed what to him and many of his
contemporaries seemed to be the death throes of Western civilisation.
Thus, in "Los nueve monstruos" his personal inability to cope is now
shared by mankind in general. As man loses control of his world, the
poet sees the floodgates burst open and suffering and misery spread
with nightmarish rapidity, turning a once-ordered world on its head
and reducing it to chaos:

> Y desgraciadamente,
> el dolor crece en el mundo a cada rato,
> crece a treinta minutos por segundo, paso a paso [...]
>
> Crece la desdicha, hermanos hombres,
> más pronto que la máquina, a diez máquinas, y crece
> con la res de Rousseau, con nuestras barbas;
> crece el mal por razones que ignoramos
> y es una inundación con propios líquidos,
> con propio barro y propia nube sólida!
>
> (And unfortunately,
> pain grows in the world every moment,
> grows at thirty minutes a second, step by step [...]
>
> Misfortune grows, brother men,
> faster than the engine, at the speed of ten engines, and it
>   grows
> with Rousseau's cow, with our beards;
> evil grows for reasons we don't know
> and it's a flood with its own liquids,
> its own mud and its own solid cloud!)

"La rueda del hambriento", a poem set against the background of the Depression, expresses through the persona of a starving beggar not only the plight of the unemployed masses but that of a humanity whose traditional values have failed it. The beggar's pleas for a stone on which to rest and bread to appease his hunger go unanswered and he is left alone to brood on his destitution:

> Una piedra en que sentarme
> ¿no habrá ahora para mí? [...]
> Un pedazo de pan, ¿tampoco habrá ahora para mí? [...]
> pero dadme
> en español
> algo, en fin, de beber, de comer, de vivir, de reposarse,
> y después me iré ...
> Hallo una extraña forma, está muy rota
> y sucia mi camisa
> y ya no tengo nada, esto es horrendo.
>
> (A stone to sit down on,
> isn't there even that for me any more? [...]
> A piece of bread, isn't there that for me now either? [...]
> but give me
> in Spanish
> something, in short, to drink, to eat, to live, to rest,
> and then I'll go away ...
> I notice a strange shape, my shirt's
> all torn and filthy
> and I've nothing left, this is horrendous.)

Parodying the Lord's Prayer and St. Matthew's Gospel — "Everyone that asks, will receive ..." (7. 8-11) —, the poem is both an ironic comment on the death of God in the modern world and an expression of humanity's hunger for a new faith which would nourish it emotionally, provide a solid basis for existence and incorporate the alienated individual into a united human family.

Up to a point Vallejo found that faith in Communism. His later work abandons the visionary poetics of *Trilce* and his ideal of a super-reality gives way to that of a world transformed and redeemed by socialist revolution. Many of his later poems are overtly political in character and others have political undertones, but Vallejo never subordinated art to politics and what makes his work superior to the bulk of political poetry produced in Peru and elsewhere is that it is not put at the service of an ideological message but integrates politics into it as an intrinsic dimension of his human experience and personal world-view. The fifteen poems of *España, aparta de mí este cáliz* rank among the best written on the Spanish Civil War because Vallejo projects his own inner world on to that conflict and because the historical events are transformed into a symbolic enactment of humanity's struggle to build a better world. The Spanish Republic is presented as a symbol of the socialist society of the future which will reproduce on a universal scale the atmosphere of the family home of the poet's own childhood, while the workers and peasants of the Republican militia represent a new breed of men who have transcended the egoism of bourgeois individualism to think and act in collective terms for the common good. *España, aparta de mí este cáliz*, in fact, constitutes a complement to *Poemas humanos*, for while the latter consists mainly of anguished monologues on the absurdity of the human condition, it looks forward to a redeemed future. Here Vallejo turns to the Bible for his inspiration, adopting the tone of a prophet to announce the coming of a new Jerusalem brought into being by the sacrifice of a modern-day Christ in the shape of the worker militiaman, a socialist paradise in which a united humanity working together in solidarity will deploy the resources of science and technology to transform the conditions of life:

> ¡Entrelazándose hablarán los mudos, los tullidos andarán!
> ¡Verán, ya de regreso, los ciegos
> y palpitando escucharán los sordos! [. . .]
> ¡Sólo la muerte morirá!
>
> (Embracing one another, the dumb will speak, the lame will walk!
> The returning blind will see
> and, quivering, the deaf will hear! [. . .]
> Only death will die!)

However, faith did not come easily to Vallejo, for he was unable to free himself from metaphysical needs which a materialistic doctrine like Marxism could never satisfy and the optimistic prophecies of *España, aparta de mí este cáliz* are offset in *Poemas humanos* by compositions expressing his personal anguish in face of life. That anguish was to become more acute as he felt life begin to slip away from him and "Un pilar soportando consuelos . . . " presents an ironic picture of a Marxist desperately turning to religion for comfort as he is seized by panic at the prospect of death. The poem shows him on his knees in a church whose pillars stand as symbol of the moral support which religion offers to those who are about to pass through the dark door of death, and though the weary, disillusioned side of his personality looks on sceptically and dismisses prayer as a waste of breath, his thirst for immortality beyond the grave leads him to drink greedily from the chalice of hope:

Un pilar soportando consuelos,
pilar otro,
pilar en duplicado, pilaroso
y como nieto de una puerta oscura.
Ruido perdido, el uno, oyendo al borde del cansancio;
bebiendo, el otro, dos a dos, con asas.

(A pillar supporting solace,
another pillar,
pillar in duplicate, pillarish
and like the grandchild of a dark door.
Wasted noise, the one, listening on the edge of exhaustion;
drinking, the other, two by two, with handles.)

In the end he is too honest to delude himself, but, nonetheless, the poem illustrates the existential drama Vallejo lived through in his final years and the failure of Marxism to resolve it. Hence it is not surprising that, while he admired the party militants who devoted body and soul to the cause, he should feel himself incapable of such total commitment. Thus, in "Salutación angélica", after placing the Russian Bolshevik on a pedestal as the embodiment of socialist virtues, he confesses his inability to match his revolutionary dedication, for he is but an ordinary mortal subject to ordinary human weaknesses and there lurks within him a doubting *alter ego* which prevents him from seeing things with the Bolshevik's clear-sighted vision and from following in his footsteps:

Y digo, bolchevique, tomando esta flaqueza
en su feroz linaje de exhalación terrestre:
hijo natural del bien y del mal
y viviendo tal vez por vanidad, para que digan,
me dan tus simultáneas estaturas mucha pena,
puesto que tú no ignoras en quién se me hace tarde diariamente,
en quién estoy callado y medio tuerto.

(And I say, Bolshevik, taking this weakness
in its savage lineage of terrestrial exhalation:
as a natural child of good and evil
and perhaps living out of vanity, so that people will talk,
your simultaneous statures grieve me,
for you can't but know the person within whom I'm kept late
         every day,
within whom I'm silent and half-blind in one eye.)

Furthermore, Vallejo was torn between an emotional need to believe in man and a jaundiced view of human nature which made it difficult for him to persuade himself that man was capable of improving his lot. These conflicting attitudes come into opposition in

"Considerando en frío ...", where the poet coldly and rationally analyses the human condition and accumulates evidence to prove to himself that man is a miserable animal beyond redemption, only to end up hugging the human animal in a fraternal embrace as his feelings get the better of him:

> le hago una seña,
> viene,
> y le doy un abrazo, emocionado.
> ¡Qué más da! Emocionado ... Emocionado ...
>
> (I signal to him,
> he comes over,
> and I give him a hug, moved.
> So what! Moved ... Moved ...)

Yet though Vallejo's instinctive solidarity with his fellows and his emotional need to believe were to triumph over his scepticism, his political optimism suffered a severe buffeting as the revolutionary movement was crushed in China and then in Spain and the Russian Revolution lapsed into Stalinist Terror. At moments the thwarting of the cause in which he had placed all his hopes leads him to succumb to despair. Thus the world of which he takes his leave in "Despedida recordando un adiós" is one which seems to him to be collapsing in chaos, an absurd world where Marxism is but another failed system:

> Adiós, hermanos san pedros,
> heráclitos, erasmos, espinozas!
> Adiós, tristes obispos bolcheviques!
> Adiós, gobernadores en desorden!
>
> (Goodbye, brother saint peters,
> heraclituses, erasmuses, spinozas!
> Goodbye, sad bolshevik bishops!
> Goodbye, governors in disorder!)

However, the final image that emerges of Vallejo is of a man who, as defeat and death stare him in the face, clings desperately to a belief in the ultimate and inevitable triumph of Socialism. Reluctantly recognising the impending fall of the Spanish Republic and the failure of the attempt to build in Spain a new society which would be a mother to the masses, Vallejo, in the title-poem of *España, aparta de mí este cáliz*, urges those who survive him to continue working and struggling to make that society a reality:

> ... si la madre
> España cae —digo, es un decir—
> salid, niños del mundo; id a buscarla! ...

(... if mother
Spain should fall — I'm just supposing —,
go out, children of the world; go out and look for her!)

During his lifetime Vallejo had little influence on Peruvian poetry, for it was only after his death and as his international reputation grew that he achieved recognition in his own country. Indeed, it is symptomatic of the conservatism of the Limeñan literary environment in the early twenties that 1922 saw the official coronation of Chocano as national poet while the publication of *Trilce* went virtually unnoticed, and it is surely not without significance either that the most innovative poets of the period were provincials and that after a brief sojourn in the capital they opted to move abroad. However, the second half of the decade was to bring an avant-garde breakthrough. The years 1926-27 saw the emergence of half-a-dozen short-lived avant-garde reviews, but the most important vehicle for the diffusion of the new aesthetic was *Amauta* (1926-30), whose editor, José Carlos Mariátegui, was unstinting in his encouragement of new writers and tendencies.[7] A leading role was played, too, by Xavier Abril (b. 1905), who did much to promote Surrealism in Peru with the poems and essays which he published in *Amauta*.[8]

One of the main tendencies of the period was a current of *indigenista* poetry which had its antecedents in González Prada and Vallejo's *Los heraldos negros* (concretely the section entitled "Nostalgias imperiales") and was part of the literary expression of the *indigenista* movement of those years. A feature of this poetry was the attempt to combine native themes with avant-garde techniques, an enterprise justified on the grounds that "revolutionary" content went hand in hand with "revolutionary" form. The outstanding representative of this tendency was Alejandro Peralta (1899-1973), a native of Puno. Peralta's most important works are his two early books, *Ande* (1926) and *Kollao* (1934), for though he started publishing again in 1968 after a long silence, his later production shows no significant development.[9]

[7] See Mirla Alcibíades, "Mariátegui, *Amauta* y la vanguardia literaria", *RevCrit*, 15 (1982), 123-39.

[8] Though Abril can hardly be classified as a major poet, his work is of considerable interest because of the influence he had at the time. See *Difícil trabajo (Antología 1926-1930)* (Madrid: Plutarco, 1935); *Descubrimiento del alba* (Front, 1937).

[9] See Alejandro Peralta, *Poesía de entretiempo* (Andimar, 1968), a volume which includes *Ande* and *Kollao*; *Tierra-Aire* (Minerva, 1971); *Al filo del tránsito* (Instituto Puneño de Cultura, 1974). See also Alberto Tauro, *El indigenismo a través de la poesía de Alejandro Peralta* (Compañía de Impresiones y Publicidad, 1935); Graciela Palau de Nemes, "La poesía indigenista de vanguardia de Alejandro Peralta", *RevIb*, 110/111 (1980), 205-16.

Peralta's work is characterised by his love of the sierra, its people and its culture, and as one would expect in poetry of this kind, it makes heavy use of Quechua vocabulary that is part of the everyday language of the region. For the most part it celebrates the Andean way of life through evocations of landscape or costumbrist vignettes, but it voices, too, solidarity with the downtrodden Indian peasantry and outrage at their suffering. This social strain, more marked in *Kollao* than in *Ande*, is at its most effective in poems like "El indio Antonio" and "Barro trágico" where the poet limits himself to depicting scenes of hardship and leaves the reader to draw his own conclusions. More often, however, the poems tend to lapse into prosaic denunciations of injustice accompanied by prophecies of forthcoming revolution, and on the whole they are less successful than those which convey the feel of Andean life.

In keeping with avant-garde fashion Peralta's poetry is written in free verse and suppresses punctuation, but in the main it is fairly traditional in language and syntax and its novelty rests largely on the reduction of the poem to an unconnected sequence of images and in its use of onomatopoeia and graphic devices such as capitalisation and unusual distributions of words on the page. In "Travesía andinista", for example, these techniques are successfully exploited to convey the experience of a long journey on horseback across the Andes. Likewise "Las bodas de la Martina" effectively evokes the sound of Andean popular music and the uninhibited atmosphere of a native wedding feast:

EL CHARANGO SALE A GRITAR A LA PUERTA
SE HA CASADO LA MARTINA
. . . . .
Toda la noche la música sobre los cerros
          como sankayos
          como clavelinas
BOM BOM BOM BOM
Ahora es el bombo que levanta terrales de alegría
. . . . .
Los novios están bailando un wayñu de llamaradas
LA MARTINA LA MARTINA LA MARTINA
LA MARTINA LA MARTINA LA MARTINA
        la
         mar
          ti
          na
El alba está cantando en las vertientes

(THE *CHARANGO* COMES OUT TO SHOUT AT THE DOOR
OUR MARTINA HAS GOT MARRIED
.....
All night the music over the hills
                    like *sankayos*
                    like marigolds
BOOM BOOM BOOM BOOM
Now it's the drum that raises clouds of joy
.....
The bride and groom are dancing a blazing *wayñu*
OUR MARTINA OUR MARTINA OUR MARTINA
OUR MARTINA OUR MARTINA OUR MARTINA
         our
              mar
                 ti
                    na
Dawn is singing on the slopes)

At its best, then, Peralta's poetry does succeed in expressing local themes by means of avant-garde techniques. All too often, however, his concern for novelty creates images that are so forced as to be absurd, such as the one evoking daybreak over Lake Titicaca:

> ... el sol desde su aeronave
> arroja bombas de magnesio
>
> (... from its airship the sun
> hurls magnesium bombs)

More generally the reader is left with an impression of incongruity that a poet seeking to give expression to a reality that is essentially non-Western should do so with techniques that were the West's latest fashion. In the end, therefore, the enterprise undertaken by Peralta and other *indigenista* poets has to be deemed an experiment that failed.

Very different and much more accomplished is the work of Peralta's fellow Puneñan, Carlos Oquendo de Amat (1905-36).[10] Oquendo produced only one book, *5 metros de poemas* (1927), for he appears to have given up writing poetry after joining the Communist Party in 1930, but on the strength of that brief collection of eighteen poems and a handful of poems published in magazines he ranks as

[10] See Carlos Oquendo de Amat, *5 metros de poemas* (Decantar, 1969). See also Carlos Meneses, *Tránsito de Oquendo de Amat* (Las Palmas: Inventarios Provisionales, 1973); Luis Monguió, "Un vanguardista peruano: Carlos Oquendo de Amat", in *Homenaje a Luis Leal*, ed. D.W. Bleznick and J.O. Valencia (Madrid: Insula, 1978), pp. 203-14; Julio Ortega, *Figuración de la persona*, pp. 151-56.

one of his country's best poets. His poetry displays most of the features associated with the avant-garde: an up-to-date vocabulary reflecting the urban, technological and cosmopolitan character of modern life; disconnected sequences of novel images; the dislocation of logic and grammar; graphic devices and unusual typographical arrangements which convey the poem's sense visually. In some respects it is very much a product of its epoch, but it escapes the shallow trendiness of so much poetry of the period in that these techniques are harnessed to the expression of his own personal world. That world is, above all, a world of the imagination. Oquendo's family moved to Lima when he was a child and both his parents died young, leaving him orphaned at the age of sixteen. Most of his life he lived in penury, but he steadfastly refused to give up his freedom by taking a job; his health, too, was poor and he was only thirty when he died of tuberculosis. Significantly, though, none of the hardships of Oquendo's daily life are mentioned in his work, though two poems, "Cuarto de los espejos" and "Poema del manicomio", give expression to the anguish and uncertainty of adolescence. For Oquendo's poetry creates its own alternative reality in which the poet finds the fulfilment lacking in the everyday world.

Oquendo's poetry is marked by a child-like sense of illusion that is reminiscent of Eguren. Many of his compositions have the same deceptive simplicity as the older poet's work and he shares his ingenuous pleasure in the contemplation of a world transformed into a wonderland by the imagination. In "Jardín", for example, an autumn garden, watered by the gaze of a child, undergoes a magical metamorphosis, a process which is conveyed visually by the typography, with a long line suggesting a stream of water and the capitals of the final line vigorous growth sprouting suddenly from the confined space of the penultimate:

> Un niño echa el agua de su mirada
> y en un rincón
> **LA LUNA CRECERA COMO UNA PLANTA**

> (A child pours the water of his gaze
> and in a corner
> **THE MOON WILL GROW LIKE A PLANT**)

For Oquendo, as for Eguren, the poetic imagination is a means of penetrating beyond the surface of things to the beauty and harmony that lie behind them and poetry itself is a re-creation and a celebration of that hidden order. Thus, "Poema al lado del sueño" conjures up a marvellous landscape which has a distinctly child-like quality, with grazing elephants with flowers for eyes and an angel playing hoop with the rivers, and into which the poet himself is integrated as another element of nature:

> Parque salido de un sabor admirable
> Cantos colgados expresamente de un árbol
> Arboles plantados en los lagos cuyo fruto es una estrella
> Lagos de tela restaurada que se abren como sombrillas
> Tú estás aquí como la brisa o como un pájaro
> En tu sueño pastan elefantes con ojos de flor
> Y un ángel rodará los ríos como aros
> Eres casi de verdad
> pues para ti la lluvia es un íntimo aparato para medir el cambio
> moú Abel tel ven Abel en el té
> Distribuyes signos astrónomicos entre tus tarjetas de visita.

> (A park emerging from an admirable flavour
> Songs expressly hanging from a tree
> Trees planted in lakes bearing stars as fruit
> Lakes of restored cloth opening like parasols
> You are here like the breeze or like a bird
> In your dream graze elephants with flower-eyes
> And an angel will roll the rivers as if they were hoops
> You are almost real
> for for you the rain is a private apparatus for measuring change
> moú Abel tel ven Abel en el té[11]
> You distribute astronomic signs among your visiting cards.)

At the end of the poem the poet presents himself as a magician, for that vision, real but unreal (casi de verdad), has been conjured up by his magic spell (suggested by the garble of the penultimate line), which has the same life-giving powers as the falling rain.

Though Oquendo's poetry is in no way autobiographical, it does seem to reflect something of his situation as a young man of provincial background living in a city increasingly open to cosmopolitan influence. Alongside an ultra-modern vocabulary evoking the bustle, novelty and excitement of the twentieth-century city, there abound in his poems words and images referring to the world of nature. A number of poems, indeed, seem to look backwards to the tranquillity, stability and intimacy of a pre-industrial world. The poetry still has a Romantic-Modernist flavour to it on occasion, but it is not so much a literary anachronism as an expression of an

---

[11] The garble of this line is impossible to translate.

emotional attitude, for running through the book is a note of tenderness quite uncharacteristic of the avant-garde. Thus, "Madre" pays homage to the poet's mother in a manner reminiscent of Vallejo and it is to her that the volume is dedicated. Of his love poems, "Aldeanita" and "Campo" harp back to a rural world and the others associate the woman with nature, as in "Poema", where she not only embodies the beauty and harmony of the world but humanises the urban environment.

On the other hand, Oquendo's attitude towards modern city-life is essentially one of child-like delight and excitement, and what many have regarded as an alienating concrete jungle is transformed by his fantasy into a wonderland as marvellous as the natural world. Thus, "Réclame" views modern commercialism as an amusing game and in "Film de los paisajes" the bewildering changes of modern life become episodes in a swift-moving film. The bustling activity of the modern city is evoked, above all, in "New York", where the typographical arrangement conveys simultaneously an impression of a street junction, of flowing traffic and of the ubiquitous advertising hoardings:

El tráfico
escribe
una carta de novia

T
I
M
E
Los teléfonos   I   Diez corredores
son depósitos de licor S   desnudos en la Underwood
M
O
N
E
Y

(The traffic
writes
a love letter

```
                    T
                    I
                    M
                    E
The telephones      I      Ten naked
are liquor stores   S      runners in the Underwood
                    M
                    O
                    N
                    E
                    Y)
```

Typography is again exploited to suggest the excited curiosity and admiration of the public as they crane to catch a glimpse of one of the stars of the cinema screen, an embodiment of the glamour of modern life:

Mary Pickford sube por la mirada del administrador

```
              Para observarla
        HE   SA LI   DO
        RE   PE TI   DO
        POR  25 VENTA-
                    NAS
```

(Mary Pickford goes up the manager's gaze

```
                To watch her
        I'VE  COME      OUT
        RE    PEAT      ED
        AT    25   WINDOW
                        SILLS)
```

Above all, Oquendo's vision of New York is of a city full of endless exciting possibilities and as day breaks at the end of the poem, the morning appears bearing a sign offering itself for hire to the awakening population to do with it what they will.

The poem which perhaps best typifies Oquendo's work is "Mar", where he adopts the persona of a carefree sailor who has a woman in every port but whose only love is the sea:

```
Yo tenía 5 mujeres          (I had 5 women
y una sola querida          and only one beloved

        El Mar                      The Sea)
```

For Oquendo life, lived as art, is a great adventure on which he embarks with joyful illusion, confident of the power of the poetic imagination to surpass all existential limitations. Thus, the horizon, symbol of those limitations, is jokingly depicted as a wild beast captured and put on public show, and the poem ends with the announcement of a panacea in the form of sea-pills representing involvement in the adventure of life:

> El Horizonte —que hacía tanto daño—
> se exhibe
> en el hotel Cry
> > Y el doctor Leclerk
> > oficina cosmopolita del bien
> > obsequia pastillas de mar.

> (The Horizon — which did so much harm —
> is on show
> in the Cry Hotel
> > And Doctor Leclerk's
> > cosmopolitan bureau of happiness
> > gives out complimentary sea-pills.)

Significantly, too, a line of the same poem is boxed off in the form of a poster prohibiting sadness:

> | Se prohibe estar triste |
> | --- |

> | (It is forbidden to be sad) |
> | --- |

For Oquendo conceives poetry as fun, a game, an adventure. His is a poetry which relishes the savour of its own music and imagery. It delights, too, in verbal jokes and visual games, the two being combined in the following example where an advertisement defines poets as the product of their typewriter and an ascending lift is described as bringing the moon a copy of the poet's work as a present:

> r   Novedad
> o   Todos los poetas han salido de la tecla U. de la Underwood
> s
> n
> e
> c
> s
> a
> n
> u   compró para la luna 5 metros de poemas

(r   Latest
o   All the poets have come from the U key of the Underwood
t
a
v
e
l
e
n
a   bought the moon 5 metres of poems)

Indeed, the volume itself is packaged as a game. The title jokingly puts poetry on sale as just another commodity to be bought by the metre, and the book consists of a single folding sheet of paper which the reader is invited to open as if he were peeling a fruit. Furthermore, it is organised as if it were a cinema show, with a ten-minute interval. Such games are not gratuitous, of course, but an intrinsic part of an alternative reality created by the poetic imagination.

A striking contrast with the limpid, outward-going poetry of Oquendo is formed by the hermetic verse of Emilio Adolfo Westphalen (b. 1911), the author of *Las ínsulas extrañas* (1933) and *Abolición de la muerte* (1935).[12] A man of wide culture, Westphalen assimilated the surrealist aesthetic and combined it with an awareness of Spanish poetic tradition to create his own very personal brand of poetry. His poems are long monologues without titles or punctuation to guide the reader, whose first impression is that he is following the chaotic flow of the poet's subconscious. This is a highly visual poetry constructed on images, sometimes grouped in sequences, sometimes replacing one another in quick succession, and often linked by association of concept or of sound. It is, too, a poetry that is remarkably fluid and musical, particularly in the second book, where the irregular versification of the first gives way to a greater formal symmetry. The reader, in fact, is swept along from image to image by the force of the poetic emotion and finds himself immersed in a strange imaginative world which captivates him but escapes his understanding. Gradually, however, certain patterns begin to emerge. In the main the images are the classical ones of poetic tradition,

---

[12] See Emilio Adolfo Westphalen, *Otra imagen deleznable* ... (Mexico City: Fondo de Cultura Económica, 1980), a volume which includes both his main books; *Máximas y mínimas de sapiencia pedestre* (Lisbon: n.p., 1982); *Arriba bajo el cielo* (Lisbon: n.p., 1982). See also *Creación & Crítica*, 20 (1977), a volume devoted to Westphalen; James Higgins, "Westphalen, Moro y la poética surrealista", *Cielo Abierto*, 29 (1984), 16-26; Julio Ortega, *Figuración de la persona*, pp. 165-71; Roberto Paoli, "Westphalen o la desconfianza en la palabra", in *Estudios sobre literatura peruana contemporánea*, pp. 95-103.

images of earth, sea, air, fire, and most of the poems revolve around the figure of a beloved who seems to be consubstantial with the elements. It becomes clear, too, that far from being the chaotic outflow of the subconscious, the poems are manipulated by a consummate artist who is in complete control of his material. Westphalen's mastery as a poet, indeed, rests precisely on his achievement of a perfect equilibrium between intensely felt emotion and artistic control of that emotion.

Westphalen himself provides us with a key to his hermetic poetic universe in the epigraphs which precede both books. The first, from San Juan de la Cruz, links his work with the tradition of Spanish mystic poetry, and the second, from André Breton, with Surrealism, which postulated what might be described as a secular mysticism with a super-reality as its goal. Westphalen, in fact, may be regarded as a visionary poet in the symbolist-surrealist tradition represented in Peru by Eguren and the Vallejo of *Trilce*. For him also the act of poetic creation is an attempt to surpass the limitations of ordinary life and attain a state of unity with the world. The fifth poem of *Las ínsulas extrañas* evokes the image of a tree raising itself up to the heavens and banging against the sky as a symbol of earth-bound existence rebelling against its limitations and striving to transcend them:

> Un árbol se eleva hasta el extremo de los cielos que lo cobijan
> Golpea con dispersa voz
> El árbol contra el cielo contra el árbol

> (A tree raises itself up to the very limit of the heavens that roof it
> It beats with dispersed voice
> The tree against the sky against the tree)

Identifying with the tree, the poet expresses his own yearning for transcendence in terms of a burning thirst:

> Agua
> La garganta de fuego agua agua
> Matado por el fuego

> (Water
> The throat on fire water water
> Killed by the fire)

The poem traces the build-up of that thirst till, in a climactic final section, it is quenched as he is transported to a realm where all things outgrow their limitations and become fused in unity. Here alliteration and chaotic enumeration combine to convey a sense of babbling ecstasy as the poet's being is immersed in a cosmic harmony:

> Crece el árbol
> Ya no cabe en el cielo en el alma
> Crece el árbol
> Otra hoja
> Ya no cabe el alma en el árbol en el agua
> Ya no cabe el agua en el alma en el cielo en el canto en el agua
> Otra alma
> Y nada de alma
> Hojas gotas ramas almas
> Agua agua agua agua
> Matado por el agua

> (The tree grows
> It no longer fits in the sky in the soul
> The tree grows
> Another leaf
> The soul no longer fits in the tree in the water
> The water no longer fits in the soul in the sky in the song in the
>   water
> Another soul
> And no soul
> Leaves drops branches souls
> Water water water water
> Killed by the water)

As has been suggested, most of Westphalen's poems are love poems, but the love affair to which they refer is one that is over and lost in the past. Thus, the seventh poem of *Las ínsulas extrañas* laments the empty meaninglessness of the poet's life now that the beloved has gone out of it:

> Se despega una nada tras otra
> Crece una nada sobre nada [...]
> Me deslumbra tanta noche
> La muerte que mira con los ojos de los vivos
> Los muertos que hablan con los loros de los vivos

> (One nothing peels off after another
> A nothing grows on nothing [...]
> I'm dazzled by so much night
> Death gazing with the eyes of the living
> The dead speaking with the parrots of the living)

"Andando el tiempo", the opening poem of *Las ínsulas extrañas*, sets the work in the context of a world ruled by the inexorable march of time and "Hojas secas para tapar ..." is constructed around the image of autumn, a symbol of the inevitable erosion of life by death and decay, a process which makes a mockery of human activity, for all that men close their eyes to it:

> Tal vez nunca se ha dado más el otoño a la angustia del hombre
> Los periódicos anuncian una buena cocinera
> Un canario
> O un perro amaestrado en el arte de pelar las cebollas
> Nadie dice buenos días al cortejo fúnebre
> Ni a los bueyes asesinados para satisfacer una conclusión

> (Autumn has perhaps never lent itself more to the anguish of man
> The newspapers advertise a good cook
> A canary
> Or a dog trained in the art of peeling onions
> No one says good morning to the funeral procession
> Nor to the oxen murdered to satisfy a conclusion)

All of Westphalen's poetry is to be seen in that context, as a struggle against time and death, as a "recherche du temps perdu" in which the poet attempts to recuperate the happiness of lost love through memory and the poetic imagination. In *Las ínsulas extrañas* that enterprise has mixed fortunes. Sometimes it is successful, as in "La mañana alza el río la cabellera . . .", but in other poems the attempt to conjure up the image of the absent beloved ends in failure and she remains lost to him in the dark night of oblivion:

> Ya no encuentro tu recuerdo
> Otra noche sube por tu silencio
> Nada para los ojos
> Nada para las manos
> Nada para el dolor
> Nada para el amor
> Por qué te había de ocultar el silencio
> Por qué te habían de perder mis manos y mis ojos
> Por qué te habían de perder mi amor y mi amor
> Otra noche baja por tu silencio

> (I can no longer find the memory of you
> Another night rises out of your silence
> Nothing for the eyes
> Nothing for the hands
> Nothing for the pain
> Nothing for my love
> Why did silence have to hide you
> Why did my hands and my eyes have to lose you
> Why did my love and my love have to lose you
> Another night descends from your silence)

In *Abolición de la muerte*, on the other hand, memory generally proves triumphant, abolishing time and death as it dredges the figure of the beloved and the happiness associated with her out of the mists of the past. In some cases, notably in "Marismas llenas de corales ...", a complex interplay of tenses attests to the struggle between memory and time, but in others temporal barriers are erased as the image of the woman materialises out of the past to revitalise him in a moment that is qualitatively eternal:

> Has venido pesada como el rocío sobre las flores del jarrón
> Has venido para borrar tu venida
> Estandarte de siglos clavado en nuestro pecho

> (You have come with the weight of the dew on the flowers in the
>   vase
> You have come to erase your coming
> The banner of centuries thrust into our breast)

However, Westphalen's poems are more than a mere reliving of the past and more than conventional love poems. The absent beloved is consistently presented in terms which suggest that she is, above all, a symbol of a lost cosmic harmony which the poet seeks to recapture through the poetic imagination. Indeed, poems seven and eight of *Abolición de la muerte*, which might be regarded as constituting his poetics, describe his efforts to grasp the elusive image of the absent beloved in a manner reminiscent of the mystics' quest for union with the godhead. The tone of the first is one of optimistic affirmation. He pursues her image with the same persistence with which time dogs man, confident of being able to transcend it:

> Te he seguido como nos persiguen los días
> Con la seguridad de irlos dejando en el camino

> (I have followed you as the days pursue us
> With the certainty of leaving them on the road behind)

The phrase "Te he seguido" repeats itself at strategic points throughout the poem, conveying a sense of a relentless quest of cosmic proportions, and in the final lines he is still pursuing her, with the faith that phantoms can materialise and that she is there, intangible but real, just beyond reach:

> Te sigo como los fantasmas dejan de serlo
> Con el descanso de verte torre de arena
> Sensible al menor soplo u oscilación de los planetas
> Pero siempre de pie y nunca más lejos
> Que al otro lado de la mano

(I follow you as the phantoms cease to be such
With the respite of seeing you as a tower of sand
Sensitive to the planets' slightest puff or oscillation
But always standing and never further
Than the other side of my hand)

Poem eight, on the other hand, is fraught with uncertainty as he succumbs to despair as her image eludes him and then recovers his optimism as he gears all his faculties to apprehending her, only to give way to doubt again:

La otra margen acaso no he de alcanzar
Ya que no tengo manos que se cojan
De lo que está acordado para el perecimiento
Ni pies que pesen sobre tanto olvido
De huesos muertos y flores muertas

(Perhaps I'm not to reach the other shore
Since I don't have hands to grasp
What is ordained to perish
Nor feet to place weight on so much oblivion
Of dead bones and dead flowers)

The poem ends on a note of appeal and significantly the figure of the beloved is here metamorphosed into that of the great rose, a symbol of the absolute:

Rosa grande ya es hora de detenerte
El estío suena como un deshielo por los corazones
Y las alboradas tiemblan como los árboles al despertarse
Las salidas están guardadas
Rosa grande ¿no has de caer?

(Great Rose it's time now for you to stop
The summer sounds like a thaw in men's hearts
And the dawns tremble like the trees on awakening
The exits are guarded
Great rose won't you fall?)

The uncertainty of this poem is resolved, however, in the final poem of the volume where the beloved materialises. Here, as in all the poems, the beloved is an embodiment of the natural world and in his union with her the poet attains an ecstatic sense of oneness with the cosmos:

Tú como la laguna y yo como el ojo
Que uno y otro se compenetran
Tal el árbol y la brisa tal el sueño y el mundo [. . .]
Es la gloria caída a nuestros pies

Es el triunfo llegado como un crepúsculo subterráneo
Cambiando de estación en el corazón del azogue
Como una rosa ahogada entre nuestros brazos
O como el mar naciendo de tus labios

(You like the pool and I like the eye
Interpenetrating the one and the other
The same as the tree and the breeze the dream and the world [...]
It's glory fallen at our feet
It's triumph arriving like a subterranean twilight
Changing station in the heart of quicksilver
Like a rose smothered in our arms
Or like the sea born from your lips)

After 1935 Westphalen lapsed into silence and though in the 1970s he intermittently started writing again, his later poetry compares unfavourably with his two major books.[13] The explanation of that long silence is to be found perhaps in a later poem, "Poema inútil", which expresses a loss of faith in language to do more than serve the practical needs of everyday life:

Empeño manco este esforzarse en juntar palabras
Que no se parecen ni a la cascada ni al remanso,
Que menos trasmiten el ajetreo del vivir [...]

Qué será el poema sino castillo derrumbado antes de erigido,
Inocua obra de escribano o poetastro diligente,
Una sombra que no se atreve a aniquilarse a sí misma.

(It's a flawed enterprise this striving to put together words
Which resemble neither the falls nor the backwater,
And which convey even less the hustle and bustle of living [...]

What will the poem be but a castle demolished before it's erected,
The innocuous work of a diligent clerk or poetaster,
A shadow that hasn't the courage to obliterate itself.)

Those sentiments, however, are disproved by his own earlier work, which has earned him a place in the front rank of the poetry of his country and, indeed, of Spanish America as a whole.

While several poets flirted with Surrealism, Peru did not have a surrealist movement as such, but it was a Peruvian, César Moro (1903-56), who had the distinction of being the only Latin American directly involved with the surrealist activity in Paris in the late twenties and early thirties, an involvement which he later continued

---

[13] However, Westphalen continued to make a major contribution to Peruvian cultural life as editor of the journals *Las Moradas* (1947-49) and *Amaru* (1967-71).

in Mexico, where he resided from 1938 to 1948.[14] The rejection of the alienating reality in which he was born and brought up in order to assume another felt to be more authentic is perhaps the key to Moro's life and career. Detesting his native city, which he labelled "Lima la horrible", he abandoned Peru in his youth and spent most of his life in voluntary exile before returning to live out his last years as a lonely, marginal figure. He dropped his given name — Alfredo Quispez Asín — and adopted a pseudonym, and with the exception of *La tortuga ecuestre*, written in 1938-39 and published posthumously in 1957, he chose to write his work in French. It is, however, on the basis of his Spanish verse that his contribution to Peruvian poetry has to be assessed.

In one of his letters Moro vehemently rejects the "real" world, the practical world of "reason" in which Capitalism and Marxism compete with each other to dehumanise the individual:

¿Cómo no seguir en los sitios de peligro donde no caben ni salvación ni regreso? Tanto peor si la "realidad" vence una vez y otra y convence a los eternos convencidos trayendo entre los brazos verdaderos despojos: el hierro y el cemento o la hoz y el martillo como argumentos definitivos para justificar la prodigiosa bestialización de la vida humana.
Ese mundo no es el nuestro.

(What else but to continue in the places of danger where there's no room for salvation or return? So much the worse if "reality" keeps winning, bringing armfuls of veritable dross to convince the eternally convinced: iron and cement or the hammer and sickle as definitive arguments to justify the prodigious bestialisation of human life.
That world isn't ours.)

Like his fellow surrealists Moro regarded poetry as an alternative way of life lived on the margin of a comfortable but alienating civilisation and devoted to the passionate pursuit of a super-reality.

[14] See César Moro, *Obra poética* (INC, 1980); *La tortuga ecuestre y otros textos* (Caracas: Monte Avila, 1976); *Los anteojos de azufre* (San Marcos, 1958); *Couleur de bas-rêves tête de nègre* (Lisbon: Altaforte, 1983); *The Scandalous Life of César Moro, in his own words*, trans. Philip Ward (New York-Cambridge: The Oleander Press, 1976); *Vida de poeta (algunas cartas de César Moro escritas en la Ciudad de México entre 1943 y 1948)* (Lisbon: n.p., 1983). See also André Coyné, *César Moro* (Torres Aguirre, 1956); id., "César Moro entre Lima, París y México", in *Convergencias/divergencias/incidencias*, ed. Julio Ortega (Barcelona: Tusquets, 1972-73), pp. 215-27; id., "Al margen", in *Palabra de escándalo*, ed. Julio Ortega (Barcelona: Tusquets, 1974), pp. 448-51; id., "César Moro: el hilo de Ariadna", *Insula*, 332/333 (July-Aug. 1974), 3 and 12; Américo Ferrari, "Moro, el extranjero", *Hueso Húmero*, 2 (1979), 106-09; James Higgins, *The Poet in Peru*, pp. 123-44; Julio Ortega, *Figuración de la persona*, pp. 117-28; Roberto Paoli, "La lengua escandalosa de César Moro", in *Estudios sobre literatura peruana contemporánea*, pp. 131-38.

Most of the thirteen poems which make up *La tortuga ecuestre* are love poems, inspired, it seems, by a passionate homosexual affair, though the lover to whom they are addressed appears in female guise. However, as in the case of Westphalen, they deal not so much with an actual amorous experience as with the poet's attempts to summon and possess the image of the beloved, who ultimately personifies Poetry, an elusive super-reality pursued with a lover's passion and grasped by means of the imagination in the poetic act, producing an experience of fulfilment as complete and intense as that associated with love. Poetry, the beloved, appears as a phantom conjured up by the poet's imagination to fill him with ecstasy and transform existence in a qualitatively eternal moment:

> Apareces
> La vida es cierta
> [...] tus pies transitan
> Abriendo huellas indelebles
> Donde puede leerse la historia del mundo
> Y el porvenir del universo
> Y ese ligarse luminoso de mi vida
> A tu existencia

> (You appear
> Life is certain
> [...] your feet traverse
> Making indelible footprints
> In which the history of the world
> And the future of the universe can be read
> And that luminous linking of my life
> To your existence)

As an emblem of his poetics Moro adopts the figure of the madman in "A vista perdida", a poem where chaotic enumeration, the absence of punctuation and perplexing surrealist imagery create an overall impression of incoherence which is particularly appropriate to the subject of madness:

> No renunciaré jamás al lujo insolente al desenfreno suntuoso de
>   pelos como fasces finísimas colgadas de cuerdas y de sables
> Los paisajes de la saliva inmensos y con pequeños cañones de
>   plumasfuentes
> El tornasol violento de la saliva
> La palabra designando el objeto propuesto por su contrario
> El árbol como una lamparilla mínima
> La pérdida de las facultades y la adquisición de la demencia
> El lenguaje afásico y sus perspectivas embriagadoras
> La logoclonia el tic la rabia el bostezo interminable
> La estereotipia el pensamiento prolijo

> (I'll never abjure the impudent luxury the sumptuous wildness
>   of hair like the finest fasces hanging from cords and sables
> The immense landscapes of saliva with small fountain-pen
>   cannons
> Saliva's violent sunflower
> The word designating the object proposed by its opposite
> The tree as the minutest of lamps
> The loss of faculties and the acquisition of madness
> Aphasiac language and its intoxicating perspectives
> Logoclonia tics rages interminable yawning
> Stereotyping prolix trains of thought)

The poem is a profession of faith. The title (Lost to Sight) suggests that what society regards as madness is in fact the vehicle for discovering the hidden world that the eye cannot see, the marvellous landscapes which lie beyond the bounds of our rational faculties, a super-reality which can be apprehended only by means of a total derangement of the senses. Renouncing reason, Moro dons the wildly dishevelled hair of the madman as a symbol of aristocratic distinction and revels in the limitless landscapes which unfold before the lunatic who drools at the mouth. For him madness is not the sickness it is generally held to be but a privileged state which gives free rein to the imagination, permitting the contemplation of a secret universal order as it perceives relationships between the most disparate objects. After a eulogy of stupor, the rapture induced by the spectacle of the super-reality the everyday world becomes when beheld through eyes unblinkered by reason, the poem ends with a delirious exaltation of madness:

> El grandioso crepúsculo boreal del pensamiento esquizofrénico
> La sublime interpretación delirante de la realidad
> No renunciaré jamás al lujo primordial de tus caídas vertiginosas
>   oh locura de diamante

> (The grandiose boreal twilight of schizophrenic thought
> The divine delirious interpretation of reality
> I'll never abjure the primeval luxury of your giddy fallings oh
>   diamond-like madness)

For the dark regions of unreason are lit up by the aurora borealis of a super-reality and the sublime reveals itself to the disordered vision of the mind unfettered by reason. Moro, therefore, pledges himself never to forsake the cult of madness which affords such rich spiritual treasures.

Likewise, in "La vida escandalosa de César Moro", the poet undertakes a symbolic pilgrimage to the tomb of one of his spiritual forefathers, the eccentric Ludwig II of Bavaria, who lived life as fantasy and converted his fantasies into reality by constructing extravagant castles on the banks of the Rhine. That pilgrimage takes the form of a descent into the depths of his own subconscious, an excursion which ends in a triumphant moment of epiphany:

El viento se levanta sobre la tumba real
Luis II de Bavaria despierta entre los escombros del mundo
Y sale a visitarme trayendo a través del bosque circundante
Un tigre moribundo
Los árboles vuelan a ser semillas y el bosque desaparece
Y se cubre de niebla rastrera
Miríadas de insectos ahora en libertad ensordecen el aire
Al paso de los dos más hermosos tigres del mundo

(The wind rises over the royal tomb
Ludwig II of Bavaria awakens amid the debris of the world
And comes out to visit me bringing through the surrounding
        forest
A dying tiger
The trees vanish to become seeds and the forest disappears
And is covered by a hanging mist
Myriads of insects now at liberty deafen the air
At the approach of the two most beautiful tigers in the world)

At that moment history is abolished. Rising from the grave, Ludwig comes to the poet leading a moribund tiger, symbol both of a natural harmony which our civilisation has all but totally destroyed and of the human spirit atrophied by reason. The world reverts to its primeval origins and the deafening buzz of insects swarming over prehistoric swamplands celebrates freedom from unnatural restraints and the recovery of an original state of unity. The spirits of the two soul-mates, Ludwig and Moro, come together in communion and, restored to wholeness and harmony with their environment, stalk the world in unison in the shape of two beautiful tigers. Thus the poetic experience heals the scision between man and his universe and, if only momentarily, affords the poet the unmitigated joy of being at one with a world which is a harmonious whole.

Moro thus continues the visionary tradition that is perhaps the dominant strain of Peruvian poetry in the twenties and thirties. However, while Eguren and Westphalen were content to turn their backs on society to embark on a personal quest for another reality, Moro, like Vallejo in *Trilce* and like his fellow surrealists, saw the artist as a revolutionary waging a campaign of subversion aimed at undermining established values and liberating mankind from its spiritual shackles. In "A vista perdida" the image of the lunatic going around firing "small fountain-pen cannons" establishes a parallel between the madman's irreverent and outrageous conduct and the activity of the poet, who likewise wields the pen to cultivate a poetry of the irrational to wage war on conventional values. Similarly, "La vida escandalosa de César Moro" asserts the poet's determination to follow the example of the eccentric Ludwig II and to lead a life dictated not by reason but by his own inner impulses, a life-style which, the title (The Scandalous Life of César Moro) indicates, will shock and scandalise bourgeois society. The same poem implies, too, that each poetic experience, each descent into the subconscious, effectively, if only temporarily, abolishes the rational world and, by undermining the values on which our civilisation is based, fore-shadows and prepares for the total extinction of that civilisation. Indeed, "Visión de pianos apolillados cayendo en ruinas", the opening poem of the volume, is a prophetic vision of civilisation's demise. Poetry, though a seemingly harmless activity, a mere "minuscule volcano", is evoked as the force which will precipitate the process of destruction, and the final image, ironically equating the wise men of reason with performing dogs as they deliberate on means of renovating a culture that is irremediably moribund, implies that the only fresh life likely to flourish on that barren ground is the vegetation that will spring up to overgrow its ruins:

> Serás un volcán minúsculo más bello que tres perros sedientos
> haciéndose reverencias y recomendaciones sobre la
> manera de hacer crecer el trigo en pianos fuera de uso

> (You will be a miniscule volcano more beautiful than three thirsty
> dogs bowing to one another and exchanging recommen-
> dations on the way to make wheat grow on disused pianos)

However, in contrast to the optimistic aggressiveness of this poem, the last text of the volume, "Varios leones al crepúsculo lamen la corteza rugosa de la tortuga ecuestre", depicts a world whose natural beauty and harmony have been destroyed by the inexorable spread of a rationalistic and materialistic civilisation. The final refuge of instinct, it is implied, is the inner world of the artist's subconscious, and the poet stands alone as a last line of resistance, waging a lonely underground campaign for a more authentic life. Hence the title (At Dusk Various Lions Lick the Rough Shell of the Equestrian Turtle) shows him on the defensive. The equestrian turtle, a symbol of the forces of the subconscious which have been the vehicle of the poetic adventure, is here crouched inside its shell as it attracts the attention of a group of lions representative of society's uncomprehending and potentially violent response. The final line, however, brings the poetic adventure to a close with a gesture of defiance, establishing an opposition between the poet's nocturnal world of unreason, whose darkness is lit up by dazzling visions of Poetry, and the hated daytime world of bourgeois society, that unholy alliance of reason and religion proclaimed by the Angelus bells of noon, at the sound of which he spits with scorn:

> una caballera desnuda flameante en la noche al mediodía en el
>   sitio en que invariablemente escupo cuando se aproxima
>   el Angelus
>
> (a naked head of hair flamboyant in the night at midday in the
>   place where I invariably spit at the approach of the
>   Angelus)

The fluidity of Moro's verse and the powerfulness of his imagery combine to convey an emotional impact that makes *La tortuga ecuestre* an impressive work by any standard, and with Vallejo, Oquendo and Westphalen he constitutes a quartet of poets of which countries larger and more developed than Peru would be entitled to be proud.[15] Indeed, if Eguren initiated a Peruvian poetic tradition, it was the avant-garde who put that tradition on a firm footing, and the self-confidence that modern Peruvian poets have derived from having a Vallejo behind them has been compared to having a gun without having to use it.[16] Vallejo, of course, is a quite exceptional figure who belongs indisputably in the first rank of world literature. The true measure of Peruvian poetry of the avant-garde period, however, is that in addition to throwing up a genius of his calibre, it produced strength in depth with figures of the stature of Oquendo, Westphalen and Moro.

---

[15] A lesser figure worthy of mention is Enrique Peña Barrenechea (b. 1904). While Peña flirted briefly with the avant-garde aesthetic, he is essentially a poet in the main tradition of Spanish poetry. See Enrique Peña Barrenechea, *Obra poética* (Mejía Baca, 1977). See also Javier Sologuren, "Visión y forma secreta en la poesía de Enrique Peña Barrenechea", *Lexis*, 5 (1981), 183-86; Various, "Homenaje a Enrique Peña Barrenechea", *Cielo Abierto*, 30 (1984), 2-11.

[16] See Antonio Cornejo Polar et al., *Narración y poesía en el Perú* (Hueso Húmero, 1982), p. 95.

CHAPTER 5

THE BLOSSOMING (c.1940-c.1970)

Part I
The New Narrative

For the most part Peruvian fiction in the first half of the twentieth century was in the traditional realist mould and to a large extent it was the work of authors whose literary formation was limited and for whom literature was a part-time activity. However, the fifties saw the emergence of a group of young writers who, while still committed to depicting the social reality of their country, were concerned to bring a new professionalism to literary activity and to modernise literary expression.[1] Most of the members of this group were university-educated, they were familiar with the great figures of world literature and they enjoyed the additional advantage of regular contact and discussion among themselves. Emblematic of this new literary awareness was the study of the work of Faulkner which Carlos Zavaleta wrote as his doctoral thesis. The outcome of that awareness was a neo-realism which attempted to renovate and update Peruvian narrative by incorporating the technical developments of mainstream modern Western fiction.

The new fiction was predominantly urban. It was so for the obvious reason that the experience of most of the writers concerned was that of the city-dweller. However, it also reflects major socio-economic changes that had been taking place in the country. The

[1] See Mario Castro Arenas, "La nueva novela peruana", *Cuadernos Hispano-americanos*, 138 (1961), 307-29; Antonio Cornejo Polar, "Hipótesis sobre la narrativa peruana última", *Hueso Húmero*, 3 (1979), 45-64; Carlos E. Zavaleta, "Narradores peruanos: la generación de los cincuenta. Un testimonio", *Cuadernos Hispano-americanos*, 302 (1975), 454-63.

forties and fifties saw a massive shift of population from rural areas to the towns as migrants flocked to the increasingly industrialised coast in search of work and a better life. Lima's population swelled from half-a-million in 1940 to close on two million in the early sixties, and the shanty towns which proliferated around the capital became a visible symbol both of the difficulties of assimilating the rural influx and of the nation's basic social and economic problems. Not surprisingly, therefore, the central theme of the new fiction is the tensions and frustrations of life in an over-populated city in an underdeveloped country.[2]

The work which perhaps best exemplifies the spirit underlying all of this literature is the non-fictional *Lima la horrible* (1964). Its author, Sebastián Salazar Bondy (1924-65), was himself one of the pioneers of modern urban fiction in that the stories of *Náufragos y sobrevivientes* (1954) and its expanded second edition (1955) portray the grey and precarious existence of Lima's lower middle classes.[3] Unfortunately, there and in *Pobre gente de París* (1958), a collection of stories about Latin Americans in France, he appears as a very minor talent indeed and he did not live to complete the novel *Alférez Arce, Teniente Arce, Capitán Arce* that might have required revision of his status as a fiction writer. However, in *Lima la horrible* he was to capture the mood of a whole generation. Here Salazar undertakes a personal analysis of Peruvian society similar to the interpretative studies of the national situation of other Latin American countries made by authors such as Ezequiel Martínez Estrada and Octavio Paz. He argues that Limeñans' view of their city has been falsified by a series of comfortable illusions based on the myth of a spurious viceregal golden age, that the structures, attitudes and injustices of colonial society have persisted into the modern period and that the

---

[2] The perspective of the generation of the fifties was essentially middle-class. However, an authentically working-class vision of Peruvian social reality is provided by Julián Huanay (1907-69) in *El retoño* (1950), a novel based on the author's own experiences and recounting the adventures of a young provincial boy who runs away from home to make his way to Lima. Within its obvious limitations it is a well-written book and deserves more attention than it has hitherto received. See Julián Huanay, *El retoño* (Casa de la Cultura del Perú, 1969).

[3] See Sebastián Salazar Bondy, *Lima la horrible* (Mexico City: Era, 1964); *Náufragos y sobrevivientes* (Club del Libro Peruano, 1954; 2nd ed., Círculo de Novelistas Peruanos, 1955); *Pobre gente de París* (Mejía Baca, 1958); *Dios en el cafetín* (Populibros Peruanos, 1964); *Alférez Arce, Teniente Arce, Capitán Arce* (Casa de la Cultura del Perú, 1969). See also Tomás G. Escajadillo, "Sebastián como narrador, no como estatua", *Revista Peruana de Cultura*, 7/8 (1966), 98-129; Wolfgang A. Luchting, "Sebastián Salazar Bondy's only novel", *Iberoromania*, 1 (1974), 155-69; Mario Vargas Llosa, "Sebastián Salazar Bondy y la vocación del escritor en el Perú", in *Contra viento y marea* (Barcelona: Seix Barral, 1983), pp. 89-113.

time has come to face up to the "horrible" reality behind the myth. *Lima la horrible* could well be taken as an emblem of the urban fiction which flourished in the fifties and sixties. For, in keeping with Salazar's prescription, writers of that period challenge complacent assumptions about the Peruvian capital and expose various aspects of the squalid reality they gloss over.

In the vanguard of the new fiction was Enrique Congrains Martín (b. 1932), who was the first writer to portray the hardships and frustrated ambitions of the new urban proletariat.[4] Social-realist in character, most of the stories of *Lima, hora cero* (1954) and *Kikuyo* (1955) depict the squalid living conditions of Lima's crowded *barriadas* and the struggle of the provincial immigrants to make a living in the capital. Artistically, the most accomplished and effective of these stories is "El niño de Junto al Cielo", where a young boy's painful initiation into the ways of the world reflects the bitter disillusionment experienced by the immigrant population. Fresh from the provinces, Esteban lives in a hilltop *barriada* to which he gives the name Junto al Cielo (Next to Heaven) and from which he descends in a state of unworldly innocence to explore the capital. There he finds a banknote in the street and is persuaded by another boy to go into business with him buying and selling newspapers and magazines, only to have his partner disappear with the profits. Esteban thus receives a lesson in the ways of capitalist society, which first seduces and corrupts him with the lure of wealth and then leaves him cheated and disenchanted.

However, Congrains' most important work is the novel *No una sino muchas muertes* (1957). Set on waste ground adjoining the *barriadas*, it recounts thirty-six hours in the life of Maruja, a young girl who works as a cook in a *lavadero* (bottle-washing establishment) run by a miserly old woman and her half-breed husband with a labour force of twenty-odd enslaved idiots. Here Congrains reveals to us the hidden face of Lima, a marginal world beyond the fringes of society, a world that is literally and metaphorically a wasteland. In this environment Maruja's only escape from her dreary, soul-destroying routine is through sexual promiscuity, and the other main characters, a gang of adolescent boys, lead an aimless day-to-day existence, living by scavenging or odd jobs or petty thieving.

---

[4] See Enrique Congrains Martín, *Lima, hora cero* (Círculo de Novelistas Peruanos, 1954); *Kikuyo* (Círculo de Novelistas Peruanos, 1955); *No una sino muchas muertes* (Barcelona: Planeta, 1975). See also James Higgins, "A Forgotten Peruvian Novelist: Enrique Congrains Martín", *Iberoromania*, 2 (1971), 112-20; Wolfgang A. Luchting, *Escritores peruanos ¿qué piensan, qué dicen?* (Ecoma, 1977), pp. 63-81.

Ambitious to improve her lot, Maruja sees her opportunity when she makes contact with the gang and proposes that they set up their own *lavadero*. She then leads the gang in an assault on her work-place to carry off the idiots and in a second raid to seize the materials, but when they discover that the old woman's husband has murdered her and run off with her savings, the boys abandon the project and go in pursuit of the money. Accustomed to living on whatever turns up, they cannot think in the long term and are dazzled by a windfall which they will soon squander. The gang thus remain trapped in their futile existence because they are so conditioned by their environment that they are incapable of seeing the way out of it, while Maruja's ambitions are frustrated because in her world there is no one to help her to realise them. All of the characters are, therefore, victims of their environment.

No una sino muchas muertes takes up a major theme of the European nineteenth-century novel, that of the poor but ambitious young protagonist who struggles to climb in society by dint of talent, energy and will. Where it differs is that in this case the protagonist not only belongs to the lowest strata of the proletariat but is also a woman. Congrains was a militant Trotskyist and an early champion of women's liberation and in Maruja he has created a character who rebels against the condition determined for her by her class and sex. She stands apart from others in her circle because of her ambition and her will to achieve it. That ambition is not primarily for money or status but for a position of independence in which she can fulfil herself as a human being. When she glimpses her opportunity she is quick to seize it and thanks to her intelligence, courage and determination she imposes her will on the gang and becomes its guiding force. In contrast the young men of the gang are moral cowards who passively accept the conditions life imposes upon them. Short-sighted and inert, they have to be led and even then, when they are confronted by difficulties, they let themselves be daunted and opt for the easy way out. In the end Maruja is thwarted by their inadequacies, but she refuses to be deterred and, accepting the experience as a lesson for the future, sets off for the city to renew there her quest for a better life. Though a story of individual rebellion, the novel can also be interpreted on another level as an allegory of revolution, with Maruja representing the revolutionary spirit and the gang the masses who turn against the forces of capitalism (the old woman) to seize control of the means of production (the idiots). If so interpreted, it offers a dismal view of the capacity of the lower orders to take effective political action to alter the socio-economic structure and its final implication would seem to be that radical change requires an élite of dedicated militants to direct and manipulate the passive majority towards revolutionary goals.

Like Congrains' short stories *No una sino muchas muertes* is basically a social-realist work. However, like the best of his stories, it is also much more than a documentary, its real theme being the universal one of man's struggle for self-determination and self-fulfilment. Stylistically, too, it goes beyond a simple realism in that Congrains brings a poetic dimension to his narrative by employing a series of symbols as recurrent motifs. Thus, for example, the fluorescent tube which Maruja finds on the rubbish dump represents her ambition which somehow remains intact in adverse circumstances. Fire, too, is a symbol of her burning ambition, while the gulley at the foot of the *lavadero* is associated with the rut of drudgery and the depths of unfulfilment, and dust with cowardice. On the whole such symbolism is effective, but at times it tends to be overdone. Indeed, though generally well-written, the novel suffers from a number of flaws. In the main Maruja is a well-drawn and convincing character, but she displays an intellectual ability to formulate her thoughts that is somewhat implausible in a person of her background. There is, too, a fundamental contradiction between the individualistic values which she embodies and the revolutionary ideal which she is clearly intended to represent. And on the allegorical level it is difficult for the reader to stomach the idea that human beings can be regarded even symbolically as mere instruments of production, particularly in a novel with socialist pretensions. Nonetheless, despite its defects, *No una sino muchas muertes* is an estimable minor novel and it is a considerable loss to Peruvian letters that Congrains subsequently abandoned creative writing for other activities.[5]

Sharing Congrains' strong political commitment, Oswaldo Reynoso (b. 1932) focuses attention on another section of urban society, the alienated youth of the lower middle classes.[6] The adolescent protagonists of *Los inocentes* (1961), a volume of short stories later

---

[5] Congrains was later to publish *Guerra en el Cono Sur* (Ecoma, 1979), a fictional reportage set in the future and dealing with a war arising out of territorial disputes involving Argentina, Chile and Peru.

[6] See Oswaldo Reynoso, *Los inocentes* (La Rama Florida, 1961); *En octubre no hay milagros* (Waman Puma, 1966); *El escarabajo y el hombre* (Univ. Nac. de Educación, 1970). See also Wolfgang A. Luchting, *Escritores peruanos ¿qué piensan, qué dicen?*, pp. 83-104.

reissued as *Lima en rock*, and of the novel *El escarabajo y el hombre* (1970) are rebels without a cause. Reacting against the grey drudgery of their parents' lives, they reject the values of the older generation and seek a more exciting and fulfilling life-style but since they are trapped by their socio-economic circumstances they merely drift into vice and delinquency. A feature of Reynoso's prose is the reproduction of the slang of this alienated generation, a language which constitutes a rejection of the established order and expresses their own particular world-view. His experimentation with narrative technique is most evident in the later novel where the narrative, a rambling soliloquy in colloquial speech, is broken by an essay sequence and a series of Beckett-like dialogues, both of which centre on the efforts of an allegorical beetle to push a ball of excrement across a busy road and which situate the story in the context of man's struggle against alienating social structures.

However, Reynoso's most substantial and most important work is *En octubre no hay milagros* (1965), a novel set against the background of the annual procession of Our Lord of the Miracles when the population of Lima unites in a single mass to make public demonstration of its faith. The reality of class and economic divisions which lies behind this appearance of social cohesion is ruthlessly exposed by a narrative which follows twelve hours in the lives of two families from different ends of the social scale. On the one hand, Don Manuel, a prominent member of the oligarchy and the country's leading financier, engineers a political and economic crisis which brings down the government and enables him and his accomplices to set up another of their choosing. On the other, Don Lucho Colmenares, a clerk in one of the great man's banks, has received an order to vacate the modest flat where he and his family have lived for twenty years, because one of Don Manuel's companies has bought up the building with the object of constructing a new block of luxury flats on the site, and faced with immediate eviction, he tramps across the whole of Lima in an unsuccessful search for accommodation he can afford. The religious faith manifested in the procession is also exposed as an example of the false values propagated by the ruling élite as an instrument of social control. Don Manuel is a committed defender of the Christian way of life, but the immorality of his private life (he is a homosexual who preys on the youth of the poorer districts of the capital) parallels his corruption in the public sphere (his manipulation of the political and economic life of the nation) and in a society ruled by him and his kind the miracle

Don Lucho's wife prays for never materialises. However, behind the procession's display of collective faith Peruvian society is seen to be in a state of crisis which is reflected in the tensions and conflicts within both families, and the possibility of an imminent upheaval is suggested by Don Manuel's humiliation and desertion by his proletarian lover and by the attack which the berserk Miguel Colmenares launches against the statue of Christ carried in the procession. The main weakness of *En octubre no hay milagros* is that while Reynoso is at home when handling lower-middle-class characters and successfully conveys their hardships and frustrations, his characterisation of the oligarchy is simplistic and degenerates into caricature. Yet, despite that, it remains a powerful novel whose savage indictment of contemporary Peruvian society makes a strong impact on the reader.

While the new fiction was primarily urban, it was not exclusively so. If, as has been seen, regionalism was slow to establish itself in Peru, there was in the forties and fifties and beyond a proliferation of regionalist fiction of a traditional realist/costumbrist kind, most of it mediocre in quality. However, the fifties saw the emergence of a new type of regionalism as young writers like Vargas Vicuña and Zavaleta developed new ways of treating rural life. In contrast to traditional regionalist writers, Vargas Vicuña and Zavaleta do not present "realistic" or picturesque accounts of local geography, customs and types, nor do they dwell on the social and economic backwardness of the provinces. For their concern is not with the external aspects of regional reality but to convey the essence of rural life and to do so they adopt a new narrative approach.

Eleodoro Vargas Vicuña (b. 1924) is the author of two slim collections of short stories, *Nahuín* (1953) and *Taita Cristo* (1963).[7] Yet the slimness of his production is more than offset by its high quality. Vargas Vicuña was born in Cerro de Pasco and his stories are set in a small isolated village in the Andean countryside where he spent his childhood. The tales introduce us into a world on the margin of history where the modern-day peasants of the underdeveloped Peruvian sierra re-enact the joys and hardships of all peasantries down through the ages. They are narrated by one of the villagers, who sometimes is protagonist and other times witness of

---

[7] These were later republished, with some additional narratives, as a single volume. See Eleodoro Vargas Vicuña, *Ñahuin* (Milla Batres, 1976). See also Antonio Cornejo Polar, "Apunte sobre 'Esa vez del huaico' de Vargas Vicuña", *Lexis*, V, 1 (1981), 215-20; Wolfgang A. Luchting, "Vargas Vicuña, ¿predecesor técnico de Mario Vargas Llosa?", in *Pasos a desnivel* (Caracas: Monte Ávila, 1971), pp. 332-64.

the action. However, they depart from the canons of traditional realism in that no concessions are made to the reader in the form of background descriptions and explanations and the narrative tends to consist of sequences of images and perceptions as events are presented through the consciousness of the narrator. Furthermore, though the language is based on the everyday speech of the sierra, it has been artistically reworked and is charged with poetic intensity. Hence the reader is forced actively to involve himself and in return is rewarded by a more immediate understanding of the rural world.

Underlying Vargas Vicuña's stories is a sense of the hard and frequently tragic existence of a peasantry struggling to wrest a living from an inhospitable environment. Thus, "Esa vez del huaico" is the tale of a man whose world falls apart when he loses his home and his wife as the result of a sudden flood, while "Sequía nomás" is a poetic monologue expressing the collective despair of the community as it agonises under a drought. Other narratives show how adversity often brings out the worst in human nature. In "La Mañuca Suárez" folk lose the habit of sympathising with others' misfortunes in the wake of an earth tremor which devastates the village, and malicious tongues spread wicked gossip about a widow's innocent visits to the parish priest for comfort. Similarly, "Memoria por Raúl Muñoz Mieses" tells of the collective murder of a stranger whom the superstitious villagers blame for a drought. Yet other stories convey a sense of how life goes on in spite of tragedy. In "Tata Mayo" a pair of young lovers are drawn together again when their first child dies at birth, and in "En la altura" a husband who thinks the end of the world has come when he discovers his wife in incestuous intercourse with her brother, learns to come to terms with it. In the end what Vargas Vicuña's stories reveal is humanity's capacity to endure.

The tragic nature of rural life and the endurance of the rural population are given their most powerful expression in "Taita Cristo", Vargas Vicuña's masterpiece. The story is set in Holy Week, the period of the year, we are told, when the people, familiar with suffering, identify most closely with Christ. It revolves around a change introduced into the traditional Good Friday procession when Alejandro Guerrero, who for thirty-nine years has been a bearer of one of the tableaux, reluctantly yields to pressure and submits to being replaced by his son. When the latter collapses under the strain, the old man undertakes to make atonement by shouldering the huge wooden cross normally carried by several men. As he relives the ordeal of Christ his original motivation — the wish to vindicate his family's honour and to prove that he is not the worn-out old man people believe — and that of the townsfolk in encouraging him — the urge to atone for their error in tampering with custom and to prove the manhood of the town to outsiders — fade into the background. For his struggle with the cross becomes a ritual re-enactment of the eternal suffering of man struggling to overcome his own limitations and the hardships life imposes on him. The enthralled onlookers will him along every painful step of the way, for the burden he is shouldering is their burden, and when, at the end of his efforts, he falls dead, defeated yet victorious, the whole town is uplifted and fortified. In the final lines the significance of his feat is brought out by his senile mother who feels confusedly that his death is a birth. For his sacrifice, like that of Christ, represents redemption in that it confirms man's ability to triumph over adversity.

Born in Caraz in 1928, Carlos E. Zavaleta spent his childhood in the sierra and subsequently moved to the provincial city of Tarma and later to Lima and his literary production embraces all three settings.[8] A more prolific writer than Congrains, Reynoso or Vargas Vicuña, he is the author of three novels and of several collections of short stories, but his work is uneven in quality and his reputation rests mainly on his early narratives portraying life in small rural Andean communities. Here Zavaleta explores the whole system of rural values and traditions to show the tragedy of human under-development in a narrow and conservative environment. To do so he eschews long descriptions of milieu and employs an austere style which builds up atmosphere by means of a poetic transformation of reality. And the rural world is presented from the inside as the author retreats into the background to let characters and events speak for themselves, with the attendant use of multiple viewpoints, interior monologues and temporal restructurings.

Emblematic of Zavaleta's new brand of regionalism is the title-story of *La batalla* (1954), an account of a festival in which a giant condor is tied between stakes with only its head allowed to move freely and contestants take turns at striking it with their fists as they ride past on horseback. The colourful spectacle which the young

---

[8] See Carlos E. Zavaleta, *El cínico* (San Marcos, 1948); *El Cristo Villenas* (Lluvia, 1983), a volume which includes *La batalla* (1954) and *El Cristo Villenas* (1955); *Los Ingar* (Mejía Baca/Villanueva, 1955; Lluvia, 1983); *Unas manos violentas* (Ediciones Peruanas 1958); *Muchas caras del amor* (Moncloa, 1966; Lluvia, 1984); *Niebla cerrada* (Mexico City: Joaquín Mortiz, 1970); *Los aprendices* (Buenos Aires: Crisis, 1974; Mosca Azul, 1977); *La marea del tiempo* (Lluvia, 1982); *Retratos turbios* (Peisa, 1982). See also Wolfgang A. Luchting, *Escritores peruanos ¿qué piensan, qué dicen?*, pp. 21-33.

visitor from Lima has come to see proves not to be the expected piece of picturesque costumbrism but a grotesque orgy of bestial brutality embracing the whole community from the most prominent notables to the humblest Indians. In effect the festival is presented as a ritualisation of the cult of machismo and violence that is inherent in the rural way of life and, under the influence of alcohol and the excitement of danger, the participants are degraded to a level below that of the ferocious bird of prey they are torturing. Yet neither is the story an overt denunciation of rural backwardness, for these are conclusions which the reader is left to draw for himself. The young Limeñan's reaction to the events depicted remains unvoiced and the cultural gulf between rural Peru and the modern world is merely insinuated when he slips silently away before the end, leaving his more primitive compatriots to pursue their still unsated lust for violence.

An equally impressive tale is *El Cristo Villenas*, published separately in 1955 and dealing with the hold of superstition over the minds of the rural population. When Villenas, a popular local figure, dies of horrible burns after falling into a vat of boiling *chicha* (maize liquor), gossip compares his agony to that of Christ and over the years his legend becomes confused with that of Jesus till the two are completely identified in local folklore. The significance of the story is brought out when a passing stranger challenges the authenticity of both legends. For he is looked upon with horror as if he were the Anti-Christ, yet as he departs the child narrator associates him with the freedom of the open plains. Thus, like the violence of "La batalla", superstition is shown to be part of a traditional way of life that restricts the development of the human personality.

The violence of rural life is again the theme of the short novel *Los Ingar* (1955), which revolves around a long-standing feud between the Ingar family and the mayor and governor of the small town of Corongo. Though it seems that the latter fear the Ingar as a threat to their political power and that they have designs on the family's best land, the origins of the feud are never made clear and it is on the authorities' persecution of their enemies that the novel concentrates. They have Sheesha, the head of the household, arrested on a trumped-up charge but are obliged to release him when the whole family turns up in force with a witness who can prove his innocence. They then send one of their thugs to provoke a fight and the two elder brothers are forced to flee when the police come after them. Finally the youngest son, Llica, is arrested on another false charge and the narrative ends in tragedy when he is shot trying to escape. The novel thus reveals the squalid nature of small-town politics, which revolve around personalities and families rather than ideologies, where power is sought and exploited for personal ends and where all parties are only too ready to resort to force to achieve their objectives. Yet though on the surface the Ingar appear to be victims unjustly persecuted, they are to a large extent the agents of their own misfortunes. They are a fighting family always squabbling among themselves as well as with their enemies and though they openly sneer at the corruption of the authorities, the fact that Sheesha declines an invitation to be governor suggests that they are less concerned with cleaning up the town than with fighting their feud. Ultimately, therefore, the real theme is the senselessness and self-destructiveness of the violence that seems to be part of the fabric of rural life. From the outset Zavaleta builds up an atmosphere of violence and inevitable tragedy reminiscent of the plays of Lorca. The novel opens with a violent scene in which one of the brothers beats up an enemy and an air of impending disaster is created by the repeated appearances of the widowed mother, sick with anxiety for the safety of her sons. Above all, a sense of tragedy is brought out by the fact that events are presented through the eyes of the youngest son whom we see suppressing the gentler side of his nature as he absorbs the attitudes of his elder brothers and tries to live up to their macho image, and when he is shot down in the last paragraph his death represents the culmination of all the forces that have been at play in the book, as the vicious circle of violence within which he is caught finally closes in on him, leaving the reader with a sense of tragic and pointless waste.

If Congrains, Reynoso, Vargas Vicuña and Zavaleta have all produced estimable work, the outstanding figure of the generation of the fifties is undoubtedly Julio Ramón Ribeyro (b. 1929). Ribeyro stands apart from his contemporaries in that, with the exception of a two-year interval in the late fifties, he has lived in Europe since 1954. There he has pursued his literary vocation with commendable constancy, venturing into the essay and the theatre as well as producing three novels and some sixty-four short stories.[9] The novels

---

[9] See Julio Ramón Ribeyro, *La palabra del mudo*, 3 vols. (Milla Batres, 1973-77); *Crónica de San Gabriel* (Milla Batres, 1974); *Los geniecillos dominicales* (Milla Batres, 1973); *Cambio de guardia* (Milla Batres, 1976). For his essays see *La caza sutil* (Milla Batres, 1976); *Prosas apátridas aumentadas* (Milla Batres, 1978). See also María Rosario Alfani, "Escritura en contumacia: la escritura horizontal de Julio Ramón Ribeyro", *RevCrit*, 10 (1979), 137-42; Ileana Banchero de Seminario, "Un micro-

and more than two thirds of the stories are set in the Peru of his early adolescence and offer a vision of his native society as seen from the detachment of Europe. At the same time, however, they deal with universal themes and bear the stamp of a highly personal world-view, for, wryly sceptical about man's ability to control or understand his world, Ribeyro portrays a humanity whose illusions are repeatedly negated by reality and whose hopes and ambitions end in failure and frustration. Artistically, he is an accomplished, if conservative, writer, more concerned with effectiveness than with formal experimentation or technical innovation, and writing in a clear, simple, economical style which exploits irony, symbolism and narrative patterns to enrich the basic realism of his fiction by suggesting levels of significance beyond the literal. Partly because of the inaccessibility of his early books and partly because he has remained on the margin of the experimental fiction that has been the predominant fashion in recent decades, his work received little attention outside Peru until fairly recently, but increasingly he has come to be recognised as a major Spanish American writer, at least in the field of the short story.

Ribeyro's first novel, *Crónica de San Gabriel* (1960), represents an important contribution to the renovation of regionalist fiction. The protagonist/narrator Luis, an orphaned teenager, leaves coastal Lima, where he has lived all his life, to spend some time with distant relatives on their San Gabriel estate in the northern sierra. There he finds himself disorientated in a strange, disconcerting world. At first his disorientation is caused by the immensity of the landscape, but increasingly what perplexes him is the strange conduct of the

mundo que refleja un macromundo (Análisis de la novela *Crónica de San Gabriel* de Julio Ramón Ribeyro)", *Humanidades*, 5 (1972-73), 85-92; Antonio Cornejo Polar, "*Los geniecillos dominicales*: sus fortunas y adversidades", in *La novela peruana: siete estudios*, pp. 145-58; Graciela Coulson, "Los cuentos de Ribeyro", *Cuadernos Americanos*, 194 (1974), 220-26; Dianne Douglas, "The Demythification of Reality in the Narrative of Julio Ramón Ribeyro", Diss. Oklahoma 1981 (Univ. Microfilms, 1983); Dick C. Gerdes, "La obra literaria de Julio Ramón Ribeyro en la novelística peruana contemporánea", Diss. Kansas 1976 (Univ. Microfilms, 1980); Luis Loayza, "Regreso a San Gabriel", *Hueso Húmero*, 8 (1981), 66-79; Wolfgang A. Luchting, *Julio Ramón Ribeyro y sus dobles* (INC, 1971); id., "Una historia edificante: 'Al pie del acantilado', de Julio Ramón Ribeyro", *Hispamérica*, 15 (1976), 3-13; id., *Escritores peruanos ¿qué piensan, qué dicen?*, pp. 43-61; id., "Los mecanismos de la ambigüedad: 'La juventud en la otra ribera' de Julio Ramón Ribeyro", *Iberoromania*, 17 (1983), 131-50; Julio Ortega, "Los cuentos de Ribeyro", *Cuadernos Hispanoamericanos*, 417 (1985), 128-45; Jorge Rodríguez Padrón, "Julio Ramón Ribeyro o el placer de contar", *Cielo Abierto*, 25 (1983), 2-10; Phyllis Rodríguez-Peralta, "Counterpoint and Contrast in Julio Ramón Ribeyro's Two Novels", *Hispania*, 62 (1979), 619-25; Augusto Tamayo Vargas, "Julio Ramón Ribeyro: un narrador urbano en sus cuentos", *CIILI*, II, 1161-75; Luis Fernando Vidal, "Ribeyro y los espejos repetidos", *RevCrit*, 1 (1975), 73-88.

inhabitants of San Gabriel, and particularly of his cousin Leticia. In contrast to many early Spanish American regionalist writers, Ribeyro places his emphasis not on nature but on the human landscape. Behind the majesty of the Andes, the apparent placidness of country life, the boisterous good humour and open-handed hospitality of the locals, Luis discovers a world of injustice, hidden passions, tensions, betrayals and frustration. *Crónica de San Gabriel* is thus a novel of initiation relating Luis's loss of innocence as he becomes aware of the nature of the world. It is also a novel which destroys the myth of idyllic country life, and throughout it the sea is a recurrent motif evoked as a symbol of a freedom that is not to be found in the suffocating atmosphere of the mountains.

However, *Crónica de San Gabriel* is, above all, a novel about the break-up of a social order, the decline of the traditional land-owning oligarchy. At first that order seems to be still intact. The family lord it over the Indians in the traditional manner and Leonardo keeps lavish open house for all who pass through. But the evidence of remorseless decline is there. A strain of abnormality runs through the family, the result of intermarriage and exemplified by Jacinto, a living symbol of the decadence of a race. Only the weary Leonardo has any interest in the land or in the running of the estate. Most of the others, like Felipe, work for a salary and have no commitment to the estate, which is losing money. Moreover, the family is rent by dissensions and betrayals in the form of adulterous relationships. They unite momentarily in common cause when the hacienda is threatened by rioting Indians and again when an earthquake causes destruction, but when these dangers have passed they revert to the old pattern of squabbles and betrayals, and the final collapse of their order is announced when Leonardo is forced to sell off his timber and to mortgage the estate. One by one the members of the family depart, deserting the sinking ship, and the various betrayals that have taken place culminate when Leonardo's wife runs off with Felipe. Throughout the book the situation of the family and its class has been personified by Leticia, who alternates between moods of domineering haughtiness and frightened uncertainty about where she is going; now the cause of her progressively worsening nervous depression is revealed to be a secret pregnancy, and when she suffers a miscarriage we are left in doubt as to whether she will recover.

Ribeyro switches from the provinces to his home ground in *Los geniecillos dominicales* (1965), a novel which, like the work of Congrains and Reynoso, has as its central theme the dissatisfaction and frustration experienced by the marginal sectors of Lima society. In this case, however, the protagonist's background is very different, for he is the heir of a once-prominent family that has come down in the world, and the ironic tone of the narrative introduces an unaccustomed vein of humour into an urban fiction generally characterised by its seriousness. Weary of the insipid existence to which he is condemned by his family's impoverishment and the humdrum routine of office work, Ludo abandons his job and embarks on a series of adventures in the quest for a more exciting and fulfilling life. Unfortunately his adventures all end in frustration and defeat and the novel, in fact, reads like a kind of parody of the quest for the Holy Grail as he lurches from disaster to disaster. An orgy organised by him and his friends turns out to be a fiasco; an incursion into the capital's night life in pursuit of forbidden pleasures merely takes him from one drab, depressing brothel to another; an idealised affair with the prostitute Estrella ends when his money runs out; and the ideal woven around his childhood sweetheart Walkiria is shattered when he encounters her again after an absence of several years. Significantly, Ludo's adventures often bring him into confrontation with dwarves, for they seem to be an absurd incarnation of the mediocrity and malevolence of an environment that frustrates and eventually crushes him.

If *Los geniecillos dominicales* is a funny novel, its humour is tinged with pathos. Like *Crónica de San Gabriel* it is a novel of social decadence depicting the decline of once-flourishing families that have been unable to adapt to changing times and reflecting the situation of Ribeyro's own family.[10] The feckless Ludo and his companions are as much the victims of their own failings as of the limitations of their environment. The upper-class counterparts of the adolescent gang in *No una sino muchas muertes*, they have been rendered equally impotent by their social conditioning. Caught in an ambivalent social position as economic outcasts from the class to which they belong by birth and upbringing, they are unable to come to terms with reality and feel entitled to a life-style which their financial position does not permit. Moreover, their formation and

[10] The decline of the Ribeyro family and of the old élite in face of the emergence of a new, dynamic capitalist class is portrayed symbolically in the story "El ropero, los viejos y la muerte" (1972). Alberto Wagner de Reyna (b. 1915), an older writer standing apart from the generation of the fifties, deals with a similar theme in *Como todos en la tierra (Los Villalta)* (Ediciones del Sol, 1962), a long novel spanning the decade from the early thirties to the early forties and tracing the decomposition of one of Lima's old ruling families.

outlook have left them totally unequipped for the struggle for life. Mostly students with literary inclinations, they are completely impractical and lack the ambition, energy, determination and initiative to make their way in the world and instead weakly and passively allow themselves to be carried along by events. Thus, though Ludo tries his hand at various jobs, he is a failure at all of them and never sticks to any one for more than a few weeks and he is powerless to halt the decline of his family's fortunes.

On the literary front, too, Ludo and his friends are pathetic failures. They form part of a group of young intellectuals, protégés of the university professor, Doctor Rostalínez, and through them Ribeyro satirises the literary world of Lima, or at least a sector of it. Typifying the sterility of the Limeñan intellectual, Rostalínez has for years been reputed to be writing an important tome which never materialises, and his protégés suffer from the same barrenness, for though they sit around in cafés and bars discussing literature, arguing about their ideas and speaking of their plans, they lack both the experience and understanding of the real world and the dedication and perseverance to carry their projects to fruition. Emblematic of this unproductiveness is the review which the group plans to publish and which they pretentiously see as the mouthpiece of their generation, but its appearance — always imminent — is repeatedly postponed and by the end of the novel it has still not seen the light of day. What emerges from the novel, therefore, is a picture of a literary scene in which writers never write and projects remain unrealised, a picture which perhaps explains Ribeyro's decision to escape the Limeñan environment and makes all the more commendable his own achievements and those of the other members of the generation of the fifties.

Ribeyro makes a rare incursion into the realm of political fiction with *Cambio de guardia*, a novel written between 1964 and 1966, though not published until 1976. Revolving around a chain of events leading up to a *coup d'état* which brings an army general to power, the novel is loosely based on the Odría revolution, but Ribeyro's concern is not so much to chronicle a concrete historical event as to depict certain constants of Peruvian socio-political life. As the title indicates, the *coup* we see engineered is merely the latest replay of the oligarchy's standard manoeuvre to protect its interests and keep intact the country's power structure. Writing in a detached, almost clinical style, Ribeyro shows the mechanism of power at work to hush up shady business deals and sexual scandals, to immobilise or eliminate political opposition and finally to bring about a change of government that will perpetuate corruption, injustice and exploitation. What emerges is a very depressing picture of Peruvian socio-political life and if the novel seems merely a rehash of the same old, familiar story, the point that it is making is precisely that that story never changes. Perhaps its most original feature is its structure. The narrative is fragmented, consisting of a series of brief narrative sequences, many of them occurring simultaneously, which go together to form a mosaic interweaving several stories and involving a huge cast of characters. By means of this structure Ribeyro succeeds in conveying an impression of the complexity of modern urban society, where individuals live in the isolation of their own little circles yet interrelate and affect one another's lives in unsuspected ways. Such a society is shown to be so bewilderingly complex that it is often impossible to determine who is responsible for a particular action, as is exemplified by the mystery surrounding the death of a newspaper editor whose murder might have been the work of political enemies or of either of two jealous husbands. Indeed, events are seen to be often the result not of design but of a confluence of accidents, so that, for example, the Negro Luque finds himself charged with a murder he did not commit because he happens to have fallen foul of people in high places and to have been in the wrong place at the wrong time. Inevitably, *Cambio de guardia* invites comparison with Vargas Llosa's *Conversación en La Catedral* (1969), which deals with a similar subject,[11] and, unfortunately, it has to be said that Ribeyro fares badly in that comparison, for *Los geniecillos dominicales* and *Cambio de guardia* are both flawed works which reveal that he has never fully mastered the novel genre.

Though a novelist of some distinction, Ribeyro is much more at home with the short story and he is without doubt Peru's foremost exponent of that genre. Like the novels, the stories, gathered together in the three volumes of *La palabra del mudo*, build up a picture of a Peru in the throes of economic and social change yet which, paradoxically, remains fundamentally unaltered. For, beneath the superficial changes taking place in the country, Ribeyro has an eye for constants in national life. Thus, deep-rooted social divisions are

---

[11] Mention should be made here of another member of the generation of the fifties, Luis Loayza (b. 1934), whose fine minor novel, *Una piel de serpiente* (Populibros Peruanos, 1964), depicts the Odría dictatorship and gives expression to the disillusionment of the generation that grew up under it. Loayza has also published *El avaro* (Villanueva, 1955).

highlighted in "Los moribundos" (1961), a tale set in a frontier town against the background of the 1940 war with Ecuador. Not only is class and racial exploitation dramatised by the contrast between the suffering of two wounded soldiers (both Indians though on opposing sides) and the victory celebrations of the local establishment, but the ultimate realities of class interest and allegiance underlying hollow nationalistic jingoism are laid bare by the fact that, while an Ecuadorean bar-owner rubs shoulders with the celebrating Peruvians, the Quechua-speaking Peruvian soldier is unable to communicate with his "compatriots" and dies comforted by his "enemy". Similarly, the sordid nature of Peruvian public life is encapsulated in "El banquete" (1958), the tale of a provincial landowner, Fernando Pasamano, who invests his whole fortune in offering a sumptuous banquet for the President with the aim of obtaining a diplomatic post in Europe and the construction of a railway link to his estates, and who succeeds in gaining promises from the President only to discover that, while the banquet was in progress, a *coup* has brought a change of government. The story, in effect, is a tale of the biter bitten, for Pasamano is defeated by the very capriciousness of the political system which he sought to exploit and the *coup* which undoes his plans merely reflects the instability of a corrupt system in which groups and individuals vie to seize power for their own ends.

At the same time, Ribeyro reveals as illusory the progress represented by the socio-economic changes which were transforming the country. In much of his early work he coincides with Congrains in the depiction of the struggles and hardships of the marginated lower classes of an expanding Lima. Indeed, perhaps the most striking piece of urban fiction produced in the fifties is the title-story of his first work, *Los gallinazos sin plumas* (1955). Set in the *barriadas*, it is the tale of two young brothers who are obliged by their grandfather, Don Santos, to scavenge alongside the vultures on the city's rubbish dumps for food to fatten his pig, which he hopes to sell for a huge profit. When illness prevents them from doing so, he feeds their dog to the starving pig, whereupon one of them attacks him and he stumbles into the pen and is himself devoured. What we are shown, therefore, is the unacceptable face of capitalism, the cruelly primitive world of poverty and squalor that lies behind Lima's civilised and affluent facade. That marginal world is also presented as a kind of distorting mirror reflecting in exaggerated outline the characteristics of the city itself. Aspiring to a place in capitalist society, the marginated are seen to adopt its values, and in his obsession with reaping a profit from his investment and in his inhuman treatment of his grandsons Don Santos grotesquely apes the attitudes and behaviour of the capitalist businessman. The pig, indeed, comes to be a symbol of a monstrous system which brings out the worst in men's nature by fomenting their greed, and when it eventually devours the old man it merely completes its destruction of him as a human being. And when the two boys make their way into the city to be swallowed up by its gigantic jaw, it is made clear that they, too, are destined to fall victims to a system which condemns the weak to abject misery and dehumanises those who adopt its values.

However, stories of this kind are not typical of Ribeyro's production as a whole and, in the main, his stories focus on the middle classes and portray attitudes of mind with a combination of humour and pathos that is perhaps the most characteristic note of his fiction. His middle-class characters tend to be outsiders, also-rans in the capitalist rat race, not only because they are handicapped by socio-economic disadvantages but also because they lack the qualities necessary for success. Often, too, their failure in the struggle for life is paralleled by a failure in the sphere of human relationships in a society which has no time for the inadequate. One such character is Arístedes, the chronically timid protagonist of "Una aventura nocturna" (1958). A forty-year old bachelor without friends, he has long since resigned himself to his lot and spends his evenings walking the streets on his own. Passing an empty café late one night, he thinks his luck has changed when the proprietress makes up to him, only to be disabused when, after getting him to clear the tables, she shuts the door in his face. A more complex and contradictory character is Alfredo, the protagonist of "De color modesto" (1961). Like Ludo in *Los geniecillos dominicales*, he is a young man with artistic leanings who occupies an ambivalent social position as an impoverished member of Miraflores' upper middle classes. He likes to think that he despises the frivolous values of the bourgeoisie but cannot help envying the affluence and self-assurance of his contemporaries and, above all, their success with women. At a fashionable party he is made painfully aware of his own inadequacies by his inability to find a dancing partner and as a last resort forces a Negro maid to dance with him. In the ensuing scandal he sees his action as a heroic gesture of rebellion and he leaves the house with her determined to pursue the relationship in defiance of convention, but when he comes to realise the inevitable consequences he loses his nerve and ditches her. Alfredo thus proves as incapable of genuine rebellion as he is of achieving social success, and in the end he merely exploits and hurts a social inferior in the worst tradition of his class.

One of Ribeyro's favourite themes is self-delusion of the kind indulged in by Alfredo. Some of his best stories portray lower-middle-class characters who, trapped in precarious financial circumstances and in a rut of soul-destroying mediocrity, nurse an ideal image of themselves which their situation and personality make them incapable of living up to. Typical of such characters is Pablo Saldaña, the protagonist of "Explicaciones a un cabo de servicio" (1957). The story has the form of a monologue in which Pablo, under escort to the police station for his failure to pay a bar bill, tries to persuade the arresting officer that it has all been a dreadful mistake. As he does so, there emerges an ironic contrast between the image he projects and the person he unwittingly reveals himself to be. In dire straits as a result of being unemployed for five months, he had been out searching for a job and met up with an old acquaintance who was in the same situation. Over a few drinks they conceived a scheme for going into business together. They lacked money, of course, but they had ideas and that was their true capital and it would be easy enough to find others to put up the cash, and, firing each other's enthusiasm, they decided on a name for the company, designed the offices and planned how they would spend the profits. Pablo then slipped out to have business cards printed, only to have his friend disappear, leaving him to pay the bill. Now he tries to convince the policeman that he is not a nobody but an important businessman and to prove it he shows him his card, the only material outcome of the illusory project, but he is steered relentlessly into the police station to confront the reality which even to the end he refuses to face. Pablo thus comes across as a pathetic fantasiser who is as much the victim of his own unrealistic pretensions as of his socio-economic position. As such he seems to personify a mentality which Ribeyro sees as pervading all classes of Peruvian society and as being one of the main causes of the country's backwardness, and his fantastic project might be interpreted as a symbol of a national unwillingness to come to terms with reality, a tendency which leads Peruvians to embrace instant solutions to deep-rooted problems and to be carried away by words, ideals and programmes, no matter how impractical they may be.

Yet if Ribeyro's fiction reflects a Peruvian reality, he is a writer who is also very much concerned to detect the universal in the local, and his stories communicate a world-view that is sardonically pessimistic. Again and again they portray characters who, like Pasamano, are unable to control events and find their ambitions thwarted by an unpredictable world, or who, like Pablo Saldaña, see their illusions — or delusions — negated by an implacable reality. That world-view is conveyed, too, by certain recurrent story patterns which invite symbolic interpretation. Some stories have a cyclical structure in which the protagonists' attempts to achieve self-determination are frustrated, leaving them trapped in their original unsatisfactory circumstances. A typical example is "De color modesto", where Alfredo rejects the standards of his middle-class background only to end up conforming when the full implications of his rebelliousness become apparent. Another favourite pattern is the story of initiation, in which characters are introduced to the cruel realities of life. One such case is "Una medalla para Virginia" (1965), set in Paita. Fêted as a heroine for saving the mayor's wife from drowning, the young protagonist discovers that the rescue was far from being an unalloyed blessing, since the mayor has lost interest in his ageing spouse and the couple are trapped in an unhappy marriage, and when he makes covert advances to her a subtle set of parallels suggests that her own future fate is prefigured in that of the discarded older woman. The aptly named heroine thus metaphorically loses her virginity.

Other stories move away from specifically Peruvian settings or abandon social observation to enter the terrain of the metaphysical in a manner reminiscent of Borges, posing inexplicable enigmas symbolic of the inscrutability of the world. Thus, in "Ridder y el pisapapeles" (1971) a Peruvian living in Antwerp visits the home of a Belgian novelist and discovers on his desk the paperweight which he himself threw out in Lima ten years previously and which mysteriously landed in the novelist's yard. A series of parallels suggests that the two men are somehow connected, and other stories, like "Demetrio" (1953) and "Doblaje" (1955), similarly involve mysterious doubles who may or may not be products of fantasy but who in either case imply the existence of phenomena beyond ordinary comprehension. The intractable incomprehensibility of the world is again the theme of "Silvio en el rosedal" (1976), whose eponymous protagonist seeks to read his destiny in the design formed by a bed of roses in the garden of his newly inherited country estate. His various speculations merely prove to be a source of bewilderment, anguish and frustration and in the end he comes to terms with life by accepting the futility of trying to decipher its meaning. The story may thus perhaps be read as the ultimate statement of Ribeyro's position with regard to a world which he sees as being beyond man's ability to control or understand.

On balance it has to be recognised that the generation of the fifties met with only limited success in its attempt to bring a new professionalism to Peruvian fiction, for, with the exception of Ribeyro and Zavaleta, who maintained a constant literary activity, it seems quickly to have run out of steam, a phenomenon that is largely explained by the underdeveloped state of the Peruvian book industry, which made it dishearteningly difficult for authors to publish and even more difficult to reach a wide and educated reading public.[12] Yet the achievements of that generation should not be underestimated, for it did significantly transform Peruvian fiction by modernising narrative technique and, above all, by introducing a new "professional" awareness of the importance of technique. It thus helped to establish a new attitude to the creation of fiction and initiated a process that was to culminate in the emergence of two novelists of international stature.

The first of these writers was an old dog with the adaptability to learn new tricks. As has been seen, José María Arguedas had already established himself as a leading figure in the literary representation of Indian culture with *Agua* (1935) and *Yawar Fiesta* (1941).[13] After a prolonged silence broken only by *Diamantes y pedernales* (1954), a

---

[12] This topic will be discussed more fully on pp. 319-20.

[13] See José María Arguedas, *Obras completas*, 5 vols. (Horizonte, 1983); *Los ríos profundos* (Caracas: Biblioteca Ayacucho, 1978); *Los ríos profundos*, ed. William Rowe (Oxford: Pergamon, 1973); *Deep Rivers*, trans. Frances Horning Barraclough (Austin and London: Univ. of Texas Press, 1978); *El Sexto* (Mejía Baca, 1961); *Todas las sangres* (Buenos Aires: Losada, 1964); *El zorro de arriba y el zorro de abajo* (Buenos Aires: Losada, 1971). For a discussion of Arguedas' early work and the relevant bibliography, see pp.137-43. See also Sara Castro Klarén, *El mundo mágico de José María Arguedas* (Instituto de Estudios Peruanos, 1973); Antonio Cornejo Polar, *Los universos narrativos de José María Arguedas* (Buenos Aires: Losada, 1973); Alberto Escobar, *José María Arguedas, el desmitificador del indio* (Chicago: Univ. of Chicago Center for Latin American Studies, 1981); id., *Arguedas o la utopía de la lengua* (Instituto de Estudios Peruanos, 1984); Juan Larco, ed., *Recopilación de textos sobre José María Arguedas* (Havana: Casa de las Américas, 1976); Martin Lienhard, *Cultura popular andina y forma novelesca: zorros y danzantes en la última novela de Arguedas* (Latinoamericana/Tarea, 1981); Gladys C. Marín, *La experiencia americana de José María Arguedas* (Buenos Aires: Fernando García Cambeiro, 1973); Silverio Muñoz, *José María Arguedas y el mito de la salvación por la cultura* (Minneapolis: Instituto para el Estudio de Ideología y Literatura, 1980); Julio Ortega, *Texto, comunicación y cultura: Los ríos profundos de José María Arguedas* (CEDEP, 1982); Edgardo J. Pantigoso, *La rebelión contra el indigenismo y la afirmación del pueblo en el mundo de José María Arguedas* (Mejía Baca, 1981); William Rowe, *Mito e ideología en la obra de José María Arguedas* (INC, 1979); Pedro Trigo/Gustavo Gutiérrez, *Arguedas: mito, historia y religión/Entre las calandarias* (Centro de Estudios y Publicaciones, 1982); Antonio Urrello, *José María Arguedas: el nuevo rostro del indio* (Mejía Baca, 1974). See also *Review* (New York), 25/26 (1980); *Revista Iberoamericana*, 122 (1983).

somewhat mediocre long short story, his career took off again in 1958 with the publication of *Los ríos profundos*, which is generally regarded as his best novel. That silence was the result of a deep psychological crisis which seems to have had its roots in his own personal sense of alienation and in his pessimism with regard to his country's future, and in a sense *Los ríos profundos* may be viewed as a working-out of that crisis. The novel takes up again the basic theme of *Agua*, the predicament of a young boy caught between the worlds of the whites and the Indians, but, in common with Vargas Vicuña and Zavaleta and the Mexican Juan Rulfo, Arguedas develops a new mode of treating regional life. That new style — already present in embryonic form in his earlier work — is essentially lyrical in character and draws heavily on popular myth.

The predicament of the child narrator is essentially that of Arguedas himself. Brought up among the Indians, Ernesto looks back on the period spent in an *ayllu* (Indian community) as the happiest of his life. There his relationships with others were marked by tenderness and, imbibing the Indians' magical-religious view of reality, he enjoyed a sense of integration with the world. But now, when he moves to Abancay to receive the education that will equip him to take his place in white society, he finds himself cut off from the beloved world of his early childhood. Built on the lands of an hacienda, the town lives under the shadow of the oppressive social order represented by the *latifundistas*. The *colonos* whom he visits seem to have lost their cultural tradition and have been reduced to such a degree of abject servility that they recoil from any contact. The Church-run school where he is a boarder is one whose function is to provide an education for the sons of the land-owning class and its values are those of the class it serves. The air of sexual repression which hangs over the school reflects the oppressiveness of the social order, and the aggressive violence of white society is embodied in the bully Lleras and manifests itself, too, in the brutal violations of the half-witted serving woman, *la opa*. In such an atmosphere Ernesto finds himself completely alienated. His experiences sever his relationship with the natural order and he is left feeling desperately alone and disorientated.

What sustains him is the comfort he derives from the spiritual world of the Indian. To escape from the oppressive atmosphere of the school and to recharge himself emotionally, he visits the *chicherías* (liquor stores) of the poor district to listen to Indian music and makes frequent trips out of town to renew his bonds with nature. In the school itself he has the comfort of his *zumbayllu*, a magical spinning-top endowed with the power to conjure up a whole natural order linked by a chain of magical relationships and with which he feels himself integrated as he plays with the toy. One of the main virtues of *Los ríos profundos* is that it offers a fuller and richer picture of Quechua culture than any of Arguedas' other works. It is not just that the novel abounds in observations on Quechua music, language and folklore. Above all, it conveys the functioning of magical-religious thought and by showing it at work in Ernesto's mind gives it the immediacy of subjective experience. A substantial part of the novel consists of descriptive passages but rather than factual depictions of settings these are lyrical evocations linking the protagonist emotionally with the natural world and revealing the unifying chain of secret magical relationships perceived by him. A significant evolution in Arguedas' style is that, abandoning the linguistic experiments of *Agua* and *Yawar Fiesta*, he here opts for a correct Spanish skilfully manipulated to capture that magic reality. It is perhaps his greatest achievement as a writer that he has managed to convey the sensibility of the Quechua people to the outside world by successfully translating its modes of thought into Spanish.

For most of the novel Ernesto's position is an ambivalent one as he confusedly adapts to his new circumstances. He is partially absorbed into white society, for though he feels himself to be different, many of his attitudes are those of the class to which he belongs by birth and his teachers and comrades embrace him as one of their own. Furthermore, his experiences conspire to undermine his faith in Indian values by calling into question their effectiveness in the world of the whites. It is not just that at every turn he sees the Indian people downtrodden and humiliated. Even the divine forces of nature seem to be defeated when they come into confrontation with white culture, so that, for example, another of his magical toys loses its powers after being blessed in the school chapel.

In the latter part of the novel, however, there takes place a series of events which further estrange Ernesto from the world of the whites and consolidate his allegiance to that of the Indians. First the *chicheras* (female liquor-vendors) challenge the established order by breaking into the government salt warehouses and distributing the contents among the poor. Then the *colonos* rise in rebellion in the climactic final chapter where, believing that the plague which has broken out among them is a supernatural being which can be destroyed only by a special mass said for them in Abancay, they march on the city and force the authorities to accede to their demands. The novel thus ends with a victory of the Indians over the social order, a triumph that is paralleled on the internal plane by Ernesto's unreserved adherence to Quechua cultural values. Through-out the book his identification with the *chicheras* and the Indians was more than solidarity with the social aspirations of the downtrodden. For the central theme of *Los ríos profundos* is existential rather than social, though the two dimensions are obviously closely linked. What is in conflict are not just two social orders but two ways of life, and on the outcome of that conflict depended Ernesto's faith in the Quechua values he has grown to live by. In a very real sense his personal salvation hinged on the ability of the Indians to assert the validity of their culture by asserting themselves socially. Now, with the victory of the *colonos*, his faith is vindicated.

Nonetheless, the novel's ending is somewhat problematic. On one level, if Ernesto appears to have resolved his inner conflict by embracing Quechua culture with complete faith in its effectiveness, he clearly faces a future fraught with tensions since he must assume its values in the alien world of the whites. On another, there is a pathetic disproportion between the strength the *colonos* acquire and the tragically limited purpose to which it is put. As in *Yawar Fiesta*, the Indians' magical-religious outlook reveals itself to be both a strength and a weakness, for if it gives them the capacity to challenge the established order and win, it also substitutes a mythical enemy for the real enemy (the society which forces them to live in subhuman conditions) and diverts them from the struggle to achieve effective political objectives. However, it would seem that Arguedas was concerned to demonstrate that the Indians have the potential to assert themselves socially and politically in that the strength they display in rebelling for religious reasons is capable of being harnessed to a social and political consciousness. Likewise, Ernesto's faith in Quechua culture would seem to reflect Arguedas' own new-found confidence in the ability of that culture not only to survive but to spread beyond its traditional geographical boundaries to permeate and change the character of Peruvian society as a whole.

The optimism which characterises the final chapter of *Los ríos profundos* is even more marked in Arguedas' third major novel, *Todas las sangres* (1964).[14] His longest and most ambitious work, it reflects the changes which had been taking place in Peru from the

---

[14] In the interval Arguedas had published *El Sexto* (1961), a novel based on his experience as a political prisoner.

mid-fifties onwards with the spread of industrial development, the advent of a more liberal political climate and the growth of a new militancy among workers and peasants. Like *Yawar Fiesta* but on a much larger scale, it attempts to give a complete overall picture of the complex and changing social pattern of the sierra and to pinpoint the direction in which Andean society is moving.

The novel portrays the break-up of traditional feudal society under the impact of change, a process dramatised by the dissensions within the Aragón de Peralta family and the suicide of Don Andrés and by the decline and eventual abandonment of the once-prosperous mining town of San Pedro. The main cause of this disruption of the old order is the intrusion of the forces of modern capitalism, represented in the early part of the novel by Fermín Aragón de Peralta. In the pursuit of his ambitions he is coldly calculating and totally ruthless and unscrupulous, but his plans to develop the mine of Apark'ora involve him in a struggle with international capital in the shape of the Consortium and such is the influence it exerts over the nation's political and economic institutions that it is able to block his attempts to secure financial backing and he is obliged to sell out for a minority share in the mine. At this stage Fermín becomes a spokesman for Acción Popular's capitalist-reformist ideology as he resolves to combat his country's backwardness by investing his newly acquired millions in a fish-meal company on the coast and in a scheme to introduce modern farming methods on his estate in the sierra. The development of Peru and the emancipation of the Indian depend on breaking down the feudalism of the sierra by incorporating the Indian into a modern technological society, he argues, and that can be achieved only by a progressive national capitalism independent of foreign imperialism. In terms of characterisation, however, Fermín's metamorphosis from ruthless capitalist to idealistic patriot is unconvincing and unsubstantiated by anything other than his own claims. One of the major weaknesses of the novel, in fact, lies in its portrayal of the capitalist class, for here Arguedas was dealing with a world outside his personal experience and his treatment of it is marked by obvious superficiality and caricature.

Fermín's brother Bruno, on the other hand, is the most complex and best drawn character in the novel, confirming that Arguedas is more at home when dealing with members of traditional Andean society. A conservative landowner of the old school and fanatically religious, Bruno regards the economic forces which are transforming the sierra as the enemy of God corrupting men's souls and disrupting the divinely ordained order. In him the crisis of feudal society manifests itself in a personal crisis. Tormented by guilt at his lechery and his complicity in his father's ruin, he seeks to atone for his sins by fulfilling his God-given duty to protect the Indians against the corrupting influence of the outside world. He grants privileges to his *colonos* to prevent them from drifting away to the coastal towns and, realising that he and his class have themselves contributed to the break-up of the old order by their cruel despotism, he takes the neighbouring community of Paraybamba under his protection. Yet Bruno's motives are not quite what he and others believe them to be. His religious fanaticism, in fact, disguises an instinct of class self-preservation, for he is acceding to change in order to salvage what he can of the old order. Such a policy, however, is fraught with contradiction, for his actions have the effect of raising the Indians' expectations and rousing them to disaffection, thereby hastening the collapse of the world he seeks to preserve. Unaware of this, Bruno experiences peace of mind for the first time in his new relationship with the Indians, paralleled by release from his lechery achieved through his love of Vicenta. However, his contentment is destroyed by the triumph of the Consortium, and in an insane attempt to wreak divine retribution on those responsible for the evils which have undermined the traditional order from within and without, he resolves to kill Fermín and Lucas, the most reactionary and cruel of the local *hacendados*. Significantly, he succeeds only in eliminating the latter whilst the former survives the attempt on his life, for Bruno's story illustrates that when a dominant class belatedly makes concessions in order to forestall change it succeeds only in precipitating its own destruction.

While the traditional order of the sierra is falling apart, the Indians not only remain intact as a group but grow in strength as they develop a new consciousness represented in the novel by Rendón Wilka. A *comunero* of Lahuaymarca, Rendón has had the benefit of an elementary education and several years in Lima studying the white man's society at first hand, experiences which have prepared him for the role of leader of his people. On his return he acquires positions of influence among the whites, first as overseer in Fermín's mine and then as foreman on Bruno's estates. At the same time, with the help of a team of young followers, he busies himself organising and politicising the Indians of the region.

Central to Rendón's strategy is the belief that the non-Indian sectors of Peru have no understanding of the Indian and that consequently the latter must retain his independence *vis-à-vis* other groups and carve out his own future. Thus while he is willing to learn from the left-wing political parties and to cooperate with them where there are advantages to be gained, he dismisses their policies and aims as being irrelevant to the real interests and goals of the Indian. Similarly the alliances he establishes with Fermín and Bruno are tactical alliances from which the Indian reaps concrete benefits without compromising his independence. The essence of his ideology is that the Indian must retain the cultural tradition that has been his main source of strength, while freeing himself from the old superstitions that have helped to keep him in subservience. In particular he believes that the Indian must retain his communal organisation, but that he must acquire a political consciousness and learn to adapt to modern industrial society.

By the end of the novel Rendón has mobilised the Indians into a powerful force. The success with which the *colonos* adapt to work in the mine under his leadership has demonstrated that the Indian peasant is capable of taking his place in industrial society. The Indians in the mine have organised themselves with the other workers and go on strike; the *colonos* of several haciendas have expelled the landowners and taken over the land; Bruno's former estates have been reorganised on a communal basis; Paraybamba has re-established itself as an independent community; the *comuneros* of Lahuaymarca have occupied the abandoned town of San Pedro. And when the Indians stand firm in face of the troops sent in to suppress them, Rendón is able to accept his execution calmly, secure in the knowledge that the forces which he has set in motion cannot be halted.

In *Todas las sangres* we see the Indians mobilise to shake off the shackles of feudal servitude and Quechua culture transform itself to meet the challenge of the modern age. However, the weakness of the novel is that while it convincingly portrays the break-up of the traditional order, its rosy view of the future glosses over a number of crucial questions. The community is envisaged by Arguedas as the means by which Quechua culture can survive in modern conditions, its ideal of fraternal and cooperative labour being presented as a viable alternative to capitalist relations of production. Yet, if we see the community ideal function successfully in the mine, we are not told *how* it is to replace capitalism. Furthermore, the alliance between the Indians and the national capitalism of Fermín against the common enemy, international capital, disguises a conflict of aims, since one of the goals of Fermín's capitalism is to destroy the traditions which are the basis of Rendón's programme. Above all, despite the optimism of the last pages, we are not told how the stranglehold of international capital is to be broken.

In the event Peru's subsequent development was to negate Arguedas' optimistic view of the future, for the following years saw the triumph of the capitalist ethos with a process of industrial expansion that brought with it the erosion of traditional values and ways of life. Arguedas' disillusionment with these developments coincided with a recurrence of the psychological crisis he had suffered in the forties and in his despair he was driven to contemplate suicide. His last, uncompleted novel, *El zorro de arriba y el zorro de abajo*, published posthumously in 1971, represents an attempt both to come to terms with the new situation in which the country found itself and to fight off death by forcing himself to write. The narrative is interspersed with sections of diary in which he recalls past experiences and preoccupations, recounts his struggle against the temptation of suicide and comments on the novel he is writing and on the difficulties he is encountering. It would seem, in fact, that when creativity failed him he had recourse to the diary in an attempt to keep on writing. Unfortunately he was never able to finish the novel and committed suicide in November 1969.

The new reality with which Arguedas seeks to come to terms in *El zorro de arriba y el zorro de abajo* was epitomised by Chimbote, the once-tranquil coastal port which was transformed into a boom town by the expansion of the fish-meal industry and a massive influx of labour from the sierra and other parts of the country. In the novel Chimbote represents the realisation of the capitalist dream of Fermín Aragón de Peralta and the frustration of the new future announced by Rendón Wilka. It is a city to which men are drawn by the lure of wealth, encouraged by the example of the mysterious Braschi who has risen from humble origins to be a captain of industry, and where money is squandered recklessly in ostentatious display of affluence. But it is also a chaotic world made up of thousands of individuals whose only common concern is the pursuit of personal ambition, a world whose lack of social cohesion is highlighted by the fragmented narrative and by the wide variety of Spanish spoken by the characters, a world so seemingly senseless that the madman Moncada is the only person able to make sense of it. Moreover, beneath the surface affluence many have been unable to get in on the boom and live in miserable squalor in the *barriadas* surrounding the town, while power and wealth are effectively concentrated in the hands of magnates like Braschi, who use violence, blackmail and bribery to frustrate trade union organisation and promote consumerism, typified by the proliferation of bars and brothels, to claw back workers' earnings. Above all, the atmosphere of Chimbote is one which corrupts, as is indicated by the recurrent image which depicts the coast as a harlot, whose sex organ is the sea, and the Indian migrants' loss of their cultural identity in their new environment is illustrated by the case of Asto, who equates social advancement with the adoption of the manners of the coastal *criollos* and the abandonment of all that identifies him as a *serrano*.

Yet within this pessimistic panorama there are those who resist and struggle to preserve their integrity as human beings and to survive with dignity. Of these the most memorable is the former miner Esteban de la Cruz, whose determination to spit up the coal dust that clogs his lungs represents a heroic refusal to be beaten and a rejection of the prevailing corruption, and a spirit of resistance among the exploited is manifested by the millenarian utterances of Hilario Caullama, who echoes the myth of Inkarrí to foretell the eventual destruction of capitalism. Moreover, the pervasive and insidious presence throughout the novel of manifestations of Quechua culture suggests the ability of that culture not only to survive in an alien environment but also significantly to influence the development of national culture. In particular, the novel has a mythological dimension in the form of interpolated conversations between the two foxes of the title, characters from Quechua folklore embodying the spirit of sierra and coast. Their meeting parallels the coming together of Peru's two cultures in Chimbote and their dialogue points forward to a new phase in their relationship. It is suggested that the chaos of Chimbote is like the chaos preceding creation, that the port is the melting pot out of which a new Peru will emerge through a process of transculturation, a process whereby Quechua culture will be modified but the country as a whole "Indianised". Here we see Arguedas desperately clinging to faith in the future in face of a reality which horrified him, but his decision to abandon the novel and commit suicide would seem to confirm that in his heart he was convinced that the Peru he saw emerging was one in which he himself could not live.

For some critics *El zorro de arriba y el zorro de abajo* is a failed novel, not only because it remained unfinished, but also because the existing text is so amorphous that it is doubtful if it could ever have been brought to a successful conclusion. For others it is an

experimental novel of the most radical kind, one which, focusing
coastal Peru from an Andean perspective and aimed at a potential
new reading public of educated *serrano* immigrants, seeks to subvert
and "Indianise" the essentially European medium of the novel by
developing a style of "oral writing" that transposes popular Quechua
art forms to the printed page and is structured on Andean organising
principles.[15] In either case, it is a very moving book and one which is
indispensable for an understanding of the development of a writer
whose major works make him one of Peru's two greatest novelists.

The other is Mario Vargas Llosa (b. 1936), who began his literary
career with *Los jefes* (1959), a promising if unexceptional volume of
short stories, and went on to achieve international renown after
winning the prestigious Biblioteca Breve prize in Spain with his first
novel, *La ciudad y los perros* (1963).[16] Vargas Llosa was the first

[15] In particular, see Lienhard.

[16] See Mario Vargas Llosa, *Los jefes. Los cachorros* (Madrid: Alianza, 1978); *La
ciudad y los perros* (Barcelona: Seix Barral, 1963); *The Time of the Hero*, trans.
Lysander Kemp (New York: Harper and Row, 1979); *La Casa Verde* (Barcelona: Seix
Barral, 1966); *The Green House*, trans. Gregory Rabassa (London: Cape, 1969);
Conversación en La Catedral (Barcelona: Seix Barral, 1969); *Conversation in the
Cathedral*, trans. Gregory Rabassa (New York: Harper and Row, 1974); *Pantaleón y
las visitadoras* (Barcelona: Seix Barral, 1973); *Captain Pantoja and the Special Service*,
trans. Gregory Kolovakos and Ronald Christ (London: Cape, 1978); *La tía Julia y el
escribidor* (Barcelona: Seix Barral, 1977); *Aunt Julia and the Scriptwriter*, trans. Helen
R. Lane (London: Picador, 1984); *La guerra del fin del mundo* (Barcelona: Seix Barral,
1981); *The War of the End of the World*, trans. Helen R. Lane (London: Faber, 1985).
For his journalism see *Contra viento y marea* (Barcelona: Seix Barral, 1983). Vargas
Llosa's other works include literary criticism and the plays *La Señorita de Tacna*
(Barcelona: Seix Barral, 1981) and *Kathie y el hipopótamo* (Barcelona: Seix Barral,
1983). See also María Rosa Alonso et al., *Agresión a la realidad: Mario Vargas Llosa*
(Las Palmas: Inventarios Provisionales, 1971); Rosa Boldori, *Mario Vargas Llosa y la
literatura en el Perú de hoy* (Santa Fe, Argentina: Colmegna, 1969); id., *Vargas Llosa:
un narrador y sus demonios* (Buenos Aires: Fernando García Cambeiro, 1974); Ricardo
Cano Gaviria, *El buitre y el ave fénix, conversaciones con Mario Vargas Llosa*
(Barcelona: Anagrama, 1972); Sara Castro Klarén, "Fragmentation and Alienation in
La Casa Verde", *Modern Language Notes*, 87 (1972), 286-99; Claudio Cifuentes
Aldunate, *"Conversación en La Catedral": Poética de un fracaso (análisis texto-
estructural)* (Odense: Odense Univ. Press, 1982); Antonio Cornejo Polar, "*La guerra
del fin del mundo*: sentido (y sinsentido) de la historia", *Hispamérica*, 31 (1982), 3-14;
Luis A. Díez, *Mario Vargas Llosa's Pursuit of the Total Novel* (Cuernavaca, Mexico:
Centro Inter-cultural de Documentación, 1970); id., ed., *Asedios a Vargas Llosa*
(Santiago de Chile: Editorial Universitaria, 1972); Mary Jane Fenwick, *Dependency
Theory and Literary Analysis: Reflections on Vargas Llosa's "The Green House"*
(Minneapolis: Institute for the Study of Ideologies and Literature, 1981); Casto M.
Fernández, *Aproximación formal a la novelística de Vargas Llosa* (Madrid: Editora
Nacional, 1977); David P. Gallagher, *Modern Latin American Literature* (Oxford:
Oxford Univ. Press., 1973), pp. 122-43; Helmy F. Giacoman and José Miguel Oviedo,
eds., *Homenaje a Mario Vargas Llosa* (New York: Las Américas, 1971); Luis Harss and
Barbara Dohmann, "Mario Vargas Llosa or the Revolving Door", in *Into the
Mainstream* (New York: Harper, 1967), pp. 342-76; Phillip Johnson, "Vargas Llosa's
Conversación en La Catedral: A Study of Frustration and Failure in Peru",
Symposium, 30 (1976), 203-12; Marvin A. Lewis, *From Lima to Leticia. The Peruvian*

Peruvian novelist to be a genuinely international figure, ranking with Gabriel García Márquez, Julio Cortázar and Carlos Fuentes as one of the leading representatives of the so-called new Latin American novel and writing for a market that was no longer purely local. He was also the country's first truly professional novelist, partly because he had the good fortune to enjoy an unprecedented editorial success generated by the fashionable "boom" in Latin American fiction, but, above all, because of his exemplary sense of commitment to his art.

In part Vargas Llosa's work may be seen as a culmination of the process of literary renovation initiated by the generation of the fifties, but at the same time he was much more attuned than his compatriots to contemporary literary trends, having lived in Europe for a number of years, and he was much more radical in his technical experimentation. Yet he stands out among the new Spanish American novelists in that he is very much a writer in the tradition of the great European realists of the nineteenth century. His three major works — *La ciudad y los perros* (1963), *La Casa Verde* (1966) and *Conversación en La Catedral* (1969) — are social novels on a grand scale and his frequently reiterated ambition has been to write a total novel, one reflecting all levels of a given reality. By abandoning conventional approaches to narration, plot, chronology and character, he, like his fellow new novelists, questions the assumptions on which realism has traditionally rested, presenting the world not as ordered and stable but as too complex and elusive to be grasped. Simultaneously, however, his fiction enlarges the traditional concept of realism by conveying a sense of the bewildering complexity of reality. Seeking to avoid giving the impression that he is in a privileged position to explain the world he is describing to the reader, the author abandons the stance of omniscient narrator and withdraws

Novels of Mario Vargas Llosa (Lanham: Univ. Press of America, 1983); Wolfgang A. Luchting, *Mario Vargas Llosa: Desarticulador de realidades* (Bogotá: Plaza y Janés, 1978); José Luis Martín, *La narrativa de Vargas Llosa. Acercamiento estilístico* (Madrid: Gredos, 1974); Duarte Mimoso-Ruiz, "*La guerra del fin del mundo* et l'aventure messianique de Canudos: la raison prise au piège", *Les Langues Néo-Latines*, 243 (1982), 95-117; José Miguel Oviedo, *Mario Vargas Llosa. La invención de una realidad*, 3rd ed. (Barcelona: Seix Barral, 1982); Angel Rama, "*La guerra del fin del mundo*", *Eco* (Bogotá), 246 (1982), 600-40; María L. Rodríguez Lee, *Juegos sociológicos en la narrativa de Mario Vargas Llosa* (Miami: Universal, 1984); Charles Rossman and Alan Warren Friedman, eds., *Mario Vargas Llosa. A Collection of Critical Essays* (Austin and London: Univ. of Texas Press, 1978); Joseph Sommers, *Literature and Ideology: Vargas Llosa's Novelistic Evaluation of Militarism* (New York: New York Univ. Ibero-American Language and Area Centre Ocasional Papers No. 15, 1975); Peter Standish, *Vargas Llosa: La ciudad y los perros*, Critical Guides to Spanish Texts 33 (London: Grant and Cutler, 1983); Mario Vargas Llosa, *La historia secreta de una novela* (Barcelona: Tusquets, 1971).

into the background by employing techniques, such as interior monologue, dialogue, the use of intermediaries, which distance him from the narrative, and by having recourse to multiple narrators and multiple points of view he highlights the subjective nature of reality. Vargas Llosa's novels also abandon the linear, chronological sequence of conventional fiction, presenting a disconnected narrative which changes in form, style, time, place and protagonists every few pages, so that reality is presented not in an artificially ordered manner but in bits and pieces, as it comes in real life, and it is only at the end of the novel that the reader, with hindsight, is able to piece everything together. His novels also depart from the traditional treatment of the human personality as something stable and consistent. The fragmented narrative shows the characters responding to immediate situations, without analysis of psychological motivation or explanation of actions, and they respond to different circumstances in ways so contradictory that at times they seem to have two distinct identities. At the same time the novels are constructed with consummate artistry. Montage enriches the reader's view of reality, for narrative units are arranged in such a way that they bring fresh perspectives to bear on one another and are mutually illuminating. Moreover, the novels' apparent disorder disguises a narrative pattern which in its intricacy is comparable to a labyrinth. That structural labyrinth might be said to function as a gigantic metaphor of the bewildering existential labyrinth which the characters inhabit.

In keeping with the author's belief that it is the novelist's task to present a critical view of the world, *La ciudad y los perros* (1963) is a savage indictment of Peruvian society. Though most of the action takes place in the Leoncio Prado Academy, a secondary school run by the military, the book is dominated by the presence of Lima in the background, and the Academy, in fact, is presented as a microcosm of the larger society, for it brings together characters from all social backgrounds and its values reflect those of the society it serves in its role of preparing the cadets to take up their place in the outside world. There the cadets are subjected to a discipline that is calculated to inculcate in them a respect for authority, hierarchy, the established order, and when they leave at the end of the novel, it is to occupy the social position they were born into in a society rigidly stratified by class.

Vargas Llosa has asserted that violence is at the very roots of life in Peru, since it is a country where the individual makes his way by imposing himself on others and where ultimately the system rests on the oppression of one group by another, and in the novel violence is virtually a way of life. It is, in fact, to teach their sons to be men that parents send them to the Academy, whose educational system is based on the premise that to survive the rough-and-tumble of life boys must learn to defend and assert themselves. The boys themselves readily fall in with the general cult of machismo and evolve their own society where the strong lord it over the weak. Machismo, in fact, is their passport to mutual acceptance and they learn to suppress or conceal the softer side of their natures and to behave with ostentatious toughness in the presence of their comrades. One of the effects of Vargas Llosa's technique of continually switching between third-person narration and monologue (interior or spoken) is to bring out the gulf between the public persona adopted by the boys and their sensitive and vulnerable inner self and to highlight how for them social intercourse involves the jettisoning of their better instincts and the distortion of their true selves. This is shown most dramatically — if not entirely convincingly — by the double presentation of Jaguar, whose "tough guy" image is unmasked at the end of the novel when it is revealed that the anonymous timid and sensitive boy who has been narrating the story of his early life in the first person is the same aggressive bully we have seen ruling the roost in the school.

Image, in fact, is one of the main features of the society depicted in the novel, a hypocritical, dishonest society professing values which are necessary to keep the system functioning but which no one really believes in or lives by. Thus, the officers parrot the military virtues of patriotism, duty and discipline and seek to instil them in the cadets, but when Arana is shot dead during an exercise, they shirk their responsibility and are concerned only to hush the matter up to prevent a scandal which would damage the Academy's prestige and prejudice their own careers. Their dishonesty has its corollary among the cadets, who learn to use their wits to find ways of circumventing the strict discipline to which they are subjected, behaviour condoned by one of the officers as part of the business of growing up to be men. It is accepted, therefore, as the normal pattern of life, in society as in the Academy, that men pay lip-service to rules and regulations while dodging them whenever they can.

As the title indicates, *La ciudad y los perros* is a novel of adolescence tracing the painful process of growing up as the young cadets adapt to the reality of their social environment. In such a violent society the sensitive and timid Arana is a friendless misfit who is bullied and humiliated by everyone, and after being broken as a person he is eventually murdered when despair drives him to denounce a classmate for the theft of an examination paper. The other two protagonists find themselves at odds with the social order only to come to terms with it in the end. Alberto confronts in the Academy a moment of truth which determines the kind of person he grows up to be. Though his quickness of wit and tongue enable him to cover it up behind a mask of self-assurance, he is a sensitive boy tormented by a sense of insecurity caused by his feelings of sexual inadequacy and by the break-up of his home as a result of his father's philandering, and he reacts against the insensitive egoism and moral hypocrisy of his wealthy, upper-middle-class parents. He makes a stand for honesty and decency when he denounces Arana's death to the authorities as murder, but he lacks the moral courage to stick to his guns and backs down under pressure. From that moment his growth as a human being is stunted and when he leaves the Academy it is to step into his father's shoes. The social order is thus seen to perpetuate itself from one generation to another, not only because it pressurises individuals into conformity, but also because of the human weaknesses of those individuals. Jaguar, too, is beaten into submission, but his is a somewhat different case. Rebelling against the hardness of the world by paying back violence with violence, he adopts a tough, invulnerable persona as an over-compensation for the sensitive, vulnerable person that he is. The product of a lower-middle-class home, he drifts into delinquency and in the Academy he imposes himself as top dog among the cadets and leader in the war against authority. However, in the aftermath of his liquidation of Arana, he comes to realise that he is set on a course which isolates him from the friendship of others and will eventually lead him to prison, and the end of the novel finds him settled down as a respectable married bank-clerk. Yet if in social terms Jaguar submits and ends up accepting the position determined for him by his class background, the fact remains that he makes a positive choice and adopts a life-style appropriate to his true character. In human terms, therefore, his apparent conformity represents a victory over the pressures of his environment.

La ciudad y los perros still retains many features of the traditional novel: it develops a story-line, with exposition, climax and denouement; the characters are placed in context, with detailed accounts of their background; and the greater part of the story is recounted by an omniscient narrator who presents settings and events and takes us inside the minds of the characters. However, on to these traditional elements Vargas Llosa grafts modern novelistic techniques. Most strikingly, the narrative is fragmented, with constant shifts in time, place, characters and points of view. At the same time the omniscient narration is complemented by two first-person accounts, Boa's interior monologues, which give us an ordinary cadet's view of events in the Academy, and the reminiscences of an anonymous speaker whom a surprise ending reveals to be Jaguar, obliging us to re-evaluate our reading of the novel.

In *La Casa Verde* (1966) Vargas Llosa turns his attention from the capital to focus on life in the interior of the country. The novel has five main story-lines spanning a period of some forty years and unfolds in two settings: the provincial city of Piura on the north-west coast and the jungle department of Amazonas. One of the effects of the novel's fragmented narrative structure is to convey a view of Peru as a country divided. Not only are the two regions geographically and culturally isolated from each other, but society is divided by race and class, for the inhabitants of La Mangachería, Piura's lower-class district, feel themselves to be a community apart, while the Indian tribes of the jungle exist on the fringes of civilisation.

The two stories set on the coast build up a picture of Piura as a parochial, narrow-minded provincial town. The first concerns a brothel — the Green House of the title — which stands as a symbol of freedom, excitement and vitality in conflict with conservative morality. Opened by a mysterious stranger, Don Anselmo, it poses a challenge to Piura's puritan mores and is eventually burned down by the respectable women of the town, incited by the local priest, only to be reopened later by Anselmo's daughter. The second story is that of the self-styled "Inconquistables", a quartet of layabouts from La Mangachería whose life is a continuous round of boozing and whoring and who embody the exaggerated sense of machismo for which Piura has always been renowned. The reverse side of their heroic image of themselves is exposed when Lituma is transferred back to Piura after leaving to join the Civil Guard in an attempt to better himself. Away from his native environment he had matured into a decent and considerate human being but on his return he succumbs to group pressure and reverts to type. During a drinking session with his friends in the brothel he allows himself to be provoked into an absurd game of Russian roulette, as a result of which he ends up in prison, and in his absence one of his friends seduces his wife and sets her to work as a prostitute. Our view of

Piura is also conveyed by the manner in which the stories are presented, for they are narrated by a voice which purports to be that of the collective consciousness of the town and what we are given is not so much actual events as events recalled and elaborated by a vulgarly sentimental mentality which converts life into soap opera.

In its portrayal of the jungle region the novel creates the impression of a vast labyrinthine world in which men never really impose their presence. Here there is no stable social order as in Piura. Civilised institutions take the form of religious missions, military outposts and trading posts and few of the characters actually settle. This social instability is reflected in the story of Fushía's journey by river, which becomes a symbol of the unsettled lives of all of the characters, and in the fragmented and intertwining structure of the narrative, which brings the characters briefly together only to separate them again.

The novel also reworks the theme of civilisation and barbarism, the former represented by the nuns and the civil and military authorities based in Santa María de Nieva. Like many novelists before him, Vargas Llosa questions the so-called civilisation that is being brought to the hinterland. The nuns take upon themselves the mission of rescuing Indian girls from ignorance and paganism, but they have to resort to using the army to remove them forcibly from their families and the story of Bonifacia illustrates the cruel fate of such girls, who are educated and taught to live in a white civilisation only to end up as maids or prostitutes to the very race that has elevated them. The corruption of the civil authorities is embodied by Julio Reátegui, the governor of Santa María, who uses his position to establish a monopoly of the rubber trade, forcing the natives to sell their rubber to him cheaply, and runs an illegal smuggling operation on the side. When Jum, an Aguaruna chief, organises his people into a cooperative to sell their rubber in Iquitos, Reátegui finds an official pretext to lead a punitive expedition against the village and Jum is brought back to Santa María for exemplary punishment. Afterwards he seeks revenge by allying himself with Reátegui's criminal competitors, but at the same time he repeatedly returns to Santa María in search of redress from the very authorities responsible for his humiliation. Jum thus stands as an archetype of the Indian's perpetual and fruitless quest for justice. The other main story concerns Fushía, a river pirate who attempts to muscle in on Reátegui's operation. Basically there is nothing to choose between the two men and indeed at one stage they worked hand in glove, but while Reátegui is a pillar of society who has the cunning to manipulate the system, Fushía is an outsider who never manages to break into respectable society and must operate on its fringe and for all his efforts he achieves very little and eventually dies of leprosy.

It would seem that one of Vargas Llosa's aims in *La Casa Verde* was to surmount the limitations of the traditional regionalist novel which flourished in Peru from the late thirties onwards and earlier in other parts of Spanish America. While the material presented is not in itself particularly different, it is presented in a manner that is artistically more effective, for he eschews the obtrusive documentation of characteristic features of regional life and conveys them instead by literary technique. Thus, for example, the jungle Indians are shown to be outsiders in the ethno-political composition of Peru by the mere fact that they lack an independent voice and narrative point of view, speaking through interpreters or being seen through the eyes of other characters. Likewise, he goes beyond the stereotypes of earlier novels to offer a more complex view of reality. Instead of a simplistic portrayal of idyllically innocent natives exploited and oppressed by evil white men, we are shown jungle Indians who are savage warriors living in subhuman conditions, exploiters whose motivation is psychologically complex and injustices which are often the consequence of chains of circumstances or ingrained attitudes rather than of deliberate policy. However, a major weakness in the novel is the imbalance between the treatment of the two regions, for while it gives an overall picture of the socio-economic order of the jungle region, in the case of Piura it focuses on social attitudes without relation to the socio-economic conditions which would explain them.

Beyond the regional the novel offers a view of the human condition. Vargas Llosa's scepticism with regard to man's ability to arrive at any truth in life is not only implicit in his novelistic technique as a whole but is highlighted by the mystery surrounding the first Green House, about which there are conflicting accounts and even doubt as to whether it existed at all. Caught up in a chaotic world, the characters are constantly on the move, searching for something which would give order and meaning to their lives, but their inability even to discover their own true selves is underlined by the fact that, like Jaguar in *La ciudad y los perros*, three of the protagonists — Don Anselmo/the Arpista; the Sergeant/Lituma; Bonifacia/the Selvática — have two quite distinct identities. All of the characters strive to rise above their circumstances and to fulfil themselves as human beings, but almost all are thwarted and end up degraded or destroyed either by themselves or by others or by some mysterious fatality inherent in life. Standing out as an epic personification of failure, Fushía mirrors the fate of most of them and in that sense his journey downriver to die in the leper colony can be viewed as a symbol of life as it is seen in what is an extremely pessimistic novel.

Artistically, *La Casa Verde* is a *tour de force* in which Vargas Llosa extends and perfects the techniques he began using in his first novel. There are five narrative threads which are developed in recurrent pattern through each of the four chapters and in the epilogue various loose ends are tied together, but individually and collectively the stories are presented in discontinuous sequence and the fragmentation of the whole is duplicated in individual sections, and ultimately it is the internal montage, with its close-knit web of criss-crossing lives and events depending on one another for their meaning, which gives the novel its coherence. A greater illusion of authorial detachment is achieved by sparing use of third-person narration and an increased use of dialogue and intermediaries. Even more than in the first novel we are given multiple perspectives and a significant new development is the employment of a kind of telescopic narrative in which a dialogue or dramatised narrative conjures up another one. A major departure is that in his ambition to achieve a total realism Vargas Llosa goes beyond the usual confines of realist fiction and attempts to add a mythical dimension through the story of the Green House, whose history is shrouded in fable, and more generally the novel is enriched by the use of symbols, the most important being the Green House itself and Fushía's river journey. Unfortunately, the mythical story of the Green House does not really gel with the rest of the novel and the cost of its incorporation into the work is a loss of artistic unity.

One of Vargas Llosa's best works is *Los cachorros* (1967), a novelette in which he returns to a social class and a theme which particularly obsessed him: the privileged upper middle class of the Miraflores district of Lima and the process of growing up and being assimilated into the adult world. It tells the story of Cuéllar, a schoolboy who is attacked by a savage dog and castrated. Thereafter his inability to lead a normal life prompts him to compensate by embarking on wild and reckless escapades which bring him to self-destruction when he is killed in a car crash. While the story functions effectively on a realistic level, physical castration is, above all, a metaphor. Cuéllar first appears as an outsider, a newcomer to the school eager to get himself accepted, and he succeeds in doing so by dint of exerting himself scholastically and socially. It is at this stage that his misfortune occurs. Symbolically, therefore, his castration is caused by social forces and represents the destruction of his personality by the pressure to conform. Subsequently his deficiency becomes a metaphor of his inability to fit in, for from then on the story focuses on two parallel themes: the unwitting cruelty of his friends, who will not let him come to terms with his condition but keep pressuring him to imitate them; and his attempts to compensate for his inadequacy by indulging in actions which will demonstrate his manhood to others.

However, this is not merely a story about Cuéllar, for his predicament focuses our attention on the society from which he is an outsider and his physical castration is a kind of distorting mirror reflecting the moral castration of that class. The privileged classes of Miraflores are portrayed as leading pampered lives in luxury homes and exclusive schools and clubs, in a sheltered world remote from the reality facing the rest of the country and where discomfort and hardship are unknown and whims always indulged. That pampered existence is reflected in the peculiarly honeyed speech of Miraflores which Vargas Llosa reproduces in the narrative. Significantly, that speech remains constant depite the ageing of the characters, implying that they fail to grow and develop as human beings and remain pampered children even in middle age.

The story is narrated by a collective voice, that of the group of schoolboys now grown to middle age, and is marked by frequent switches from "they" to "we". Cuéllar's tragedy clearly haunts them, stirring feelings of guilt for their unwitting part in his destruction, and the telling of the story represents an attempt to exorcise the ghost. The use of the third person corresponds to a desire to distance events and absolve themselves of responsibility, while the use of the first person is an unconscious recognition of involvement in Cuéllar's undoing. The collective narrator thus keeps alternating between the denial of responsibility and an unwilling admission of guilt which, insofar as the first person becomes an extended "we", involves the reader — society at large — in responsibility for Cuéllar's plight.

Vargas Llosa's major work is undoubtedly the monumental *Conversación en La Catedral* (1969). The novel pivots around a four-hour conversation betweeen Santiago Zavala, the black sheep of an oligarchic family, and the Negro Ambrosio, the former family chauffeur. The whole novel, in fact, is made up of dialogue and narrative units generated in waves by this central conversation, for the two men's review of their past lives sparks off inner thoughts and recollections and conjures up other conversations and dramatised episodes. Here the various techniques which Vargas Llosa had developed in his earlier novels are carried to their furthest extreme and exploited to their fullest potential. Since the novel is based largely on conversations skilfully identified by leit-motifs and individualised speech patterns, the authorial presence is virtually imperceptible and we are presented with a seemingly autonomous narrative. The fragmentation of the narrrative is further intensified because the interlocking parallel stories are told not only in alternating sections of a chapter but often simultaneously on a page by means of parallel dialogues, but with consummate artistry these apparently disparate elements are juxtaposed in such a way that they always interact and they are assembled in such a way that they contribute to the overall picture.

Artistically the most accomplished of Vargas Llosa's novels, *Conversación en La Catedral* is also the one in which he comes closest to realising his ambition of writing a total novel. Indeed, it is perhaps the most complete picture of non-Andean Peru to be found in that country's literature. The main narrative covers a period of approximately fifteen years (1948-63), our view of each main character is temporally all-encompassing and we have the impression of seeing a whole era evolve before our eyes. Geographically the novel encompasses the various districts of the capital and extends beyond it to provincial cities like Arequipa, Cuzco, Pucallpa, Ica, Camaná, Trujillo and Puno. The multitude of characters in the book represents a wide range of social and ethnic groups, and we are introduced into the worlds of politics, journalism, the military, student life and Lima night-life. Indeed, the only social groups not portrayed in detail are the industrial working classes and the Indians of the sierra, and their exclusion, it could be argued, is entirely consistent with the margination of those groups in real life.

The image which we are offered of the country is a bitterly pessimistic one. Peru appears as a "país jodido", a nation corrupted and degraded. In part the novel is a testament of the dictatorship of General Odría (1948-56), whose regime, if it rested ultimately on repression, was characterised above all by its wholesale corruption, and Vargas Llosa himself has stated that the *ochenio* (eight-year period) contaminated the whole of Peruvian society and left his generation totally disillusioned with their country. However, politics is only one dimension of the reality treated in the novel. Moreover, if it is set mainly during the *ochenio*, it also extends into the constitutional presidency of Manuel Prado (1956-62) and the early days of Fernando Belaúnde's term of office and there is no evidence of any fundamental change, a fact which is highlighted by the novel's temporal shufflings, which often leave us confused as to under which president events are taking place. What we are presented with, in fact, is a chicken-and-egg situation. For if we are shown the contaminating influence of the *ochenio*, the dictatorship is also seen as a manifestation of deep-rooted ills in Peruvian society.

Odría himself makes only a brief appearance in the novel. The regime is represented by his fictional Minister for Internal Affairs, Cayo Bermúdez, and the oligarchy, its main source of support, by the wealthy businessman, Fermín Zavala. The gulf between image and reality is indicated from the outset, for the cathedral of the title proves not to be a magnificent church but a seedy bar-cum-brothel where the conversation between Santiago and Ambrosio takes place. Subsequently we discover that the two pillars of the establishment, Cayo and Fermín, are respectively an impotent voyeur who pays lesbian prostitutes to perform for him and a notorious homosexual. Likewise, we see the regime posing as the guarantee of law, order and progress and staging an election to present a democratic image to the outside world, but we also see Cayo deploy strong-arm methods to eliminate the Apra and Communist opposition and use bribery and blackmail to ensure the support of influential groups and individuals. Perhaps the most striking feature of the political scene depicted in the novel is the complete absence of ideology. Self-interest is the name of the game and accommodation is the means by which it is achieved. The regime, in fact, is an alliance of interest groups and its survival depends on its keeping the various groups satisfied. Tensions exist. Cayo, a middle-class *cholo* who owes his rise to personal contacts, has a chip on his shoulder against the white oligarchs and indeed one of his main motivations seems to be to pay back in kind the class that has humiliated him all his life, while Fermín has nothing but contempt for the racial and social inferiors with whom he is obliged to cooperate. The two men hate each other, but they work together and treat each other with apparent respect, Cayo because the regime needs the support of the oligarchy, and Fermín because in general terms the regime creates the conditions for capitalist development and, more particularly, brings him lucrative contracts. The prevailing attitude is exemplified by Cayo, whose view of politics is completely cynical and who devotes himself to amassing money while he can, knowing that sooner or later he must fall from office. Eventually he does fall, betrayed by his former allies, but not before he has salted away a tidy fortune and after a period of exile he is able to return to a comfortable retirement in Lima. For his part Fermín supports the regime only as long as it suits his interests, and if he loses his contracts when he makes the miscalculation of switching his support too soon, he regains them when Cayo falls from power, and though the family fortunes decline under Prado they are restored with the advent of Belaúnde. Thus the only changes that we see on the Peruvian political scene are the regroupings of interests among the dominant classes. Yet even those classes are victims of the system which they manipulate, for in their private lives Cayo and Fermín are failures as pathetic and unhappy as any of the characters from the lower orders. Indeed the voyeurism of the one and the homosexuality of the other seem to symbolise the sterility of a socio-political order which not only does not operate for the common good but stultifies all those caught up in it.

A sense of hopelessness is created by the fact that the main opponents of the regime, the Apristas, have been effectively neutralised and appear only on the fringes of the novel while the lower-class characters who take centre-stage are passive and unpoliticised. The only anti-government activity on which the novel focuses are the plottings of the student revolutionaries of San Marcos and they come across as naive idealists merely playing at politics and easy meat for Cayo, as is underlined by the technique of allowing them a few pages before burying them in the labyrinthine structure of the novel. For their part the representatives of the lower classes never question the social system but accommodate themselves to it, trying to get on within it as best they can. Some actively help to perpetuate the social order by following Cayo's example and selling their services as political thugs. Others have been so conditioned by their circumstances that they passively accept their inferiority and are grateful for whatever crumbs are thrown their way. The most extreme case is the servile Ambrosio, who out of a sense of respect, gratitude and devotion submits to a homosexual relationship with Fermín and ruins his own life by murdering the prostitute who blackmails his master. Even to the very last, when he has been reduced to the miserable existence of a dog-catcher, he rejects all criticism of the master who has abused and abandoned him, and the passive resignation of his final words brings the novel to a very gloomy conclusion.

The fact that every character in the novel, irrespective of social origins, experiences defeat and failure is a reflection of the life-destroying nature of the social order. However, it is above all the central character, Santiago Zavala, who embodies the disillusionment of the author's own generation. The inevitability of failure in such an environment is highlighted by the fact that we are shown the defeated, disillusioned thirty-year-old before the idealistic youth and that on the opening page he equates his own downhill slide with that of Peru. In his adolescence Santiago rebels against his family's bourgeois life-style and values, partly because he feels stifled by them and partly because he is disgusted by the social system which they uphold. However, his predicament is that he is a rebel without a cause. At the University of San Marcos he becomes involved in left-wing politics but is never able to commit himself fully. Objectively his doubts are justified, given the ineffectuality of student politics as depicted in the novel, but they reflect, too, his personal weakness, his class formation and the lack of commitment of the nation as a whole to any cause or ideology. Nonetheless, when he is arrested by the police and then freed because of his father's influence, he refuses to return to the fold and opts instead for a career in journalism. Unfortunately this does not represent a real alternative either, for he finds himself working for the government newspaper and seems doomed to spend the rest of his days reporting on trivia. Eventually he settles down to the monotonous and mediocre life of a *petit bourgeois*, married to a girl from the lower middle classes. Leading a tedious, soul-destroying existence, he is gnawed by a sense of frustration and masochistically tortures himself over the waste of his life. Santiago is an unheroic character in an unheroic society and like everyone else in the novel accommodates himself to the system and succumbs to the general mediocrity. Yet, if he achieves nothing positive, he at least demonstrates a moral superiority by choosing to be a drop-out and stubbornly refusing to conform to the values and life-style of his class. In that he represents the one positive note in the novel and alleviates somewhat its overriding pessimism.

Pantaleón y las visitadoras (1973) and *La tía Julia y el escribidor* (1977) represent a new phase in Vargas Llosa's novelistic career in that they move away from the structural complexity of his earlier works to a relatively straightforward narrative that makes few demands on the reader. At the same time Vargas Llosa abandons his hitherto uniformly serious and solemn tone in favour of humour.

Pantaleón y las visitadoras recounts the hilarious adventures of an army officer entrusted with the task of organising a prostitution service for the sex-starved garrisons in jungle areas, a macabre counterpoint being provided by the history of a fanatical religious sect. *La tía Julia y el escribidor* is the story of Vargas Llosa's discovery of his vocation as a writer, thanks in large part to his love affair with and marriage to a divorcee fifteen years his senior, which enables him to assert his independence of social and family pressures, and to the influence of a scriptwriter of radio soap operas who sets him an example of total professional commitment. Written with Vargas Llosa's habitual professionalism, both novels are immensely readable and very funny, but, it has to be admitted, they are also rather lightweight when judged against the high standards he had previously set.

In his most recent work, *La guerra del fin del mundo* (1981), Vargas Llosa continues to cultivate the simpler, more accessible style of his second phase but returns to the novel on the grand scale.[17] However, this novel is a new departure in that for the first time he goes beyond the portrayal of Peruvian reality to tackle a subject representative of the reality of Latin America as a whole. A historical novel of epic proportions, it is set in Brazil and is a reworking of Euclides da Cunha's *Os Sertões* (1902), an account of the rebellion of the peasants of the poverty-stricken backlands of the North-East led by Antonio Conselheiro, "the Counsellor". The latter was an itinerant preacher who acquired a fanatical following among the inhabitants of the backlands and in 1890 he established a community in Canudos. Subsequently he clashed with the state and ecclesiastical authorities and, mistakenly fearing the movement to be monarchist subversion, the republican government sent in the army to suppress it and in 1897 the settlement was destroyed after a long and bloody campaign. In his re-creation of the story of the Counsellor Vargas Llosa narrates the personal histories of a number of his followers and his impact on them. The Counsellor not only appeals to the mysticism of the simple backlanders, offering them spiritual compensation for the poverty of their existence, but gives a sense of identity to a people who are the nation's pariahs. In that sense the epic of the backlanders is the epic of all the marginated peoples of Latin America in their quest for an identity and a voice. Likewise the

---

[17] In fact, Vargas Llosa has since published two new novels, *Historia de Mayta* (Barcelona: Seix Barral, 1984) and *¿Quién mató a Palomino Molero?* (Barcelona: Seix Barral, 1986). Unfortunately, they appeared too late to receive discussion in this book.

tragedy of Canudos is that of all Latin America. For the backlanders suffer the fate of all minority cultures in the continent, since in the centres of power the politicians and middle classes reduce everything to the terms of their own world-view and ideology and, interpreting the backlanders' struggle for self-expression as a threat to the established order, they think only of suppressing it.

In counterpoint to the marginated peasants of the world's end that is the backlands, the novel tells the story of several characters from the reader's own world. These include politicians and military commanders, but the two principal figures are a journalist accompanying the army on the Canudos campaign and Galileo Gall, a globe-trotting Scottish anarchist and phrenologist. All his life Gall has searched and toiled in vain for the revolution of his intellectual ideals and, thinking to find it at last in Canudos, he makes his way there to observe it at first hand and to lend his services. Significantly, he never succeeds in reaching Canudos, for between his intellectual view of revolution and the aspirations of the peasants of the backlands there exists a gulf as wide as that separating the latter from the middle classes of Rio. For his part the short-sighted journalist would seem to represent the uncommitted intellectual and it is only after he has fallen in with the Counsellor's followers and, having lost his spectacles, sees things through their eyes, that he comes to an understanding of the events of Canudos and of himself. *La guerra del fin del mundo* could thus be described as a saga of the aspirations and struggle of the marginated peoples of Latin America and an examination of the diverse attitudes of the middle classes towards that struggle. It is undoubtedly Vargas Llosa's most important work after *Conversación en La Catedral* and confirms his status as one of Latin America's major novelists, meriting comparison with Alejo Carpentier's *El siglo de las luces* as one of the continent's great historical novels. It is also a further indication of the extent to which Peruvian fiction has progressed since the tardy establishment of a novelistic tradition. For, thanks in no small measure to the efforts of the generation of the fifties, Peruvian authors have developed a genuine artistic awareness and in Arguedas, Vargas Llosa and Ribeyro the country has produced writers who by any standards must be regarded as outstanding.

Part II
Poetry Pure and Impure

In the years after 1940 the single most important poetic current in Peru was what is often loosely and inaccurately referred to as "pure poetry". Cultivated by artists from cultured backgrounds whose influences tended to be European and whose interests were abstract and philosophical, it was a poetry which ignored the surrounding local reality to concern itself with the poet's own inner life. Essentially it was a continuation of the visionary poetics which, in the avant-garde epoch, had established itself as one of the major traditions of Peruvian verse, for it conceived poetry as the pursuit of an alternative, absolute reality beyond the contingency of the temporal world. It was also characterised by its preoccupation with form and by its aspiration to stylistic perfection as a means of expressing that ideal reality.

The leading representative of this tendency was Martín Adán (1908-85), who is widely regarded as Peru's greatest poet after Vallejo.[1] Chronologically Adán belongs to the avant-garde generation and in fact he first came to prominence in the late twenties and his early poetry, like his novel *La casa de cartón* (1929), was written in the avant-garde manner. Subsequently, however, in *La rosa de la espinela* (1939), a collection of *décimas*, and *Travesía de extramares* (1950), a volume of sonnets, he was to abandon the avant-garde poetics in favour of an art which, while exploiting "modern" techniques, was based on discipline and order and a respect for tradition. In these works Adán employs a recondite lexicon, including archaisms and technical terms, and conceptual devices, reminiscent of the mystics and metaphysical poets, to create a complex, hermetic poetry that is

---

[1] See Martín Adán, *Obra poética* (INC, 1971); *Obra poética*, ed. Ricardo Silva-Santisteban (Edubanco, 1980); *Obras en prosa*, ed. Ricardo Silva-Santisteban (Edubanco, 1982). See also Edmundo Bendezú Aibar, *La poética de Martín Adán* (Villanueva, 1969); José Antonio Bravo, "Un soneto de Martín Adán. Análisis semántico del soneto 'Declamato come in coda', *Cielo Abierto*, 8 (1980), 45-51; James Higgins, *The Poet in Peru*, pp. 145-66; John Kinsella, "The Tragic and its Consolation: A Study of the Work of Martín Adán", Diss. Liverpool 1977; Mirko Lauer, *Los exilios interiores: una introducción a Martín Adán* (Hueso Húmero, 1983); Julio Ortega, *Figuración de la persona*, pp. 158-64; Roberto Paoli, "Lo hiperformal y lo informal de Martín Adán", in *Estudios sobre literatura peruana contemporánea*, pp. 139-50; Hubert P. Weller, *Bibliografía analítica y anotada de y sobre Martín Adán (Rafael de la Fuente Benavides) (1927-74)* (INC, 1975); id., "The Poetry of Martín Adán", in *Romance Literary Studies. Homage to Harvey L. Johnson*, ed. M.A. Wellington and M. O'Nan (Potomac: Porrúa Turanzas, 1979), pp. 151-60.

extremely rich and dense in meaning. At the same time it is a poetry which makes a powerful emotional impact on the reader and intensity of feeling is conveyed by graphic effects and the masterly manipulation of rhythmic patterns. Indeed, one of the great achievements of Adán's poetry is that it encompasses and communicates the dynamism and disorder of the life of the emotions within an artistic order of rigorous formal perfection.

Adán may be regarded as a visionary poet in the tradition previously discussed. Like Eguren he turned his back on the world to devote himself exclusively to poetry and like Moro he dropped his given name — Rafael de la Fuente Benavides — and adopted a pseudonym in a symbolic renunciation of one kind of reality for another, and the nautical metaphor of the title of his major work, *Travesía de extramares*, defines poetry as an adventure in which the poet embarks on a lonely voyage of exploration of the other side of life, a journey into the unknown in quest of the undiscovered land of the absolute. His poetics finds its clearest expression in that volume in the first of three sonnets addressed to Alberto Ureta, who is held up as a model of the poet he aspires to be:

—Deidad que rige frondas te ha inspirado,
¡Oh paloma pasmada y sacra oreja!,
El verso de rumor que nunca deja
Huïr del seno obscuro el albo alado.

—Venero la flexión de tu costado
Hacia la voz de lumbre, el alta ceja,
El torcido mirar, la impresa queja
De mortal que no alcanza lo dictado ...

—Sombra del ser divino, la figura
Sin término, refléjase en ardura
De humana faz que enseñas, dolorosa ...

—¡Que ser poeta es oír las sumas voces,
El pecho herido por un haz de goces,
Mientras la mano lo narrar no ösa!

(The deity who rules the foliage has inspired in you,
Oh enraptured dove and sacred ear!,
The murmuring verse which never allows
The white winged creature to flee the dark breast.

I revere the turning of your body
Towards the voice of light, the raised eyebrow,
The straining gaze, the imprinted groan
Of the mortal who cannot grasp what is dictated.

The shadow of the divine being, the image
Without end, is reflected in the distress
Of the human face which you painfully display.

For to be a poet is to hear the voices from on high,
The breast wounded by an abundance of pleasures
Which the hand doesn't dare narrate!)

That poetics is linked to the ancient tradition which regarded the poet as a seer, a prophet, an interpreter of the gods. Ureta is presented as a priest whose "sacred ear" is an antenna picking up the voice of the deity, and the ecstasy he experiences as the divine spirit enters his soul is conveyed by the metaphor of the enraptured dove. Yet, as he observes his master in an attitude of straining contemplation, Adán notes on his lips the groan that his poetry will record, a groan of impotence at his inability as a human to put into words the message dictated to him from on high. This, the final tercet explains, is the nature of the poetic activity. The poet is privileged to experience a mystic ecstasy so overwhelming that it renders him incapable of expressing it, so that if he knows the joy of contemplating the infinite, he also suffers the torment of not having at his disposal a language capable of translating that transcendental experience.

The poems of *Travesía de extramares* revolve around the poet's pursuit of an ineffable ideal reality. "Senza tempo. Affrettando ad libitum", for example, is a triumphant celebration of the moment of epiphany which is the goal of his poetics and represents an attempt to achieve what he himself deems to be impossible, to convey that experience in verse:

> —¡Mi estupor ... ¡quédateme ... quedo ... cada
> Instante! ... ¡mi agnición ... porque me pasmo! ...
> ¡Mi epifanía! ... cegóme orgasmo! ...
> ¡Vaciedad de mi pecho desbordada! ...
>
> —¡Básteme infinidad de mi emanada ...
> Catástasis allende el metaplasmo! ...
> ¡Que no conciba ... yo el que me despasmo ...
> Entelequia ... testigo de mi nada! ...
>
> —¿Mi éxtasi ... estáteme! ... ¡inste ostento
> Que no instó en este instante! ... ¡tú consistas
> En mí, o seas dios que se me añade! ...
>
> —¡Divina vanidad ... onde me ausento
> De aquel que en vano estoy ... donde me distas,
> Yo Alguno! ... ¡dúrame, Mi Eternidade!

(My stupefaction! ... stay with me ... stock-still ... instant
After instant! ... my agnition ... because I'm awestruck! ...
My epiphany! ... orgasm blinded me! ...
Overflowing emptiness of my breast! ...

Let it suffice me, this infinity of my emanated soul ...
Catastasis beyond metaplasm! ...
Let entelechy ... witness of my nothingness ...
Not conceive ... I who unastounds me! ...

My ecstasy ... stay with me! ... Insistent be the monstrosity
That wasn't insistent in this instant! ... whether you consist
Of me or be a god who adds himself to me! ...

Divine vanity ... where I absent myself
From him who I am in vain ... where you're far from me,
Someone I! ... endure for me, My Eternity!)

As in mystic poetry, conceptual conceits here serve to express a transcendental experience which runs counter to our accustomed habits of thought. Thus, in the opening stanza, the poet experiences self-recognition (agnition) as he loses consciousness in a mystic swoon; an ineffable harmony manifests itself to him visibly (epiphany) in an orgasm which blinds him; he is simultaneously purged and filled to overflowing. At the same time, archaisms and rare words gleaned from dictionaries (agnición, catástasis, metaplasmo, entelequia) convey by their very strangeness the extraordinary nature of that experience and confer upon it an appropriate air of solemnity. The poetic delirium is given an artistic order by the sonnet form, which in a sense freezes this fleeting moment like the figures on Keats's Grecian Urn. Yet Adán also manages to communicate the dynamism of the experience and the emotional upheaval it produces. The poem is something of a paradox in that it is a sonnet without a regular rhythm, and this rhythmical irregularity creates a frenzied effect, so that the poem appears as a series of verbal explosions, stammering exclamations wrenched from the poet by the emotional impact of the poetic experience. Alliteration and enjambment create a sense of urgency (ll. 1-2) and this is redoubled at the moment (ll. 9-10) when the experience reaches its climax and begins to decline. The poem thus achieves the remarkable feat of encompassing disorder within a symmetrical form and movement within a rigid structure.

Adán's sense of tradition is apparent in his choice of the rose as one of the central symbols of his work. *La rosa de la espinela* and a sequence of eight sonnets in *Travesía de extramares* are, in fact, dedicated to that flower. These poems, like the work of his Symbolist predecessors, seem to be based on the Neo-Platonic theory according to which the spiritual manifests itself in the material and the objects of the real world are ciphers of the essences of the ideal world, so that the poet, through contemplation of the former, can at certain privileged moments glimpse behind them the archetypal essences of which they are but imperfect copies. Thus the rose, a consecrated symbol of transient earthly beauty, is a cipher of the archetypal Rose, symbol of eternal spiritual beauty,and at given moments the poet is able to perceive in the real rose the presence of the ideal Rose, the dazzling archetype of whose nature it partakes but of which it is only a pale reflection.

As so often in Adán's poetry, paradox is again the keynote of the sonnets to the Rose. Thus, in "Quarta ripresa", the tantalising elusiveness of the absolute is conveyed by the notion that the Rose which is the object of the poet's passion can flourish only by remaining invisible to him:

> —La que nace, es la rosa inesperada;
> La que muere, es la rosa consentida;
> Sólo al no parecer pasa la vida,
> Porque viento letal es la mirada.
>
> —¡Cuánta segura rosa no es en nada! ...
> ¡Si no es sino la rosa presentida! ...
> ¡Si Dios sopla a la rosa y a la vida
> Por el ojo del ciego ... rosa amada! ...
>
> —Triste y tierna, la rosa verdadera
> Es el triste y el tierno sin figura,
> Ninguna imagen a la luz primera.
>
> —Deseándola deshójase el deseo
> Y quien la viere olvida, y ella dura ...
> ¡Ay, que es así la Rosa, y no la veo! ...
>
> (She who is born is the rose unexpected;
> She who dies is the rose pampered;
> Only by not appearing does she live her life,
> For a lethal wind is the human gaze.
>
> How much sure rose exists nowhere! ...
> For only the intuited rose exists! ...
> For God breathes on the rose and on life
> Through the blind man's eye ... beloved rose! ...
>
> Sad and tender, the authentic rose
> Is the sad and tender man without form,
> Presenting no image to the morning light.

> Desiring her desire deflowers itself
> And when he who would see her forgets, she endures ...
> Alas, such is the Rose, and I cannot see her! ...)

The Rose can and does manifest itself to man, but it cannot be called into being and is born into the world unbidden and when least expected. Moreover, he can catch only a fleeting glimpse of it, for when he seeks to retain the vision it is extinguished like a pampered creature smothered by too much attention. Once exposed to the lethal wind of the human gaze the Rose withers as surely as any earthly flower. Hence, though obliged to adore the Rose platonically from afar, the poet recognises in the final tercet that the desire to possess it is counter-productive, since like a brutal act of rape possession desecrates the object of one's desire. Thus, the paradox which torments the poet is that it is only by renouncing the wish to possess it that he can hope to behold the unsullied Rose of his dreams.

It has already been observed that the title of *Travesía de extramares* defines art as an exploration of the uncharted seas of the shadowy side of life. The nautical metaphor is, in fact, a recurrent one and the voyage constitutes one of the central themes of the book. Adán's sense of carrying on a noble tradition is again manifest in "Leit-motiv", where Chopin — to whom the volume, subtitled *Sonetos a Chopin*, is addressed and following whom many of the poems bear as titles technical terms of musical composition which serve to establish the tone — is held up as a model of the artist who has successfully accomplished his mission and is portrayed as the master of a well-equipped ship steering a majestic course. In "Frase in polacca per piano" Adán's own poetic adventure is likewise viewed in a heroic light as, guided by the pole-star of the great composer's example, his ship makes its stately way over the ocean towards the undiscovered land of the absolute. By contrast, "Quadratura subita in preludio" records his despair as his ship runs adrift and he feels himself incapable of measuring up to the ideals which he has set himself. This sense of failure to realise his high poetic ideals is perhaps the dominant note of the volume and in some poems it leads Adán to meditate on death and to nurse the hope that beyond the tomb he will enjoy the authentic life which has proved so elusive on earth. Significantly, the volume is brought to a close by "Volta subito", a poem where death is represented by the mythical ferryman, Charon, and which indicates that the poet's voyage of exploration must inevitably take him into the nether regions since his quest for the infinite can be fully realised only in the world beyond the grave:

—¡Compás de la Bogada de Caronte,
Tú libérame ya de sutileza,
Madre y caudal de lágrima que empieza
En mí y no para ni en el horizonte!

—¡Dame tú ceguedad con que yo afronte
Rumbo infinible de vida y belleza! ...
¡Y la mudez con que el eterno expresa! ...
¡Y el mi cadáver la tu boza apronte!

—¡Más no discurra yo sobre la linfa,
Ni rebusque ni finja, en haz o seno
De insondable hora, nenúfar o ninfa!

—¡De los ojos del muerto, mi mirada
Paire en faceta a luz cristalizada
Y yo mire belleza así sereno!

(Rhythm of the stroke of Charon's oar,
Free me at last from subtlety,
Source and river of a tear that begins
In me and doesn't stop flowing even at the horizon!

Grant me blindness with which to confront
The never-ending route of life and beauty! ...
And the dumbness with which the eternal give voice! ...
And quickly let my corpse cast off your moorings!

Let me roam no more on the lymph,
Nor on the surface or in the depths of unfathomable time
Seek or feign water-lily or nymph!

Through dead man's eyes let my gaze
Rest becalmed on a light-crystallised facet
That I may behold beauty thus serene!)

The tercets express his weariness with the artistic adventure which has him scouring the oceans for the beauty which, like the water-lily, manifests itself on the surface of the temporal world or, like the water-nymph, is concealed in the unfathomable depths of eternity beneath the temporal, a beauty which his poetry can only simulate since it is beyond his power as a mere human to reproduce it in his verse. He longs, therefore, for the world beyond the grave where, through the eyes of a dead man, his gaze, like a ship at rest on an ocean whose surface appears in the sunlight as smooth and dazzling as a precious stone, can linger in serene contemplation of absolute beauty. Thus, despite his failure fully to achieve his poetic goals, Adán ends the volume on an optimistic note with a view of death reminiscent of Eguren.

Subsequently, however, Adán was to undergo a crisis of confidence with regard to poetry and life and his verse was to take on a note of acute existential anguish. This change of tone was to be paralleled, too, by a change in his poetic manner, for though the poems retain their emotional intensity and conceptual complexity, he was to abandon the rigorous discipline of traditional forms in favour of long rambling monologues, and his language was to become less recondite and a more direct expression of his feelings. This new phase of his career begins with *Escrito a ciegas* (1961), a long poetic epistle in which he struggles to take stock of his life. He confesses to a loss of confidence in his previous poetic beliefs. His life as a poet was devoted to the pursuit of a higher state of being, but though he still yearns for it, that is a state in which he no longer has faith and as a result poetry has become for him nothing more than an expression of the pain and frustration which life causes him:

> ¿Qué es la Palabra
> Sino vario y vano grito?
>
> (What is the Word
> But a varying, vain scream?)

For his life he has come to see as empty and meaningless, simply "una palabra más" (one more word) in a world made up of "nadas acumuladas" (accumulated nothings), a world that is "sombra apenas de apetito de algo" (barely the shadow of the appetite for something). With a tone of weary disillusionment which irony saves from lapsing into morbid self-pity, he presents himself as man who no longer believes in or understands anything but merely soldiers on as best he can:

> No soy ninguno que sabe.
> Soy el uno que ya no cree
> Ni en el hombre,
> Ni en la mujer,
> Ni en la casa de un solo piso,
> Ni en el panqueque con miel.
> No soy más que una palabra
> Volada de la sien,
> Y que procura compadecerse
> Y anidar en algún alto tal vez
> De la primavera lóbrega
> Del ser
> No me preguntes más,
> Que ya no sé ...

(I'm not anyone who knows.
I'm the one who no longer believes
Either in man
Or in woman
Or in the single-storey house
Or in the pancake with honey.
I'm no more than a word
Exploded from the brain,
And trying to fit in
And to nest perhaps on some height
Of the gloomy spring
Of being.
Don't ask me any more,
For I don't know any longer ...)

However, the most important work of this phase of Adán's poetry
is *La mano desasida (Canto a Machu Picchu)* (1964) which, like its
sequel *La piedra absoluta* (1966), is a long monologue addressed to
the ancient Inca mountain city of Machu Picchu, in which he
discourses on the mystery of the human condition. The apparent
shapelessness of the poem corresponds to that of life itself and it
continually ebbs and flows as it builds up a series of oppositions
between transience and permanence, transcendence and contingency
and voices conflicting attitudes of irony, euphoria and despair.
Tension is always present in the oscillation between positive
assertions and statements of hesitancy and doubt, and paradox and
other conceptual conceits are again the main devices used by Adán to
express complex levels of thought and feeling, while reiterative
enumeration translates the impassioned nature of this poetry and
reiterative interrogation the urgency behind the poet's quest for
meaning in a world of confusion. Machu Picchu is a multi-faceted
symbol which ultimately represents life itself in all its complexity. At
times the ancient Inca city and the mountain on which it stands seem
to embody a solid durability which makes the poet acutely aware of
human mortality and insignificance, and at others the stones of this
ruined and abandoned city are viewed as a monument to death's
sway over life. Sometimes this marvel created by the hand of man
seems to represent man's striving to rise above the limits of his
human condition, but its ruins also mirror human imperfection.
Nonetheless, it offers hope and encouragement to the poet's deepest
longings by seeming to represent the absolute, to be a manifestation
of the infinite on earth, but the recurrent motif of the vainly grasping
hand which gives the book its title indicates that the infinite remains
stubbornly beyond his reach, and on other occasions he dismisses

Machu Picchu as just another mountain onto which he has projected his desires or repudiates the kind of eternity it represents as being an inhuman denial of life. Yet Machu Picchu, poised as it appears to be on the frontier betweeen earthly reality and the infinite, seems to hold the key to ultimate truth. However, what that truth is remains undiscovered. Though the meaning of life seems to be contained within the stones of Machu Picchu, the poet is never able to decipher it, for it tantalises him with the promise of a revelation that never materialises and where he hoped for luminous certainty he finds only pervasive ambiguity:

> Eres la duda cierta y la misma vida,
> Eres lo humano y macizo de cielo y nube,
> Eres lo infinito que se está,
> Y eres la palabra que huye.

> (You are certain doubt and life itself,
> You are humanity and solidity of sky and cloud,
> You are the infinite that remains,
> And you are the word that flees.)

Ultimately, therefore, Machu Picchu stands as a symbol of the insoluble enigma of life.

The last phase of Adán's career is marked by a return to the sonnet form in the collections *Mi Darío* (1966-67) and *Diario de poeta* (1966-73). These poems continue to express the central theme of Adán's work, a desperate craving for the absolute, but they are dominated, above all, by feelings of futility, solitude and despair and by an anguished awareness of the inevitability of death. Indeed, it would seem that Adán reverted to the sonnet form as a means of imposing an order onto the emotional chaos that characterises this final stage of his poetry. On the whole the poems do not contain the dense symbolism of his earlier verse but tend to be a more direct expression of his growing sense of anguish in face of life, and a weary sense of frustration and disillusionment is often conveyed by means of a vocabulary which emphasises the mundane and squalid aspects of daily life. Thus, in one poem, the spiritual failure of his life is expressed by an image depicting his soul as a drunken, degraded pariah:

> ¡Todo tan simple y trágico, Rubén ... el alma mía,
> La que mea tal vez y golpea a otra puerta
> Con el golpe redondo del ebrio que se guía!

> (Everything so simple and tragic, Rubén ... my soul,
> It that pisses perhaps and knocks at another door
> With the emphatic knock of a drunk seeking directions!)

This tormented experience of life is accompanied by a decreasing ability to understand himself or the world around him and by a growing realisation that wisdom limits itself to an acceptance of death as the only ultimate truth:

> ¡Ay, cuánto no sé nada y me abandono
> A discurso de necio ... de persona
> Que dice que lo sabe, y desatina! ...
>
> ¿Qué otro saber que de lección divina
> De vivo que a su muerte se abandona ...
> Seña y paso de despaciosa ruina! ...
>
> (Alas, how much I know nothing and abandon myself
> To the discourse of the idiot ... of the person
> Who says he knows, and talks nonsense! ...
>
> What other wisdom but that of the divine lesson
> Of the living man who abandons himself to his death ...
> Token and gait of slow, protracted ruin! ...)

Among the new generation of poets who emerged in the forties and foremost exponents of this type of poetry are Jorge Eduardo Eielson and Javier Sologuren. A painter and sculptor as well as a poet, Jorge Eduardo Eielson (b. 1924) produced a series of slim volumes of verse from 1942 through to the mid-fifties, an output of varied range and evolving style that demonstrates a permanent quest for a renovation of poetic forms.[2] His is a work totally detached from the local reality of his native country. Symptomatic of that detachment is the fact that since the late forties he has been resident in Europe and that for a long time much of his work remained unpublished and unknown. That detachment is manifest in *Reinos* (1944), a work in which the richness of the language, the musical fluidity of the verse and the creation of new perspectives by means of unusual yet seemingly natural images combine to make it one of the most impressive collections produced in Peru. Here the rural settings, the refined vocabulary and a predilection for classical devices such as hyperbaton introduce us into a poetic universe that is literary and timeless. Needless to say, this is combined with contemporary techniques to

---

[2] See Jorge Eduardo Eielson, *Poesía escrita* (INC, 1976); *Noche oscura del cuerpo* (Paris: Altaforte, 1983). See also Abelardo Oquendo, "Eielson: remontando la poesía de papel" (interview), *Hueso Húmero*, 10 (1981), 3-10; Julio Ortega, *Figuración de la persona*, pp. 172-77; José Miguel Oviedo, "Jorge Eduardo Eielson o el abismo de la negación", *Cuadernos Hispanoamericanos*, 417 (1985), 191-96; Roberto Paoli, "Exilio vital y exilio verbal en Eielson", in *Estudios sobre literatura peruana contemporánea*, pp. 103-13; Eduardo Urdanivia Bertarelli, "Los *Reinos* de Jorge Eduardo Eielson", *RevCrit*, 13 (1981), 71-79.

create a poetry that is both personal and part of the modern Western tradition.

The world-view which emerges from these sixteen poems is a bleakly pessimistic one. Thus, the opening poem, a modern-day version of the myth of Adam and Eve, unfolds not in paradise but in a world that has been blighted, seemingly cursed by the ire of God:

> Sobre los puros valles, eléctricos sotos,
> Tras las ciudades que un ángel diluye
> En el cielo, cargado de heces sombrías y santas,
> El joven oscuro defiende a la joven.
> Contemplan allí al verde, arcaico Señor
> De los cedros, reinar furtivo en sus telas,
> Guiar la nube esmeralda y sonora del mar
> Por el bosque, o besar los abetos de Dios,
> Orinados por los ángeles, la luna y las estrellas:
> Manzanas de amor en la yedra de muerte
> Ve el joven, solemnes y áureos cubiertos
> En la fronda maldita, que un ciervo de vidrio estremece.
> La joven, que nada es ya en èl polvo sombrío,
> Sino un cielo puro y lejano, recuerda su tumba,
> Llueve e irrumpe en los brazos del joven
> En un rayo muy suave de santa o paloma.

> (Over pure valleys and electric copses,
> Behind cities adulterated by an angel
> In a sky laden with sombre, sacred scum,
> The anonymous young man defends his young woman.
> There they behold the green, archaic Lord
> Of the cedars reigning furtively on his canvases,
> Guiding the sea's sonorous, emerald cloud
> Through the forest, or kissing God's firs,
> Urinated upon by the angels, the moon and the stars:
> Apples of love on the ivy of death
> Sees the young man, solemn, golden meals
> In the accursed frond stirred by a glass deer.
> The young woman, nothing now in the sombre dust
> but a pure, distant sky, remembers her tomb,
> Rains and bursts into the arms of the young man
> In a gentle ray of saint or dove.)

This image of a blighted world would seem to reflect the tragedy that afflicted the poet's own life — the death of people close to him, which is a theme of other poems in the collection — and the horrific destruction wreaked by the Second World War, which is the theme of the prose poem *Antígona* (1945). As the dust clouds of destruction hang over the world the ancient lord of the forest, the pagan spirit of life, now reigns only furtively and the terrified human couple live on the defensive. The poem ends, however, with an affirmation of life as the archetypal couple rebel against the condition the world imposes upon them and seek salvation in each other's arms.

The affirmation of life in a desolate world is perhaps the central theme of *Reinos* and, with love, art is viewed as one of the ways in which man can assert himself over the forces of chaos and death. "Parque para un hombre dormido" introduces the solitary figure of the poet in a bleak winter landscape where he suffers the anguish of his human condition, aware of his essential loneliness and of his puniness and vulnerability in an alien world:

> Cerebro de la noche, ojo dorado
> De cascabel que tiemblas en el pino, escuchad:
> Yo soy el que llora y escribe en el invierno.
>
> Palomas y níveas gradas húndense en mi memoria,
> Y ante mi cabeza de sangre pensando
> Moradas de piedra abren sus plumas, estremecidas.
> Aún caído, entre begonias de hielo, muevo
> El hacha de la lluvia y blandos frutos
> Y hojas desveladas hiélanse a mi golpe.
> Amo mi cráneo como a un balcón
> Doblado sobre un negro precipicio del Señor.
>
> Labro los astros a mi lado ¡oh noche!
> Y en la mesa de las tierras el poema
> Que rueda entre los muertos y, encendido, los corona.
> Pues por todo va mi sombra tal la gloria
> De hueso, cera y humus que me postra, majestuoso,
> Sobre el bello césped, en los dioses abrasado.
>
> Amo, así, este cráneo mío, en su ceniza, como al mundo
> En cuyos fríos parques la eternidad es el mismo
> Hombre de mármol que vela en una estatua
> O que se tiende, oscuro y sin amor, sobre la yerba.
>
> (Brain of night, golden eye
> trembling like a bell on the pine, listen:
> I am the one who weeps and writes in winter.
>
> Doves and snowy terraces sink into my memory
> and, before my head of thinking blood,
> dwellings of stone open their feathers with a shiver.
> Even fallen, drowsing among frosty begonias,
> I wield the rain's axe and tender fruit
> and restless leaves freeze at my touch;
> I love my skull bent thus like a balcony
> perched over one of the Lord's black precipices.
>
> I fashion the stars at my side, oh night!,
> and on the table of the lands the poem

that rolls around among the dead and bursts into flames to
    crown them,
for my shadow goes everywhere like the glory
of bone, wax and humus which prostrates me in majesty
on the beautiful turf, burning in the fire of the gods.

Thus do I love this skull of mine, in its ashes, as I love the world
in whose cold parks eternity is the selfsame
man of marble who keeps watch on a statue
or stretches out, obscure and loveless, on the grass.)

Yet in his consciousness he possesses a power to raise himself above
his condition of weak mortal of flesh and blood. His mind is able to
absorb the world around him, to take possession of it, to control and
reshape it, and, like God gazing on the original void, to create order
out of chaos. Thus, by means of the poetic imagination the poet joins
the ranks of the gods by creating cosmic harmony out of desolation
and by fixing that qualitatively eternal moment forever in his art,
symbolised by the marble statue in the park.

If *Reinos* is very much the creation of an alienated intellectual
withdrawn into a private world of his own, Eielson's work subsequently evolved towards a greater involvement in the everyday
reality of the world around him. Though something of this evolution
is evident in *Bacanal* (1946) and *Doble diamante* (1947), his last two
books written in Lima, it is most marked in the poetry produced in
Europe and particularly in *Habitación en Roma* (1951-54), his most
ambitious collection after *Reinos*. In many ways Eielson's European
experience seems to have been similar to that of Vallejo. In Rome he
was to know the loneliness of life in an alien city and the hardship of
the daily struggle for life and he was brought face to face with the
spectacle of human squalor and misery. He became acutely aware,
too, of the extent to which man lived at an animal level, dominated by
physical needs and appetites. His work is marked by an acute
existential anguish in the midst of which he retains a desperate
longing to transcend the limitations of his human condition.
Paralleling this development, the poetry becomes more confessional
in tone and looser in structure, with a style that is more simple and
direct and a language that is more colloquial and less literary. All of
this is exemplified in "Azul ultramar", where his own personal
situation is identified with that of the Italian capital. The poem opens
with an appeal to the ancient god of the Mediterranean to grant him a
life that is more than mere physical existence and to restore Rome to
its former glory as a spiritual and cultural centre. He feels trapped in
a chaotic, senseless world where he is relentlessly pursued by the dark

night of despair and his attempts to escape it merely lead him into the error of seeking an illusory spiritual fulfilment in the pleasures of the flesh. His search for his own authentic self is linked to his attempt to discover the true soul of Rome, but the Rome that was and all that it represented are buried beneath the ugliness and pollution of a modern metropolis that enshrines the soulless materialism of Western capitalism:

esta ciudad con casas	(this city with houses
con restaurantes	with restaurants
con automóviles	with cars
con fábricas y cinemas	with factories and cinemas
teatros y cementerios	theatres and cemeteries
y escandalosos	and outrageous
avisos luminosos	luminous signs
para anunciar a dios con insistencia	insistently advertising god
con deslumbrantes criaturas	with dazzling creatures
de papel policromado	of multicoloured paper
que devoran coca-cola	guzzling coca-cola
bien helada	well chilled
con espantosos remates	with appalling sales
de vestidos usados	of second-hand clothes
sexo y acción	sex and action
heroísmo y pasión	heroism and passion
technicolor por doquier	technicolor all over the place
con elegantes	with elegant
señores que sonríen y sonríen	gentlemen who smile and smile
y operarios que trabajan y trabajan	and factory hands who work and work
con miserables avenidas	with miserable avenues
que huelen a ropa sucia	that smell of dirty clothes
y miserable ropa sucia	and miserable dirty clothes
que huele a puro mármol	that smell the very same as marble
(tal y cual como tu cuerpo	[just like your body
criatura	child
fabuloso bajo el ruido de mil klaxons	fabulous beneath the din of a thousand horns
y motores encendidos)	and revving engines])

In "Poema para ser leído de pie en el autobús entre la Puerta Flamínea y el Tritone" he comes to feel the futility of writing poetry. Persuaded of the empty vanity of a life that never rises above the elemental humdrum of day-to-day existence, he has nothing positive left to offer his readers. All that remains is his persistent aspiration to a reality superior to that which the world affords him:

pero de nada sirve	(but it's utterly useless
de nada sirve escribir	utterly useless to write
siempre sobre sí mismo	always about oneself
o de lo que no se tiene	or about what one doesn't have
o se recuerda solamente	or only remembers
o se desea solamente	or only desires
yo no tengo nada	I have nothing
nada repito	nothing I repeat
nada que ofreceros	nothing to offer you
nada bueno sin duda	nothing good undoubtedly
ni nada malo tampoco	and nothing bad either
nada en la mirada	nothing in my gaze
nada en la garganta	nothing in my throat
nada entre los brazos	nothing in my arms
nada en los bolsillos	nothing in my pockets
ni en el pensamiento	nor in my mind
sino mi corazón sonando alto alto	except my heart booming loud loud
entre las nubes	among the clouds
como un cañonazo	like a shell from a cannon)

Another feature of Eielson's later poetry is experimentation with forms of expression in an attempt to transcend the limitations of language. Each of the poems of *Tema y variaciones* (1950) is an example of such experimentation. "Solo de sol", for instance, uses alliteration to exploit the sound of words and create a play of associations. "Variaciones en torno a un vaso de agua" consists of six couplets which repeat the same words in varying order. Eielson also experiments with the visual possibilities of the text by creating what he calls "word sculptures", the best example being "Poesía en forma de pájaro" which reproduces pictorially the image of a bird. This experimentation appears to have been accompanied by a progressive loss of confidence in language as a means of expression, a crisis clearly illustrated by the last poem of *Mutatis mutandis* (1954):

> escribo algo
> algo todavía
> algo más aún
> añado palabras   pájaros
> hojas secas   viento
> borro palabras nuevamente
> borro pájaros   hojas secas   viento
> escribo algo todavía
> vuelvo a añadir palabras
> palabras otra vez
> palabras aún
> además pájaros   hojas secas   viento

```
borro palabras nuevamente
borro pájaros        hojas secas      viento
borro todo por fin
no escribo nada
```

(I write something
something more
something more still
I add words   birds
dry leaves   wind
I erase words again
I erase birds   dry leaves   wind
I write something more
again I add words
more words
still more words
birds as well   dry leaves   wind
I erase words again
I erase birds   dry leaves   wind
finally I erase everything
I don't write anything)

Eielson's poetic career virtually came to an end with that volume. For though he was to continue his formal experiments in five brief collections, they are slight works of dubious merit and thereafter he abandoned poetry to devote himself to the visual arts. The subsequent publication of *Noche oscura del cuerpo* (1983) does not, it seems, represent a breaking of his poetic silence, for the poems appear to belong to the fifties, being similar in manner and tone to those of *Habitación en Roma*. Parodying the mysticism of San Juan de la Cruz, the book shows the poet trapped in the dark night of existential nihilism, frustrated in his yearning for sexual union and verbal communication and regarding living and writing poetry as naught but masturbation.

Javier Sologuren (b. 1921) has played a major role in stimulating poetic activity in Peru through his work as a publisher and editor.[3] He is also one of his country's outstanding poets and since the publication of his first volume in 1944 his poetry has shown a steady and consistent development, as is indicated by the retention of the title *Vida continua* for three successive editions of his collected works.[4] His poetic production is not large, but it is characterised by a

---

[3] Many young Peruvian poets were first published in editions produced by La Rama Florida, an enterprise founded and directed by Sologuren. As editor he has compiled anthologies of Peruvian poetry.

[4] See Javier Sologuren, *Vida continua* (La Rama Florida/Biblioteca Universitaria, 1966); *Vida continua* (INC, 1971); *Folios de el Enamorado y la Muerte* (Caracas: Monte

polished refinement born of a rigorous artistic consciousness. His early poetry is that of a man who turns his back on the real world to withdraw into solitary contemplation in the quest for essential reality. Thus, the title of his first volume, *El morador* (1944), defines him as an inhabitant of a region on the margin of the world, one which, as the poetic imagination strips objects of their contingency and lays bare their essence, transforms itself into a realm of absolute beauty outside time. The poet

> alcanza su motivo y su paisaje
> en la linde del mundo (en incipiente
> aventura del párpado yacente)
> viéndolo todo, y todo sin su traje.

> (attains his motif and his landscape
> at the world's boundary [in incipient
> adventure of the recumbent eyelid]
> seeing all, and all without its clothing)

The formal perfection of the poems of this volume, achieved by a masterly use of classical verse forms and metres and by the exquisiteness of the language, mirrors the perfection of that ideal reality. A typical example is the title-poem:

> Resplandeciente umbela el sueño vierte
> entre perlas que el légamo detiene;
> en leve ascenso de la tez se cierne
> la tiniebla de seda de los peces.

> Desde esa fuente que silencia el quieto
> peso de la marea: caed, caed,
> lentos caed glomérulos, desiertos
> seres bermejos entre tenue verde.

> Ved perfectas arenas los reflejos
> de yedra en el silencio; sedimentos
> de transparentes huesos en la piedra.

> Ved el entero helecho en las paredes
> de yacentes murciélagos, y ved
> que en ese pez el tiempo se nivela.

> (Fantasy casts a resplendent umbel
> among pearls stuck fast in the slime;

Avila, 1980); *Vida continua (1945-1980)* (Mexico City: Premià, 1981). See also Abelardo Oquendo, "Sologuren: la poesía y la vida", *Amaru*, 5 (1968), 56-61/reprinted as prologue to *Vida continua* (INC, 1971); Julio Ortega, *Figuración de la persona*, pp. 177-82; Roberto Paoli, "Palabra y silencio en las texturas de Sologuren", in *Estudios sobre literatura peruana contemporánea*, pp. 113-23; Luis Hernán Ramírez, *Estilo y poesía de Javier Sologuren* (Biblioteca Universitaria, 1967).

in a slight heightening of the complexion
hovers the silken shadow of the fishes.

From that fountain silenced by the placid
heaviness of the tide: fall, fall,
slowly fall, glomerules, red beings
isolated among subdued green.

Behold, perfect sands, the reflections
of ivy in the silence; sediments
of transparent bones in the stone.

Behold the sturdy fern in the walls
of recumbent bats, and behold
how in that fish time is levelled.)

The atmosphere is one of absolute peace and tranquillity, a perfect
calm far removed from the hustle and bustle and disturbing passions
of the human world. The landscape is completely under the control
of the poetic imagination which, in the opening lines, intervenes to
rearrange it and subsequently, through imperatives, directs the
actions of its various components. It is, too, a landscape in which the
laws of the everyday world are abolished, so that fountains can spray
glomerules and silence reflect ivy, a landscape perceived as total
harmony in which time comes to a standstill.

Though *Detenimientos* (1947) reveals an evolution in the direction
of freer verse forms, including prose poems, Sologuren's poetics
remains essentially the same in this second book. As the title
indicates, the volume celebrates those moments when time freezes
and essential reality is glimpsed by the poetic vision in some
apparently trivial phenomenon of the surrounding world. The
philosophy underlying the poems would seem to be that summed up
in the words of Keats:

> "Beauty is truth, truth beauty," — that is all
> Ye know on earth, and all ye need to know.

Thus, in "Morir" the poet feels that it would be sweet to die at just
such a moment:

Morir viendo el sol a través de gaseosas laderas.
Morir como una rosa cortada al fuego de la noche.
Morir bajo una lluvia de sedosas escamas.
Morir en las fragantes olas de unas sienes sensibles.
Morir en esta ciudadela esculpida en una desierta mañana.
Morir llevado por el mar que respira contra los muros de mi casa.
Morir en una súbita burbuja de amor a punto de no ser más que
     vacío [. . .]

Morir sintiendo que en la tierra aún son hermosas la sangre, el
    desorden y el sueño.

(To die seeing the sun across gaseous hillsides.
To die like a rose clipped in the fire of night.
To die beneath a rainfall of silken flakes.
To die in the fragrant waves of sensitive temples.
To die in this citadel sculptured in a desolate morning.
To die carried off by the sea that breathes against the walls of my
    house.
To die in a sudden bubble of love on the point of being no more
    than emptiness [...]
To die feeling that on earth blood, disorder and dreams are still
    beautiful.)

Estancias (1960) marks an important change in Sologuren's work
in that the solitary poet now emerges from his isolation and his
poetry opens out to embrace a world it had previously shunned. The
key to this new outward-looking attitude would seem to be love. The
last two poems of the volume celebrate the love between man and
woman, who discover that "the world is companionship", and the
fruit of their union, the sons through whom the poet rediscovers the
child's trusting acceptance of the world and his innocent sense of
illusion in face of life. Significantly, the poems of this volume have
the form of dialogues in which the poet enters into communication
with the elements, cosmic forces, the faculties of the human spirit, the
diverse manifestations of the world which he now embraces. One
such dialogue is addressed to the sea, symbol of the elemental force of
life in rhythm with which his own blood pulsates:

Giro, Mar, sobre tu aliento.
De ti salí, hacia ti vuelvo.
Soy tu fábula, tu espuma;
y tu anhelo, tu sueño
indescifrable
me palpita en la marea
de la sangre.

(I rotate, Sea, on your respiration.
From you I emerged, to you I return.
I am your fable, your foam;
and your yearning,
your indecipherable dream,
palpitates in the tide
of my blood.)

However, as in Sologuren's previous work, the reality transmitted by
these poems is one which has been distilled by the poetic vision, so

that the world which the poet embraces is one which has been disembodied and reduced to its essences, and this is reflected in the concision of the poems and in the language, which has now shed all preciosity in favour of an austere simplicity. What is conveyed is a vision of harmonious world in which everything has its place. Thus, the tree of poem 9 is evoked as an altar where the world communes in cosmic harmony:

> Arbol, altar de ramas,
> de pájaros, de hojas,
> de sombra rumorosa;
> en tu ofrenda callada,
> en tu sereno anhelo,
> hay soledad poblada
> de luz de tierra y cielo.

> (Tree, altar of branches,
> of birds, of leaves,
> of murmuring shade;
> in your silent offering,
> in your serene yearning,
> there is solitude populated
> by light of earth and sky.)

However, already in *Otoño, endechas* (1959) a note of anguish had begun to creep into Sologuren's work in poems like "No, todo no ha de ser ceniza de mi nombre" and "Poesía", and that note was to become more pronounced in *La gruta de la sirena* (1961), particularly in "Tema garcileño" and "Te alisas, amor, las alas . . .". The best of his later work are long meditative poems in which he attempts to reconcile his desire for harmony with the disturbing realities which obtrude more and more on his optimistic vision. *Recinto* (1967) is built around an extended metaphor in which archeological exca-vation symbolises man's striving to decipher the mystery of life and the secret of what lies beyond the grave, and life and art are viewed as being governed by the impulse to transcend human limitations and give lasting meaning to mortal existence. The concluding section of the poem comes to an acceptance of existence as an endless process in which that impulse is the driving force of a cycle which continually revolves on itself without purpose or transcendence as life and death ceaselessly feed on each other. This view of life is reflected in the circular pattern of the poem, whose last lines echo those of the beginning, and the chaotic enumeration of the concluding section reduces all existence to the same ultimately inconsequential level. Yet there is a calm equanimity in the poet's acceptance of this state of

affairs and if his final words imply a recognition of the meaninglessness of his life and his poetry, they also imply a willingness to
continue to embrace both with undiminished enthusiasm:

> porque todo es origen
>
> nuestro polvo nuestro oro
> el crujiente muerto y vivo
> hacinamiento de las hojas
> el brazo tendido hacia la vida
> las aguas hostiles de la charca [. . .]
> las cien mil hojas secas
> y el estar decidido
> a extraer de ellas el poema
> y todo oscilando
> rodando
> circulando
>
> (for everything is origin
>
> our dust our gold
> the creaking dead and living
> pile of the leaves
> the arm stretched out towards life
> the pool's hostile waters [. . .]
> the hundred thousand dry leaves
> and the resolve
> to extract from them the poem
> and everything flickering
> moving
> circulating)

"La hora", another long reflective piece on the human condition,
shows a new awareness of and concern at the realities of the modern
age and the poet's anguish is exacerbated by the blind folly of a
technologically advanced humanity seemingly bent on self-destruction:

> asistimos a una apoteósica danza de la muerte
> al espectáculo del siglo
> con comparsas masivas
> y coreografías de inenarrable pesadilla
> con nubes de cercenado esplendor
> pero eficazmente radiactivas
> los megatones miden
> sus méritos artísticos
>
> (we're witnessing an apotheosic dance of death
> the spectacle of the century
> with massive parades
> and inexpressibly nightmarish choreographies
> with clouds of stunted splendour

> but efficiently radioactive
> the megatons measure
> their artistic merit)

Yet, in spite of everything, Sologuren refuses to despair and this, the last poem of the 1981 edition of *Vida continua*, ends with a tenacious affirmation of faith in man and life:

> sin embargo no entierro la esperanza
>
> (yet I don't bury hope)

Two other poets were to continue the same poetic tradition. Leopoldo Chariarse (b. 1928) began writing in the forties and published his first book, *Los ríos de la noche*, in 1952.[5] However, following his departure for Europe in that same year, he virtually disappeared from view and remained relatively unknown until the publication of his collected poetry in 1975 in an edition that included two new books, *La cena en el jardín* (1972) and *Los sonetos de Spoleto* (1973). Now recognised as an important poet, he went on to confirm his reputation with *Himnos* (1984). Thematically Chariarse's range is limited, but stylistically he is something of a virtuoso. His work is characterised not only by a progressive perfecting of his technique but also by a variety of forms and manners. Thus, fairly clear and simple songs alternate with conceptually dense and complex compositions, while the traditional sonnets of *Los sonetos de Spoleto* stand in contrast to the free-verse poems of *La cena en el jardín*, which abandon punctuation and experiment with spatial arrangements. Above all, Chariarse's early musical training manifests itself in the subtle, unobtrusive musicality of his verse.

In the main Chariarse shuns geographical and historical references and introduces us into a landscape that is literary and atemporal. Markedly elegiac in tone, his poetry harps back to a lost paradise in the form of a romantic idyll of adolescence, one of the most poignant expressions of his sense of loss at his inexplicable expulsion from that youthful paradise being the title-poem of *La cena en el jardín*. The bulk of his work, in fact, is made up of love poems addressed to an unnamed woman, who would seem to symbolise an unworldly ideal of beauty and communion briefly glimpsed before being snatched away to leave the poet stranded in the lonely alienation of everyday reality. Some contrast the short-lived fulfilment of the past with the

---

[5] See Leopoldo Chariarse, *La cena en el jardín* (INC, 1975); *Himnos* (separata de *Lienzo*, Univ. de Lima, 1984).

desolation of the present. Others conceive the idyll as remaining intact and capable of being conjured up and re-experienced by the poetic imagination despite the separation of the lovers in time and space:

> Del vacío de la mirada surgen
> tus rasgos y un camino en la noche
>   por donde voy y vengo buscándote
> en las tinieblas vibra el olor de sándalo
> de tus cabellos y oigo tu voz
> y la inmensidad de tus ojos
> se abre ante mí creciente
>   con el dulzor de lejanos días
> y si de algo me sirvió el ser poeta
> si cada objeto se hizo instrumento en mis manos
> de música para alcanzar tu oído
>   fue a fin de que al fin vinieras
> tú que te acercas y alejas con el secreto
> de las palabras no dichas
> mi laúd y tu silencio

> (From the void of my gaze rise up
> your features and a road in the night
>   along which I come and go seeking you
> in the darkness vibrates the sandalwood perfume
> of your hair and I hear your voice
> and the immensity of your eyes
> opens before me growing
>   with the sweetness of distant days
> and if being a poet was of any use to me
> if every object became in my hands an instrument
> for making music to reach your ears
>   it was so that at last you would come
> you who approach and recede with the secret
> of words unspoken
> my lute and your silence)

In the poetry written in Europe a second major theme that comes to the fore is that of a rootless journeying and of a restless questing for some ineffable ideal. Yet in the end that ideal is invariably linked with the long-lost beloved and the poet's quest is revealed as another way of seeking to recover that lost paradise. The key to Chariarse's whole work is perhaps provided by "Tithonus a la aurora", the magnificent closing poem of *Los ríos de la noche*. Here the poet sees himself as being punished by the gods for the sin of wishing to be more than human, condemned to be eternally haunted by the image of an impossible ideal inspired by his erstwhile beloved but which no

earthly woman, not even she, can live up to, an ideal too absolute to
be attainable on earth:

> Hace ya muchos años que vivo
> y que me duele tu mirada en los ojos.
> Año tras año sin descanso la lluvia me roe,
> ¡oh, si pudiera ahogarme bajo la dulce tierra,
> bajo su cabellera oscura, de árboles poblada!
> Pero tú me abandonas en brazos del viento
> que me envuelve en aromas nuevos
> a mí, el irremediablemente lejano,
> el sombrío y olvidado, de cuyos escombros se alimentan las
>   horas
> como cuervos venidos para la venganza divina [. . .]
> Tú amas a los mortales. ¿Cómo puedes amarme
> a mí, que renuncié a su efímera condición adorable
> para hacerme un residuo de eterna servidumbre?

> (It's many years now that I've been living
> and that your gaze has been hurting my eyes.
> Year after year without respite the rain gnaws me,
> oh, if I could but smother myself beneath the sweet earth,
> beneath its dark hair, covered in trees!
> But you abandon me to the arms of the wind
> which wraps me in new aromas,
> me, the irremediably distant,
> the sombre and forgotten one, on whose debris the hours feed
> like crows come to wreak divine vengeance [. . .]
> You love mortals. How can you love me,
> me who renounced their ephemeral adorable condition
> to make of myself a residue of eternal servitude?

Like Chariarse, Francisco Bendezú (b. 1928) began writing in the
forties, though he did not publish in book form until the sixties.[6]
Though a committed communist who suffered imprisonment and
exile as a result of his political militancy, Bendezú has always
shunned politics in his verse. It is no accident that his poetry abounds
in allusions to the plastic arts and that his major work, *Cantos* (1971),
is a magnificently produced volume including five colour repro-
ductions of paintings by Giorgio de Chirico, for he conceives art as
the creation of a timeless ideal reality of absolute beauty beyond the
imperfections of the ordinary world. The poem which perhaps best

---

[6] See Francisco Bendezú, *Arte Menor* (Escuela Nac. de Bellas Artes, 1960); *Los años*
(La Rama Florida, 1961; 2nd [definitive] ed., Ministerio de Educación Pública del
Perú, 1961); *Cantos* (La Rama Florida, 1971). See also Roberto Paoli, "El paroxismo
verbal de Francisco Bendezú", in *Estudios sobre literatura peruana contemporánea*, pp.
160-62.

typifies his work is "Nostalgia de lo infinito", a poetic transposition
of one of Chirico's paintings, in which reiterative enumeration
translates the painter's — and the poet's — striving to stretch
upwards beyond the bounds of the real world to the infinite:

> Más allá de la distancia,
> más allá del polvo, más allá del cielo,
> tus banderolas deliran. Más allá del viento
> y la luna indescifrable de la nieve.
> Más allá de marismas azules y acuarios inundados [...]
> Más allá del polen.
> Más allá de las cenizas.
> En la nada.

> (Beyond the distance,
> beyond the dust, beyond the sky,
> your banderoles flutter deliriously. Beyond the wind
> and the indecipherable moon of the snow.
> Beyond blue marshes and flooded aquaria [...]
> Beyond the pollen.
> Beyond the ashes.
> In the void.)

The lines quoted illustrate one of the basic features of Bendezú's
style, the development of a metaphor by means of an anaphoric
scheme which gradually intensifies its sense. Another is his liking for
recondite vocabulary, of which his work is a veritable treasury. The
combined effect is to work a kind of magical enchantment which
transports us from everyday reality into a realm of mystery and
beauty. Yet both features also point to another affinity with the
plastic arts, for this is a poetry that treats words and images as
beautiful objects to be lovingly caressed and savoured with pleasure.

The central theme of Bendezú's poetry is the poet's yearning for
the unattainable woman worshipped from a distance, a recurring
figure who both represents a real hunger for companionship and
stands as a symbol of the ideal enunciated in "Nostalgia de lo
infinito". In "Muchachas de Roma" the unattainable woman takes
the form of all the girls whom the poet admires from afar as they pass
him in the street, and a recurring and emblematic image is that of the
statue, a symbol of the object of his erotic desires and of frustrated
union. Out of that unsatisfied longing Bendezú has created compositions of rare beauty, but poems like "Oda a la tarde" betray the
acute loneliness that underlies his work and weariness with living
vicariously is expressed in "Súplica", a desperate plea for the woman
of his dreams to materialise in the real world:

¡Oh, sal de los espejos,
reverdece en las sábanas de lino,
atraviesa los tabiques y los muros,
aparécete de pronto en las más ciegas estancias
o el balcón más desolado!

(Oh, come out of the mirrors,
flourish again in the linen sheets,
pass through partitions and walls,
appear suddenly in the darkest rooms
or the most desolate balcony!)

Often ranked among the so-called "pure poets" are figures like Sebastián Salazar Bondy and Blanca Varela for whom poetry is essentially an expression of their personal preoccupations and view of life. However, while such a classification does serve to distinguish them from the politically committed poets of the period, it is erroneous and misleading and it would be more appropriate to regard their work as being existential in character. For whereas the poets hitherto discussed view poetry as the pursuit of an alternative reality, the work of both these artists is very much rooted in the real world and in everyday life. Indeed, in "Otro reino" Salazar explicitly distances himself from poets who claim that their kingdom is not of this world, and in "La vie en rose" he states that life

... es lo único que verdaderamente me interesa
pues es más perfecta que los sueños.

(... is the only thing which truly interests me
for it's more perfect than dreams.)

An apt description of the poetry of Sebastián Salazar Bondy (1924-65) is provided by the title of the volume *Confidencia en alta voz* (1960), for his is a confessional poetry, somewhat in the manner of the Argentinian Jorge Luis Borges by whom he seems to have been influenced, a poetry in which he gives testimony of his personal encounter with the world.[7] His early books, *Voz desde la vigilia* (1944), *Cuaderno de la persona oscura* (1946) and *Máscara que duerme* (1949), suffer from an over-mannered and stilted use of language, but from *Los ojos del pródigo* (1951) onwards he discovered a voice of his own, developing a simpler, more natural, almost conversational style which was to find its best expression in the posthumously published *El tacto de la araña*.

---

[7] See Sebastián Salazar Bondy, *Poemas*, vol. III of *Obras* (Moncloa, 1967). See also Luis Loayza, "La poesía de Sebastián Salazar Bondy", *Amaru*, 6 (1968), 71-76; Javier Sologuren, *Tres poetas, tres obras*, pp. 75-105.

The tone of Salazar's poetry is set by the poem "Confidencia en alta voz":

> Pertenezco a una raza sentimental,
> a una patria fatigada por sus penas,
> a una tierra cuyas flores culminan al anochecer,
> pero amo mis desventuras,
> tengo mi orgullo, doy vivas a la vida bajo este cielo mortal
> y soy como una nave que avanza hacia una isla de fuego.

> (I belong to a sentimental race,
> to a country worn out by its troubles,
> to a land whose flowers reach full bloom at nightfall,
> but I love my misfortunes,
> I have my pride, I give three cheers for life beneath this mortal sky
> and I'm like a ship advancing towards an island of fire.)

This is a poetry that is unashamedly sentimental in character, bearing witness to his strong emotional attachment to the people and places who make up his world, and the values it celebrates are above all those of love, friendship, goodwill among human beings. Many of his poems are love poems. Others are nostalgic reminiscences of his childhood home or tender evocations of his own family. Others express his love of Lima and Peru. Yet this is not to say that Salazar looks at the world through rose-tinted spectacles. Indeed, his dominant tone is perhaps one of melancholy. A consciousness of time, particularly acute in his later work as he felt the approach of death, makes him starkly aware of the precariousness of all things human. He saw with sorrow the growing alienation and isolation of the individual caused by urban and technological development. Above all, he was acutely conscious of the squalor and misery he saw all around him in Lima and of the political oppression and social injustice that were the unacceptable face of his beloved country. Hence his poetry, particularly in the later period, embraces social themes quite naturally, denouncing social evils, not from the standpoint of a political ideology, but because he feels them personally as an offence to life and a blight on the country he loves. Thus, the seven poems of the posthumously published *Sombras como cosas sólidas* trace a socio-political history of Peru which prompts an anguished question:

> ¿Para qué,
> pero para qué fue descubierta esta última morada salvaje?

> (For what,
> for what purpose was this last savage land discovered?)

Ultimately Salazar viewed life as tragic but beautiful. In "Testamento ológrafo" he sardonically bequeaths a last image of himself as a man wasted away by illness, gazing sadly on a city which frustrates the hopes and dreams of its inhabitants and looking back on a life of frantic activity that has achieved only half-realised ambitions. Yet the image that impresses itself on the reader is of a man possessed of a tremendous love of life and committed to living it to the full in spite of all its imperfections:

> Dejo mi sombra,
> una afilada aguja que hiere la calle
> y con tristes ojos examina los muros,
> las ventanas de reja donde hubo incapaces amores,
> el cielo sin cielo de mi ciudad.
> Dejo mis dedos espectrales
> que recorrieron teclas, vientres, aguas, párpados de miel
> y por los que descendió la escritura
> como una virgen de alma deshilachada.
> Dejo mi ovoide cabeza, mis patas de araña,
> mi traje quemado por la ceniza de los presagios,
> descolorido por el fuego del libro nocturno.
> Dejo mis alas a medio batir, mi máquina
> que como un pequeño caballo galopó año tras año
> en busca de la fuente del orgullo donde la muerte muere.
> Dejo varias libretas agusanadas por la pereza,
> unas cuantas díscolas imágenes del mundo
> y entre grandes relámpagos algún llanto
> que tuve como un poco de sucio polvo en los dientes
>
> Acepta esto, recógelo en tu falda como unas migas,
> da de comer al olvido con tan frágil manjar.
>
> (I leave my shadow,
> a sharp needle that wounds the street
> and with sad eyes examines the walls,
> the grilled windows where love was impotent,
> my city's skyless sky.
> I leave my ghostly fingers
> that touched keys, bellies, waters, eyelids of honey
> and from which the writing came
> like a virgin with her soul in shreds.
> I leave my egg-shaped head, my spider's legs,
> my suit burnt by the ash of foreboding,
> discoloured by the fire of nocturnal books.
> I leave my wings in mid-flight, my typewriter
> that galloped like a small horse year after year
> in search of the fount of pride where death dies.
> I leave several notebooks wormeaten by sloth,
> a few mischievous images of the world

and among great lightning flashes the odd tear
that I had like a speck of dirty dust in the teeth.

Take it, gather it up in your skirt like crumbs
and feed oblivion with so frugal a dish.)

Blanca Varela (b. 1926), Peru's foremost woman poet,[8] published her first book in 1959 and has since followed it up with three other volumes in which a more or less consistent view of life finds an increasingly accomplished artistic expression.[9] The dominant note of her poetry is one of rebellious dissatisfaction with the conditions of life as, with a mixture of sadness and irony, her lucid consciousness cuts through the veil of comfortable illusions to lay bare its unpleasant underside, yet that same lucidity never allows her to lapse into facile romantic posturing but forces her to recognise the contradictory nature of the world and of human beings, to question and criticise her own attitudes and to face up to life with honesty and resilience.

In some poems Varela's native city of Lima is the object of a love-hate relationship. Thus, in the title-poem of *Valses y otras falsas confesiones* (1972) Lima, evoked through snatches of popular song, is identified with shallow *criollo* sentimentality and qualified as a squalid, shameless tramp of a mother whose mawkish love of her children is the other side of her neglect of them:

> No sé si te amo o te aborrezco
> porque vuelvo
> sólo para nombrarte desde adentro
> desde este mar sin olas
> para llamarte madre sin lágrimas
> impúdica
> amada a la distancia
> remordimiento y caricia
> leprosa desdentada
> mía

---

[8] Other leading women poets are Lola Thorne (b. 1931) [*Cuentos para Puck* (San Marcos, 1951); *De lunes a viernes* (Imago, 1961); *La edad natural* (Buenos Aires: Zona, 1965); *El litigio de la noche* (San Marcos, 1980)] and Cecilia Bustamante (b. 1934) [*Poesía* (Flora, 1963); *Nuevos poemas y Audiencia* (Flora, 1965); *El nombre de las cosas* (Montevideo: Alfa, 1970); *Discernimiento* (Mexico City: Premià, 1982)].

[9] See Blanca Varela, *Ese puerto existe* (Xalapa: Univ. Veracruzana, 1959); *Luz de día* (La Rama Florida, 1963); *Valses y otras falsas confesiones* (INC, 1972); *Canto villano* (Arybalo, 1978). See also Cristina Graves, "Con el ángel entre los dedos", *Hueso Húmero*, 4 (1980), 93-101; Edgar O'Hara, "Blanca Varela en aire, tierra y agua", *Cielo Abierto*, 24 (1983), 19-24; Julio Ortega, *Figuración de la persona*, pp. 196-201; José Miguel Oviedo, "Blanca Varela o la persistencia de la memoria", *Diálogos* (Mexico City), 89 (1979), 15-20.

> (I don't know if I love you or hate you
> for I've come back
> only to name you from within
> from this sea without waves
> to call you mother without tears
> shameless
> loved at a distance
> remorse and caresses
> leprous toothless
> mine)

Yet the counterpoint sections of the poem depict New York as being equally squalid and uncaring and one of the effects of quoting snatches of popular song is to convey the poet's nostalgic affection for her home town, so that the ultimate irony, as she herself recognises in the title, is that she identifies with Lima by virtue of the very sentimentality she despises in it.

Other poems are written out of woman's experience and present a critical view of the female condition. Thus "Nadie sabe mis cosas", another poem from the same collection evoking the plight of the wife abandoned by the philandering husband, conveys woman's cruel dependence on man, though at the same time appreciation is shown of the trap that marriage can represent for the male. More feminist is "Vals del Angelus", also from the same book, where the female persona addresses herself to the dominant male who has set himself up as God and calls him to account for what he has made of woman:

> Ve lo que has hecho de mí, la santa más pobre del museo, la de la última sala, junto a las letrinas, la de la herida negra como un ojo bajo el seno izquierdo [. . .]
>
> Así te he visto, virtiendo plomo derretido en las orejas inocentes, castrando bueyes, arrastrando tu azucena, tu inmaculado miembro, en la sangre de los mataderos. Disfrazado de [. . .] general en Bolivia, de tanquista en Vietnam, de eunuco en la puerta de los burdeles de la plaza México [. . .]
>
> Ve lo que has hecho de mí.
>
> Aquí estoy por tu mano en esta ineludible cámara de tortura, guiándome con sangre y con gemidos, ciega por obra y gracia de tu divina baba.
>
> (See what you've made of me, the most wretched saint in the museum, her of the last room, next to the toilets, her of the black wound like an eye beneath the left breast [. . .]
>
> So I've seen you, pouring molten lead into innocent ears, castrating oxen, trailing your lily, your immaculate member, through the blood

of slaughterhouses. Disguised as [. . .] general in Bolivia, tank-driver
in Vietnam, eunuch at the door of the brothels of Mexico Square [. . .]

See what you've made of me.

Here I am by your hand in this inescapable torture chamber, guiding
myself with blood and moans, blinded by grace and handiwork of
your divine slobber.)

However, rather than launch into a blanket denunciation of the male
of the species, Varela identifies oppressed womanhood with all
oppressed groups, and if the poem is subversively feminist it is also
critical of women in that the servility of the poetic persona implies
that they have invited subjection by their passiveness and their
vocation for martyrdom.

However, it is above all the human condition which is the subject
of Varela's poetry. In "Auvers-sur-Oise", the concluding poem of
Valses y otras falsas confesiones, the mutilated Van Gogh, unable to
distinguish the sound of music, is portrayed as a symbol of alienated
man, a fallen angel excluded from a paradise of whose existence he
can no longer even be sure, yet who stubbornly refuses to accept the
fact of his banishment and persists in hungering after a state of
absolute being which his human limitations deny him. Likewise, the
title-poem of *Canto villano* (1978) evokes the meagre diet of the poor
as a metaphor of the unsatisfying nature of existence in a meaningless
world, and "Camino a Babel", the final poem of the same book,
depicts the poet's search for meaning as a journey into senseless
confusion. It is in this latter poem that Varela gives what is perhaps
the clearest expression of her world-view:

> y sucedió también que
> fatigados los comediantes
> se retiraron hasta la muerte
> y las carpas del circo se abatieron ante el viento
> implacable
> de la realidad cotidiana.
> y si me preguntan diré [. . .
> . . .] que nosotros
> los poetas los amnésicos los tristes
> los sobrevivientes de la vida
> no caemos tan fácilmente en la trampa
> y que
> pasado presente y futuro
> son nuestro cuerpo
> una cruz sin el éxtasis gratificante del calvario
>
> (and it also happened that
> the weary actors

retired to death
and the circus tents collapsed
before the implacable wind
of everyday reality.
and if you ask me I'll say [...
...] that we
the poets the amnesiacs the sad
life's survivors
don't fall so easily into the trap
and that
past present and future
are our body
a cross without the gratifying ecstasy of calvary)

Reworking the age-old metaphor of life as a stage to convey the absurdity of human existence, the poet here refuses to allow herself to be deluded into falling into the trap of believing life to be anything more transcendental than mere physical existence.

Yet if Varela's lucidity reveals life to be a sham, it also recognises that it must go on. "Hasta la desesperación requiere un cierto orden" (Even despair requires a certain order), begins "Del orden de las cosas", the opening poem of *Luz de día* (1963), and those words sum up the basic attitude underlying all her work, for, for her, life is essentially a question of coping with despair and ultimately she regards existence as an art form which consists of inventing illusions in order to survive, of living life as if it were meaningful while all the time being conscious that it is not. Thus "Antes del día", another poem from the same book, employs the imagery of childbirth to convey her view of existence as a constant struggle to create something out of the sterility of our lives. The same vital attitude is reformulated in the final section of "Camino a Babel" where, mimicking the formula of oriental religious incantation in a climactic enumeration that mirrors the construction of the Tower of Babel, she addresses herself as the only divinity in whom she believes and persuades herself that she has the power to conquer the heavens, and if the poem's last line reveals a lucid consciousness that her spiritual questing must inevitably bring her back face to face with the existential void, also implied is a stubborn willingness to shrug off failure and to begin the process anew:

ayúdame mantra purísima
divinidad del esófago y el píloro.

si golpeas infinitas veces tu cabeza contra lo imposible
eres el imposible

el otro lado [...]
el nadador contra la corriente
el que asciende de mar a río
de río a cielo
de cielo a luz
de luz a nada.

(help me mantra most pure
divinity of the oesophagus and the pylorus.

if you keep endlessly knocking your head against the
    impossible
you are the impossible
the other side [...]
the swimmer against the current
he who ascends from sea to river
from river to sky
from sky to light
from light to void.)

In the panorama of Peruvian poetry in the years after 1940 a special place is occupied by Mario Florián (b. 1917), whose work represents a continuation of the *indigenista* tradition of Peralta.[10] Of humble peasant stock, Florián grew up in a remote country district of the Cajamarca region of the northern sierra before moving to Lima where he pursued university studies and entered the teaching profession. His poetry reflects his origins. Particularly in his earlier work and most notably in *Urpi* (1944), his most accomplished book, he sings of the landscape and agricultural activities of the Andes in simple but highly lyrical poems marked by a feeling for the earth and the people who cultivate it. He practises, too, a folk poetry that has its roots in popular oral tradition, Spanish as well as Andean. Such poems are characterised by their simplicity of tone, by a tenderness of feeling that is peculiarly Andean, by the introduction into the Spanish of Quechua expressions that are part of everyday rural vocabulary, by imagery drawn from the flora and fauna of the Andean landscape, and by their musical quality. A good example is the following love poem:

        Pastorala.
        Pastorala.
        Más hermosa que la luz de la nieve,

---

[10] Florián is a prolific writer with over twenty volumes of verse to his name. For his most important works, see *Poesía (1940-1950)* (Villanueva, 1954); *Obra poética escogida (1940-1976)* (Studium, 1977). His most recent books are *Habla de Pedro Palana* (1980) and *La sangre del pueblo magisterial* (1984), both privately published.

más que la luz del agua enamorada,
más que la luz danzando en los arco iris.
Pastorala.
Pastorala.

¿Qué labio de kukulí es más dulce,
qué lágrima de quena más mielada
que tu canto que cae como lluvia
pequeña, pequeñita, sobre flores?
Pastorala.
Pastorala.

....
Por amansar tus ojos, tu sonrisa,
perdido entre la luz de tu manada
está mi corazón, en forma de allqo,
cuidándote, lamiéndote, llorándote ...
Pastorala.
Pastorala.

(Country girl.
Country girl.
More beautiful than the light of the snow
or the light enamoured of the water
or the light dancing on the rainbows.
Country girl.
Country girl.

What cooing of the turtle-dove is sweeter,
what weeping of the quena flute more honeyed
than your song that falls like rain
finely, ever so finely, on the flowers?
Country girl.
Country girl.

....
To win your look, your smile,
my heart, in the shape of a dog,
roams lost amid the light of your flock,
watching over you, licking you, weeping for you ...
Country girl.
Country girl.)

Exuding a delightful freshness, these poems successfully convey
the spirit of the rural Andean world. Understandably, however,
Florián felt that a full appreciation of that world could only be
communicated by giving account of the misery its inhabitants had to
endure and increasingly it was to be social poetry that was to become
the dominant strain of his work. Writing as the spokesman of the
downtrodden peasant masses of Peru, Florián evokes their grinding

poverty and suffering, denounces the feudal land-owning oligarchy and preaches the forthcoming revolution when the peasant will come into his own again. Thus in the eponymous hero of *Pedro Palana* (1965) he creates a symbol of the eternal suffering and tenacious resistance of the Andean peasant:

> Pedro Palana, te saludo.
> Pedro Palana, mido tu cuerpo.
> Persona débil. Fuerte.
> Viejísimo en la tierra,
> como los ríos, como los llamas,
> como las grandes chontas de la selva ...
> Trueno del tiempo, forma
> de eternidad doliente en barro humano.

> (Pedro Palana, I salute you.
> Pedro Palana, I measure your body.
> A weak person. Strong.
> Ancient on the earth,
> like the rivers, like the llamas,
> like the great chonta trees of the jungle ...
> Time's thunder, the shape
> of suffering eternity in human clay.)

Other books, like the recent *La sangre del pueblo magisterial* (1984), which was inspired by the 1979 schoolteachers' strike, sing of the wider class struggle. Unfortunately, however, it has to be said that this side of Florián's work compares unfavourably with his earlier verse.

Florián's social poems are, in fact, fairly representative of a current of committed poetry which had been prevalent in Peru since the twenties and which, on the whole, produced little of literary value. The fifties were to see an upsurge of such poetry in the wake of the overthrow of the short-lived democratic government of José Luis Bustamante in 1948 and the establishment of the dictatorship of General Odría. The social poets were strongly critical of the so-called "pure poets" for their failure to confront the social and political realities of the country. They themselves conceived poetry as an instrument of political change and wielded it to denounce injustice and to preach revolutionary values. Stylistically, they shunned complex imagery and employed a simple, direct language in a plain-speaking attempt to reveal socio-political "truth", and since they aspired to reach a wide, largely non-literary public, their poetry also had a distinctive oral quality which made it suitable for declamation. In the main, however, they merely succeeded in presenting a naively simplistic view of reality whose ingenuousness was to be exposed by the subsequent course of history, and because their poetry tended to limit itself to the unquestioning assertion of a political faith, it lacked the complexity, tension, profundity and dynamism of that of their principal model, César Vallejo. Stylistically, their verse was not only heavily influenced by Vallejo and the great Chilean poet Pablo Neruda, but it was often so in a way that was blatant and unassimilated, to the extent that some critics came to regard Vallejo's influence on Peruvian poetry as being positively harmful, and it tended, too, to be tediously repetitious and cliché-ridden and often reduced itself to strident diatribe or effusive declarations of political optimism. Nonetheless, it would be unfair to dismiss all committed poetry of the period as unworthy of serious consideration and in Alejandro Romualdo and Juan Gonzalo Rose that tendency threw up two figures of considerable stature.[11] Significantly, what sets them apart from other poets of this kind is their artistic awareness and a sense of a personal voice behind the political rhetoric of the poems.

A native of Trujillo, Alejandro Romualdo (b. 1926) had established a name for himself as a fine poet in the manner of Rilke when in *Poesía concreta* (1954) he abandoned his earlier poetics in favour of a committed poetry.[12] "A otra cosa", the opening poem of that book, marks his break not only with his own previous work but also with the type of poetry that was predominant in Peru at that time. Reacting with impatience to his fellow poets' withdrawal into introspective isolation and to the anguished pessimism of their work, he mimics the famous death-sentence pronounced on Modernism by the Mexican Enrique González Martínez as he invites them to emerge into the real world and to overcome their alienation by participating in the struggle to create a better society:

---

[11] Also deserving mention is Manuel Scorza (1928-83); see *Poesía incompleta* (Mexico City: UNAM, 1976). Nor would any survey of social poetry of the period be complete without at least some reference to the self-educated working-class poet Leoncio Bueno (b. 1921), whose poetry gives testimony of the life and struggles of the working classes. See *Al pie del yunque* (Grupo intelectual 1 de mayo, 1966); *Este Gran Capitán* (Tungar, 1968); *Pastor de truenos* (Tungar, 1968); *Invasión poderosa* (Tungar, 1970); *Rebuzno propio* (Arte-Reda, 1976); *La guerra de los runas* (Tungar, 1980).

[12] See Alejandro Romualdo, *Poesía (1945-1954)* (Mejía Baca/Villanueva, 1954); *Edición extraordinaria* (Ediciones Cuadernos Trimestrales de Poesía, 1958); *Como Dios manda* (Mexico City: Joaquín Mortiz, 1967); *El movimiento y el sueño* (Viva Voz, 1971); *Cuarto mundo* (Buenos Aires: Losada, 1972). See also Mirko Lauer and Abelardo Oquendo, "'Yo de esta sociedad no podía esperar nada': una conversación con Romualdo", *Hueso Húmero*, 11 (1981), 3-27; Julio Ortega, *Figuración de la persona*, pp. 182-90.

Basta ya de agonía. No me importa
la soledad, la angustia ni la nada.
Estoy harto de escombros y de sombras.
Quiero salir al sol. Verle la cara

al mundo [...]

Déjense de sollozos y peleen
para que los señores sean hombres.
Tuérzanle el llanto a la melancolía.

(Enough now of agony. I don't care two hoots
about loneliness, anguish or the void.
I'm fed up with shadows and ruins.
I want to go out into the sun. To see the world's

face [...]

Cast off tears and fight
to make our lords and masters men.
Strangle melancholy's sobbing.)

The other poems of the volume are, above all, an assertion of a newly found optimism with regard to life, an optimism born of a political faith promising the redemption of the world through revolution, and significantly many of them have the form of litanies or hymns. The direct influence of Vallejo is evident in this book, but Romualdo was to outgrow that influence in *Edición extraordinaria* (1958) where, in his best poem, "Canto coral a Túpac Amaru, que es la libertad", he finds in the historical figure of Tupac Amaru a symbol to express his faith in inevitable and irreversible social revolution:

Lo harán volar
con dinamita. En masa,
lo cargarán, lo arrastrarán. A golpes
le llenarán de pólvora la boca.
Lo volarán: ¡y no podrán matarlo! [...]

Querrán volarlo y no podrán volarlo.
Querrán romperlo y no podrán romperlo.
Querrán matarlo y no podrán matarlo.

Al tercer día de los sufrimientos,
cuando se crea todo consumado,
gritando ¡libertad! sobre la tierra,
ha de volver.
         Y no podrán matarlo.

(They'll blow him up
with dynamite. In a body,
they'll carry him, they'll drag him. By force

they'll stuff his mouth with gunpowder.
They'll blow him up: and they won't be able to kill him! [...]
They'll try to blow him up and they won't be able to.
They'll try to smash him and they won't be able to.
They'll try to kill him and they won't be able to.

On the third day of suffering,
when they think it's all over and done,
shouting "Liberty!" throughout the earth,
he'll return.
    And they won't be able to kill him.)

Throughout his career Romualdo has demonstrated a preoccupation with form and a willingness to experiment, but above all, what gives his poetry its impact is that behind the political rhetoric the reader senses a personal response to the world in his passionate affirmation of faith in life.

Born in Tacna, Juan Gonzalo Rose (1928-83) militated in the ranks of the Apra and Communist parties and suffered a period of political exile in Mexico, where his first book was published in 1954.[13] At times Rose is capable of exaltant declamation, as in "Voz de orden" which is a call to revolutionary action and for the subordination of individuality to the cause of the proletariat. More generally, however, the tone of his poety is restrained and his language austere and concise. On the whole, too, his political verse tends to be rooted in personal experience. Thus, in "Mi pueblo era de arena", he finds in the arid coastal landscape of his childhood an image of his country thirsting for social justice:

Caminé por la costa de mi patria
buscando los pezones
de la estatua del agua;
fantasmas de gaviotas me seguían
persiguiendo la sed de mis sandalias;
y en todas partes sólo
me encontré con la arena,
tiranía y arena,
arena y muerte,
hombres que se pudrían en las cárceles
con la mirada roja de venganza y arena.

(I tramped the coast of my country
seeking the teats
of the statue of water;

---

[13] See Juan Gonzalo Rose, *La luz armada* (Mexico City: Humanismo, 1954); *Obra poética* (INC, 1974).

phantom gulls followed me
pursuing the thirst of my sandals;
and everywhere I went
I found only sand,
tyranny and sand,
sand and death,
men rotting in the gaols,
their eyes red with vengeance and sand.)

Alternating with Rose's political verse is another strain of poetry in which he gives lyrical expression to personal emotions, most notably in the love poems of *Simple canción* (1960). Some of his best poems are to be found in *Cantos desde lejos* (1957) where compositions like "Las cartas secuestradas" and "El vaso" voice the exiled poet's nostalgia for his childhood home with a melancholy tenderness reminiscent of Valdelomar and Vallejo. The two sides of his work are brought together in that volume in the moving "Carta a María Teresa", a poetic epistle in which he attempts to explain to his little sister what motivated him to bring pain to their mother by embarking on a life of political activism:

> Para ti debo ser, pequeña hermana,
> el hombre malo que hace llorar a mamá [...]
>
> Mas una tarde, hermana,
> te han de herir en la calle
> los juguetes ajenos;
> la risa de los pobres
> ceñirá tu cintura
> y andando de puntillas
> llegará tu perdón.
>
> (For you, little sister, I must be
> the evil man who makes mummy weep [...]
>
> But one of these afternoons, sister,
> other folks' toys
> will hurt you in the street;
> the laughter of the poor
> will encircle your waist
> and walking on tiptoe
> your forgiveness will come to me.)

Later Rose was to reveal himself to be a poet of unsuspected range in books like *Las comarcas* (1964), a collection of prose poems celebrating the peoples and landscapes of the American continent, and *Cuarentena* (1968), where he takes stock of his life on reaching middle age, and in *Informe al Rey y otros libros secretos* (1967) he was to develop a more sophisticated type of social poetry. Dedicated to Guamán Poma de Ayala, the book is, in effect, another "new chronicle", an alternative, demystificatory history of Peru offering a caustic criticism of national life. Thus, "Fe, Esperanza y Caridad" ironically questions the benefits that the Christian religion has brought the country:

> Aquí, mi Rey, se ven por todas partes
> monasterios e iglesias
> bellamente tallados [...]
> ¿Dónde se alzan los templos
> del idólatra, del que no tuvo tiempo
> para pensar en su alma
> porque sus tripas eran
> más vacías de carne
> que el sagrado misterio?

> (Here, my lord King, beautifully wrought
> monasteries and churches
> are everywhere to be seen [...]
> Where stand the temples
> of the idolater, of him who hadn't time
> to think about his soul
> because his guts were
> more empty of flesh
> than the sacred mystery?)

On the whole, though, the socially committed poetry of the period was markedly inferior to that produced by the so-called "pure poets". Nonetheless, despite the continuation of what I prefer to call the visionary tradition by the likes of Chariarse and Bendezú, there was towards the sixties a movement away from the type of poetry that turned its back on the world to concern itself with its own alternative reality. As has been seen, the evolution of the work of Adán, Eielson and Sologuren was marked by a progressive loss of confidence in their original poetics and by a growing sense of anguish in face of life. The existential poetry of Salazar Bondy and Varela confronted the problems of the human condition and, at least in the case of the former, revealed an awareness of social realities without being overtly political. And the committed poets, for all their limitations, brought to the fore a socio-political situation that could no longer be ignored. Finally, in the late fifties there were to emerge poets like Wáshington Delgado and Pablo Guevara who bridged the gap between subjective and social poetry by producing a work which not only combined the expression of personal emotion with a preoccupation with socio-political realities but focused the poet's own personal situation in the context of social and historical processes.

A native of Cuzco, Wáshington Delgado (b. 1927) has lived all his adult life in Lima where he works as a professor of literature in San Marcos University. His collected poetry, comprising seven books spanning the period 1951-1970, was published in that latter year under the title *Un mundo dividido*.[14] Quietly meditative in tone and restrained and deceptively simple in its language, his work expresses the drama of a left-wing intellectual alienated in a country that is politically and socially backward. Significantly two of his books are entitled *El extranjero* (1956) and *Destierro por vida* (1970), for underlying all of his poetry is his sense of being an exile in his own country since Peru has never been for him a true homeland with which he can identify with pride. Thus in the title-poem of the former book he peruses the country's history and traditions in search of some positive value which would restore his faith in it, but in the past he can find nothing worthy of respect to offer him hope for the future:

> Pregunto por mi patria
> y mi esperanza busca una palabra, el nombre
> de una ciudad antigua, de una calle pequeña,
> de una fecha de victoria o desolación [...]
>
> Si toda esperanza surge del pasado
> nada en verdad poseo ...
>
> (I ask for my country
> and my hope seeks a word, the name
> of an ancient city, of a small street,
> the date of a victory or a disaster [...]
>
> If all hope springs from the past
> I truly possess nothing ...)

Delgado's poetry tends to oscillate between two poles. On the one hand, recognising as he does in "El ciudadano en su rincón" that he is just another man in the street powerless to do anything to change the world at large, he arrives at a *modus vivendi* with his environment, withdrawing into his own little corner to live his life as best he can,

---

[14] See Wáshington Delgado, *Un mundo dividido* (Casa de la Cultura del Perú, 1970). The dates cited for individual books are those given in this volume and not those of the original editions. See also Matyás Horanyi, "El mundo dividido de Wáshington Delgado", *Cuadernos Hispanoamericanos*, 300 (1975), 519-42; Julio Ortega, *Figuración de la persona*, pp. 190-96; Javier Sologuren, *Tres poetas, tres obras*, pp. 41-73.

striving to be an honest, decent, affable human being, cultivating his intellectual and artistic activities, and snatching at such fulfilment as comes his way in the form of the love of his wife and the simple pleasures of life. Much of his verse is private poetry reflecting on the human condition. In poems like "La condición humana", "Dromedario" and "Necesidad de la vida y el sueño" that condition is viewed as an absurdity. Yet in an absurd world Delgado finds pleasure and meaning in the humble, elemental things that men take for granted but which give life its charm and make it worth living. Thus the volume *Parque* (1967) is devoted entirely to the celebration of the many faces of nature enjoyed in a city park, an oasis of peace and beauty in the midst of an overcrowded, polluted and disorientating urban environment.

However, this retreat into isolation is a stance which Delgado clearly feels uneasy about. In "Poema moral" he recognises that, by opting out and cultivating a safe poetry acceptable to the ruling establishment, he has followed the same line of least resistance as the rest of society, that he has, in effect, sold his soul to the powers that be and connived at the perpetuation of an unjust social order. And in "Monólogo del habitante", after a critical examination of his life as a man and a poet, he acknowledges its sterility and abandons the isolation of his room to participate in the political struggle to build a better world:

> Qué inútil es
> la soledad y qué inútil el amor
> ciego, individual y melancólico,
> refugiado en los parques, hundido en los versos
> de Bécquer o arrinconado en una cama
> tan inútil como el amor, como la soledad [...]
>
> Mi habitación de nada sirve.
> La posteridad me espera en la calle.
> Mi monólogo ha terminado.
>
> (How useless is
> solitude and how useless love,
> blind, individual and melancholic,
> hiding in the parks, immersed in the verses
> of Bécquer or cornered in a bed
> as useless as love, as solitude [...]
>
> My room serves no purpose.
> Posterity awaits me in the street.
> My monologue has finished.)

The other pole of Delgado's work is, in fact, a social poetry denouncing injustice and voicing his commitment to the class struggle, sometimes in a serious moral tone, sometimes employing an irreverent irony to debunk the values underpinning socio-economic domination. "Historia del Perú" demystifies national history, caustically dismissing it as "twenty words that say nothing", while other poems, like "En el valle de sombras" and "Canción de la tierra", exploit the myth of a pre-Columbian Golden Age to evoke by contrast the evils of contemporary Peru and to prefigure a future redeemed by socialist revolution. "Los pensamientos puros" calls the representatives of the established order to account, announcing that the day of retribution is at hand, and "El día venidero" is a profession of faith in a new world in the making. In such poems Delgado seems to have been infected by the mood of revolutionary optimism that swept Latin America in the years leading up to and following the Cuban Revolution. But it was his misfortune to live in a country and a period where historical reality was to make a mockery of such revolutionary hopes and he was too honest to refuse to face the facts. Thus, against a background of the defeat of the guerrilla movement of the sixties, "Canción del amante de la libertad" speaks of the frustration of his hopes for a liberated future.

It should be emphasised that these two kinds of poetry, private and social, do not correspond to different phases of Delgado's work but coexist side by side. Nor is it simply a question of their being equally legitimate expressions of opposite sides of his personality, though, of course, they are. Above all, they reveal two conflicting attitudes towards public life, one of disenchanted withdrawal, the other of passionate involvement. The moral and intellectual dilemma of the man pulled in both directions at once is particularly well treated in the magnificent "Pluralidad de los mundos". On the one hand, the poet presents himself as someone who turns his back on the world to live in the more satisfying worlds of books, his justification being his total scepticism about man's ability to alter the course of history:

Leo los libros de Marx y sé	(I read Marx and know
que la historia se repite	that history repeats itself
y es una farsa	and is a farce
como para llorar.	to weep over.
Los retratos acaricio	I caress the photos
de mis hijos que han de morir	of my children who will die
en medio de los nuevos basurales.	surrounded by new rubbish dumps.)

On the other, the heroic example of those with the commitment to fight and die to transform society highlights the senseless sterility of his own solitary intellectual activity:

> En las montañas, los hombres
> mueren y combaten,
> yo enciendo un cigarrillo y lo reparto
> entre cincuenta mundos
> sin sentido.

> (In the mountains men
> are dying and fighting,
> I light a cigarette and scatter it
> over fifty worlds
> without meaning.)

No other Peruvian poet has expressed as honestly as Delgado has done the tension between the ardent longing for socio-political change and the recognition that such hopes were wishful thinking in the conditions prevailing in the fifties and sixties. "Globe Trotter" brings his collected poetry to a despairing conclusion by presenting the poet as a pilgrim stranded in a barren desert from which he can find no way out. And yet while he acknowledges that the various paths he has followed have led nowhere and that all he has succeeded in doing has been to add his "small sadnesses" to the "pain of centuries", he persists in other poems such as "Difícil soneto" in believing in the future as the only thing he has left to him:

> Vivo para mañana y eso es todo.
> Y eso no es nada. Y, sin embargo, es
> la única luz que alumbra este soneto.

> (I live for tomorrow and that's all.
> And that's nothing. And, yet, it's
> the only light that brightens up this sonnet.)

Though his work has received little critical attention, Pablo Guevara (b. 1930) anticipated later developments in Peruvian poetry and was a major influence on the new generations of poets who emerged in the sixties and seventies.[15] The decisive influence on his own poetry seems to have been the years he spent in Europe in the late fifties. As a result of that experience his work evolved towards a consideration of the destiny of the individual within the context of

---

[15] See Pablo Guevara, *Retorno a la creatura* (Madrid: Cooperación Intelectual, 1957); *Los habitantes* (La Rama Florida, 1965); *Crónicas contra los bribones* (Milla Batres, 1967); *Hotel del Cuzco y otras provincias del Perú* (INC, 1972). See also Julio Ortega, *Figuración de la persona*, pp. 201-06; Armando Zubizarreta, "La elegía de la derrota anónima", *Razón y Fábula* (Bogotá), 12 (1969), 53-62.

historical processes. At the same time, under the influence of Anglo-Saxon poetry, he abandoned the concept of the poem as an encapsulating stylistic unit in favour of a more open and loosely structured type of poem incorporating disparate discourses and tones. This was precisely the direction in which Peruvian poetry was to move from the sixties onwards.

Nonetheless, despite the evolution mentioned, there is a marked consistency in Guevara's poetry. His first volume, *Retorno a la creatura* (1957), includes a moving elegy to his father, a humble shoemaker whose life was an obscure story of failure. Other early poems, like "Lealtad" from the same collection, celebrate loyalty between friends, or, like "Los sapos" and "Las tortugas" from *Los habitantes* (1965), oppose nature to the city. All of Guevara's work, in effect, is a vindication of the values of decency and goodness of ordinary men and women in opposition to the selfishness and cruelty of those who rule over them, and of natural instincts in opposition to the stultifying and dehumanising codes imposed by man-made civilisation represented by the city.

Guevara's European experience is reflected in *Los habitantes* and in *Crónicas contra los bribones* (1967). In the great cities of the old continent he was to find himself at the heart of a civilisation which had imposed its values, institutions and way of life on the world, a civilisation based on the senseless pursuit of wealth and power, on selfish rapaciousness and cruel domination, a civilisation which, he felt, not only inflicted untold material hardship and suffering on the weak and defenceless but stifled and distorted the development of the human personality. Thus, though he understands full well that it is institutionalised violence which ensures the survival of that order, he voices in "Los burgueses son bestias" the sadness and outrage of a man unable to conceive how a system so manifestly absurd and inhuman should have persisted down through the ages:

> Oh mundo de la necesidad,
> ¿eres acaso inmortal?
> "Los burgueses son bestias,
> los burgueses son bestias,"
> lo digo cada día, pero es
> por los ejércitos del mundo
> que el Orden Burgués supervive.
>
> Nunca lo dejé de saber,
> nunca lo dejé de saber,
> pero debo poder enfrentarme
> al rinoceronte que bufa

en Place Vendôme desde 1871
—año de derrota de la Comuna—,
a través de las mareas
que ascienden y descienden,
¡años de la crueldad y la estupidez!

(Oh world of necessity,
are you perhaps eternal?
"The bourgeois are beasts,
the bourgeois are beasts,"
I repeat every day, yet it's
because of the world's armies
that the bourgeois order survives.

I've never ceased to be aware of it,
I've never ceased to be aware of it,
but I have to be able to face
the rhinoceros that's been bellowing
in Place Vendôme since 1871
— the year the Commune was defeated —,
across the tides
that ebb and flow,
years of cruelty and stupidity!)

Yet in a world blighted by the evils of capitalism, art is seen as an affirmation of life in poems like "Botticelli" and "Giotto", and in others lovers are conceived as waging a resistance campaign in defence of human values. *Crónicas contra los bribones*, dedicated to "the child and woman, divine", raises up ordinary human love and family life in opposition to the ruthless scheming of the ambitious. Significantly, "Nietos y abuelos", the closing poem of the book and one set in Peru, contrasts the peaceful contentment of humble fisherfolk bringing back a hard-earned catch with the piracy by which capitalist entrepreneurs make their profits.

In *Hotel del Cuzco y otras provincias del Perú* (1972) Guevara focuses more directly on the reality of his own country, though the book's central section situates it in a wider context by renewing his assault on Western civilisation's dehumanising values and institutions. The other two sections present contrasting visions of the Peruvian provinces and capital. In "La mazamorra morada" the typical Limeñan sweet of the title becomes a symbol of the sickly blandness of the *criollo* character which over the centuries has passively accepted social injustice and found distraction in diversions and religion. Evoking the urban underdevelopment characteristic of the Third World, the poem personifies Lima as a backward, simple-minded young girl living in squalor and incapacitated for the full life represented by love and whose occasional false pregnancies symbolise a promise of progress and reform that never materialise. By contrast, in "Hotel del Cuzco", the ancient capital of the Inca Empire, once the "navel of the world", is seen as the cradle of coming revolution, whose unwitting vanguard are the humble, long-suffering natives who have never accepted the dominant culture and stubbornly endure and cling to their own ways while awaiting the day when they will come into their own again. Underlying the book is a passionate belief in the urgent need to overthrow the established order. Significantly, it closes with a poem entitled "Hay que luchar" (It's necessary to fight) and the opening poem voices allegiance with the guerrilla movement. Significantly, too, that first poem identifies the *guerrilleros* with the Huns who, in opposition to the time-honoured view of them, are seen as the heroes of an alternative history, the history of ordinary, anonymous men and women and of their struggle against the unjust social orders imposed by the powerful:

> Llegaron al punto
> en que se volvió a demostrar
> que lo habitual y lo cotidiano
> > *es la Historia*
> y que vahos, sudores, llagas, imprecaciones,
> pies como globos, diarreas, caídas, maldiciones
> a través de muchos kilómetros sin testimonios
> > *son la Historia,*
> > *otra Historia,*
> y destruyeron el Imperio Romano
> > y su injusta *PAX.*

> (They reached the point
> where it was proved again
> that the everyday and commonplace
> > *is History*
> and that stink, sweat, sores, oaths,
> feet like balloons, diarrhoea, falls, curses
> over many unrecorded kilometres
> > *are History,*
> > *another History*
> and they destroyed the Roman Empire
> > and its unjust *PAX.*)

However, of the poets who emerged in the fifties the outstanding figure is undoubtedly Carlos Germán Belli (b. 1927), whose major books are *El pie sobre el cuello* (1964), *Por el monte abajo* (1966) and

Canciones y otros poemas (1982).[16] Temperamentally apolitical, Belli
is concerned above all with his own personal predicament, the
mundane drama of a humble member of the middle classes struggling
to make his way in the world. For many years he worked as a
government employee and his poetry voices the humiliations and
frustrations of the office-worker caught in the daily grind of a dull,
soul-destroying job which earns him barely enough to support his
family, whose circumstances deny him the possibility of fulfilling
himself as a human being, who sees before him no prospect but a
lifetime of unrewarding and demoralising toil. To express that
predicament he developed a personal and original style combining
elements derived from Spanish Golden-Age poetry — a classical or
archaic vocabulary; a disconcerting syntax characterised by hyperbaton and ellipsis; the frequent use of reiterative epithets; a
predilection for the hendecasyllable and heptasyllable — with
contemporary themes and modern language and imagery. In his best
poems the end result is an emotionally charged and artistically
accomplished poetry in which the personal acquires a universal value
and social criticism is made much more effectively than in most
directly political verse of the period.

Underlying Belli's work is a view of the world similar to that of
Vallejo, that of a cruelly competitive world where only the strong
survive and in face of which he feels hopelessly inadequate. Thus one
poem presents birth as a catastrophe and evokes the apprehension of
the foetus as it reluctantly emerges from the shelter of the womb into
a cold, alien world where it is the lot of the weak to be victimised:

> Frunce el feto su frente
> y sus cejas enarca cuando pasa
> del luminoso vientre
> al albergue terreno,
> do se truecan sin tasa
> la luz en niebla, la cisterna en cieno;

[16] See Carlos Germán Belli, *Poemas* (1958), *Dentro & Fuera* (1960), ¡*Oh Hada
Cibernética!* (1961), *El pie sobre el cuello* (1964), *Por el monte abajo* (1966), all in *El pie
sobre el cuello* (Montevideo: Alfa, 1967); *Sextinas y otros poemas* (Santiago de Chile:
Universitaria, 1970); *El libro de los nones*, in ¡*Oh Hada Cibernética!* (Caracas: Monte
Avila, 1971); *En alabanza del bolo alimenticio* (Mexico City: Premià, 1979); *Canciones y
otros poemas* (Mexico City: Premià, 1982). See also James Higgins, *The Poet in Peru*,
pp. 46-64; W.N. Hill, *Tradición y modernidad en la poesía de Carlos Germán Belli*
(Madrid: Pliegos, 1984); Francisco Lasarte, "Pastoral and Counter-pastoral: The
Dynamics of Belli's Poetic Despair", *Modern Language Notes*, 94 (1979), 301-20; Julio
Ortega, *Figuración de la persona*, pp. 129-36; Roberto Paoli, "Razón de ser del
neoclasicismo de Carlos Germán Belli", in *Estudios sobre literatura peruana contemporánea*, pp. 151-59; Javier Sologuren, *Tres poetas, tres obras*, pp. 7-40.

y abandonar le duele al fin el claustro,
en que no rugen ni cierzo ni austro,
y verse aun despeñado
desde el más alto risco,
cual un feto no amado,
por tartamudo o cojo o manco o bizco.

(The foetus fiercely frowns
and arches its eyebrows as it passes
from the luminous womb
to its earthly abode,
where, beyond measure, light
turns to mist, the reservoir to slime;
and it pains it finally to abandon the cloister,
in which neither north nor south wind howls,
and to look forward, to boot, to being dashed
from the highest crag
as a foetus unloved,
for being a stammerer, a cripple, maimed or cross-eyed.)

A series of poems dedicated to his spastic brother Alfonso sees in the latter's infirmity evidence of the fundamental injustice of life which capriciously favours some and discriminates against others, and far from attenuating that injustice, the society depicted in his verse reflects and accentuates it. In "Segregación No. 1" Peru is viewed as a country where the poor skulk underground while on the earth above a small privileged class owns everything, manages everything in its own interest and enjoys all the advantages of wealth and power, and various poems are based on a contrast between the poet's hardships and frustrations and the affluence and well-being of others. Thus he is able to establish a parallel between his own position and that of his brother, for, born without the qualities to triumph in the social rat race, he languishes in a condition of economic servitude which, like Alfonso's paralysis, prevents him from leading a free and full existence and exposes him to the domination of others. For Belli poetry seems to be a kind of personal catharsis, a means of purging the pain that life causes, for his verse reveals a tendency to wallow in misery, abounding in imagery of hyperbolic horror which translates spiritual suffering into physical terms and presents the poet as the most humiliated and downtrodden of men. While Vallejo expresses his inadequacy in face of life through the persona of the child, the persona here adopted is that of the eternal loser, the poor weakling whose lot it is to be pushed around and trampled on by others stronger than he and to look on sadly and enviously as they carry off the prizes on which he has set his heart.

Even his artistic leanings are a liability, for they have no practical worth in a competitive world and his lack of a practical turn of mind relegates him to the bottom of the social ladder. Thus, to the unhappy poet it seems that all the books he has read and all the culture he has acquired serve only to feed the lice of his poverty:

> ¿Cuál mano, Marcio, cuál peine
> arrojará alguna vez
> de tu cabelludo cuero
> tantas arraigadas liendres?
> Pues tus piojuelos engullen
> no el polvo de las afueras,
> ni de tu cuero la grasa,
> sino la clara primicia
> de las mil lecturas varias,
> que en ti, Marcio, de los libros
> por tus ojos hasta el buche
> del insecto pasar suele,
> confinándote a la zaga,
> no sólo del piojo, no,
> mas sí de sus huevecillos.
>
> (What hand, Marcio, what comb
> will one day cast out
> from your hairy hide
> so many embedded nits?
> For your lice devour
> not the dust on the outside,
> nor the fat of your skin,
> but the juicy fruit
> of the thousand varied readings,
> which in you, Marcio, is wont to pass
> from the books, through your eyes,
> to the insect's belly,
> confining you to the rear,
> not just of the louse, no,
> but even of its tiny eggs.)

Employing classical language, metres and techniques, Belli introduces us in his verse into a stylised rural world reminiscent of much Spanish poetry of the Golden Age. The poet, after the manner of Garcilaso in his "Eglogas", appears as a shepherd tending his sheep in the valley. The characters often bear classical names such as Marcio, Anfriso, Filis, and their world is ruled by mythological deities. Happiness is conceived in terms of pagan *joie de vivre* and bucolic frolicking in the fields, but the tone of the poems tends to be elegiac. On one level this stylised pastoral world stands as a poetic symbol of Peru seen as a country which is still basically feudal. References to the mistiness of the valley identify it as the valley of Lima, and it is presented as a cold, arid, inhospitable land where the poet-shepherd is the serf of cruel feudal lords, toiling in a bondage that excludes even the vision of higher things:

> ... en el globo sublunar yacía,
> en los cepos cautivo
> del neblinoso valle de mi cuna.
>
> (... I languished on the sublunar globe,
> captive in the traps
> of the misty valley of my birth.)

As a counterpoint to this feudal valley of tears Belli frequently evokes the image of Bética, an earthly paradise with all the characteristics of the *beatus ille* of classical literature, a green, fertile, pleasant arcadia where more fortunate shepherds live in liberty and abundance and enjoy a permanent idyll of love. A compendium of all the poet's desires, Bética is a projection of his dreams of independence and personal fulfilment, but since the land in which he lives is very different, it is ultimately a poetic device which serves to highlight by contrast his frustration and the imperfections of his own world. Thus the pagan pleasures in which Betic shepherds are able to indulge are experiences he has never known and which he can only envy from afar:

> nosotros [...] no vamos
> por el valle gritando:
> ¡que viva el vino!, ¡que viva la cópula!
>
> (we [...] don't run
> about the valley shouting,
> "Long live wine! Long live copulation!")

Anachronism is an important element in Belli's work in that within the archaic pastoral world of his poetry are to be found the trappings of a modern urban civilisation, an anomaly reflecting the uneven development of Third World countries. Hence, if Peru appears in his poetry as a society which is still basically feudal, it appears also as a modern society ruled by impersonal economic laws which reduce the individual to a mere cog in the socio-economic machine. To symbolise these modern economic forces Belli installs as the supreme deity of his poetic world an invented personage, Fisco, the god of income, to whom man offers up the sacrifice of his labours in the hope of winning the blessing of his generosity. Thus, the poet prostrates himself at the altar of Fisco only to see his offering scorned:

> Tal cual un can fiel a su dueño sólo,
> así a tus plantas por la vil pitanza
> que dan tus arcas, cuán cosido vivo,
>   año tras año.
>
> Pues por el monto destos bofes míos,
> migas me lanzas como si no humanos
> fuéramos yo, mi dama y mis hijuelas,
>   mas sólo hormigas.
>
> (Like a dog faithful only to its master,
> for the vile pittance doled out from your coffers,
> how bound I live to the soles of your feet,
>   year after year.
>
> For in exchange for these slogged-out guts of mine,
> crumbs you toss me as if we weren't human,
> myself, my lady and my little daughters,
>   but merely ants.)

Set in opposition to Fisco is the Hada Cibernética, a kind of fairy godmother personifying the technology of the future which will redeem man from the slavery of work. Thus, impatiently awaiting her coming, the poet calls on her to destroy the inhuman commercial system represented by the exchanges:

> ¡Oh Hada Cibernética!,
> cuándo de un soplo asolarás las lonjas,
> que cautivo me tienen,
> y me libres al fin
> para que yo entonces pueda
> dedicarme a buscar una mujer
> dulce como el azúcar,
> suave como la seda,
> y comérmela en pedacitos,
> y gritar después:
> "¡abajo la lonja del azúcar,
> abajo la lonja de la seda!"
>
> (Oh Cybernetic Fairy,
> when with one blow will you raze the exchanges,
> which hold me captive
> and free me at last
> so that I can then devote myself
> to seeking a woman
> sweet as sugar,
> soft as silk,
> and eat her all up in little pieces,

and afterwards shout:
"Down with the sugar exchange,
down with the silk exchange!")

Yet if the Hada Cibernética is a vehicle for the expression of the poet's dreams of liberation and fulfilment, she is also another Godot who never arrives and hence, like Bética, she ultimately serves to emphasise his unhappy servitude.

At times Belli's stylised classical manner serves to create a picture of a feudal society and at others to highlight by contrast the baseness of modern life. On other occasions, however, the interplay of the archaic and the contemporary, the classical and the colloquial, is much more complex. Thus, "Cupido y Fisco" is based on a tension between modern and ancient, between the mundane and the noble, between the poet's real situation and the allegorical expression of it:

El sol, la luna y el terrestre globo
recorrí cuánto arriba abajo ansioso,
del ara en pos de los antiguos dioses
    Cupido y Fisco.

Asaz temprano comenzó este caso,
cuando bisoño era y tener quería
un cuerpo y alma de mujer en casa,
    y un buen salario.

Ya por doquiera perseguí cual loco
mañana, tarde, noche a bella Filis,
mas mis hocicos su desdén cuán fiero
    restregó siempre.

Ya letra a letra el abecé retuve,
que a la pirámide del torvo Fisco
presto lleváronme, y de cuyas bases
    salir no puedo.

Ahora, en fin, en la madura, ahora
¡ay!, ¿por qué migas en amor y paga,
si desde tiempo yo a Cupido y Fisco
    cosido yazgo?

(The sun, the moon and the terrestrial globe
I anxiously traversed from top to bottom
on the trail of the altar of the ancient gods
    Cupid and Revenue.

It began very early, this affair,
when I was still green and wanted to have
the body and soul of a woman in the house
    and a good salary.

Here I pursued the beautiful Phyllis
morning, noon and night like a madman,
but her scorn so cruel she always rubbed
        in my snout.

There I crammed the alphabet letter by letter,
for they soon came and carried me off
to stern Revenue's pyramid, from whose depths
        I cannot escape.

Now, at the end of it, in full maturity, now,
alas!, why only crumbs in love and pay,
if for many a year I've lain bound
        to Cupid and Revenue?)

The humble and mundane ambitions expressed in the second stanza
are elevated by being transposed to a stylised world of antiquity
where the poet's poverty and alienation are attributed to the cruelty
of the gods and his efforts to realise his mediocre aspirations become
a quest for noble ideals as heroic in its way as the adventures of the
knights errant of old. At the same time, however, the allegory is
repeatedly undermined by phrases which bring the poem back down
to earth, so that, for example, the second stanza reduces the epic
quest of the first to commonplace longings, while in the third the
image of scorn being rubbed in the poet's snout exposes the beautiful
lady of his dreams as a class-conscious snob and his platonic love for
her as the humiliating frustration of animal lust. Belli's best poetry,
in fact, creates a tension between two contradictory views of the daily
economic struggle, dignifying it as an epic struggle of the human
spirit to triumph over adversity while simultaneously emphasising
the squalid meanness of a routine which degrades the individual and
prevents him from realising his humanity.

The poetic language of Belli's most recent book, *Canciones y otros
poemas* (1982), is essentially the same as that of his earlier work, but
the poems tend to be longer and more discursive and reflective and
they turn away from social reality to take on a decidedly metaphysical
character. A key poem is "En la cima de la edad", where the poet,
having reached the mountaintop of middle age, surveys his life and
ponders what lies ahead of him at the end of his journey. The whole
book, in fact, is dominated by an obsessive desire to possess a world
that he feels to be slipping out of his grasp. This desire manifests itself
in love poems of a markedly erotic nature, where sexual intercourse is
seen as the truest form of human self-expression and communion,
and the woman vainly worshipped from afar is identified with a

fulfilment desperately yearned for but never attained. Elsewhere, as in the magnificent "El ansia de saber todo", Belli voices an urgently felt need to penetrate the mystery of life and to discover an absolute that would not only give meaning and plenitude to his remaining years but assure him of eternal bliss in the after-world. His wish is

> ... enterarse de todo de una vez:
> cuál es la fuente y cuál es el Leteo,
> y en qué punto del universo azul
> la inalcanzable ninfa será hallada
> (aún no vista por la mente obtusa);
> y antes de oír atónito
> el ruin ruido del río tenebroso,
> por último saber
> si el amor que acá empieza en cuerpo y alma,
> en tal estado seguirá en la muerte.

> (... to ascertain everything once and for all:
> which is the source and which is the Lethe,
> and in what point of the azure universe
> is to be found the unattainable nymph
> [still unseen by the obtuse mind];
> and before hearing with awe
> the sinister sound of the gloomy river,
> to know finally
> if the love that begins here in body and soul
> will continue in that state in death.)

Other compositions reflect on the nature and significance of the poetic activity. Thus, "Asir la forma que se va" views artistic creation as an affirmation of life, since aesthetic form is something intrinsically pleasurable, and as an expression of the human longing to cling to life in face of death, since it is an attempt to give lasting shape to what is inevitably slipping away from us. And in "La canción inculta" Belli is able to console himself with the thought that poetry confers a kind of immortality, since it will always be read by future generations:

> pues se perpetuará
> no en los infolios deleznables todos,
> mas en algunas otras
> almas que no han nacido todavía,
> y le abrirán su seno por entero.

> (for it will perpetuate itself,
> not in folios which moulder one and all,
> but in a few other
> souls not yet born
> who will receive it in bosoms opened wide.)

The claims which Belli here makes for poetry are well justified in his own case, for not only has he developed a distinctive personal voice which sets him apart from other Spanish-speaking poets of his age, but his masterly manipulation of language and rhythm translates essentially limited and mundane themes into a verse of universal and lasting significance. Yet his words might be applied with equal justification to Peruvian poetry as a whole during this period. For if the avant-garde era saw the establishment of a solid poetic tradition, the forties and fifties threw up a remarkable generation of poets whose general standard is unmatched anywhere in Latin America. It is the misfortune of those poets and the world's loss that, because of the parlously underdeveloped nature of the Peruvian book industry,[17] their work remains relatively little known outside their own country.

[17] For a discussion of this topic, see pp.319-20

CHAPTER 6

THE CONTEMPORARY THEATRE

Though the genre has a long history stretching back to the early years of the colonial period and even to pre-Columbian times, the theatre has never really flourished in Latin America. The explanation would seem to lie in a chicken-and-egg situation arising out of the continent's underdevelopment: few cities have been able to count on an educated public large enough to support commercial theatre or on professional companies to create a theatre-going public. In such circumstances plays have tended to have very short runs, the majority of those staged have tended to be prestigious foreign works, and the production of national drama has been effectively stifled. Indeed, it is only in recent decades that concerted efforts have been made to establish national theatres and by then the potential mass public had already been captured by the cinema. As a result the Latin American theatre is very much a minority interest.

In the case of Peru the situation has been particularly grave, for there the theatre went into a long decline after the death of Manuel Ascensio Segura.[1] Throughout most of the first half of the twentieth century, in fact, there was a dearth of theatrical groups to stage serious drama and such local theatre as was produced was largely a

---

[1] On twentieth-century drama, see Robert J. Morris, *The Contemporary Peruvian Theatre* (Lubbock, Texas: Texas Tech Press, 1977); Arthur Natella, Jr., *The New Theatre of Peru* (New York: Senda Nueva, 1982); Carlos Miguel Suárez Radillo, "Poesía y realidad social en el teatro peruano contemporáneo", in *Lo social en el teatro hispano-americano contemporáneo* (Caracas: Equinoccio, 1976), pp. 39-61.

continuation of the costumbrist tradition of the nineteenth century, with José Chioino (1898-1960) succeeding Leonidas Yerovi as the main representative of that trend.[2] However, the late thirties and early forties saw a renewal of interest in the stage and efforts were made by artists and intellectuals to revive the national theatre and to bring it into line with international trends. Support and stimulus were given by the government, which funded the Compañía Nacional de Comedias, established in 1945, and in 1946 inaugurated an annual national theatre prize. Other new and energetic theatrical groups were the Asociación de Artistas Aficionados (1938) and the Teatro de la Universidad de San Marcos (1941), and the foundation in 1946 of the Escuela Nacional de Arte Escénico (later to become the Instituto de Arte Dramático) did much to promote training in the dramatic arts. In this new climate the beginning of a theatrical renaissance came in 1946-47 with the appearance in the space of fourteen months of three award-winning plays: Percy Gibson Parra's *Esa luna que empieza* (1946), Juan Ríos' *Don Quijote* (1946) and Sebastián Salazar Bondy's *Amor, gran laberinto* (1947). These plays mark not only a revival of the Peruvian theatre but also a new direction, for all three break with the costumbrist tradition, abandon realism in favour of a non-mimetic representation of reality and are concerned with universal rather than local themes.

Esa luna que empieza, the only play of Percy Gibson Parra (b. 1908), was co-winner of the Premio Nacional de Teatro in 1946.[3] A three-act poetic drama or, as Gibson himself labels it, "poema escénico", it is a lyrical representation of the eternal truths of human existence viewed as an unchanging cycle. It is structured around the daily life of a small fishing village, but the setting is not localised, dramatic conflict and intrigue are eschewed, and the characters are archetypal figures rather than individuals in their own right. Bruno, a sea-captain, sets out on a voyage, leaving his pregnant wife Alba in the care of her brother Dionisio, a student teacher; the latter becomes involved in the eternal love triangle but eventually succeeds in winning the affection of Aura in face of the competition of the artist El; finally, the birth of Alba's son coincides with the news of Bruno's

---

[2] Chioino's main works during this period were *Retorno* (1923), *La divina canción* (1923), *Una vez en la vida* (1927) and *Novio de emergencia* (1928). They appear never to have been published.

[3] See Percy Gibson Parra, *Esa luna que empieza*, in *Teatro peruano contemporáneo*, ed. José Hesse Murga (Madrid: Aguilar, 1959), pp. 27-85. See also Hernán Vidal, "*Esa luna que empieza* y Maeterlinck: la contemporaneidad modernista", *Latin American Theatre Review*, 6 (1973), 5-11.

death at sea. The situations developed in the play are clearly symbolic. Thus, Bruno's final voyage represents man's journey towards death, while the rivalry between Dionisio and El reflects different attitudes towards life, the one embodying social involvement and an ideal of progress, the other the attempt to give permanence to the fleetingness of existence through artistic creation. The dramatic structure itself encapsulates the theme of the cyclical nature of existence, the involvement in life implied by the love triangle of the middle act being enclosed by death and birth depicted in the first and last. The play's meaning is further reinforced by a series of symbols: the phases of the moon mirror the eternal laws of life; the sea symbolises the origins of life and the unknown that lies at the end of it; fishing-nets represent the web of existence. The symbolism, indeed, is perhaps rather too explicit for *Esa luna que empieza* to be an entirely successful work, but Gibson displays undoubted poetic and dramatic gifts and it is a great pity that he did not pursue his career as a playwright.

In contrast Juan Ríos Rey (b. 1914), who shared the 1946 Premio Nacional with Gibson, went on to produce a total of eight plays and to win the prize a further four times.[4] Written in blank verse, *Don Quijote* is a poetic re-creation of episodes from Cervantes' novel, with the twist at the end that the hero refuses to give up his dream and succeeds in communicating it to Sancho and others. Despite its success and its importance in the development of the Peruvian theatre, it is a play with glaring deficiencies and certainly not the best that its author has written. It relies too heavily on the original novel, is too episodic and is cluttered by too many characters, and, above all, it is spoiled by the tendency towards poetic verbosity that mars much of Ríos' theatre. Ríos appears to have been much influenced by César Vallejo, but that influence was largely pernicious, for adopting almost systematically the technique of reiterative accumulation that was a feature of the poet's later work, he carries it to an extreme of rhetorical over-emphasis and self-indulgence and his dialogues often lack naturalness. However, *Don Quijote* establishes a dramatic pattern that Ríos was to develop and improve upon in subsequent plays. Like Gibson, he is concerned to express universal truths and seeks to do so through the creation of poetic myths. With the

---

[4] See Juan Ríos Rey, *Teatro* (n.p., 1961); *Ayar Manko*, in *Teatro peruano contemporáneo*, ed. José Hesse Murga, pp. 95-182. *El mar* (1954) is the only one of Ríos' plays not to have been published. See also Morris, pp. 14-28; Natella, pp. 83-107.

exception of *Los desesperados* (1951),[5] all of his plays are poetic dramas set in the past and are reworkings of well-known historical episodes or cultural myths, sometimes of both in combination. Underlying his work is a sense of the ultimate futility of existence. What gives a meaning to man's life is the struggle for noble ideals which will live on after him, as exemplified by Don Quixote. Conversely, as in *El reino sobre las tumbas* (1949), *Los bufones* (1949) and *La selva* (1950), selfish emotions like envy, hatred, lust and ambition are sterile and lead only to a disillusioned awareness of the emptiness of life. In *El fuego* (1948) and *Los desesperados* (1951) these themes are related to the political struggle for a just society. A combatant on the Republican side in the Spanish Civil War, Ríos believed in the revolutionary ideal but was troubled by the eternal dilemma of ends and means. Both plays deal with revolutionary situations. *El fuego* is structured around an attempt to overthrow a military dictatorship in an unnamed Andean republic in the early years after independence, and explores the ideological conflict between the compassionate and idealistic Captain, who seeks to inspire others with his dream of social justice, and the embittered Fugitive, who advocates unrelenting hatred and ruthless violence as the only means of effecting social change. The same subject is treated much more successfully in *Los desesperados*, which represents a departure for Ríos in that it is his only realistic drama, is set in modern times and is written in prose. The action again takes place in an unnamed country but is clearly based on the abortive Apra *coup* of 3 October 1948. Luciano is an uncompromising militant totally dedicated to the party cause and convinced that only bloody revolution can change an unjust and repressive society. Events seem to vindicate that attitude, but the traumatic effect of terrorism on the young man who carries out an assassination on his instructions and the inhuman way in which he uses people as instruments of the cause call its validity into question. The play thus dramatises an issue of great relevance both to the Peru of the period and to the whole modern age.

Los desesperados is one of Ríos' finest plays and is surpassed only by *Ayar Manko* (1952), the fullest and most effective expression of his world-view. Here Ríos uses characters and events from Peru's pre-Columbian past as raw material to forge a poetic myth encapsulating

---

[5] Most of Ríos' plays underwent substantial revision. In all cases the date given is that of the original version. The revised version of *Los desesperados* won the Premio Nacional de Teatro in 1960.

his vision of man's history and what he believed to be his true destiny. Setting the scene, he conjures up an image of the Inca Empire as an ordered society bound together by a collective spirit and animated by the ideal of creating a world of peace, harmony and plenty. However, the order of that world is disrupted by the violent passions of Ayar Auka, the eldest son of the dying Inca. Devoured by jealousy and ambition for power and egged on by the treacherous Ayar Uchu, his *alter ego*, Ayar Auka cannot accept his father's decision that his brother Ayar Kachi should be the new ruler and secretly has him murdered in order to assume the throne himself. As Inca he betrays the values of his race, for to maintain himself in power he installs a reign of terror and, when forced against his will to embark on a campaign of expansion, he forsakes the policy of benevolent imperialism and wreaks devastation on neighbouring tribes. His evil actions are seen as being counter-productive, however, for he is unable to enjoy the fruits of power since, like Macbeth, he is tormented by his conscience and lives in fear of retribution. Eventually he is deposed by the noble-minded Ayar Manko, the youngest of the four brothers, who restores order to the Inca world and sets his people on the rightful path once more. Ayar Auka would thus seem to represent the course that human history has taken, a course which has deviated from what ought to have been man's true mission on earth and has led to social oppression and individual alienation, while Ayar Manko, who effects a conciliation with the defeated tribes and proclaims that they are all brothers and must work together as a single people to cultivate the earth, embodies what Ríos saw as the authentic revolutionary spirit. Thematically *Ayar Manko* is clearly an important play. Technically it suffers from Ríos' habitual tendency to verbosity and over-emphasis, but these defects are offset by powerful dialogue, some fine lyrical passages, skilful use of poetic symbols and interpolated song and ballet, effective dramatic construction and, above all, excellent characterisation. Not only does Ríos' overall production constitute a substantial contribution to the development of the Peruvian theatre, but *Ayar Manko* and *Los desesperados* reveal him to be a much underrated dramatist.

No individual did more to promote a vigorous and modern theatre in Peru than Sebastián Salazar Bondy (1924-65).[6] Salazar was the

---

[6] See Sebastián Salazar Bondy, *Comedias y juguetes* and *Piezas dramáticas*, vols. I and II of *Obras* (Moncloa, 1967). See also Juan Caballero, *El teatro de Sebastián Salazar Bondy* (García Ribeyro, 1975); Wolfgang A. Luchting, "*El rabdomante* o el escepticismo burgués", *Mundo Nuevo*, 33 (1969), 38-44; Morris, pp. 28-40; Natella, pp. 31-74; José Miguel Oviedo, "Sebastián Salazar Bondy en su teatro", in Salazar Bondy, *Obras*, II, 9-33.

country's leading theatre critic of the fifties, in 1951 he was responsible for reorganising the Ministry of Education's theatrical division, he was the inspiration behind the founding of the Club de Teatro group in 1953 and he was directly involved in theatrical productions as director and artistic adviser. His own dramatic output consists of ten major works, eleven brief one-act plays, and a reworking of the classic *Ollantay* in collaboration with César Miró. While Ríos' work is remarkably consistent in themes and manner, Salazar's theatre is varied in character, for his career was marked by continual experimentation as he sought simultaneously to find the form that best suited him and to renovate the national theatre. Nonetheless, there are two main sides to his work, corresponding to the two facets of his own personality and to two dramatic concepts. On the one hand, he conceived theatre as entertainment, as light-hearted play, and on the other, he saw it as a vehicle for the critical portrayal of the society in which he lived. Throughout his career those two attitudes struggled against each other for the upper hand and, unfortunately, he never really succeeded in harmonising them.

Salazar made his theatrical debut with *Amor, gran laberinto*, which won the 1947 Premio Nacional de Teatro. An allegorical farce with grotesque, puppet-like figures in the style of Valle-Inclán, it is set in the imaginary country of Vientreameno and mirrors the depressing reality of Latin America's political history, in which hopes of social justice have repeatedly been defrauded by an endless series of so-called revolutions. Finding his advances spurned by the wife of the ruling Baron, the discontented police chief Jerónimez wreaks revenge by heading a popular revolution which takes over the palace and condemns the former rulers to be servants of the new masters. However, the revolution merely turns things on their head without changing anything and in the end the Baron regains power with the support of the very populace who had rebelled against him. An epilogue delivers a warning against false revolutionaries who act out of purely selfish motives and suggests that the people still await authentic leaders who will give direction to their revolutionary aspirations. Though an innovatory work in the Peruvian context, the play is less than successful. The dialogues are frequently artificial and stilted and the language exaggeratedly archaic; the denouement is so inadequately justified as to appear contrived; and, above all, it is a farce that fails to be funny because of the heavy emphasis on the social allegory, which is spelt out rather too solemnly and explicitly.

In the following years Salazar went on to cultivate a realistic type of theatre with two historical pieces, *Rodil* (1954) and *Flora Tristán* (1959), and the social dramas *No hay isla feliz* (1954) and *Algo que quiere morir* (1956). The historical plays reflect the author's growing political radicalism. General Rodil, the protagonist of Spain's last stand against the forces of independence, is a symbol of the intransigent defence of conservative tradition, while Flora Tristán, a French-Peruvian who was an early champion of women and workers' rights, represents a new progressive spirit. *Rodil* is one of Salazar's best constructed works, but the latter play, consisting of three separate dialogues corresponding to three stages in the heroine's life, lacks unity and dramatic force. The social dramas depict the frustration of the hopes and ambitions of the aspiring lower middle classes. In *No hay isla feliz* the settlers of a small coastal village struggle for years to build up the community and to create a decent life for their families, only to see their dreams shattered at a stroke by faceless government bureaucrats who decide that the planned highway extension should bypass the town. The play also introduces the theme of the generation conflict, in which Salazar saw a symptom of the crisis Peruvian society was undergoing and which he explores more fully in *Algo que quiere morir*. Here the world of an immigrant couple, who by dint of hard work have built up a successful small business, is brought down around them by the waywardness of their children, whose raised expectations lead them to reject the traditional values of their parents and to nurse desires and ambitions they lack the means to satisfy. Unfortunately, neither of the social dramas is an artistic success. Technically *No hay isla feliz* is one of Salazar's weakest works, and though *Algo que quiere morir* is a considerable improvement in that respect, it too is marred by some over-dramatisation and by the excessive sentimentality of the denouement.

In the late fifties Salazar's career entered a new phase with a series of four satirical-costumbrist comedies which represent an attempt to create a modern national theatre on the model of the French popular theatre, whose vitality greatly impressed him during a brief stay in France in 1956, but which also mark a return to the tradition of Segura. This phase was initiated by *Dos viejas van por la calle* (1959), which again introduces the theme of generational conflict through the story of the efforts of two elderly spinsters to mould their young nephew in the image of their own traditional social standards and of their eventual ejection from their home by his domineering bride. On the costumbrist level the play is a success, but its great weakness is that by enclosing the play in a prologue and an epilogue depicting the pathetic destitution of the elderly sisters, Salazar seeks to impose on it a social message — the uncaring treatment of the old by the young — which the dramatic action does not justify. His next two comedies, *El fabricante de deudas* (1963) and *La escuela de los chismes* (1965), are based on two classics of the European theatre, Balzac's *Le faiseur* and Sheridan's *School for Scandal*, which are adapted to the Limeñan scene. In the first the capitalist financial system is effectively satirised through the wheeling and dealing of the cynical Obedot, but the latter is a rather conventional and superficial portrayal of Limeñan society's love of malicious gossip. The musical comedy *Ifigenia en el mercado*, staged posthumously in 1966, brings a new dimension to Salazar's popular theatre, but while it is effective entertainment it is ultimately no more than a mildly satirical and somewhat sentimental dramatisation of the disillusioning experiences of a naive provincial girl brought face to face with the deceitfulness of the inhabitants of the capital. Indeed, while Salazar's realistic works tend to be rather heavy-handed in conveying their social message, his popular comedies, with the exception of *El fabricante de deudas*, present a satire that is very much diluted.

Just before his death Salazar wrote *El rabdomante*, an extended one-act play which is perhaps his best work and was posthumously awarded the 1965 Premio Nacional de Teatro. Abandoning the popular comedy, he here creates an allegorical drama which is usually considered as marking yet another new departure but could equally be regarded as a return to the manner with which he began his theatrical career. Like *Amor, gran laberinto* it is constructed around a symbolic situation reflecting the socio-political reality not only of Peru but of the whole Latin American continent. The wretched inhabitants of an unnamed province suffer from a prolonged drought, symbol of the deprivation of social justice, till a water-diviner, representing the figure of the artist, shows them how to find water for themselves, whereupon they rise up and massacre their rulers and then kill their benefactor. Written at a time when the example of Cuba seemed to be inspiring a continental movement towards revolution, the play is an important statement on the artist's position in society. Salazar saw it as the artist's role to promote revolutionary values but he was realistic enough to recognise that, as a product of the middle classes, he was destined to be devoured by the very revolution he helped set in motion. Yet if *El rabdomante* is a significant work, it is too slight to be a great one. Indeed, in contrast to Ríos, Salazar is a very overrated dramatist, for if *Rodil, El fabricante de deudas* and *El rabdomante* are estimable works, he failed to produce one really outstanding play. Ultimately, therefore, he is destined to be remembered as the stimulator of a theatrical revival rather than as a major dramatist.

Meanwhile the fifties saw an increase in theatrical activity with the staging of foreign plays by touring companies and the emergence of new theatrical groups such as the Teatro de la Universidad Católica (1951), the Club de Teatro (1953) and Histrión (1956), and towards the end of the decade the national theatre was given a boost by the success of two plays by local dramatists. First Enrique Solari Swayne's *Collacocha*, written in 1955, won an international award in Mexico in 1958 and went on to receive acclaim throughout Latin America, and subsequently Julio Ramón Ribeyro's *Vida y pasión de Santiago el pajarero*, written in 1958 and premiered in 1960, proved enormously popular with Lima audiences.[7]

In *Collacocha* Enrique Solari Swayne (b. 1915) brings to the stage one of the great themes of Latin American fiction, that of man's struggle to dominate the continent's hostile natural environment.[8] The play is both a call to Peruvians to work to build a brave new future and an affirmation of faith in their ability to do so. The protagonist Echecopar, the engineer in charge of the construction of a series of tunnels through the Andes, is an idealist and a man of action. An anti-establishment figure, he rejects the values of Limeñan society preoccupied only with status and soft living, and he has nothing but contempt for politicians and businessmen, who in their concern to promote their own interest ignore the plight of the masses. But he is equally impatient of intellectuals who harp on about the human condition and of left-wing ideologues who theorise about the class struggle. Animated by a deep sense of mission, he is convinced that only practical action will bring progress to the country and free its population from ignorance and misery. Symbol of that progress is the tunnel at Collacocha, the last link in a road

---

[7] Another, more modest success of this period was *Muerte de Atahualpa* by Bernardo Roca Rey (b. 1918), who, though very much a secondary dramatist, had earlier made a significant contribution to the revival of the national theatre with three plays produced in the late forties. His last and best work, *Muerte de Atahualpa* dates from 1951, but was not staged until 1957, when it won the Premio Nacional de Teatro. See *Teatro peruano contemporáneo*, ed. José Hesse Murga, pp. 181-201.

[8] See Enrique Solari Swayne, *Collacocha*, in *Teatro peruano contemporáneo*, ed. José Hesse Murga, pp. 307-99. Solari is also the author of *La mazorca* (1965) and *Ayax Telamonio* (1968), both of which have remained unpublished. See also Morris, pp. 44-49; Natella, pp. 75-82.

system joining jungle and coast. The first act presents Echecopar as a dynamic figure whose dedication and ability to inspire his workers have enabled him to achieve that extraordinary engineering feat. In the second act, however, unpredictable nature strikes back as water from a mountain lagoon seeps downwards, causing a violent cave-in which claims the lives of 180 workers. Here, at the moment of greatest peril, Echecopar reveals himself at his most impressive as, putting the workers' safety before his own, he remains at his post to coordinate the evacuation. The third act shows him haunted by guilt for the deaths for which he holds himself responsible, but the project is carried on by his assistant Fernández and Echecopar's life's work is justified as the first lorry is driven through the new tunnel. *Collacocha* is a play of considerable dramatic force and its let's-roll-up-our-sleeves attitude to the problems of underdevelopment is a welcome change from the usual woolly ideological approach. However, Echecopar comes across as a larger-than-life figure with a tiresome tendency to indulge in declamatory tirades, and the final act is something of an anti-climax after the drama of the one preceding it. Above all, it is a very simplistic and naively optimistic work. Therein, one suspects, lies the secret of its popularity.

A very different kind of play is *Vida y pasión de Santiago el pajarero* by Julio Ramón Ribeyro (b. 1929), a work in six scenes based on a *tradición* of Ricardo Palma concerning an eighteenth-century visionary who believed that he had discovered the secret of flight.[9] In Ribeyro's adaptation Santiago's dream of flying is inspired by the birds he sells for a living and is encouraged by the rhymester and the sculptor, his bohemian associates, but it is opposed by his fiancée Rosaluz, who urges him to concentrate his attention on establishing a solid financial and social position and eventually leaves him to take up with the aristocratic Duque de San Carlos. The hero submits a plan for a flying machine to Viceroy Amat with a request for financial backing, but in the centre-piece of the play the obscurantist professor of mathematics at San Marcos University, Don Cosme Bueno, holds it up to public ridicule. Undaunted, he resolves to pursue his project but comes to grief when his neighbour, a barber greedy to gain possession of his shop, announces to the public that he is to stage a

---

[9] Ribeyro is the author of a further seven plays, the most important of which is the as yet unstaged *Atusparia* (1981). See Julio Ramón Ribeyro, *Teatro* (INC, 1975); *Atusparia* (Rikchay Perú, 1981). See also Wolfgang A. Luchting, *Julio Ramón Ribeyro y sus dobles* (INC, 1971), pp. 87-122; id., "El *Teatro* de Julio Ramón Ribeyro", *Hispamérica*, 31 (1982), 93-100; Morris, pp. 49-52.

demonstration of human flight. When Santiago protests that he is not yet ready to do so, the crowd, feeling itself cheated, marches him up to a hilltop and forces him off the edge. Ribeyro departs from Palma's original by making Santiago a bird-seller instead of a tailor, by giving him a fictitious fiancée and fictitious associates and by inventing his own denouement. More importantly, by portraying a suffocating environment that stifles creative activity he offers an image of colonial Lima very different from that presented by Palma. Above all, while the *tradición* is essentially a simple historical reconstruction, Ribeyro transforms the story of the historical figure into an allegorical representation of the situation of the artist in contemporary Peru. Santiago is clearly a personification of the artist, his dream of flight symbolising creative aspiration, but, in keeping with the cultural backwardness of an underdeveloped country, he is very much an incipient artist still not sure of his vocation — with his fiancée and his shop he still has a foot in the everyday world — nor sure of where he is going. And no sooner does he formulate his dream than the whole of society seems to conspire to thwart his pursuit of it. He has to resist emotional pressure to conform from his fiancée, the voice of bourgeois common sense and materialism. The conservatism of the intellectual establishment denies him encouragement and support. His unworldliness makes him an easy victim of the *viveza* of the grasping and unscrupulous businessmen represented by the barber. And finally he is pilloried and destroyed by a public which demands to be entertained. Like all of Ribeyro's theatre *Vida y pasión de Santiago el pajarero* suffers from certain dramatic weaknesses which betray its author's lack of theatrical experience.[10] Yet, despite that, it is among the best of Peruvian plays, with effective dialogue, superb characterisation and some marvellous *tours de force* such as the episode of Don Cosme's report.

Since the early sixties there have been renewed attempts to popularise the theatre. At an individual level sterling work has been done by figures such as Sara Joffré (b. 1935) and Víctor Zavala (b. 1932). Joffré is herself a dramatist of some distinction with six one-act plays to her credit,[11] but her main contribution to her country's

---

[10] The same is true of the theatre of his fellow fiction-writer, Mario Vargas Llosa. See *La Señorita de Tacna* (Barcelona: Seix Barral, 1981); *Kathie y el hipopótamo* (Barcelona: Seix Barral, 1983).

[11] See Sara Joffré, *Cuento alrededor de un círculo de espuma. En el jardín de Mónica* (Exprinter, 1962); *Una obligación*, in Cinco autores, *Teatro peruano* (Ediciones Homero Teatro de Grillos, 1974), pp. 59-77. Her other plays remain unpublished. See also Morris, pp. 80-90.

theatre has been as founder of Homero, Teatro de Grillos, a theatrical group for children which has become an institution in Lima and has enjoyed successful tours of the provinces. Zavala, a professor of literature at the University of Huánuco, is the author of seven one-act social dramas depicting the oppression and exploitation of the Indian, but his originality lies in the fact that his work is aimed at the rural masses rather than at sophisticated city audiences and it has been successfully performed in rural areas.[12] Official recognition of the need for state support came with the creation in 1971 of a government-funded Teatro Nacional Popular to promote every aspect of the dramatic arts throughout the country. For many years the Teatro de la Universidad de San Marcos has seen it as part of its function to take its productions to the *barriadas* of Lima and to the provinces. The Teatro de la Universidad Católica was prominent in pioneering experimental theatre, and various companies have drawn in the public by staging adaptations of well-known works of fiction. Peru is still far from having a flourishing theatre by European standards. Nonetheless, recent years have shown evidence of a new vitality and today the Peruvian theatre is in a healthier state than it has ever been, with a number of well-established companies in the capital and other companies in the main provincial cities.

In the same period several new playwrights have come to the fore, such as Juan Rivera Saavedra (b. 1930), Elena Portocarrero, Sarina Helfgott (b. 1941), Gregor Díaz (b. 1933) and Julio Ortega (b. 1942), as well as the above-mentioned Joffré and Zavala.[13] However, the major dramatist of recent years is unquestionably Alonso Alegría (b. 1940), whose *El cruce sobre el Niágara*, written in 1968, won the prestigious Casa de las Américas drama award in Cuba in 1969.[14]

---

[12] See Víctor Zavala, *Teatro campesino* (Univ. Nac. de Educación, 1969). See also Morris, pp. 90-95.

[13] Only part of the work of these authors has been published. See Juan Rivera Saavedra, *Teatro de humor negro* (Arte Futuro, 1967)/Elena Portocarrero, *La corcova. Hoy no, mañana tampoco* (Caballo de Troya, 1966)/Sarina Helfgott, *Teatro* (Teatro de la Univ. Católica, 1967)/Gregor Díaz, *Los del cuatro*, in *Teatro contemporáneo hispanoamericano*, ed. Orlando Rodríguez-Sardiñas and Carlos Miguel Suárez Radillo (Madrid: Escelicer, 1971), I, 513-604/Julio Ortega, *Teatro* (Teatro de la Univ. Católica, 1965); *La campana*, in *Teatro breve hispanoamericano contemporáneo*, ed. Carlos Solórzano (Madrid: Aguilar, 1970), pp. 71-76. Plays by Saavedra, Helfgott and Díaz are also included in Cinco autores, *Teatro peruano* (Ediciones Homero Teatro de Grillos, 1974). On Ortega, see Morris, pp. 62-73.

[14] See Alonso Alegría, *El cruce sobre el Niágara* (Havana: Casa de las Américas, 1969). An earlier work, *Remigio el huaquero* (1965), remains unpublished. See also Nora Eidelberg, "Los procedimientos de ruptura en *El cruce sobre el Niágara* de Alonso Alegría", *RevCrit*, 13 (1981), 113-20; Morris, pp. 73-79; Grazia Sanguineti de Ferrero, "*El cruce sobre el Niágara*, pieza simbólica", *Lexis*, V, 1 (1981), 221-27.

Consisting of six scenes and a prologue, the play is based on the exploits of Blondin (1824-97), the French tightrope walker whose most famous achievement was his crossing of the Niagara Falls on a wire, a feat he performed several times with variations. The only two characters are Blondin and Carlo, a young fan who accuses his hero of having become a mere showman and urges him to attempt more challenging feats which will test his courage and skill. He suggests that a man like Blondin could walk on air if he applied his mind to it and that that is the goal he ought to set himself. This the acrobat dismisses as fantasy, but recognising the truth of the criticism levelled against him, he undertakes to carry Carlo across the Falls on his shoulders. After weeks of training the two men achieve such perfect mental and physical coordination that they feel that they constitute a single being, whom they christen Icarón, and in the triumphant final scene they not only accomplish the feat but experience such an exhilarating sense of confidence in their powers that they feel capable of stepping off the wire and walking towards the sun. Alegría thus affirms the infinite potential of the human spirit, man's ability to go beyond the limits of what seems possible to ever greater achievements. Such optimism suggests an obvious parallel with *Collacocha*, but in fact the play has closer affinities with the Theatre of the Absurd and, in particular, with *Waiting for Godot*, a work which Alegría successfully staged as a director. Indeed, *El cruce sobre el Niágara* could be regarded as a response to the disillusioned world-view of the Theatre of the Absurd. As such it is an emblematic work, expressing the Third World's faith in the future in contrast to the weary disenchantment of writers of the developed Western countries.

The whole play is dominated by the central symbol of Niagara, whose great chasm represents both the abyss of existential emptiness and the unknown which beckons man with its infinite possibilities. Isolated and dissatisfied figures at the outset, Blondin and Carlo give a meaning to their lives and achieve self-fulfilment by working together to attain a common goal and striving to transcend human limitations. Yet far from being a simple allegory, it is a play rich in suggestiveness and susceptible of interpretation on various levels. Blondin and Carlo share in common the urge to tread untrodden ground but in every other respect they are complementary opposites who could be viewed as each other's *alter ego*. Blondin is the embodiment of artistic talent, of the creative spirit which expresses itself instinctively and unconsciously, but he is an artist who has never realised his full potential because he lacks the mental awareness to channel his natural gifts towards clearly defined goals. Carlo, on the other hand, is a man of intellectual vision but does not possess the creative powers to convert his vision into reality. It is only when they come together and fuse into a single being that they succeed in surpassing themselves, and it is thus implied that artistic and intellectual achievement is the privilege of those who learn to develop and harmonise all of their faculties. But Blondin and Carlo are also individuals in their own right, the one a man of action providing strength and physical skills, the other a man of ideas contributing vision and stimulus, and the story of their joint venture is also a kind of parable showing how men can rise above themselves and achieve the seemingly impossible when individuals work together in a spirit of cooperation and solidarity. *El cruce sobre el Niágara* is thus a play of universal significance and one which consciously sets out to be so. It is also a well-written work, with dialogue that is controlled yet imaginative, and Alegría's professional experience as a producer and director has made it technically the most accomplished of Peruvian plays. In all respects, therefore, it marks the culmination of Peru's theatrical revival.

In conclusion, there can be no doubt that since the 1940s the Peruvian theatre has made considerable strides. Theatrical activity has increased, more and better works have been written, productions have become more professional, the theatre has become more popular. Nonetheless, such progress as has been achieved is relative and drama continues to be the poor relation of the literary genres. Despite not unsuccessful attempts to popularise the theatre, the country still suffers from a lack of a public of sufficient size to support commercial theatre except on a very modest scale, and the continuing paucity of official support means that the various semi-professional groups have to struggle to keep their heads above water. In such circumstances it is hardly surprising that, while Peruvian dramatists have produced a number of unquestionably fine plays such as Ríos' *Ayar Manko* and *Los desesperados*, Salazar's *El rabdomante*, Ribeyro's *Vida y pasión de Santiago el pajarero* and Alegría's *El cruce sobre el Niágara*, on the whole they have failed to match the achievements of the country's poets and novelists in terms of both quantity and quality.

CHAPTER 7
FRESH GROWTH (c.1960-1984)

Part I
The New Narrative Mark II

In the panorama of contemporary Peruvian fiction special mention must be made of a novel by the poet Jorge Eduardo Eielson (b. 1921) which, though not published until 1971, was actually written between 1955 and 1957 and anticipates many of the innovatory narrative techniques of the new novel of the sixties and seventies. This is *El cuerpo de Giulia-no*, a work in the tradition of Adán's *La casa de cartón* recounting the story of an expatriate Peruvian artist who is prompted by the suicide of his mistress to take stock of his life.[1] Written in an austere style, the novel has the form of a monologue addressed to Giulia by the narrator in an attempt at self-justification. It does not follow a chronological sequence but leaps back and forth, jumbling and interrelating people and incidents from different periods of his life, and since his is an experience which in large part has been lived on an imaginative level, the real events he describes are interwoven with fantasy.

The narrator's recollections go back to his childhood and adolescence in Peru, where he was brought up by his widowed mother and his uncle Miguel, who ran the family estate in the mountains. A sensitive and imaginative boy, he did not have it in him to be the "man" his mother kept urging him to be and he hated his uncle, a coarse, domineering man who tyrannised the Indians under

---

[1] See Jorge Eduardo Eielson, *El cuerpo de Giulia-no* (Mexico City: Joaquín Mortiz, 1971).

his charge and was concerned only with making the property pay. Rebelling against the future his mother had planned out for him, he refused to settle down to marriage and a career or to take over the administration of the estate and instead opted to be an artist and moved to Europe. There he shared a bohemian existence with Giulia, an Italian model-cum-prostitute, whom he saw as an ally in his personal war against bourgeois values. Central to his life has been the pursuit of an ineffable ideal of beauty and harmony associated in his mind with certain incidents from his adolescence. The first was a tender and ecstatic sexual experience with Mayana, an innocent young Indian girl. The second involved Giuliano, a poor boy of Italian extraction from a neighbouring property, a handsome Adonis in whose company he spent an idyllic afternoon bathing nude in the river and with whom he was on the verge of having a homosexual relationship. Subsequently, however, he was to see his ideal sullied and betrayed as both were corrupted by the ugliness of the world. Shortly after his encounter with Mayana, he was an unwitting spectator of her brutal sexual degradation at the hands of his uncle and he came to realise that ahead of her lay the abjection of all women of her race. For his part Giuliano grew up to be a prosperous, self-made businessman whose obesity of physique reflected his grossness of spirit. The relationship with Giulia represents an attempt to recuperate that ideal. If Giuliano is now Giulia+ano (anus), she is Giulia-no, not Giulia but Giuliano as he was, and he regards her as a kind of goddess whose body is the incarnation of the perfection he has been seeking all his life. However, the sight of her corpse in the mortuary leaves his ideal in tatters. Beauty and harmony, it seems, cannot survive in the corrupt material world.

Her death also leads him to question himself. He becomes aware of his own egoism, which forced her to live in the image he created for her and failed to take account of her needs, and he is assailed by guilt at the thought that it was his growing coolness towards her which drove her to suicide. He comes, too, to recognise her humanity and to understand that, far from being a deity, she was a lonely, frightened creature in need of love and warmth, and that if she submitted to the role his imagination imposed upon her, it was in order to keep him. He also realises that he has been living a lie and that just as his ideal exists only in his imagination, so too his rebellion against bourgeois society has been no more than a charade, a pathetic game. Furthermore, the novel questions the validity of the written word. In a chapter devoted to a discussion of language, the narrator states that his aim is to give a truthful account of his life, but he is aware that the written word tends to become an instrument of mystification and he suspects that he has merely used people and events of his life as a pretext for exhibiting himself before a select group of fellow intellectuals. The novel thus reflects the same process of disillusionment that has already been noted in Eielson's poetry.

El cuerpo de Giulia-no is a novel which has never received the critical attention or editorial success which it deserves. By contrast, as the boom in Spanish American narrative continued into the seventies, the growing reputation of Peruvian fiction was to be confirmed by the international acclaim achieved by two writers whose respective works represent a continuation of the country's urban and regionalist fictional traditions.

Unquestionably the major Peruvian fiction-writer to emerge since Vargas Llosa, Alfredo Bryce Echenique (b. 1939) has produced in *Un mundo para Julius* (1970) one of the outstanding Spanish American novels of recent years.[2] A lengthy work set in Lima in the fifties, it offers, through the story of the childhood of a "poor little rich boy", a rare inside view of the privileged world of the oligarchy in which the author himself was brought up. The novel is, above all, a verbal *tour de force* in which Bryce displays an extraordinary talent for capturing spoken speech. Not only does the story have the form of an oral narrative recounted in a humorous and ironic tone in the language of Lima's middle and upper classes, but the narrator reproduces the discourse of his characters, sometimes directly, but more usually through free indirect speech. For Bryce's world is one created in large part by the spoken word, a world where people define themselves as much by what they say as by what they do, where most things are

[2] See Alfredo Bryce Echenique, *Cuentos completos* (Madrid: Alianza, 1981); *Un mundo para Julius* (Barcelona: Barral, 1970; Barcelona: Laia, 1979); *Tantas veces Pedro* (Madrid: Cátedra, 1981); *La vida exagerada de Martín Romaña* (Barcelona: Argos Vergara, 1981). For Bryce's journalism, see *A vuelo de buen cubero y otras crónicas* (Barcelona: Anagrama, 1977). See also Alfredo Bryce Echenique, "*Un mundo para Julius*: digresiones, preguntas y respuestas", *Les Langues Néo-Latines*, 232 (1980), 155-62; Jesús Benítez Villalba, "El mundo de Bryce Echenique a través de algunos de sus cuentos", *CIILI*, II, 1155-60; *Co-Textes* (Montpellier), 9 (1985), a volume devoted to Bryce; J. Ann Duncan, "Language as Protagonist: Tradition and Innovation in Bryce Echenique's *Un mundo para Julius*", *Forum for Modern Language Studies*, 16 (1980), 120-35; Tomás G. Escajadillo, "Bryce: elogios varios y una objeción", *RevCrit*, 6 (1977), 137-48; Mercedes López Baralt, "Otra forma de complicidad entre el autor y sus lectores: Alfredo Bryce Echenique y *Un mundo para Julius*", *Sin nombre*, 7 (1976), 50-56; Wolfgang A. Luchting, *Alfredo Bryce/Humores y malhumores* (Milla Batres, 1975); Phyllis Rodríguez-Peralta, "Narrative Access to *Un mundo para Julius*", *Revista de Estudios Hispánicos*, 3 (1983), 407-18; Paul Verdevoye, "Léxico peruano e hispanoamericano de *Un mundo para Julius*", *Les Langues Néo-Latines*, 232 (1980), 163-72.

experienced aurally, where as important as actual experience is the way in which people respond to experience by verbalising it. The overall effect of the narrative technique is simultaneously to involve us in and distance us from the world described. Though the novel is recounted mainly in the third person, the omniscient narrator is far from being a detached observer. He involves himself with his characters, puts himself in their shoes, even addresses them directly as if they were there alongside him and, like a supporter at a football match, he sides with some against others, and he also involves the reader by establishing a dialogue with him. At the same time, however, the tone of complicity established with the reader and the ironic humour of the narrative operate in the opposite direction, distancing and dissociating him and us from the image of the Limeñan oligarchy which the novel builds up from the inside, through the discourse by which that class reveals its mentality to us.

The most apolitical of writers, Bryce does not heap condemnation on an oligarchic society for which he has always retained a certain nostalgic affection, but it is presented in such a way as to stand condemned in the eyes of the reader. The world in which Julius grows up is not a static one, for the marriage of his widowed mother Susan and his stepfather Juan Lucas represents the alliance of the traditional oligarchy with the new blood of modern business interests, and Peru's changing socio-economic climate is reflected in the move from the old-fashioned palace to a modern mansion designed by the fashionable architect of the moment and in the increasingly impersonal relationship between masters and servants which replaces the old paternalism. However, we see little of Juan Lucas' business activities in the novel, for it concentrates primarily on the life-style of a class complacently enjoying the fruits of a privileged position it regards as the natural order of things. Not that there is anything vulgarly ostentatious about the world in which Juan Lucas and Susan move, for they are "beautiful people", good-looking, elegant, charming and with impeccable style and taste. Throughout the novel there are various indications of the social injustice on which the oligarchy's privilege is founded, perhaps the most subtle being a description of Julius' bedroom, known as Fort Apache, where his nanny from the sierra is daily confronted by a poster of cowboys massacring redskins. But not only are Juan Lucas and his wife blind to such injustice, but, apart from odd moments when Susan fleetingly toys with charity work, they are totally unconcerned with and even unaware of the hardship and misery all around them. For the upper classes are shown to be isolated in their own little enclave, sheltered from the world outside which they see only from the window of their limousines, and their only contact with other classes is through their servants, who, when not serving them, are conveniently tucked away in their own quarters. What the novel brings out is, above all, the emptiness and sterility of such a life-style. It is not just that it is totally frivolous or that it produces young men who, like Julius' elder brothers, are sated by the time they reach their twenties. Appearances to the contrary, Juan Lucas and Susan's elegant pursuit of pleasure is a life lived on the defensive. Just as they isolate themselves from the squalid world in which the rest of Peru lives, they retreat into a pampered and pleasurable routine to shut out the ugly side of life. Displays of genuine emotion are shunned, problems are avoided, unpleasant incidents are hushed up, corpses are slipped out the back door. Ultimately, therefore, we are presented with the image of a class which, if it is to be despised for its unthinking exploitation of the poor, is also to be pitied for its fear of assuming life in all its fullness.

This, then, is the world which Julius is destined to inherit. It is, however, one into which he never quite fits. Partly it is a question of character, for he is possessed of a natural sensitivity and curiosity of mind that set him apart from other members of the family, but partly, too, it is a consequence of his isolation within the family, for, as a youngest child largely ignored by his elder brothers and robbed of the attentions of his frivolous mother by a stepfather whom he resents, he has to turn to the servants for the affection of which he is starved. Julius takes a lively interest in the worlds outside his own and establishes bonds of affection with people outside his class. Indeed, such is his ability to empathise with the lower orders that he is capable of making gestures on their behalf against his own kind, as when he wreaks revenge on a classmate for bullying Cano, a boy from a relatively humble background, or when he steers a dead servant's coffin out the front door instead of through the back as arranged by Juan Lucas. Julius never succeeds in bridging the gulf between his own privileged world and the world that lies beyond it, for, conditioned as he is, he is repelled by its ugliness and squalor and, in any case, he always remains in the eyes of others what he is by birth. Yet neither is he at home in his own world. For he responds to people as human beings rather than as members of a social class and he is affected by experiences to which those around him make themselves insensitive. The novel, in fact, is the story of Julius' discovery of the ugly, squalid side of life from which everything in his oligarchic background conspires to shelter him. It opens with the death of his sister Cinthia, the great love of his early childhood, and it ends with the traumatic discovery that his nanny Vilma, who had been a second mother to him, has become a common prostitute in the wake of her rape by his brother Santiago and her subsequent dismissal from the family service. Devastated by that revelation, Julius loses his childhood innocence at the end of the novel and enters adolescence in tears and asking questions. What the future holds for him is left for the reader to judge, but it seems clear that, whether or not he ever succeeds in finding an alternative world, he is too sensitive to accept the values of the environment into which he has been born.

Bryce is also an important short-story writer, with the collections *Huerto cerrado* (1968) and *La felicidad ja ja* (1974) to his credit. Like *Un mundo para Julius* many of his stories revolve around outsider figures. "Con Jimmy en Paracas", the story that first made his name, is the account of a lower-middle-class boy's painful initiation into the realities of the class system during the course of a weekend at a luxury hotel by the sea, where he has been taken as a treat by his father, a salesman on a business trip paid for by the company. There he finds himself mingling with a rich classmate and his father's employers and is humiliated by the discovery of his father's servility and of the patronising attitude of the upper classes towards their inferiors. Bryce's outsiders have much in common with those of Ribeyro in that they are all losers in the rat race of life, whether because of social background or a temperamental inability to assert themselves or a combination of both, yet in their weakness and failure they demonstrate a humanity which the successful conspicuously lack. Indeed, by focusing on them Bryce is able to cast a critical light on the mechanisms, attitudes and values of the social order which marginates them. Thus, "Eisenhower y la Tiqui-tiqui-tin" is the drunken monologue of the descendant of a once-prominent family who has come down in the world, in which he rehearses the self-vindication he would like to make to the prosperous lawyer who was the inseparable friend of his youth. He comes across as a pathetic failure, lacking the qualities to triumph in a competitive world, but at the same time he reveals a sensitivity to the feelings of others which saves him as a human being, and ultimately it is the ruthless ambition and unquestioning arrogance and self-confidence of his friend that stand condemned. However, Bryce's most memorable character is the eponymous protagonist of the marvellously funny "Muerte de

Sevilla en Madrid". Sevilla is the archetypal seven-stone weakling. An orphan brought up decently and respectably in straitened circumstances by two maiden aunts, he is ugly, timid, and totally lacking in self-confidence and everything he touches goes wrong. Expecting nothing out of life, he asks only to be left alone to his own devices, but the world intrudes upon him when he unexpectedly wins a trip to Spain in a competition organised by an air-line company. The trip is an utter fiasco. He is literally sick with worry, he feels pressurised at every turn, everyone takes advantage of him, and he progresses from disaster to disaster till eventually he is driven to leap out of his hotel window. But the plane taking his corpse back home across the Atlantic crosses with another carrying the Lima manager of the Spanish air-line, now reduced to a nervous wreck by his involvement with Sevilla. Like Juan Lucas in *Un mundo para Julius*, the handsome, elegant, sophisticated, self-assured Conde de la Avenida had been the embodiment of social success till Sevilla arrived on the scene to sabotage it all by breaking down the complacent assumptions of his pampered, sheltered world and bringing him face to face with the messiness of life.

While it would be wrong to view Bryce's writing as being autobiographical, it is nonetheless clear that to a large extent his principal fictional figures are *alter egos* of the author. In that sense *Un mundo para Julius* may be regarded as a statement explaining his break with the society in which he was brought up, a break which he made in real life by moving to France, where he has devoted himself to his literary vocation while earning a living as a university teacher. More recently that break is reflected in the cosmopolitan characters and settings of his two latest novels. It is also reflected in the fact that those novels are no longer concerned with depicting a particular social environment but with expressing his own personal view of life and his personal involvement with literature. These novels, it has to be said, are something of a disappointment after *Un mundo para Julius*. The tendency to prolixity inherent in Bryce's oral style of narrative and in his predilection for humorous anecdotes here gets out of hand and the novels ramble on at disproportionate length. He is also markedly less successful in handling cosmopolitan characters and all too often they degenerate into caricatures. Nonetheless, like all of Bryce's fiction, both novels achieve the considerable feat of contriving to be simultaneously serious and highly entertaining.

Julius' childhood apprenticeship and the very title of *La felicidad ja ja* are indications that underlying the humour of Bryce's work is a painful awareness of the illusory nature of happiness and of the sadness and loneliness of the human condition. That awareness permeates *Tantas veces Pedro* (1977), the story of a kind of middle-aged Julius who has never fully grown up and come to terms with life. Irrepressibly charming and romantic, Pedro Balbuena presents himself as a man who for fifteen years has been trying to get over the great, tragic love affair of his youth through affairs with other women, and the novel in fact consists mainly of a series of highly amusing amorous adventures. Subsequently it is revealed that the great love of Pedro's life was in fact a figment of his imagination forged out of a photograph he had seen in a magazine, and that rather than seek to forget her he has been trying to find her in his various adventures. Eventually he does meet up with the woman of the photograph, but in real life his ideal proves to be selfish and frivolous and eventually ends up killing him.

Like so much modern fiction, *Tantas veces Pedro* is also a novel about novel-writing. Pedro projects himself as a failed writer who has only ever succeeded in producing one short story, partly because, while it comes easy to him to spin anecdotes in conversation, he has always lacked the discipline to put pen to paper, and partly because he has been distracted by his involvement in real life, which he claims to prefer. That, however, is contradicted by the very novel which the reader has before him, a novel in which his oral facility is transferred to the written page. Moreover, Pedro's gifts as a conversationalist are themselves an indication of his propensity and his need to invent and fantasise. Furthermore, his one short story, which is reproduced as an epilogue at the end of the novel and reveals that his youthful love affair with Sophie was an invention of his imagination, prompts the reader to ask if everything else he has told him is not equally fictitious. It would appear, then, that for Pedro, as presumably for the author, invention, the literary re-creation of reality, is both a compulsion and a way of living, one which enriches ordinary existence and compensates for its deficiencies. Ultimately, therefore, the novel is to be interpreted as an apology of Bryce's literary vocation.

The basic themes of *Tantas veces Pedro* are reworked in *La vida exagerada de Martín Romaña* (1981), the first part of a projected two-volume work entitled *Cuaderno de navegación en un sillón Voltaire*.[3] Here again a strong note of existential anguish underlies the novel's

---

[3] The second volume, *El hombre que hablaba de Octavia de Cádiz* (Barcelona: Plaza y Janés, 1985), appeared too late to receive discussion in this book.

humour. The protagonist, a young man with a highly developed sense of fun but an equally acute sense of insecurity, is a hero in the tradition of Sevilla, a kind of Peruvian Woody Allen who continually gets involved in ridiculous misadventures because in his timidity and lack of assertiveness he always allows the world to impose itself on him. The son of a wealthy oligarchic family, Martín Romaña has broken with his background and come to Paris with the dream of being a writer, but the Paris he encounters is a mean, shabby, mediocre place very different from the romantic city of his imaginings. There he becomes involved with a group of Latin American student revolutionaries who hold meetings in his flat and continually berate him for his outmoded class attitudes and his lack of a true revolutionary sense. There, too, he is joined by his sweetheart Inés, who marries him but subsequently abandons him when she tires of his lack of assertiveness and political commitment. He then takes her on a tour of Spain in an attempt to patch up the marriage, but the trip fails to produce the desired effect and he succumbs to a nervous breakdown. Like most of Bryce's fictional heroes, then, Martín Romaña suffers from a sense of inadequacy which renders him incapable of coping with life.

Yet throughout his misadventures the unassertive Romaña manages to remain true to himself in a way that others around him conspicuously fail to do. His lack of political commitment reflects an unwillingness and inability to be anything other than himself and, while Inés grows out of her revolutionary phase to settle down as the wife of a wealthy professional man and many of the radical students mature into pillars of the Latin American establishment, he continues to go his own way in his bungling fashion and eventually learns to become a writer. In his account of Romaña's painful literary apprenticeship Bryce explicitly expresses his own rejection of the pressure to write socially committed literature to which all Peruvian authors are subjected. Under such pressure his hero attempts to write a novel about labour conflicts in the Peruvian fishing industry, but the experience serves to convince him that he is equipped only to write about realities with which he is familiar, and eventually, years later, as he records in a notebook the experiences which led to his breakdown, he discovers that he is at last creating the novel he has spent most of his adult life vainly trying to write. The finished novel thus represents the realisation of a literary ambition, the reward for his tenacious determination to be a writer. It also represents the discovery of his authentic self in literature, for, unable as he is to

navigate the real world without disaster, he transcends his inadequacies in literary creation as he sails triumphantly through the
fictional world of the imagination.

Another author to achieve international success was Manuel
Scorza (1928-83), who has had novels translated into more than
twenty languges.[4] Before he turned to fiction Scorza had already
made a name for himself as a socially committed poet in the line of
Romualdo, and the same spirit animates his cycle of five novels —
Redoble por Rancas (1970), *Garabombo, el invisible* (1972), *El jinete
insomne* (1977), *Cantar de Agapito Robles* (1977) and *La tumba del
relámpago* (1979) —, which mark a significant new contribution to
indigenista fiction. These novels are essentially social-realist in
character. Not only do they record historical events — the struggles
in the late fifties and early sixties of the Indian communities of the
department of Pasco in the central Andes to defend and recover their
ancestral lands — but the main characters are drawn from real life
and, indeed, one of them, Héctor Chacón, the hero of *Redoble por
Rancas*, was released from prison by General Velasco as a result of
the publicity generated by the novel. However, at the same time
Scorza brings to his fiction techniques pioneered by the new Latin
American novel. In particular, he introduces humour, irony, gar-
gantuan hyperbole, and mythical and fantastic elements characteristic of so-called "magical realism", and the novels, which he
styles "ballads", purport, after the manner of Gabriel García
Márquez's *Cien años de soledad*, to give an epic account of historical
events as perceived by the collective popular consciousness, while
retaining an omniscient narrator to provide a wider perspective.

The social reality depicted in these novels is the feudal structure of

---

[4] See Manuel Scorza, *Redoble por Rancas* (Barcelona: Planeta, 1970; Caracas:
Monte Avila, 1977); *Drums for Rancas*, trans. Edith Grossman (London: Secker and
Warburg, 1977); *Garabombo, el invisible* (Barcelona: Planeta, 1972; Caracas: Monte
Avila, 1977); *El jinete insomne* (Caracas: Monte Avila, 1977); *Cantar de Agapito Robles*
(Caracas: Monte Avila, 1977); *La tumba del relámpago* (Mexico City: Siglo XXI, 1979);
La danza inmóvil (Barcelona: Plaza y Janés, 1983). See also Antonio Cornejo Polar,
"Sobre el 'neoindigenismo' y las novelas de Manuel Scorza", *RevIb*, 127 (1984), 549-
57; Evilio Echevarría, "La narrativa de Manuel Scorza", in *In Honor of Boyd G.
Carter*, ed. Catherine Vera and George R. McMurray (Laramie: Univ. of Wyoming,
1981), pp. 17-23; Tomás G. Escajadillo, "Scorza antes de la última batalla", *RevCrit*,
7/8 (1978), 183-91; Wilfredo Kapsoli, "*Redoble por Rancas*: historia y ficción",
Tierradentro, 2 (1984), 19-57; Oscar Rodríguez Ortiz, "Manuel Scorza: el cerco de
arriba, el cerco de abajo", in *Sobre narradores y héroes* (Caracas: Monte Avila, 1980),
pp. 75-111; Augusto Tamayo Vargas, "Manuel Scorza y un neoindigenismo",
Cuadernos Hispanoamericanos, 300 (1975), 689-93; Ada M. Teja, "El mito en *Redoble
por Rancas*: su función social", *Annali dell'Istituto Universitario Orientale: Sezione
Romanza*, 20 (1978), 257-78.

latifundismo, represented above all by the figure of Dr. Francisco Montenegro, the magistrate of the provincial capital of Yanahuanca and the leading landowner in the region, whose all-powerful status is simultaneously highlighted and debunked by means of hyperbole and ironic humour. Such is the fearful awe that he inspires that no one dares pick up a coin which he drops in the street and he is able to reclaim it a year later, and such is the power that he enjoys that he is able to abolish the official calendar and institute a whimsical one of his own. His blatantly cynical abuse of power is exemplified when the elimination of fifteen agitators by means of poison is explained away officially as a collective heart attack! The stagnation of the feudal order over which he presides manifests itself literally when the rivers cease to flow and the clouds hang motionless in the sky. At the same time, however, the forces of modern capitalism intrude into this feudal world in the form of the North American Cerro de Pasco Corporation, a mining company which controls the town of Cerro de Pasco and seems able to operate at will. With impunity it floods the lands of Indian communities to build dams to provide power for its installations. It also acquires lands, initially to feed its work-force, and then expands till it becomes one of the biggest landowners in the country. The eruption of this new and sinister force is symbolised by the sudden appearance of a fence which grows till it spans the whole world, and the disruption of the traditional order is dramatically conveyed by the apocalyptic exodus of the animals.

In a sense Scorza merely re-enacts the classic theme of *indigenista* fiction, that of downtrodden Indians waging a hopeless battle against impossible odds, for in four of the five novels the *comuneros'* attempts to assert their rights end in massacres. Yet in spite of this the overall tone of the cycle is a positive one. Despite centuries of injustice the Indian communities continue to struggle for their rights with stubborn tenacity. They produce their own mythical heroes capable of waging battle against a seemingly invincible enemy. The invisible Garabombo, representative of the ignored underdog, converts his liability into a weapon to outwit the oppressors and organise resistance under their very eyes. Raymundo Herrera, the insomniac mayor of Yanacocha, never closes his eyes in a life-long struggle to prove the community's legal title to lands that have been usurped from it. Moreover, behind what appears to be a repetitive cycle of defeat, there is in the novels a progression reflecting a growing militancy on the part of the Indians. While in *Redoble por Rancas* the community of Rancas falls victim to the expansiveness of the Cerro de Pasco Corporation and Héctor Chacón, leader of the community of Yanacocha's struggle against Montenegro, is driven by a desire for personal revenge, the other novels show the communities organising and taking collective action to recover lost lands. *Cantar de Agapito Robles* culminates in the invasion of Montenegro's estates and ends with a magical dance in which the eponymous hero's flaming poncho, symbol of a new revolutionary consciousness, burns everything in its path. *La tumba del relámpago*, the last novel of the series, shows the communities of the Centre organised in a mass movement for the coordinated take-over of estates throughout the region, only to be suppressed in the end by the military. Scorza, who himself appears as a character in the novel in his role as political secretary of the Movimiento Comunal del Perú, which lent organisational support to the peasant mobilisations of the early sixties, portrays the Indians as the vanguard of revolution in Peru let down by the failure of the orthodox left-wing parties to give them whole-hearted support. Be that as it may, the growing militancy depicted in the novels reflects a changing situation in which the Indian has ceased to be a passive victim of injustice.

Despite the popularity of Scorza's fiction, it has to be recognised that it suffers from serious flaws. Secondary stories are often well written and entertaining, but they tend to stand in their own right with little connection with the main story-line. Nor is there a consistent narrative viewpoint, for the novels oscillate between omniscient narration and eye-witness accounts and between different eye-witness narrators in a manner which undermines the cycle's pretension to be collective popular history. There is, too, a lack of unified style over the cycle as a whole. In *Redoble por Rancas* Scorza tends to go overboard in his use of techniques learned from the new Spanish American novel, with the result that while the various chapters are individual *tours de force*, collectively they are something of a hotchpotch. To a large extent that abuse is corrected in the following novels, where his use of such techniques is more disciplined and the style more unified, but he goes to the opposite extreme in *La tumba del relámpago*, which is predominantly documentary in manner and where the interventions of the omniscient narrator become excessively obtrusive. Moreover, while the fantastic and mythical elements which Scorza brings to his novels generally work effectively as literary devices, for the most part they do not introduce us to the spiritual world of the Indian as Arguedas' fiction does and they fail to convince that they are the expression of the popular view of reality that they purport to be. Yet, if Scorza's novels display many of the weaknesses of traditional *indigenista* fiction, they also share its strengths in their uncompromising exposure and denunciation of social injustice. They are, furthermore, eminently readable novels, with many memorable chapters which can be enjoyed virtually as short stories in their own right and with amusing secondary plots which enliven the narrative. Scorza's achievement — and it is not an inconsiderable one — is to have taken a subject which has traditionally been treated with extreme seriousness and solemnity and to have translated it into entertaining fiction.[5]

In Peru, as elsewhere in the continent, the boom in Spanish American fiction had a significant effect on literary activity in that, whereas previously authors were writing essentially for a small local public, it opened up a much wider market covering the whole of the Spanish-speaking world and offered, too, the possibility of translation into other languages. Yet the impression created by the world-wide popularity of the Spanish American novel in general and by the international success of writers like Vargas Llosa, Bryce and Scorza is rather misleading, for the problems confronting the aspiring writer in Peru remain fundamentally unaltered. Traditionally the major obstacle hindering the development of Peruvian letters has been the want of a sophisticated book industry, a phenomenon symptomatic of the country's general socio-economic underdevelopment.[6] Writers have always encountered difficulty in having their works published and when they have been published it has been in small editions whose circulation has been restricted and which have quickly gone out of print. Contrary to what is often asserted, it would seem that the problem is not so much the meagreness of the country's book-reading public as the failure of a book industry that is undercapitalised, lacking in professional expertise and hampered by official policies, to create an efficient system of publicity and distribution to tap the potentially large internal market and to develop an export trade. Insofar as Peruvian writers have participated in the boom, it is largely by being discovered and published abroad, for the main vehicles of the recent commercialisation of the Spanish American novel have been the major international publishing houses of

---

[5] Greatly inferior to the rest of his fiction is Scorza's last novel, *La danza inmóvil* (1983), a work set partly in Paris and partly in the Peruvian jungle and dealing with the activities and emotional conflicts of two revolutionary activists.

[6] On the Peruvian book industry see Danilo Sánchez Lihón, *El libro y la lectura en el Perú* (Mantaro-Grafital, 1978); David O. Wise, "Writing for Fewer and Fewer: Peruvian Fiction 1979-1980", *Latin American Research Review*, 18 (1983), 189-200.

Argentina, Mexico and Spain. Even today the Peruvian book industry remains as parochial and underdeveloped as ever, despite laudable isolated attempts to build solid publishing houses. 90% of all books read in Peru are imported and books produced within the country, including textbooks, average a print-run of only 3,000 copies. In the field of fiction it is still commonplace for works to appear in editions of 1,000 copies or less, and it is a revealing illustration of the state of the national book industry that while Vargas Llosa's *Pantaleón y las visitadoras*, published in Barcelona in 1973, was issued in an edition of 100,000 copies, Guillermo Thorndike's *La batalla de Lima* (1979), the last of a cycle of best-selling historical novels and financed by an investment company, was produced in a edition of only 10,000. In Peru, therefore, the average author is still writing for a small local market and hoping that one day he will have the good fortune to be discovered outside his own country, and the international status achieved by a few major figures like Vargas Llosa disguises a continuing cultural underdevelopment characteristic of the Third World.

Yet, despite such adverse conditions, the period from the late sixties to the early eighties has seen a remarkable flourishing of Peruvian fiction, thanks to the boost provided by the boom and, in particular, by the success of Vargas Llosa. Not only has the boom stimulated fictional activity, as is evidenced by the increase in the number of titles published during those years, but Peruvian writers, increasingly more sophisticated in their awareness of international trends, have been encouraged to experiment with new narrative techniques. Indeed, the emergence in this period of novelists and short-story writers such as José B. Adolph (b. 1933), Fernando Ampuero (b. 1949), Harry Belevan (b. 1945), José Antonio Bravo (b. 1938), César Calvo (b. 1940), Jorge Díaz Herrera (b. 1941), Isaac Goldemberg (b. 1945), Eduardo González Viaña (b. 1941), Miguel Gutiérrez (b. 1940), Augusto Higa (b. 1943), Edmundo de los Ríos (b. 1944), J. Edgardo Rivera Martínez (b. 1934), Guillermo Thorndike (b. 1940), Carlos Thorne (b. 1924), Luis Fernando Vidal (b. 1943) and Marcos Yauri Montero (b. 1930), attests to a new strength in depth in Peruvian fiction, comparable to that already achieved in poetry.[7]

[7] See Jorge Cornejo Polar, "Alternativas al realismo en la narrativa peruana contemporánea", *CIILI*, II, 1013-19; Wolfgang A. Luchting, "La novela peruana después de Vargas Llosa", *Revista Interamericana de Bibliografía*, 28 (1978), 275-81. See also José B. Adolph, *El retorno de Aladino* (Eudeli, 1968)*; *Hasta que la muerte*

Meriting particular mention is Luis Urteaga Cabrera (b. 1940) who, in *Los hijos del orden* (1973), employs techniques similar to those of Vargas Llosa, notably a structure based on multiple discourse, to give a view of Limeñan society reminiscent of that of Congrains and Reynoso.[8] The novel recounts an attempted break-out from the infamous Maranga reformatory for juvenile delinquents, and interspersed with the main narrative are the personal histories of the various delinquents, products of the underpriviliged world of the *barriadas* who drift into lives of petty crime. The delinquents are presented as the victims of a social order concerned only with checking the symptoms of its own disease while ignoring its root causes. Like the military academy of *La ciudad y los perros*, the reformatory itself stands as a symbol of the society it serves, being both corrupt (the staff pilfer stores and sell alcohol and drugs to the inmates) and repressive (the leaders of the break-out come to a gruesome end at the hands of the staff). The novel's main defect is that it tends to lapse into pamphleteering and, in particular, its

(Moncloa-Campodónico, 1971)*; *Invisible para las fieras* (INC, 1972)*; *La ronda de los generales* (Mosca Azul, 1973); *Cuentos del relojero abominable* (Universo, 1974)*; *Mañana fuimos felices* (INC, 1975)*/Fernando Ampuero, *Paren el mundo que acá me bajo* (Ari, 1972)*; *Mamotreto* (Ari, 1974); *Miraflores' Melody* (Serconsa, 1979); *Deliremos juntos* (Kesmes, 1979)*/Harry Belevan, *Escuchando tras la puerta* (Barcelona: Tusquets, 1975)*; *La piedra en el agua* (Barcelona: Tusquets, 1977)/José Antonio Bravo, *Las noches hundidas* (Editorialuz Sesenta, 1968); *Barrio de broncas* (Milla Batres, 1971); *Un hotel para el otoño* (El Indiano, 1977); *A la hora del tiempo* (Barcelona: Seix Barral, 1977); Edgar O'Hara, "José Antonio Bravo: la autobiografía como ejercicio narrativo", *RevCrit*, 10 (1979), 143-50/César Calvo, *Las tres mitades de Ino Moxo y otros brujos de la Amazonía* (Labor/CEDEP, 1981)/Jorge Díaz Herrera, *Alforja de ciego* (Arte/Reda, 1979)*/Isaac Goldemberg, *La vida a plazos de don Jacobo Lerner* (Libre 1, 1978; Hanover, New Hampshire: Ediciones del Norte, 1980); *The Fragmented Life of Don Jacobo Lerner*, trans. Robert S. Picciotto (New York: Persea Books, 1976); Jonathan Tittler, "*The Fragmented Life of Don Jacobo Lerner*: The Estetics of Fragmentation", in *Narrative Irony in the Contemporary Spanish-American Novel* (Ithaca and London: Cornell Univ. Press, 1984), pp. 172-85/Eduardo González Viaña, *Los peces muertos* (Trujillo: La Casa de la Poesía, 1964)*; *Batalla de Felipe en la casa de palomas* (Buenos Aires: Losada, 1970)*; *Identificación de David* (Universo, 1974)/Miguel Gutiérrez, *El viejo saurio se retira* (Milla Batres, 1968)/Augusto Higa, *Que te coma el tigre* (Lámpara de papel, 1977)*/Edmundo de los Ríos, *Los juegos verdaderos* (Mexico City: Diógenes, 1968)/J. Edgardo Rivera Martínez, *Azurita* (Lasontay, 1978)*; *Enunciación* (Lasontay, 1979)*; *Historia de Cifar y de Camilo* (Lasontay, 1981)*/Guillermo Thorndike, *Las rayas del tigre* (Mosca Azul, 1973); *1879* (Libre 1, 1977); *El viaje de Prado* (Libre 1, 1977); *Vienen los chilenos* (Promoinvest, 1978); *La batalla de Lima* (Promoinvest, 1979)/Carlos Thorne, *Los días fáciles* (Perúlee, 1960)*; *Mañana, Mao* (Buenos Aires: Losada, 1974)*; *Viva la República* (Milla Batres, 1981)/Luis Fernando Vidal, *El tiempo no es, precisamente, una botella de champán* (Ames, 1977)*/Marcos Yauri Montero, *La sal amarga de la tierra* (Piedra y Nieve, 1968; Peisa, 1974); *En otoño, después de mil años* (Havana: Casa de las Américas, 1974); *María Colón* (Villanueva, 1980); *Mañana volveré* (Lasontay, 1983). Asterisks indicate books of short stories.

[8] See Luis Urteaga Cabrera, *Los hijos del orden* (Mosca Azul, 1973).

villains emerge as shallow caricatures, but the new narrative techniques are skilfully handled and the sheer horror of the story makes a powerful impact on the reader.

A refreshing departure from the male-dominated vision of contemporary Peruvian fiction is provided by Laura Riesco (b. 1940) in *El truco de los ojos* (1978), a novel which introduces us into a feminine childhood world in middle-class Lima of the fifties.[9] A single, unbroken narrative sequence of 188 pages takes us inside the consciousness of an eight-year old girl and follows the disjointed flow of her thoughts, memories, impressions and responses to the world around her, by means of a narrative technique which keeps switching back and forth abruptly from one context to another. In contrast to other Peruvian fiction about childhood, the novel has no symbolic dimension to it and the protagonist does not rebel against her environment but is fully integrated into her small, sheltered middle-class circle. However, through her stream of consciousness we are given an insight into the social, religious and sexual conventions, attitudes and prejudices that are influencing and shaping the developing child, and ultimately what we are left with is an impression of the narrowness of the world which the Peruvian middle-class girl is destined to inherit.

However, the most interesting new development in recent years has been the appearance of fiction portraying the life and outlook of the predominantly Negroid population of Peru's arid and underdeveloped southern coastal region. This trend was pioneered by Antonio Gálvez Ronceros (b. Chincha, 1931) with the stories of *Los ermitaños* (1962) and *Monólogo desde las tinieblas* (1975),[10] but its leading representative and the most exciting new fictional talent to emerge in the last decade is Gregorio Martínez (b. Nazca, 1942).[11] In *Tierra de caléndula* (1975), a collection of stories depicting the landscape and climate of the area, its socio-economic structure and the attitudes and life-style of its inhabitants, Martínez reveals to the reader a region geographically and socially isolated from the nation's urban centres and the modern Western way of life and, adopting the perspective of the common people, presents what is very much an

[9] See Laura Riesco, *El truco de los ojos* (Milla Batres, 1978). See also Phyllis Rodríguez-Peralta, "Narrative Access to a Feminine Childhood World: A New Peruvian Novel", *Latin American Literary Review*, 17 (1980), 1-8.

[10] See Antonio Gálvez Ronceros, *Los ermitaños* (Difusora Cultural Peruana, 1962); *Monólogo desde las tinieblas* (INTI-Sol, 1975).

[11] See Gregorio Martínez, *Tierra de caléndula* (Milla Batres, 1975); *Canto de sirena* (Mosca Azul, 1977).

anti-establishment view of the world. Criticism of the established order is manifest in the disrespectful attitude of the characters towards those who wield power and authority and in the ironical manner in which the latter are portrayed in the stories. In some cases it is more direct. Thus, central government's neglect of the region is humorously treated in "Aeropuerto", where a boom in the mining industry brings two ministers to Nazca on an exceptional visit and poses the local authorities the ticklish problem of what to do about the brothel that has been installed in the disused airport building. In "La cruz de Bolívar" the action of the authorities of Nazca in pulling down the cross which the Liberator had erected in the main square mirrors the process by which the local bigwigs have seized control of the town and the arbitrary manner in which they run it. The action is resented by the ordinary townsfolk as an attack on their democratic heritage and though they dare not try to prevent it, they manifest their opposition by seizing the cross and removing it to a nearby mountaintop, where it stands as a symbol of the democratic spirit that is conspicuously missing in the public life of the town. Similarly, exploitation and class solidarity are the themes of "Cómo matar al lobo" where, behind a tale of betrayal and revenge, we glean an image of the inhuman working conditions in the *guaneras* (guano pits) and of the struggle of the workers to organise to fight for their rights.

In the main, however, the stories deal with aspects of the daily experience of the people of the region and its vigorous folk culture. Above all, they all reflect the popular speech of the area. Indeed, it is the treatment of language which constitutes the most novel feature of the book. In the monologues of his first-person narrators and even in his third-person narratives Martínez strives to capture the flavour of popular speech. It is not merely a question of realism. Rather his concern is to show that popular speech has a poetry of its own and that it is an expression of the culture of the people, of their distinctive way of being and of seeing the world, and two of the texts, written in the form of letters, seem to have no other purpose than to demonstrate that point. More than that, Martínez seeks to show that the class struggle is being waged daily on a linguistic level, "correct" speech reflecting the cultural standards which the dominant class strive to impose and colloquial speech representing the people's rejection of the dominant culture and their affirmation of their own identity. The whole book, in fact, is placed within the context of that conflict by the opposition between the first and last texts. The latter, "El hombre que sabía la verdad", reproduces pieces of advertisements, articles, public notices, a political speech and a letter, all in a correct and pretentious Spanish and reflecting the world-view of the socio-political establishment. In contrast the language of the opening text, "Eslabón perdido", not only incorporates colloquial vocabulary and imagery but breaks all the rules of conventional syntax and spelling to present a popular version of the history of Coyongo and the surrounding area. Thus, Martínez's reproduction of popular speech is clearly intended to be a vindication of the culture of the people in face of cultural imperialism. At times, it must be said, he falls into the trap of allowing his preoccupation with demonstrating the poetic qualities of popular language to take precedence over content and as literary texts some of the stories are rather feeble. On the whole, however, he remains somewhat hesitant in his infringe-ment of conventional linguistic norms, perhaps because of an awareness of the danger of unintelligibility and, with the exception of "Eslabón perdido", the language of his best stories is a compromise between the popular and the literary.

More daring and systematic in its reproduction of popular speech is *Canto de sirena* (1977), a novel which gives expression to the world-view of a man of the people in his own colloquial language laced with earthy humour. It takes the form of the reminiscences of eighty-two-years old Candelario Navarro, a Negroid peasant who has spent most of his life wandering the plains of Ica and Nazca from job to job. He recalls the history of the region and the stories of the various families who have controlled it at various times. Throughout his attitude towards his "betters" is one of healthy disrespect. A man of independent spirit with a sense of his own worth, he has always refused to let himself be pushed around and has not been afraid to beat up whites who tried to lord it over him. He is suspicious and contemptuous, too, of the political authorities, who are always making empty promises but go on exploiting the people as before, and, more generally, his down-to-earth wisdom gives him an eye for the mistaken priorities of Western civilisation, for he is unimpressed by humanity's achievement in reaching the moon when ordinary men and women live in conditions of poverty and squalor. Now nearing the end of his days, he experiences the loneliness and disillusionment of old age, but he is able to look back on a rich life that has been lived to the full. In his time he was a great womaniser and he recalls his countless sexual adventures with pleasure and humour. He was also something of a gourmet when it came to eating and he is an expert in the preparation of local culinary delights, including dishes made with cat and donkey. However, he is far from being an unthinking hedonist, for he is a man with a speculative turn of mind who has thought much about life. He took pride in his various jobs, particularly when he was working as an archeologist's assistant, and he lovingly details the skills involved and he expresses his contempt for those who have no appreciation of or respect for craftsmanship. In the course of his life he has acquired a wealth of knowledge about the medicinal properties of different plants and passes his remedies on to the reader. He also makes numerous observations on the meaning of life and here again he demonstrates an independence of mind, as when he recounts a popular version of the story of Adam and Eve and accepts the biblical version only insofar as it coincides with his experience of life. What is presented to us in the novel, therefore, is not merely the story of an old man's experiences but a way of life and an attitude to the world.

In its form as well as in its use of colloquial language *Canto de sirena* flouts established cultural norms, for it is not a novel in the traditional sense but a piece of novelised reportage, an artistic elaboration of a series of interviews with a real person, and it has no plot or narrative sequence to speak of, though the material has been organised in such a way as to build up a cumulative image of the world of the protagonist. Despite Martínez's considerable achievement in capturing popular speech and modes of thought, it cannot be said that it is entirely successful as a work of literature. For to some extent he allows the virtuoso reproduction of popular language to become an end in itself and he relies too heavily on his raw material, which tends to be lacking in artistic organisation. Martínez is clearly still feeling his way and has not yet hit on a formula to satisfy the twin demands of authenticity and literary effectiveness, but he has already done enough to prove himself an exceptionally talented writer from whom great things are to be expected in the future. His importance lies not only in that his work, in common with that of other regionalist writers, bears witness to the rich diversity of Peruvian culture, a diversity which continues to be a fact of national life even in an age which has seen the rapid spread of Western mass culture. Above all, his emergence in a literary ambience that has been traditionally middle-class brings to Peruvian fiction the fresh air of a genuinely popular perspective, and with the poets of the seventies he represents a movement towards the "democratisation" of literature which mirrors a wider process of social change that has been taking place in the country at large.

Part II
The New Poetry

The remarkable flourishing of Peruvian poetry in the forties and fifties was to continue into the sixties with the emergence of an exciting new generation of poets.[1] The sixties, indeed, mark the beginning of a new era in Peruvian poetry. For while there was no sudden break with the past nor anything approaching uniformity of poetic practice, the best poetry of those years — including that of a number of older poets who evolved in tune with the times — has a fresh and distinctive character reflecting the new mood of the period.

A feature of the sixties was a universal broadening of horizons and internationalisation of life brought about by the spread of modern systems of communication. This phenomenon was particularly marked in Peru, which not only had been traditionally isolated because of its geographical position, but under the Odría regime (1948-56) had been very much a country closed in on itself. In literature the most striking sign of changing times was the international success of Mario Vargas Llosa as one of the leading figures of the new Spanish American novel, but among the poets, too, there was to be a turning outwards, the most obvious manifestation of this being the opening up of Peruvian poetry to the influence of Anglo-Saxon poets, notably Pound and Eliot. Behind these immediate influences lay something more fundamental, for the adoption of techniques and methods learned outwith the Spanish poetic tradition represents an attempt to renovate Peruvian verse which reflects a wider aspiration to see the country emerge from underdevelopment into the mid-twentieth century. More than that, the new poets were concerned to establish their place and identity as Peruvians in the context of world culture and on that basis to assert their claim to speak universally. Hence, where formerly the poem had tended to be

[1] For a survey of poetry in the sixties and early seventies, see William Rowe "Peruvian poetry: the last ten years", *Poetry Information* (London), 9/10 (1974), 7-11. For an anthology of some of the leading poets of the sixties, with their statements on their work, see Leonidas Cevallos Mesones, ed., *Los nuevos* (Universitaria, 1967). For a selection of poetry of the sixties in English translation, see David Tipton, ed., *Peru: The New Poetry* (London: London Magazine Editions, 1970). For a selection of Peruvian poetry from the sixties to the eighties in English translation, see Edgar O'Hara and Luis Ramos García, eds., *The Newest Peruvian Poetry in Translation* (Austin: Studia Hispánica, 1979).

a separate realm inhabited only by the poet himself, it now opened out to bring in other voices in the form of the words of other writers or quotations from newspapers etc. and so to become an intertextual dialogue.

The sixties also produced a change in the socio-political climate in Peru as in the world at large. After many years of military dictatorship and right-wing regimes, a more liberal atmosphere brought a social democrat to power in the shape of Belaúnde, and an industrial boom which generated a rapid expansion of the towns was paralleled by a growing politicisation of workers and peasants. At the same time the Cuban Revolution sent a wave of revolutionary optimism throughout Latin America and was followed in Peru itself by guerrilla movements in which intellectuals from the universities took to the countryside to mobilise the peasantry. Nationally and internationally there was an exciting sense that the world was in the throes of fundamental change and that a brave new future lay just around the corner. Infected by the mood of the times, the poets of the sixties were very much concerned to reflect on national and world history and to establish where they stood in relation to it. In general they repudiated their historical heritage and the social order built on it and they identified with the revolutionary struggle both in Peru and throughout the Third World. However, any tendency to utopian idealism was to be tempered by the government's suppression of the guerrilla movements and, more directly, by the trauma of the killing of one of their number in those campaigns. In effect, the death of Javier Heraud obliged them to adopt a more sober and realistic view of contemporary historical processes and it also obliged them to re-examine their own position *vis-à-vis* those processes.

However, the change of climate in the sixties went beyond the political. The aspiration to a whole new life-style, that would be more open, free, uninhibited and qualitatively better, was expressed intellectually in the writings of Marcuse and manifested itself in diverse phenomena such as the music of the Beatles, Hippy culture and the student movements in France and the United States. Sharing that aspiration, the new poets repudiated the view that poetry was hallowed ground where only a privileged élite might tread and they repudiated, too, the academic approach to literature, regarding both as manifestations of a traditional life-style which they found stiflingly narrow and conventional. For them poetry was something vital, part of everyday life, and they effectively desacramentalised it, treating it with healthy disrespect. The new poetry shuns the rhetoric of traditional poetry in favour of a language that is simple but effective; it adopts a colloquial, conversational tone that is often ironic and deliberately prosaic; where it deems appropriate it does not hesitate to employ a narrative style or to embark on a free-flowing totalising discourse or to experiment with new forms of linguistic expression. Above all, it is a poetry which speaks without inhibition and which presupposes a dialogue with a notional reader who is "joven, cosmopolita, contestatario y culto pero sin vocación académica" (young, cosmopolitan, anti-authority and cultured but without academic vocation).[2]

Two key figures in the history of Peruvian poetry in the sixties are Javier Heraud and Luis Hernández. Javier Heraud (1942-63) was a young poet of exceptional promise who, inspired by the ideals of the Cuban Revolution, trained as a guerrilla and died tragically in an abortive campaign at the age of twenty-one.[3] The nucleus of his work are the two volumes published in his lifetime and a third published posthumously, which together constitute a kind of spiritual autobio-graphy. The tone of his brief first book, *El río* (1960), is one of youthful affirmation, expressing his confident acceptance of the adventure of life and his sense of integration with the world around him. The long title-poem, built around the metaphor of life as a river flowing towards the sea, places Heraud squarely in a Spanish poetic tradition that goes back as far as Manrique, but the traditional theme is renovated and enriched in an original and personal manner. The simplicity of his expression, reminiscent of Machado, conveys a sense of freshness and immediacy and he displays a precocious mastery of his craft in a perfectly structured rhythmic architecture based on free verse, enjambment, reiteration and oppositions. The same manner, motifs and simple metaphors are again to be found in *El viaje* (1961), but here certainty gives way to anguished doubt and confusion as the maturing poet attains a deeper and more complex awareness of the realities of the world. Thus, "El poema" is an account of a personal crisis in which he renounces the illusions of adolescence and is assailed by uncertainty about who he is and where he is going. Marvellously orchestrated in a manner reminiscent of T.S. Eliot, the

[2] Peter Elmore, "La generación del 60", *30 Días*, July 1984, p. 38. This special number devoted to the sixties provides a useful account of the background against which the new poetry emerged.

[3] See Javier Heraud, *Poesías completas* (Campodónico, 1973); this volume includes articles by Jorge Cornejo Polar, Wáshington Delgado, Gerardo Mario Goloboff, José Miguel Oviedo. See also Edgar O'Hara, *Desde Melibea* (Ruray, 1980), pp. 104-09, 149-68.

poem skilfully deploys recurrent motifs with shifting meanings and repeatedly changes focus to convey the contradictions and unresolved dilemmas with which the poet is faced. However, Heraud passes beyond doubt to a new certainty in *Estación reunida*, written in 1961 and published posthumously. Here he repudiates the world he had previously inhabited and believed in and he repudiates, too, a poetry based on solitary contemplation of self and nature in favour of a poetry with a collective focus. The destruction of his former convictions he attributes to a recognition of social reality and of the structure of power:

> Mis antiguas creencias
> (dioses, soles, paisajes interiores)
> se secaron al influjo del poder.

> (My old beliefs
> [gods, suns, interior landscapes]
> withered under the influence of Power.)

Hence, in "El nuevo viaje", he proposes to undertake a new journey which will leave behind the alienating environment of the city, associated with capitalist corruption and exploitation, and lead him to the *beatus ille* of the mountains, a symbol both of guerrilla activism and of a future utopia:

> No se puede pasear
> por las arenas
> si existen caracoles
> opresores y arañas
> submarinas.
> Y sin embargo,
> caminando un poco,
> volteando hacia la izquierda,
> se llega a las montañas
> y a los ríos.

> (You can't stroll
> along the sands
> if there are oppressor snails
> and submarine spiders.
> And yet,
> walking a little,
> turning to the left,
> you reach the mountains
> and the rivers.)

Estación reunida thus records the spiritual evolution which led Heraud to political militancy. In contrast to his earlier works, the language is at times baldly explicit and the symbolism transparent, but on the whole his ideological statements are free of rhetoric and the political implications conveyed by polyvalent images of the simple traditional type that he always favoured. How he would have developed as a poet is a matter for vain speculation, but what is beyond question is that he left behind him a work of remarkable quality for one who died so young.

A rebel of a different kind was Luis Hernández (1941-77).[4] In a sense Hernández represents a continuation of the visionary tradition of earlier generations in that he lived poetry as a way of life on the margin of society, opposing the values of art to those of a mean-spirited world. His brief first book, *Orilla* (1961), sings the joys and pain of the poet's solitary contemplation of nature, and *Charlie Melnick* (1962) is a lament on the death of a seemingly apocryphal singer, celebrating him as an example of the artist who lived only for his art. Similarly, in *Las constelaciones* (1965), "Difícil bajo la noche" portrays the artistic vocation as a curse but one which brings priceless recompense, and "Los signos del zodíaco" equates the mysteries and marvels of poetry with those of astrology. A key poem in this third volume is "El bosque de los huesos", where Hernández contrasts the excitement offered by the boundless world of culture with the stifling narrowness of the country of which he is a citizen, and speaks of the loneliness of being a poet in such a society:

> Mi país no es Grecia,
> Y yo (23) no sé si deba admirar
> Un pasado glorioso
> Que tampoco es pasado.
> Mi país es pequeño y no se extiende
> Más allá del andar de un cartero en cuatro días,
> Y a un buen tren [. . .]
> Solitarios son los actos del poeta
> Como aquellos del amor y de la muerte.

> (My country isn't Greece,
> And I [23] don't know if I should be admiring
> A glorious past
> Which in any case isn't past.
> My country is small and doesn't extend
> Beyond what a postman can walk in four days
> Or as far as a good train [. . .]
> Solitary are the acts of the poet
> Like those of love and death.)

---

[4] See Luis Hernández, *Vox horrísona* (Ames, 1978); *Obra poética completa* (punto y trama, 1983).

Most of the other poems, in fact, present him inhabiting a country of the spirit and dialoguing with his soul-mates, fellow artists of different nations and periods, such as Chopin, Beethoven, Ezra Pound. These early books show Hernández moving away from a fairly traditional style, albeit simple and unaffected, to one that is distinctively his own. One of the most marked features of that style is a playful, joky, colloquial tone. Thus, Ezra Pound is evoked, not as a grand old man to be venerated like some ancient monument, but as one of the boys who would be made to feel at home were he to drop in to his part of Lima:

> Ezra:
> Sé que si llegaras a mi barrio
> Los muchachos dirían en la esquina:
> Qué tal viejo, che' su madre . . .
>
> (Ezra:
> I know that if you were to turn up in my district
> The boys on the corner would say:
> How're things, you old son of a bitch?)

For for Hernández art was inseparable from everyday life. He embraced poetry as a life-style, leading a bohemian existence in parallel with his career as a doctor, and after *Las constelaciones* he lost interest in publishing his work, writing up his poems in notebooks which he gave away to friends. These notebooks, some twenty-eight in all, contain many repetitions and on the whole lack the polished finish of his published books. The poems, in fact, seem to have been written primarily for the poet's own pleasure, the underlying attitude being that poetry is something to be enjoyed but not taken seriously, as the following lines indicate:

> Los laureles
> Se emplean
> En los poetas
> Y en los tallarines.
>
> (Laurel leaves
> Are used
> On poets
> And noodles.)

In the main the poems continue the principal lines already noted in *Las constelaciones*. Some, like "He visto", a denunciation of the soul-destroying values of contemporary civilisation, and "Estimado General", a biting satire on militarism, voice his repudiation of society as constituted. Others carry on his dialogue with his favourite poets and composers, often treating them with affectionate disrespect and often, too, paying them the ultimate homage of plagiarising them. Various notebooks attempt a kind of spiritual autobiography in the form of a poetic narrative. The most complete of these is to be found in *Una impecable soledad* (1975) where, through the *alter ego* of the marginated pianist Shelley Alvarez, he affirms his inner world in opposition to the meaninglessness of the contingent world around him:

> Y mostraba con indiferencia el vacío de su vida; porque no era vacío, sino plenitud.

> (And with indifference he displayed the emptiness of his life; for it wasn't emptiness but plenitude.)

In the end, however, the real world was to impose itself and, after giving permission for the notebooks to be published under the title *Vox horrísona*, he died in Argentina in mysterious circumstances, probably by his own hand.

It has to be said that, while Heraud and Hernández were both talented poets, the legends surrounding their names have greatly inflated their reputations, for Heraud's work bears the signs of youthful immaturity and Hernández's later poetry too often gives the impression of being lightweight and unfinished. Nonetheless, they remain significant figures. Both anticipated a movement towards a more simple, less rhetorical style. Both were to set a trend of intertextual dialogue, Heraud by initiating it, albeit timidly, and Hernández by converting it into one of the cornerstones of his work. And both cleared the road for the poets of the sixties in other ways, Heraud by demonstrating that a preoccupation with poetic expression was compatible with the treatment of social themes, and Hernández by the adoption of a colloquial, humorous, disrespectful tone. Above all, both became emblems for the generation of the sixties, symbols in their different ways of rebellion against an outmoded social order and life-style.

It was, however, Antonio Cisneros, Rodolfo Hinostroza and Marco Martos who were to establish themselves as the major poets of the sixties.[5] Characteristic of the poetry of Antonio Cisneros (b.

---

[5] Other leading poets were César Calvo (b. 1940), *Poemas bajo tierra* (Ediciones Cuadernos Trimestrales de Poesía, 1961); *Ausencias y retardos* (La Rama Florida, 1963); *El cetro de los jóvenes* (Havana: Casa de las Américas, 1966); *Pedestal para nadie* (INC, 1975)/Juan Cristóbal (José Pardo del Arca, b. 1941), *Carta a una compañera* (n.p., 1967); *Difícil olvidar* (La Próxima Botella, 1975); *El osario de los inocentes* (Quipu, 1976); *Estación de los desamparados* (Cuadernos del Hipocampo, 1978)/ Mirko Lauer (b. 1947), *En los cínicos brazos* (La Rama Florida, 1966); *Ciudad de Lima*

1942) are the sentiment, manner and tone of "Karl Marx, died 1883 aged 65", from *Canto ceremonial contra un oso hormiguero.*[6] Here, having presented an ironic picture of the nineteenth-century bourgeois world with its cosy sense of stability and progress, its staid morality, its unquestioning assumption of the legitimacy of the capitalist order, Cisneros goes on to evoke the figure of Marx beavering away to undermine that order and renders affectionate thanks to him for spoiling the bourgeoisie's complacent sense of security:

> Ah el viejo Karl moliendo y derritiendo en la marmita los diversos
> metales [...]
> vino lo de Plaza Vendome y eso de Lenin y el montón de revueltas
> y entonces
> las damas temieron algo más que una mano en las nalgas y los
> caballeros pudieron sospechar
> que la locomotora a vapor ya no era más el rostro de la felicidad
> universal.

> "Así fue, y estoy en deuda contigo, viejo aguafiestas."

> (Ah, old Karl grinding and melting different metals in the pot [...]
> then came the Place Vendôme affair and that business of Lenin
> and a whole lot of revolts and then
> the ladies were scared of more than a pat on the rump and
> gentlemen came to suspect
> that the steam-engine was no longer the symbol of universal
> happiness.

> "That's the way it was, and I'm in your debt, old spoilsport.")

All of Cisneros' work, in fact, voices disconformity with the

(Milla Batres, 1968); *Santa Rosita y el péndulo proliferante* (INC, 1972); *Bajo continuo* (Mosca Azul, 1974); *Los asesinos de la última hora* (Mosca Azul, 1978)/Juan Ojeda (1944-74), *Ardiente sombra* (Fronda, 1963); *Elogio de los navegantes* (Trujillo: Cuadernos Trimestrales de Poesía, 1966); *Recital* (Gesta, 1970); *Eleusis* (Gárgola, 1972)/Julio Ortega (b. 1942), *De este reino* (La Rama Florida, 1964); *Tiempo en dos* (Ciempiés, 1966); *Las viñas de moro* (Universitaria, 1968); *Rituales* (Mosca Azul, 1976)/ Hildebrando Pérez (b.1941), *Epístola a Marcos Ana* (Piélago, 1963); *Aguardiente* (Havana: Casa de las Américas, 1978); *Sol de Cuba* (n.p., 1979).

[6] See Antonio Cisneros, *Destierro* (Cuadernos del Hontanar, 1961); *David* (El Timonel, 1962); *Comentarios reales* (La Rama Florida/Biblioteca Universitaria, 1964); *Canto ceremonial contra un oso hormiguero* (Havana: Casa de las Américas, 1968); *Agua que no has de beber* (Barcelona: Milla Batres, 1971); *Como higuera en un campo de golf* (INC, 1972); *El libro de Dios y de los húngaros* (Libre-1, 1978); *Crónica del Niño Jesús de Chilca* (Mexico City: Premià, 1981). For selections of his poetry in English translation, see *The Spider Hangs Too Far from the Ground*, trans. Maureen Ahern, William Rowe and David Tipton (London: Cape Goliard Press, 1970); *Helicopters in the Kingdom of Peru*, trans. Maureen Ahern, William Rowe and David Tipton (Bradford: Rivelin/Equatorial, 1981). See also Leonidas Cevallos Mesones, ed., *Los nuevos*, pp. 13-17; James Higgins, *The Poet in Peru*, pp. 65-88; Julio Ortega, *Figuración de la persona*, pp. 211-15; Enrique Russell Lamadrid, "La poesía de Antonio Cisneros: dialéctica de creación y tradición", *RevCrit*, 11 (1980), 85-106.

established social order and with the life-style of the middle classes, it tends to view his own situation within the context of history, and a devastating irony is the distinguishing feature of his style.

Cisneros' alienation from Peruvian society and its values is given indirect expression in his first major work, *Comentarios reales* (1964), which adopts the title of the famous sixteenth-century chronicle of the Inca Garcilaso de la Vega to present an alternative version of Peruvian history, one which, after the manner of Bertolt Brecht, ironically exposes hallowed traditions as myths disguising a sordid reality of dishonesty, oppression and injustice. Unlike many of his compatriots, Cisneros is too lucid and sceptical to indulge in utopian idealisations of the pre-Columbian past, which he feels, in any case, to be too remote to have any relevance to a modern city-dweller, as he indicates in "Paracas", a marvellously subtle poem of deceptive simplicity. However, what the book presents is essentially an anti-establishment version of Spanish colonialism, which set a pattern of domination and exploitation, and of the independence movement, manipulated by the Creole oligarchy in its own class interest. In poems like "Tres testimonios de Ayacucho", which purport to give a popular view of historical events, Cisneros is less than convincing. By contrast his best poems are those in which his talent for irony is deployed in laconic tone and in simple, precise language, as is the case of "Tupac Amaru relegado", which satirises the sham by which the oligarchy usurped the glory as well as the fruits of independence and then converted it into official history.

Subsequently Cisneros' poetry was to become more confessional after the manner of Robert Lowell. Thus, in *Canto ceremonial contra un oso hormiguero* (1968) his alienation is more directly expressed, though with ironic self-deprecation. In "Crónica de Lima", for example, the loss of the poet's youthful dreams and illusions, attributed to the enervating mediocrity of his native city, is related in mock-heroic tone, and the use as a structuring device of the refrain of the old *vals* "Hermelinda" ironically plays down his nostalgia for the golden days of youth by equating that nostalgia with the maudlin sentimentality of the popular song. "Poema sobre Jonás y los desalienados" takes the story of Jonah as a metaphor of the predicament of the poet, trapped and stifled by a society that is politically, economically and intellectually restrictive, but it is characteristic of Cisneros that he then went on to write a postscript, "Apéndice del poema sobre Jonás y los desalienados", in which he recognises that his moments of rebelliousness have always ended in a

whimper and that like everyone else he has accommodated himself to
the system and played his part in bolstering it up:

> Y hallándome en días tan difíciles decidí alimentar
> a la ballena que entonces me albergaba [. . .]

> (Fue la última vez que estuve duro: insulté a la ballena,
> recogí mis escasas pertenencias para buscar
> alguna habitación en otras aguas, y ya me aprestaba
> a construir un periscopio
> cuando en el techo vi hincharse como 2 soles sus pulmones
> —iguales a los nuestros
> pero estirados sobre el horizonte—, sus omóplatos
> remaban contra todos los vientos,
>   y yo solo,
> con mi camisa azul marino en una gran pradera
> donde podían abalearme desde cualquier ventana: yo el conejo,
> y los perros veloces atrás, y ningún agujero.)

> Y hallándome en días tan difíciles
> me acomodé entre las zonas más blandas y apestosas de la ballena.

> (And finding myself in such difficult times I decided to feed
> the whale that was housing me [. . .]

> [It was the last time I got tough: I insulted the whale,
> gathered up my few belongings to look for
> lodgings in other waters, and I was just getting ready
> to build a periscope
> when in the roof, like 2 suns, I saw its lungs swell up
> — just like ours
> only spread out over the horizon —, its shoulder-blades
> were rowing against all the winds,
>   and me all alone
> in my navy-blue shirt in a big field
> where they could gun me down from any window: me the rabbit,
> and the swift dogs behind, and not a single hole.]

> And finding myself in such difficult times
> I settled into the whale's softest and most pestilent regions.)

In some poems Cisneros' alienation takes the form of a sense of
stiflement caused by the stuffily conventional life-style of the middle
classes. "Soy el favorito de mis cuatro abuelos", for instance,
sarcastically derides the doubtful honour of being a favourite
grandson obliged by the pressure of family blackmail to conduct
himself like the model of bourgeois virtues he is expected to be. Other
poems are linked to the historical pieces of *Comentarios reales* in that
they relate his alienation to contemporary political history. Thus, his
disenchantment with the half-hearted reformism of the social

democrats is expressed in the title-poem, where the vices of the traditional ruling oligarchy are embodied in an incorrigible ageing homosexual, portrayed as an insatiable ant-eater preying on the unwary male population of Lima. This personification of capitalist corruption and exploitation is depicted as an antediluvian monster who has somehow outlived the historical changes that should logically have made him extinct and the poem has the form of a ritual incantation intended to scare the oligarchic beast away forever. That disenchantment is given fuller and more explicit treatment in "In memoriam", a poem on the dashing of the expectations of a brave new world created by the Cuban Revolution and the advent of Acción Popular to power in Peru. The poem evokes the climate of euphoric optimism of the early sixties and then the trauma of Heraud's death and the disillusionment of discovering that, just as the United States had mobilised its forces to contain the Cuban Revolution by blockade, so too, for all its promises of change, Belaúnde's regime was no less determined to prevent the spread of revolution to Peru:

> Y el animal fue cercado con aceite, con estacas de pino, para que
>> ninguno conociera
> su brillante pelaje, su tambor.
> Yo estuve con mi alegre ignorancia, mi rabia, mis plumas de
>> colores
> en las antiguas fiestas de la hoguera,
>>> Cuba sí, yanquis no.
> Y fue entonces que tuvimos nuestro muerto.
>
> (And the animal was encircled with oil and pine stakes, so that no
>> one might know
> its brilliant coat, its drum.
> With my joyful ignorance, my rage, my coloured feathers
> I was there at the ancient feasts around the bonfire,
>>> Cuba yes, Yankees no.
> And it was then we had our death.)

Characteristically, Cisneros plays down his disillusionment by adopting a tone of cynical worldly wisdom to suggest that he and his contemporaries were victims of their own naive idealism, but the tone becomes progressively more ironic as he passes judgement on the men who betrayed the hopes of a whole generation by offering a liberal neo-capitalist state to a country thirsting for radical social change. The "new Peru" created by Belaúnde is seen as a country whose only religion is economic progress and where rampant neo-capitalist materialism, symbolised by the pestilence of the fish-meal

factories, has choked the idealism that swept the reformist government to power.

Cisneros' disillusionment with the course of contemporary politics
was paralleled by a crisis in his private life which ended in the break-
up of his first marriage, and various poems of *Agua que no has de
beber* (1971) express a guilt-ridden disenchantment with a relationship
which he felt had trapped him in the bourgeois life-style he had
always detested. In the latter part of the sixties he exiled himself from
Peru and lived for several years in Europe, where he taught at the
universities of Southampton, Nice and Budapest. His European
experience forms the basis of several of the poems of *Canto
ceremonial contra un oso hormiguero* and of the later volumes, *Como
higuera en un campo de golf* (1972) and *El libro de Dios y de los
húngaros* (1978). Still confessional in manner, these later books
include poems dealing with personal themes such as his experience of
loneliness or the new stability brought to his life by his second
marriage, the birth of his daughter and his reconversion to Catho-
licism. However, the most interesting poems are those expressing his
response to Europe. As the title of *Como higuera en un campo de golf*
(*Like a fig-tree on a golf-course*) indicates, he was never fully at home
in Europe, being very conscious of his condition as an exotic
specimen transplanted to alien soil, a man of the Third World in the
developed imperialist West. In *Canto ceremonial contra un oso
hormiguero* the poem "Medir y pesar las diferencias a este lado del
canal" focuses on the tower blocks of the University of Southampton
as a symbol of English society, a society that is materially affluent
and culturally advanced but which is completely insular in its
attitude to the rest of the world and, in its complacent assumption of
its own superiority, conveniently forgets that its prosperity is based
on the commercial exploitation of the peoples it dismisses as
backward savages. As a citizen of the Third World Cisneros finds
himself in an ambivalent position in face of such a society, adopting a
critical stance towards its values while admiring its culture and
recognising that, in effect, the only cultural heritage available to him
is that bequeathed by the imperialist powers. Cisneros, in fact,
consistently judges European civilisation from a Third World
perspective. Thus, in *Como higuera en un campo de golf*, the first
poem of the sequence "Crónica de viaje/Crónica de viejo" complains
that everywhere in Europe he comes across "Arcos de triunfo que
celebran mi condición de esclavo, de hijo de los hombres comedores
de arroz" (Triumphal arches celebrating my condition of slave, of

son of the rice-eaters). Moreover, he always retained a strong emotional attachment to Lima and the last poem of the same sequence eagerly looks forward to his return to his native city, recognising that, no matter how oppressive and alienating he found it in the past, that is where his roots are.

On his return to Peru Cisneros associated himself with the New Left and that identification is evident in his most recent work, *Crónica del Niño Jesús de Chilca* (1981). This book represents a reworking of the project already initiated in *Comentarios reales*, being another attempt to write an alternative history. This time, however, Cisneros does not focus on national history but on the more humble saga of one small community. Moreover, whereas in the earlier volume he had been primarily intent on debunking the official version of the country's history, he now concentrates on what he regards as the real history of Peru, the unspectacular history of ordinary men and women, recounted mainly by themselves, and it is a sign of his artistic maturity that he is generally much more successful in conveying the popular consciousness. Chilca was a once-flourishing fishing and agricultural community on the coast which fell on hard times as a result of the flooding of its salt-pans by the sea and was subsequently pushed into extinction by capitalist development of the area. In the opening poem an anonymous voice tries to recall a street buried beneath the sand and in a sense the volume is an attempt to rescue from oblivion a paradise that has been lost. In the evocation of the golden age of Chilca as recalled by its few remaining survivors, we are given for the first time in Cisneros' poetry a vision of an ideal society, but it is one that avoids the risk of falling into utopianism. The good times in Chilca are, in fact, depicted as being rather modest, but sufficient to satisfy the needs of a simple people: "No era maná del cielo pero había comida para todos y amor de Dios" (It wasn't manna from heaven but there was food for everyone and love of God). The basis of Chilca's prosperity was the salt which it traded with the Indians of the sierra in return for the maintenance of the irrigation channels which brought water from the mountains, but the bases of its success as a society were the people's collective spirit, manifested in their communal organisation, and their sense of Christian brotherhood under the protection of their patron, the Infant Jesus. However, in the story of Chilca the flooding of the salt-pans takes on the proportions of a Fall. It is followed by the disintegration of the community and the Infant Jesus is seen as dying again and again with the emigration of each man and woman. At this point the book ceases to be a vision of an ideal society to become the story of all rural communities depopulated by the drift of their inhabitants to Lima. And it becomes, too, the story of communities destroyed by uncontrolled capitalist development, represented here by the reclaiming of the salt-pans by private industry and the conversion of the area into an exclusive holiday resort. Cisneros thus contrasts an ideal vision of a genuinely democratic Peru run on socialist and Christian principles with the reality of Peru as it has developed in recent decades. Yet it would be to give a false impression of the book to let it be understood that it is merely a versification of the content here outlined. For Cisneros is first and foremost a poet and one of exceptional talent, and the book demonstrates his gift for conveying complex realities in a few simple images and for condensing his thought into a symbolic expression that communicates simultaneously on sensorial, emotional and intellectual levels. Thus, the whole drama of Chilca is movingly and convincingly conveyed in "Una madre habla de su muchacho (Chilca 1967)" through the mouth of one of the community's few surviving members, a mother who sorrowfully describes her teenage son, who has grown up knowing nothing of the old days but only barren desert and the cruel world of modern capitalism:

> No es bello, pero camina con suma dignidad y tiene catorce años.
> Nació en el desierto y ni puede soñar con las calandrias en los cañaverales.
> Su infancia fue una flota de fabricantes de harina de pescado atrás del horizonte.
> Nada conoce de la Hermandad del Niño.
> La memoria de los antiguos es un reino de locos y difuntos.
> Sirve en un restaurant de San Bartolo (80 libras al mes y 2 platos calientes cada día).
> Lo despido todas las mañanas después del desayuno.
> Cuando vuelve, corta camino entre las grúas y los tractores de la Urbanizadora.
> Y teme a los mastines de medianoche.
> Aprieta una piedra en cada mano y silba una guaracha (Ladran los perros).
> Entonces le hago señas con el lamparín y recuerdo como puedo las antiguas oraciones.
>
> (He isn't handsome, but he walks with great dignity and he's fourteen years old.
> He was born in the desert and he can't even imagine the larks in the sugar-cane.
> His childhood was a fish-meal manufacturers' fleet over the horizon.

He knows nothing of the Brotherhood of the Infant.
The memory of the old folks is a kingdom of the mad and the
     deceased.
He's a waiter in a restaurant in San Bartolo [800 *soles* a month
     and 2 hot meals a day].
I see him off every morning after breakfast.
When he returns, he takes a shortcut through the Development
     Company's cranes and tractors.
And he's scared of the midnight mastiffs.
He clutches a stone in each hand and whistles a tune [The dogs
     bark].
Then I signal to him with the lamp and I remember the old
     prayers as best I can.)

Rodolfo Hinostroza (b. 1941) once complained that, while it was
accepted as normal that a T.S. Eliot should gaze at the Thames and
meditate on universal themes such as time and the vanity of life, no
one took seriously a Peruvian who stared at the Rimac and did the
same.[7] Reacting against that prejudice in his own work, Hinostroza
consciously speaks not as a local writer but as a citizen of the world.
His poetry, in fact, explores his own individual experience in relation
to the collective historical experiences of modern times, and that
contemporary experience is simultaneously related to the whole past
history of the Western world by frequent reference to cultural and
historical figures. Thus, his first book, *Consejero del lobo* (1965),
written in Cuba where he studied from 1962 to 1964, has as its
backdrop the missile crisis, when the world was poised on the brink
of total war. Several of the poems convey the psychic climate of the
period. "Del infante difunto", for instance, records the poet's
anguished realisation that childhood is behind him and irrecuperably
lost in the past. "Horacio" evokes the atmosphere of uneasy peace
and poses troubled questions about man's future. And against the
same uncertain background, "La noche" shows a group of young
people carousing on the beach, desperately clutching at life in a world
threatened with extinction. Other poems link the American blockade
of Cuba to the wider repression of the struggle for national self-
determination. Thus, "Elegía a Anakairo" is a lament on the death of
Hinostroza's fellow poet, Javier Heraud, and, more generally, on the

---

[7] See Rodolfo Hinostroza, *Consejero del lobo* (Havana: El Puente, 1965; Lima:
Fondo de Cultura Popular, 1965); *El mundo de la inteligencia* (Biblioteca Universitaria,
1967); *Contra natura* (Barcelona: Barral, 1971). Hinostroza has also published a
personal record of five years of psychoanalytical treatment in *Aprendizaje de la
limpieza* (Barcelona: Tusquets, 1978). See also Leonidas Cevallos Mesones, ed., *Los
nuevos*, pp. 65-70; Abelardo Oquendo, "Aproximación a *Contra natura*", *Textual*, 3
(1971), 67-71.

failure of the Peruvian guerrilla movement and the frustration of the dream of a liberated, egalitarian Peru. And in "Juana de Arco" the martyred Joan of Arc is invoked as a symbol both of a violent repression that has persisted down through the centuries into the present day and of hope for a liberated future for mankind. Yet though emotionally identified with the Third World's struggle for liberation, Hinostroza was always a pacifist by nature and, above all, he was acutely conscious of the contradiction between the ideal of liberation and the dictatorial intolerance of the revolutionary establishment towards those who would not toe the official line. His own ideal of a brave new world went beyond a materially developed society populated by Marxist-Leninist zombies, and a number of poems voice his disconformity with the course that the revolutionary movement was taking. Thus, in "Abel" the Cains of the modern world are seen as being the fanatical adherents of the party line who persecute their brothers for their ideological unorthodoxy. And in "La voz en la playa", an assessment of contemporary historical processes and of his own place within them, he dissociates himself from the future world in the making, which he recognises will not be his kind of world:

> Ella, la Idea, finalmente refulgirá
> como un pedazo de nieve a la luna.
> Yo no estaré. Entonces mis huesos hablarán por mí,
> y este siglo de catástrofes y trágica grandeza penderá
> ante mis ojos que vieron el fulgor de la matanza. Entonces
> querré decir que no participé y que mi amor fue más hondo [...]
> Maldeciré esta vida que atado al rejón me hizo ser lo que no era,
> y miraré con amargura a los hijos engendrados en la mujer que no
>   era
> la mía robada por el espectro de la Idea.

> (It, the Idea, will finally gleam
> like a piece of snow in the moonlight.
> I won't be there. My bones will speak for me then,
> and this century of catastrophes and tragic grandeur will dangle
> before my eyes which witnessed the glow of massacre. Then
> I'll want to say that I had no part and that my love was deeper
>   [...]
> I'll curse this life that tied me to the lance and made me what I
>   wasn't
> and I'll look bitterly at the children engendered in the wife that
>   wasn't
> mine robbed by the spectre of the Idea.)

Consejero del lobo suffers from a tendency to be over-rhetorical, but in *Contra natura* (1971), written in France where he moved in the late sixties and lived for a number of years, Hinostroza produced one of the most original and stimulating volumes of Spanish American poetry in recent years. Reflecting another collective experience, concretely the student uprisings in Paris in 1968 but more generally the whole youth movement of those years, the book is not so much a collection of individual poems as a structured whole tracing the different stages of a personal and collective quest for a more authentic existence. The opening poem, "Gambito de rey", takes the form of a running commentary on a game of chess in which the poetic persona is engaged, interspersed with reflections on the parallel game of history in which he is also involved through his emotional identification with the Third World's struggle for liberation. His loss of the chess match through ingenuous rashness is equated with the failure of the Peruvian guerrilla movement of the sixties, the outcome of which is a loss of faith in the possibility of building a brave new world by political means. Humanity, he feels, is trapped in a vicious circle from which it seems incapable of breaking out. However, his decision at the end of the poem to try his luck again employing new tactics not only translates a refusal to accept that life cannot change but points to a new approach adopted by him and by humanity in the shape of the young generation.

What that approach is is clarified in the following poems, particularly in "Imitación a Propercio", which expresses what is essentially the philosophy of the youth movement of the sixties. Addressing Caesar, the archetypal personification of political power, the poet renounces all dealings with him. He wants no truck with the order established by our civilisation, and his repudiation of everything it stands for involves the rejection not only of the capitalist system but also of revolutionary alternatives, which in the struggle for power end up by sacrificing their ideals on the altar of pragmatism and by enslaving human beings in the name of a future utopia. Hinostroza speaks here as a poet and intellectual who, while refusing to compromise with the ruling order, equally refuses to put his art at the service of any political cause and resists pressure to do so. He speaks, too, as an individual who has come to reject the reality of the pragmatists and historical determinists which he has been deceived into swallowing up till now, and to realise that there is more to life than is contained in their narrow philosophy. He also speaks as the voice of his generation, which does not seek to overthrow the existing order but to establish its own alternative order, opting to drop out

and adopt a life-style of anarchic, passive resistance to the powers
that be, a life-style devoted to the pursuit of beauty, love, harmony
and self-fulfilment. The voluntary margination of these young drop-
outs is likened to the dispersal of the Jews and they are seen as a
wandering people traversing the earth in search of the Promised
Land. Thus, the Normandy beaches where they congregate evoke a
reminiscence of the biblical story of the parting of the Red Sea and a
vision of the possibility of reaching the other shore of harmony and
self-fulfilment:

> no más la historia del Poder pero de la armonía
> millones de utopistas marchan silenciosamente
> > > NSE & O
> piedra embebida en sangre que lloramos
> > > > oh piedras levitadas
> por amor
> > la otra margen acaso alcanzaremos
> > > el mar se ha retirado y Azucena
> aguarda
> > amante incansable y ligera

> (no more the history of Power but of harmony
> millions of utopians march silently
> > > NSE & W
> stone saturated by blood that we weep
> > > > oh stones levitated
> by love
> > perhaps we'll reach the other shore
> > > the sea has withdrawn and Lily
> is waiting
> > light and tireless lover)

There is a marked progression in the book from the historical
reflections of the opening poems to compositions of an esoteric
nature. With "Dentro & Fuera" Hinostroza embarks on a kind of
mystic contemplation of the universe aimed at purifying himself of
the follies and errors of human history and at reaching a true
understanding of himself and the world. In this and other poems the
insertion of pictorial forms into the written text and the interpolation
of foreign phrases into the Spanish reflect his attempt to break out of
the vicious circle of what seems to be the human condition:

Sumersión prolongada en las formas
para emerger purificado
El equilibrio de la percepción va hacia la sagesse

la meditación sobre la armonía

y el contraste   la Videncia

es el estado natural del hombre [...]

Bocarriba
sobre la hierba fresca mirando un cielo infinito
y se ve lejos y claro

Dentro &

_____

Fuera

(Prolonged submersion in forms
to emerge purified
The equilibrium of perception moves towards la sagesse

meditation on harmony

and contrast   Clairvoyance

is man's natural state [...]

Face upwards
on the fresh grass looking at an infinite sky
one sees far and clear

Inside &

_____

Outside)

Here Hinostroza takes up the visionary tradition of Vallejo and the
surrealists. For the "counter-nature" of the title is, effectively,
another version of the latter's super-reality, an alternative reality
posed in opposition to what men have historically come to regard as
the human condition. Like them, he posits a hidden space where the

individual can simultaneously attain fulfilment of his true self and perfect harmony with his world:

> hay un espacio limpio entre las cosas
> música en los cuerpos opacos
> confío en mis sentidos
> al fondo del camino estoy yo mismo
> lleno de humores cristalinos
> algo breve como un tímpano me separa del resto de las cosas
> el perfecto equilibrio de lo vivo
> con la memoria de los cuerpos muertos.

> (there is a pure space between things
> music in opaque bodies
> I trust in my senses
> at the end of the road is myself
> full of crystalline humours
> something brief like a tympanum separates me from the rest of things
> the perfect equilibrium of the living
> with the memory of dead bodies.)

The poems are dominated by nostalgia for a lost paradise, a primeval state of integration with the world. The second piece of the sequence "Orígenes de la sublimación" traces a kind of mystic way, outlining the various stages by which man can ascend to mystical union with the cosmos. The way to that union is through love and in "Love's body" and "Contra natura", as in so much visionary poetry, eroticism is celebrated as the means of healing divisions and attaining a state of total unity.

What makes *Contra natura* different from other works in the visionary tradition is that Hinostroza's personal quest for an alternative reality is placed within a historical context and seen as a collective ideal. Indeed, in his more optimistic moments, he proclaims that with his generation history is starting off afresh as the youth of the sixties revert to the nomadic, fruit-gathering condition of primeval times before man acquired the hunter mentality that perverted human development and established the bases of our civilisation. However, in the latter part of the book realism brings him down to earth as he recognises that the task facing humanity is that of repairing the damage of millennia and that it will take more than a few idealists to reverse the course of history. Sadly he has to admit that the reign of love remains out of sight and that he and his fellow idealists cannot hope to see a change in the conditions of life but must content themselves with fleeting moments of harmony and beauty:

                    marcha sobre la tierra sin potencia
                        esta especie de amor
& la belleza basta para entrever
nunca para vivir
                    Año particularmente desventurado: 1969
                        rayonné de pouvoirs.

            (this kind of love
        marches powerless over the earth
& beauty is just enough to be glimpsed
never to be lived
                    A particularly wretched year: 1969
                        rayonné de pouvoirs.)

Here the dating of the composition is eloquent in itself, evoking as it does the collapse of the student movement and the reassertion of the established order. The poet's personal disillusionment thus goes hand in hand with the frustration of a collective ideal.

The poetry of Marco Martos (b. 1942) is more uneven in quality than that of Cisneros and Hinostroza and lacks their brilliance and inventiveness, but he is a poet who has always worked to his own strengths and at his best he stands comparison with both.[8] Like his contemporaries, he favours a colloquial, conversational tone and in his early books, particularly *Casa nuestra* (1965) but also *Cuaderno de quejas y contentamientos* (1969) and *Donde no se ama* (1974), he cultivates a deliberately prosaic anti-poetry reminiscent in some ways of that of the Chilean Nicanor Parra, though harsher and more intense. However, he stands apart from the other major poets of his generation in that, being less widely travelled and less familiar with non-Spanish literatures, he has been relatively immune to the influence of Anglo-Saxon poetry and has worked largely within the Hispanic tradition. Indeed, what distinguishes Martos, above all, is his determination to be his own man and to follow his own line, irrespective of prevailing fashions and social pressures. That determination manifests itself not only in his poetic manner but also in the position he takes up with regard to political and ideological trends, for he is distrustfully sceptical of all ideologies and mass movements. Like Cisneros and Hinostroza he reveals in his poetry a critical awareness of and a serious concern for socio-political issues. Thus,

---

[8] See Marco Martos, *Casa nuestra* (La Rama Florida/Biblioteca Universitaria, 1965); *Cuaderno de quejas y contentamientos* (Milla Batres, 1969); *Donde no se ama* (Milla Batres, 1974); *Carpe diem* (Haraui, 1979); *Carpe diem/El silbo de los aires amorosos* (Cepes, 1981). See also Leonidas Cevallos Mesones, ed., *Los nuevos*, pp. 115-17.

the title-poem of *Casa nuestra* is reminiscent of Cisneros' *Comentarios reales* in its devastating indictment of a colonial heritage that bequeathed Peru only a language, a religion and social divisions. And in *Cuaderno de quejas y contentamientos* the apparently humorous disquisition of "Hombres y moscas" on the need to eradicate flies is, in fact, a subtle allegory on the problem of combating Third World underdevelopment without falling into the clutches of foreign imperialism. But Martos is nothing if not a realist and in the poem beginning "No es la hora de Rimbaud ..." (It isn't Rimbaud's hour ...) he is scathingly scornful of the woolly idealism he saw behind Heraud's political adventurism and the youth movement of the sixties. However, whilst convinced that only effective political organisation is capable of changing the world, he confesses in "Política" that he is too sceptical by temperament to commit himself politically, and "Relaciones peligrosas" warns that the danger of unconditional commitment to any cause is that it leads to the moral trap of allowing oneself to be blackmailed into accepting and condoning injustice in the name of some greater end. Martos thus stands out as a poet who refuses to toe the fashionable line and speaks instead with an independent voice.

Indeed, in general Martos claims to speak for no one but himself, and for him poetry seems to be a means of exorcising his personal obsessions, as he indicates in *Casa nuestra*: "escribo/para calmar/ mis nervios,/casi por necesidad" (I write/to calm/my nerves,/almost from necessity). All of his poetry, in fact, expresses the anguished alienation of someone out of tune with the world around him. Like Vallejo and so many other provincial writers, Martos, a native of Piura, found it difficult to adapt to life in the capital, and in *Casa nuestra* poems like "Lima" and "Casa de pensión" express the estrangement of the lonely, intimidated outsider in a city he feels to be cold and hostile. That sense of estrangement was exacerbated by his timidity and "Quijote" conveys the emotional and erotic frustration of a young man lacking the self-assurance to make advances to women. Beyond that *Casa nuestra* manifests his disorientation in face of an unfair, senseless world that at times provokes a violent rage in him and at others suicidal thoughts:

> De mi torpe sueño
> me despiertan
> la ignorancia,
> las preguntas difíciles,
> la búsqueda de los valores.

Entonces dejo las aguas tranquilas
y me convierto
en el germen del suicidio colectivo,
en el último balido de la desesperanza,
en el corazón de las granadas en la batalla,
en el furor desencadenado,
en la angustia torpe
y sin causa aparente,
en el heraldo,
en la muerte personificada.

(From my sluggish sleep
I am wakened by
ignorance,
difficult questions,
the search for values.
Then I leave tranquil waters
and transform myself
into the germ of collective suicide,
into the ultimate bleat of despair,
into the core of the grenades on the battlefield,
into unleashed fury,
into ungainly anguish
with no apparent cause,
into the herald,
into death personified.)

Marriage was to bring a certain stability into Martos' life and in *Cuaderno de quejas y contentamientos* poems like "El telescopio más poderoso del mundo" celebrate the love of his wife who affords him a defence against the world. Yet, in spite of that, the overall tone of his poetry is, if anything, even more intensely anguished and embittered than before. Thus, "Muestra de arte rupestre" (Example of Cave Art) ironically depicts the poet as one of thousands of impecunious lower-middle-class Peruvians living on top of one another in cramped conditions no better than those of stone-age man. "Bartleby en el cementerio de elefantes" is a savage satire on the pathetic struggles of the Peruvian intellectual to pursue a life devoted to the arts in the cultural wasteland of Lima. "Casta connubi" creates, by skilful use of rhythm and onomatopoeia, a horrific picture of the trap of tedium and empty routine into which marriage can degenerate. Above all, the book expresses an impotent rage at the unfairness and stupidity of a world perceived as irremediably squalid and soul-destroying. However, what saves Martos' poetry from lapsing into despair is a black humour which enables him to exorcise his anguish by directing sarcasm not only against the world at large but also against himself and his own attitudes. Thus, in one poem from *Casa nuestra* he pokes fun at his pretensions to be a poet concerned only with his art by confessing that he likes his material comforts and is not the type to starve in a garret:

> No lo olvides:
> soy la cigarra y canto
> y pido un favor
> con la mirada puesta
> en las estrellas:
> búscame un amigo
> que me dé pan y vino,
> casa y trabajo fácil
> en los duros días
> que se acercan.
> Sé que estamos en febrero,
> pero soy una cigarra moderna,
> me estoy volviendo cauto.
>
> (Don't you forget it:
> I'm the cicada and I sing
> and with my eyes raised
> to the stars
> I ask a favour:
> find me a friend
> who'll give me bread and wine,
> lodgings and easy work
> in the hard days
> that are coming.
> I know that it's summer
> but I'm a modern cicada
> and I'm growing cautious.)

In his two most recent books, *Carpe diem* (1979) and *El silbo de los aires amorosos* (1981), Martos turns his back on contemporary social reality to focus on the age-old theme of love, the other dominant strain of his work. At the same time his poetry becomes markedly more "classical" in character, not only in the sense that it broaches time-honoured topics, but also in that it is much more concerned with form, though the norms it follows are diverse and varied, and in that, without ceasing to be conversational and colloquial, it adopts an archaic language and tone that have their roots in the Spanish poetic tradition. The poems of both books explore a range of amorous situations, but beyond these varied treatments of love there would seem to lie behind his new poetic manner the discovery of a "classical" world-view which has enabled him to overcome the desperate anguish of his earlier work and to attain a certain serenity.

For underlying the poems is a stoical acceptance of the bitter sweetness of life in a world where individual human beings are insignificant creatures who re-enact generic experiences, where happiness is something fleeting to be snatched at wherever it is to be found, and where life goes on regardless of individual suffering. That world-view is expressed in "Las cuatro estaciones", where life is seen as an unending cycle of birth-death-rebirth, and in "Correspondencias", where the poet's heart stoically hardens itself to fight against inevitable decay. However, perhaps the most revealing poem is "Viejo poeta" where, adopting the persona of a poet of old to warn the reader not to interpret his love poems in biographical terms, Martos gives voice to the scepticism underlying all of his work. Few people will read his verse and those few are more than he expected, he tells us, and in any case poetry is a futile exercise:

> Algunos leen
> sus versos, poquísimas gentes—
> abundancia sin embargo
> que no esperó
> en años mozos [...]
> Consultado el poeta,
> cabalmente elusivo,
> declara con voz cansina
> que todo amor es apócrifo
> y cualquier verso que lo celebre,
> vano esfuerzo
> que no conmueve
> a los dioses.
>
> (Some people read
> his verses, very few —
> and yet a veritable multitude
> that he dared not hope for
> in the years of his youth [...]
> When consulted the poet,
> master of elusiveness,
> declares in a weary voice
> that all love is apocryphal
> and that any verse which celebrates it
> is a vain endeavour
> which fails to move
> the gods.)

That cynicism is expressed, however, with the new-found equanimity of a man who has achieved a *modus vivendi* with the world.

Meanwhile, the late sixties had produced a development of major significance with the irruption on to the Limeñan literary scene of a generation of young poets of humble extraction, most of them from the provinces.[9] It is hardly accidental that this phenonemon should have coincided with the populist revolution headed by General Velasco (1968-75), for it was a reflection of the social changes that were taking place in the country and these new poets were, in effect, the cultural expression of the emergent provincial lower classes who were claiming a voice and a place in Peruvian society. Outsiders on the capital's cultural scene, the newcomers made common cause in opposition to what they saw as the literary establishment by banding together into groups of their own. Of these the most important was the Hora Zero movement (1970-73),[10] whose leading activists were Jorge Pimentel (b. 1944) and Juan Ramírez Ruiz (b. 1946).[11] The members of Hora Zero found an outlet for their verse by producing their own editions and magazine and by holding public recitals, but, above all, they made their presence felt by militant agitation and propaganda. In their manifestos they denounced virtually all previous Peruvian poetry as inauthentic and élitist and as serving the status quo. The most lucid exposition of their often woolly and contradictory theories is provided by Ramírez Ruiz in the essay "Poesía integral".[12] Here he advocates a poetry with the dynamism to capture and convey the vitality of everyday Latin American life, a poetry which will abandon its cloistered seclusion and go out into the streets for its inspiration and its language. This new poetry should be a totalising expression of the poet's own individual experience and of the shared collective experience of the popular classes, written from a class position and placing its subject-matter in socio-historical context. It should also stimulate social change by changing people's attitudes. Not all the poets of the period would have identified themselves with such a poetics, of course, but Ramírez Ruiz's essay does, nonetheless, capture the spirit of the new poetry of the seventies.

[9] For an anthology of the poets of the seventies, with introductory study and declarations by the poets themselves, see José Miguel Oviedo, ed., *Estos 13* (Mosca Azul, 1973). On the poetry of the seventies see Edgar O'Hara, *La palabra y la eficacia (Acercamiento a la poesía joven)* (Latinamericana/Tarea, 1984).

[10] In 1973 the group split up and its members went their separate ways. In 1977 it re-formed, though with a somewhat different membership. On Hora Zero see O'Hara, *La palabra y la eficacia*; Oviedo, *Estos 13*; Enrique Sánchez Hernani, *Exclusión y permanencia de la palabra en Hora Zero: diez años después* (Cuadernos Ruray 2, 1981).

[11] See Jorge Pimentel, *Kenacort y Valium 10* (Ediciones Hora Zero, 1979); *Ave Soul* (Madrid: El Rinoceronte, 1973); *Palomino* (Carta Socialista, 1983)/Juan Ramírez Ruiz, *Un par de vueltas por la realidad* (Ediciones Hora Zero, 1971); *Vida perpetua* (Ames, 1978).

[12] See *Un par de vueltas por la realidad*, pp. 110-18.

The new poets went further than their predecessors in the cultivation of a colloquial language and tone, virtually abolishing the distinction between prose and verse, employing slang and even obscenities, and speaking with an uninhibited frankness that refused to recognise taboos. They achieved the dynamism which Ramírez Ruiz advocated by creating poems of varying rhythms which abruptly change direction and remain open-ended. They conveyed, too, a sense of contemporary reality and of the immediacy of the real world by citing dates and even times, by use of brand names and modern technical terms, and by reference to friends and acquaintances, sometimes accompanied by addresses and telephone numbers, to particular streets, bars and cinemas, to political and cultural figures of the age and to books just read or films just seen. In practice, however, the new poets were less innovatory than they deemed themselves to be, for in essence their poetic manner is a continuation and development of that of the poets of the sixties. There is also something of a contradiction between many poets' image of themselves as the guardians of popular culture and revolutionary values and their tendency to assume in their work — and often in their life-style — the stance of bohemian rebel and outcast in the Romantic tradition. It has to be said, too, that while their poetry is charged with great emotional energy, it is often lacking in critical self-awareness and, in particular, their poems are often poorly structured and their expression over-explicit and their language of modernity has tended to degenerate into a dated rhetoric. Nonetheless, the overall standard of their verse is remarkably high and, if much of it is dispersed in magazines, they have also produced a number of fine books.[13]

One of the major talents of the period and the outstanding poet of the Hora Zero movement is Enrique Verástegui (b. 1950).[14] *En los extramuros del mundo* (1971) contraposes the alienating environment of Lima and the exhilarating world of culture, both recently encountered by the young provincial from Cañete. Several poems describe the capital as the Inferno, and "Salmo" is a hellish vision of a city populated by despairing men and women driven to neurosis by

[13] Alongside this new poetry, other poets of the seventies cultivated a more traditional poetics. Foremost among these is Armando Rojas (b. 1945), whose work carries on the traditon of "pure" or visionary poetry. See *Bosques* (Arte Reda/Casa de Cartón, 1973); *S & Q* (Paris: L'Oiseau-Felin, 1979); *El sol en el espejo* (Paris: Ceteclam, 1983).

[14] See Enrique Verástegui, *En los extramuros del mundo* (Milla Batres, 1971); *Praxis, asalto y destrucción del infierno* (Campo de concentración, 1980).

the nightmare of modern urban life. Verástegui's response is scornfully to reject the city and the Western way of life, denouncing the latter as

> ... corrupción de los que fueron elegidos como padres-gerentes
>   controlando el precio de los libros
> de la carne y toda una escala de valores que utilizo para
>   limpiarme el culo.

> (... corruption of those who were elected as fathers-managers
>   controlling the price of books
> of meat and a whole scale of values which I use to wipe my arse.)

On the other hand, the city gives access to a culture unavailable in the provinces. Even though he complains that the cost of books is beyond his pocket and he has to make do with reading them in libraries, Verástegui's poetry exudes a sense of the excitement and adventure of discovering the marvellous new universe that culture opens up to him, recalling discussions of Blake with a lover or the group celebration of Lautréamont's centenary with a soft drink. The volume includes poems inspired by paintings by Brueghel and Blake and it abounds in cultural name-dropping, but significantly those paintings are linked to personal experiences and the writers and artists cited are evoked as living beings with whom he has a personal relationship. Thus, in "Primer encuentro con Lezama", the Cuban writer Lezama Lima is evoked as a soul-mate who dropped out of the blue one day to provide him with companionship in his lonely wanderings through the city:

> ... apareciste en Lima sorpresivamente como esas pocas
>   lluvias que llegan para lavarnos de la duda
> y ahora estamos contigo en el café Palermo

> (... you appeared in Lima unexpectedly like those
>   occasional rains that come to cleanse us of doubt
> and now we're together in the Palermo café)

Given Verástegui's youthful inexperience and the narrowness of his provincial background, it is perhaps understandable that his work should betray a certain naivety. This manifests itself most notably in his tendency to strike Romantic attitudes. Thus the very title of the book defines the poet as an outcast at odds with the social order and the poems, unfolding in a marginal world of streets, parks, bars and brothels, show him leading a bohemian existence which earns him the disapproval and hostility of respectable citizens. Animated by the ambition to discover his "integral self", he exalts the disorder and squalor of low life as more authentic than the stifling orderliness of bourgeois routine and cleanses himself of the contaminating stench of commercialism and consumerism in a bohemian cultivation of the senses. Thus, paradoxically, his poetry inhabits the mire yet represents purity in a degraded world:

> En mi país la poesía ladra
> suda orina tiene sucia las axilas.
> La poesía frecuenta los burdeles
> escribe cantos silba danza mientras se mira
> ociosamente en la toilette

> (In my country poetry barks
> sweats urinates has dirty armpits.
> Poetry frequents brothels
> writes songs whistles dances while gazing
> idly at itself in the toilet)

> el mundo aún continúa siendo lavado por las lluvias,
> por palabras como éstas que son una fruta para la sed.

> (the world is still washed by the rains,
> by words like these which are thirst-quenching fruit.)

Yet beyond such Romantic attitudes Verástegui's poetry reflects the very real margination of the impecunious provincial incomer to the city. It expresses, too, a laudable determination to remain true to himself and to resist being absorbed into the system and its naivety has its positive side in a refreshingly idealistic spirit of rebellion. Thus, in "Datzibao", one of his best poems, the poet and his lover, united by their generational repudiation of the established order and by their passionate commitment to life, are seen in their love-making as striking a blow for human values against a dehumanising social system:

> y tu vida o mi vida no ruedan como esas naranjas plásticas que
>   eludimos porque tú y yo somos carne
> y nada más que un fuego incendiando este verano.
> La vida se abre como un sexo caliente bajo el roce de dedos
>   reventando millares de hojas tiernas y húmedas,
> y no dijimos nada pero exigíamos a gritos destruir la ciudad, esta
>   ciudad ese monstruo sombrío escapado de la mitología
> devorador de sueños.

> (and your life or my life don't roll like those plastic oranges which
>   we elude because you and I are flesh
> and nothing but a fire setting this summer alight.
> Life opens up a like a sex on heat beneath the friction of fingers
>   exploding thousands of soft, damp leaves,

and we said nothing but we were demanding at the top of our
   voices to destroy the city, this city that gloomy monster
   escaped from mythology
destroyer of dreams.)

Moreover, despite occasional infelicities, Verástegui is a gifted poet
with a powerful visual imagination and an ear for language and
rhythm, and his best poems are precociously mature in their handling
of emotion and in their intuitive appreciation of the ultimate sadness
of the human condition. Such is the case of the intensely moving
"Para María Luisa Rojas de Peláez . . . ", a valedictory address to his
dead grandmother, and "En el viejo libro de los cuentos de hadas", a
poem on the cruelty of life as reflected in the experience of an
unmarried mother. Unfortunately, his second book, *Praxis, asalto y
destrucción del infierno* (1980), was something of a disappointment,
being spoilt by a parade of ill-assimilated political and intellectual
theory. However, other poems published in magazines give grounds
for optimism that Verástegui will yet live up to his early promise.

  While the focus of the new poetry was predominantly urban, it was
not exclusively so. José Watanabe (b. 1946), for example, evokes the
small-town atmosphere of his native Laredo in *Album de familia*
(1971), where the ambivalent relationship of the educated, sophisticated son with his humble, traditionally-minded family and the clash
between his youthful desire for freedom and the narrow conservatism
of the provincial environment are subtly conveyed by a delicate
fusion of tenderness and irony.[15] Watanabe is one of the best poets of
the period but since *Album de familia* he has restricted himself to
publishing in magazines and, like Verástegui, he has still to
consolidate his early promise. Another kind of non-urban reality, the
magical world of nature and native myth, is evoked in the work of
Tulio Mora (b. Huancayo, 1948), whose poems published in
magazines had already earned him a reputation as a fine poet before
the appearance of *Mitología* (1977).[16] Here Mora juxtaposes the
itinerary of the alienated urban dweller, caught up in the daily
treadmill, with that of a traveller journeying through the jungle into a
world of myth, in what can be read as an exploration in quest of a
more authentic alternative to the values and way of life of Western
capitalist society. Though not an entirely successful work, *Mitología*
is one of the most ambitious books of poetry produced in Peru in

[15] See José Watanabe, *Album de familia* (Ediciones Cuadernos Trimestrales de
Poesía, 1971).
[16] See Tulio Mora, *Mitología* (Arte/Reda, 1977).

recent years and Mora's future development is to be awaited with interest.

However, despite the impact made by the new generation of poets from the provinces and by the Hora Zero group in particular, the major poet of the seventies was a Limeñan from a comfortable middle-class background. Abelardo Sánchez León (b. 1947) has combined the practice of poetry with a career as a sociologist, both activities representing a repudiation of the values of his class.[17] All of his poetry, in fact, expresses the anguished alienation of an individual estranged from the traditional, exclusive bourgeois world in which he grew up and unsure of his place in the larger, changing world of contemporary Peru. His verse tends to return again and again to the same themes and situations, but its limited range is more than compensated by its great emotional force, and through the expression of his own personal predicament he conveys more effectively than any other poet of the period a sense of the crisis of a society in the throes of change. Stylistically his work shares many general features of the poetry of the seventies, such as a language that is colloquial and frequently crude, allusions situating it in a concrete reality, and a vocabulary reflecting modern life. It is marked by a predilection for long poems, with a discourse that flows in extremely long lines and with frequent enjambments. Its rhythm is close to that of prose and, indeed, in many compositions verse is abandoned in favour of the prose poem. Imagery tends to be used sparingly, symbolic status being conferred instead on anecdotes, and his poetry, in fact, could perhaps be best described as dramatisations of situations, dramatisations which ebb and flow and are characterised by frequent changes of voice. Sánchez León's style is not particularly novel or original, for his main concern is to communicate an existential situation and he makes no claim to be an innovator in the matter of poetic expression. What distinguishes him as the outstanding poet of his generation is quite simply his sure and unobtrusive handling of his poetic techniques. That and the fact that as the author of five books he has a substantial body of work to his credit.

The title of Sánchez León's first book, *Poemas y ventanas cerradas (Poems and Closed Windows)* (1969), points to the oppressive sense of alienation that dominates his work, the alienation of someone unable

---

[17] See Abelardo Sánchez León, *Poemas y ventanas cerradas* (La Rama Florida, 1969); *Habitaciones contiguas* (Mejía Baca, 1972); *Rastro de caracol* (La Clepsidra, 1977); *Oficio de sobreviviente* (Mosca Azul, 1980); *Buen lugar para morir* (Haraui, 1984). See also Edgar O'Hara, *La palabra y la eficacia*, pp. 65-74.

to relate to his own class or to the world at large. As has been suggested, this is a poetry which reflects the drama of a society in the process of change. Thus, in "Las señoritas Godoy ..." the human side of the decline of the traditonal bourgeoisie is touchingly conveyed by the pathetic plight of two elderly genteel spinsters whose once-tranquil residential district has been transformed into a concrete jungle by urban development and the influx of the lower classes. And "¿Hasta acá llegará, hasta San Isidro?" poses the question of whether the proletarian masses swarming into Lima will ever succeed in penetrating the fortress-like enclaves of middle-class privilege. It is against that background that the poet's own predicament is placed. In "La casa del abuelo" the demolition of his grandfather's house symbolises the collapse of middle-class certainties, the erosion of the self-confidence and values of a class which regarded its domination and privilege as the natural order of things, and the old man's descendants find themselves confronted by a changing, disconcerting, frightening world with which they are unequipped to cope:

> No sólo demolieron la casa del abuelo,
> también despistaron a los nietos
> ocultando las palabras escritas en la noche [...]
> > y no quedó nada,
> ni una mirada tierna que acompañe la herencia de mano en mano,
> ni una palabra que evite el camino minado con pestes y
> > desengaños,
> ahora que débiles no soportamos las inclemencias y las tentaciones,
> cuando hemos caído tan bajo como un obstáculo en medio del
> > esfuerzo.

> (They didn't only demolish the grandfather's house,
> they also disorientated his grandchildren
> by concealing the written words in the night [...]
> > and nothing remained,
> not a tender look to accompany the inheritance from hand to
> > hand,
> not a word to avoid the road mined with plagues and
> > disenchantments,
> now that we're too weak to withstand inclemencies and
> > temptations,
> when we've fallen as low as an obstacle in the midst of endeavour.)

It is significant that "En el Chino-Chino", the opening poem of the volume, should be set in a seedy bar, for in several poems Sánchez León's repudiation of his privileged bourgeois background and his acceptance of a more egalitarian order is reflected in his immersion in a sordid world of drinking dens and brothels. But that seedy setting mirrors, too, the moral and physical squalor of the new Lima and the mess that he feels his own life to be. The poem is dominated by a sense of aimlessness as a group of friends sits drinking in the bar and when they are berated by another customer it brings to the surface the poet's latent feelings of guilt about the futility of his existence. His only self-justification — that writing poetry harms no one — fails to convince even himself:

> ¿Alguien ha muerto o perdido su trabajo por haber nosotros
>   escrito poemas
> desconocidos bajo el humo en un rincón de la Colmena,
> tratando de comprender las mil razones de la tristeza,
> del súbito desengaño, del amor perdido?
> Y en vano tratamos de apaciguar los insultos ya dichos.
> Cada palabra suya ha sido clara como una patada honesta.

> (Has anyone died or lost his job because we've written unknown
>   poems
> beneath the smoke in some corner in Colmena Avenue,
> trying to understand the thousand causes of sadness,
> of sudden disillusionment, of lost love?
> And in vain we try to appease the insults already uttered.
> Each word of his has been clear like an honest kick.)

While Sánchez León's later books show a steadily improving mastery of poetic technique, the poems consist in the main of variations on and developments of the subject-matter of his first volume. One recurrent theme, the recollection of childhood and adolescence, appears to have assumed greater importance as he has grown older, to the extent that half of his most recent book, *Buen lugar para morir* (1984), is made up of a sequence of reminiscences of his education at a prestigious English-run private school. The significance of this theme is clarified in *Rastro de caracol* (1977) by "Recordando con ira", a poem borrowing its title from John Osborne's *Look Back in Anger*. Here he recalls with bitterness an upbringing which was designed to make him take his place in a world-order that no longer exists and which has left him incapacitated for the world he now inhabits, an upbringing which, no matter how much he may have reacted against it, has shaped and marked him for life:

> sofocado, apretado en el uniforme, aprendimos a obedecer,
> respetar, amar con miedo, con vergüenza, sumisos como cabras a
>   los mayores [...]
> Qué han hecho, qué nos han hecho,

—cobardes, ofendidos, siniestros agitamos las manos,
y late el mecanismo heredándose, y de mi padrino retengo su
    recortado bigote negro, el terno oscuro,
su mano posada en mi hombro cuando arrodillado
en la frialdad del mármol miraba el altar iluminado [. . .]
y me miraba y protegía, —sereno, seguro,
armonioso con la delatora imagen de un mundo ya elaborado,
    sujeto a sus verdades,
sólido como el sonido de las pisadas en las naves del templo.

(stifled, pinched by the uniform, we learned to obey,
respect, love with fear and shame, submissive as nanny goats
    before the grown-ups [. . .]
What have they done, what have they made of us
— cowardly, offended, disastrous, we wave our hands
and the mechanism throbs, inheriting itself, and I retain the
    memory of my godfather, his clipped black moustache, his
    dark suit,
his hand placed on my shoulder as I knelt
on the coldness of the marble and looked at the illuminated altar
    [. . .]
and he watched and protected me — serene, sure,
in harmony with the tell-tale image of a world already elaborated,
    subject to his truths,
solid as the sound of footsteps on the aisles of the church.)

Thematically, Sánchez León's poetry evolves only insofar as it traces the various stages of his personal development. As the similarity of titles indicates, *Habitaciones contiguas* (*Adjoining Rooms*) (1972) is essentially a continuation of his first book, revolving around his conflictive relationship with his background and his inability to find a direction in life. Thus, "En los sótanos del columbario" presents him as an outsider at a family gathering, made conscious by the display of wealth and luxury around him of the role of poor relation to which his choice of career has relegated him, and patronised by aunts and uncles for his social concern and his cultivation of poetry, youthful aberrations which he will grow out of in time. And in "Golpes de pecho" he castigates himself for the ingenuous idealism which led him to devote four years of his life to the study of sociology only to end up in straitened financial circumstances and with a sense of his own impotence to do anything to change the world. *Rastro de caracol* (1977), written in Paris where he lived from 1973 to 1975, marks a period of pause in which he takes stock of his life. A number of poems examine the role in the world of the vocation that he has assumed. Thus, "En las caballerizas" depicts the poet as someone who is treated as an effeminate buffoon, tolerated but humiliated by a society which he is powerless to influence. Hence, in "La hora de los poemas", poetry is viewed as an essentially private activity, a refuge from the pressures and humiliations of social life, affording a freedom and fulfilment not to be found in the real world. Other poems look backwards to assess what has become of his life. Thus, in "La soledad del corredor de larga distancia", he sees in the film version of Alan Sillitoe's *The Loneliness of the Long-Distance Runner* an allegory of his university days which permitted the students a brief illusion of freedom before they were absorbed into the social system, so that for all their youthful rebelliousness his fellow students have grown into the complacent, respectable bourgeois they were programmed to be from the beginning. The implication of the poem is that, like Sillitoe's hero, the poet has kept running after breasting the tape, but the title of the volume (*Trail of the Snail*) makes it clear that he has maintained his independence not by making a heroic dash for freedom, but by crawling through life with the timid defensiveness of the snail.

Oficio de sobreviviente (1980), Sánchez León's most powerful book after *Poemas y ventanas cerradas* and perhaps his best, is an acknowledgement of defeat, of the surrender of that independence which he had struggled so hard and so long to maintain, of his absorption into the social order against which he had rebelled. Brought to heel by the need to earn a living and by his inability to find a cause into which to channel his rebelliousness, he has ended up settling into the middle-class routine that was always anathema to him. Hence, the title of the volume tells us, his life has been reduced to a precarious exercise in survival, in getting by as best he can. What that means is clarified by "Arroyo", where he achieves a kind of peace by coming to an uneasy accommodation with the world around him, living truly only in his own private universe while externally conforming to a society and way of life which he detests and which leave him dissatisfied:

> He negado lo que he asumido,
> habito en el lindero que la cabeza me permite, sin acción,
> única manera de constatar que acá se estuvo y se está.
>
> (I have denied what I have assumed,
> I inhabit the frontier that my head permits me, without action,
> the only way of proving that one was and is here.)

But he is aware enough to realise that such passiveness involves a compliant connivance in a social order which mutilates the human potential of all those caught within it, and in "La paz y la guerra" he castigates himself with savage irony:

> Querida avestruz, excelente imagen del ciudadano promedio,
> fin de semana y mis calmantes, la costumbre del excremento,
>   consigo y con el mundo
> en este país estarse en paz equivale a estarse muerto.

> (Dear ostrich, excellent image of the average citizen,
> the weekend and my tranquillisers, the habit of excretion,
>   in this country
> to be at peace with oneself and the world is the same as being dead.)

Hence, to his disgust with the world is added disgust with himself and, in "En cara", it is with self-contempt that he contemplates his reflection in the mirror:

> Hay en esa cara un sabor entrecruzado de satisfacción
>   de no estarlo
> y desvencijada vanidad de haber comprendido.
> De descubrir en las formas el aliento de vivir
>   y soportarlo,
> la manera como se consume el organismo,
> conocedor de que el destino se pudo hacer y no se hizo:
> allí la diferencia con los infelices y su secreto vínculo.

> (In that face there's a savour laced with satisfaction
>   at not being satisfied
> and rickety vanity at having understood.
> In discovering in forms the spirit to live
>   and put up with it,
> the way the organism wears itself out,
> knowing that our destiny could have been forged and wasn't:
> there's the difference with the wretches of the world and the secret
>   link.)

Too honest to delude himself that he has made anything but a failure of his life, he lives without illusions, enduring existence by going through the motions, but at the same time he recognises that even the honesty on which he prides himself is itself a form of complacency. Together with the other qualities of his work already mentioned, it is that eye for seeing through deception which marks Sánchez León out as the major voice of the seventies.

It is a sign of the vigour of Peruvian poetry that each successive generation continues to throw up a fresh crop of exciting new talent. While it is relatively easier to publish verse than fiction, either in magazines or in cheaply produced limited editions, poets nonetheless remain hampered in getting their work known by the same editorial difficulties that beset fiction-writers. Yet, in spite of that, the sheer quantity of verse produced in Peru in recent years is truly remarkable and includes a number of very fine books. Of the poets who emerged in the late seventies and early eighties the outstanding figures are perhaps Fernando Castro (b. 1952) — *Cinco rollos de plus-x* (1978) —, Mario Montalbetti (b. 1953) — *Perro negro, 31 poemas* (1978) —, Eduardo Chirinos (b. 1960) — *Cuadernos de Horacio Morell* (1981) —, and José Antonio Mazzotti (b. 1961) — *Poemas no recogidos en libro* (1981) —, who in their different ways seem to represent a move towards a more controlled and artistically self-conscious poetry in reaction to their immediate predecessors' passionate and sometimes undisciplined emphasis on vitality.[18] Another healthy trend is that, just as the seventies brought a kind of democratisation of poetry with the emergence of a generation of poets from the provincial lower classes, the last few years have seen the appearance of a growing number of women poets, of whom the most impressive is perhaps Carmen Ollé, author of *Noches de adrenalina* (1981).[19] Moreover, while the cultural life of the nation continues to be dominated by Lima, there has been a proliferation of poetry groups in provincial cities in recent decades, with Tacna in particular distinguishing itself as an important centre of poetic activity.[20] The present state of Peruvian poetry thus augurs well for the future.

[18] See Fernando Castro, *Five Rolls of Plus-X/Cinco rollos de plus-x* (Austin: Studia Hispánica, 1983; originally published in Lima in 1978 in mimeographed edition); Mario Montalbetti, *Perro negro, 31 poemas* (Arybalo, 1978); Eduardo Chirinos, *Cuadernos de Horacio Morell* (Trampa de Eustaquio, 1981); José Antonio Mazzotti, *Poemas no recogidos en libro* (Federación Universitaria de San Marcos, 1981). For an anthology of recent poetry, see Edgar O'Hara, ed., *Poesía joven de Perú* (Mexico City: Punto de Partida, 1982). See also Edgar O'Hara, *Lectura de 8 libros de la poesía peruana joven, 1980-81* (Cuadernos Ruray 3, 1981); id., *Desde Melibea*, pp. 51-97.

[19] See Carmen Ollé, *Noches de adrenalina* (Cuadernos del Hipocampo, 1981).

[20] See Edgar O'Hara, *Desde Melibea*, pp. 87-91.

GLOSSARY

Acción Popular: a reformist political party founded in 1956 under the leadership of Fernando Belaúnde Terry.

Apra: Alianza Popular Revolucionara Americana, a left-of-centre, anti-Communist party founded in 1924 under the leadership of Víctor Raúl Haya de la Torre. In the 1930s Apra emerged as the largest and most highly organised political party in Peru, but because of its revolutionary image it was prevented from gaining power by the army and the oligarchy and suffered persecution. Subsequently, in the 40s and 50s, the party was to adopt a more conciliatory image and a policy of forming tactical alliances with other parties.

barriada: squatters' settlement.

cholo: a person of mixed Indian and Spanish blood, a mestizo.

charango: a musical instrument similar to a mandolin.

colono: an Indian serf on a large estate who in return for his services is allotted a plot of land for his own use.

comunero: a member of an Indian community.

conceptismo: one of the main tendencies of Spanish Baroque literature, characterised by the cultivation of elaborate conceptual conceits.

costeño: a native of or pertaining to the coastal region of Peru.

criollo: creole. In the colonial period this term designated a native-born white person as distinguished from one born in Spain. Subsequently it came to be used to described what is typically Peruvian or, more usually, coastal or Limeñan.

culteranismo: one of the main tendencies of Spanish Baroque literature, characterised by its preciosity of style.

culterano: in the style of *culteranismo*.

hacendado: owner of a large estate.

indigenismo: a political and social movement championing the cause of the Indian. *Indigenista* literature is the literary expression of that movement.

latifundio: large estate.

latifundismo: socio-economic system based on large estates.

latifundista: owner of a large estate.

misti: white, a member of the white ruling class.

Modernism: a Spanish American literary movement which originated in the 1880s, reached its high point around the turn of the century and effectively came to an end at the time of the First World War. Modernism was heavily influenced by French Parnassianism and Symbolism and, as the name implies, represented an attempt to lift Spanish American literature into the vanguard of Western culture. In reaction to the narrow, uncultivated and unsympathetic environment of their own societies, the Modernists projected themselves as noble outcasts determinedly cultivating art for its own sake, and at the same time they were cosmopolitans who saw themselves as members of an international brotherhood dedicated to aesthetic ideals transcending national frontiers. Despite a tendency to degenerate into excessive preciosity and extravagant exoticism, Modernism implied a new dignification of literature that was to have a lasting influence and the Modernists' search for new forms of expression brought a new vitality to Spanish American letters.

serrano: a native of or pertaining to the sierra, the Andean highlands.

viveza/viveza criolla: a form of quick-witted astuteness considered to be characteristically Limeñan.

zambo: a person of mixed Negro and Indian or Negro and mestizo blood.

ABBREVIATIONS

Unless otherwise stated, the place of publication for all books mentioned is Lima. Journals are either well-known international reviews or published in Lima.

The following abbreviations have been used:

BHP:	Biblioteca Hombres del Perú (Editorial Universitaria). Each volume in this series contains two monographs.
CAP:	Colección Autores Peruanos (Editorial Universo)
CIILI:	*Memorias del XVII Congreso del Instituto Internacional de Literatura Iberoamericana*, 3 vols. (Madrid: Centro Iberoamericano de Cooperación, 1978)
INC:	Instituto Nacional de Cultura
La Católica:	Pontificia Universidad Católica del Perú
Literatura de la Emancipación:	*Literatura de la Emancipación Hispanoamericana y otros ensayos*, Memorias del XV Congreso de Literatura Iberoamericana (Lima: San Marcos, 1972)
Porras:	Instituto Raúl Porras Barrenechea
RevIb:	*Revista Iberoamericana*
RevCrit:	*Revista de Crítica Literaria Latinoamericana*
San Marcos:	Universidad Nacional Mayor de San Marcos
Univ. Microfilms:	University Microfilms International, Ann Arbor

BIBLIOGRAPHY

For the most part this bibliography is limited to books and articles dealing specifically with Peru and does not include material on Peru contained in the many existing general works on Spanish American literature. It is also limited to writings of a general nature, since bibliographies for particular authors are to be found in the relevant footnotes.

1. BIBLIOGRAPHIES

Cabel, Jesús, *Bibliografía de la poesía peruana 1965-1979* (Amaru, 1980)

Chonati, Irma, et al., *Tradición oral peruana. Hemerografía (1896-1976)* (INC, 1978)

Foster, David William, *Peruvian Literature. A Bibliography of Secondary Sources* (Westport, Connecticut, and London: Greenwood, 1981)

Rodríguez Rea, Miguel Angel, "Poesía peruana del siglo XX", *Hueso Húmero*, 7 (1980), 134-50; 8 (1981), 132-49; 9 (1981), 148-58; 14 (1982), 186-204

Sánchez, Luis Alberto, et al., *Contribución a la bibliografía de la literatura peruana* (San Marcos, 1969)

Villanueva de Puccinelli, Elsa, *Bibliografía de la novela peruana* (Biblioteca Universitaria, 1969)

2. ANTHOLOGIES

Arguedas, José María, ed., *Poesía quechua* (Buenos Aires: Editorial Universitaria, 1965)

Bendezú Aybar, Edmundo, ed., *Literatura quechua* (Caracas: Biblioteca Ayacucho, 1980)

Carrillo, Francisco, ed., *Poesía y prosa quechua*, 2nd ed. (Biblioteca Universitaria, 1968)

—, ed., *Cuento peruano 1904-1971* (Biblioteca Universitaria, 1971)

Cevallos Mesones, Leonidas, ed., *Los nuevos* (Universitaria, 1967)

Chang-Rodríguez, Raquel, ed., *Cancionero peruano del siglo XVII* (La Católica, 1983)

Cornejo Polar, Antonio, and Vidal, Luis Fernando, eds., *Nuevo cuento peruano* (Mosca Azul, 1984)

Escobar, Alberto, ed., *La narración en el Perú*, 2nd ed. (Mejía Baca, 1960)

—, ed., *Antología de la poesía peruana* (Nuevo Mundo, 1965)

—, ed., *Antología de la poesía peruana*, 2 vols. (Peisa, 1973)

González Vigil, Ricardo, ed., *El cuento peruano 1975-1979* (Copé, 1983)

Hesse Murga, José, ed., *Teatro peruano contemporáneo* (Madrid: Aguilar, 1959)

Lauer, Mirko, and Oquendo, Abelardo, eds., *Vuelta a la otra margen* (Casa de la Cultura del Perú, 1970)

—, eds., *Surrealistas y otros peruanos insulares* (Barcelona: Ocnos, 1973)

Meneses, Teodoro L., ed., *Teatro quechua colonial* (Edubanco, 1983)

Miró Quesada, Aurelio, ed., *La poesía de la Emancipación*, vol. XXIV of *Colección Documental de la Independencia del Perú* (Comisión Nac. del Sesquicentenario de la Independencia del Perú, 1971)

O'Hara, Edgar, ed., *Poesía joven de Perú* (Mexico City: Punto de Partida, 1982)

—, and Ramos García, Luis, eds., *The Newest Peruvian Poetry in Translation* (Austin: Studia Hispánica, 1979)

Oquendo, Abelardo, ed., *Narrativa peruana 1950-1970* (Madrid: Alianza, 1973)

Orrillo, Winston, and Congrains Martín, Eduardo, eds., *Antología general de la prosa en el Perú*, 2 vols. (Ecoma, 1971)

Oviedo, José Miguel, ed., *Estos 13* (Mosca Azul, 1973)

Razzeto, Mario, ed., *Poesía quechua* (Havana: Casa del las Américas, 1972)

Romualdo, Alejandro, and Salazar Bondy, Sebastián, eds., *Antología general de la poesía peruana* (Librería Internacional del Perú, 1957)

Salazar Bondy, Sebastián, ed., *Poesía quechua* (Buenos Aires: Arca/ Galerna, 1968)

Santa Cruz, Nicomedes, ed., *La décima en el Perú* (INC, 1982)

Silva-Santisteban, Ricardo, ed., *De la conquista al modernismo*, vol. II of *Poesía peruana: antología general* (Edubanco, 1984)

Sologuren, Javier, ed., *Antología general de la literatura peruana* (Mexico City: Fondo de Cultura Económica, 1981)

Stephan, Ruth, ed., *The Singing Mountaineers: Songs and Tales of the Quechua People* (Austin: Univ. of Texas Press, 1957)

Tipton, David, ed., *Peru: The New Poetry* (London: London Magazine Editions, 1970)

Toro Montalvo, César, ed., *Antología de la poesía peruana del siglo XX (Años 60/70)* (Mabú, 1978)

Vargas Ugarte, Rubén, ed., *De nuestro antiguo teatro* (Compañía de Impresiones y Publicidad, 1943; Milla Batres, 1974)

—, ed., *Nuestro romancero*, 2 vols. (Clásicos peruanos vol. IV, 1951; vol. VI, 1958)

—, ed., *Rosas de Oquendo y otros clásicos* (Clásicos peruanos vol. V, 1955)

3. LITERARY HISTORY AND CRITICISM

Adorno, Rolena, ed., *From Oral to Written Expression: Native Andean Chronicles of the Early Colonial Period* (New York: Maxwell School of Citizenship and Public Affairs, Syracuse Univ., 1982)

Aldrich, Earl M., Jr., *The Modern Short Story in Peru* (Madison: Univ. of Wisconsin Press, 1966)

Arguedas, José María, *Formación de una cultura nacional indoamericana* (Mexico City: Fondo de Cultura Económica, 1975)

—, *Señores e indios. Acerca de la cultura quechua* (Buenos Aires: Arca/ Calicanto, 1976)

Arias-Larreta, Abraham, *Literaturas aborígenes de América* (Kansas City: Indoamérica, 1968)

Arriola Grande, Maurilio, *Diccionario literario del Perú*, 2nd ed., 2 vols. (Universo, 1983)

Bacacorzo, Xavier, "El pasquín y su trascendencia en la lucha libertaria nacional", *Literatura de la Emancipación*, 16-26

Castro Arenas, Mario, "La nueva novela peruana", *Cuadernos Hispano-americanos*, 138 (1961), 307-29

—, *De Palma a Vallejo* (Populibros Peruanos, 1964)

—, *La novela peruana y la evolución social* (Cultura y Libertad, 1965)

Chang-Rodríguez, Raquel, "Sobre los cronistas indígenas del Perú y los comienzos de una escritura hispanoamericana", *RevIb*, 120/121 (1982), 533-48

Coello, Oscar, *El Perú en su literatura* (El Dorado, 1983)

Cornejo Polar, Antonio, *La novela peruana: siete estudios* (Horizonte, 1977)

—, "Hipótesis sobre la narrativa peruana última", *Hueso Húmero*, 3 (1979), 45-64

—, *La novela indigenista* (Lasontay, 1980)

—, "Historia de la literatura del Perú republicano", in *Historia del Perú*, ed. Fernando Silva Santisteban (Mejía Baca, 1980), VIII, 9-188

—, "Sobre la literatura de la emancipación en el Perú", *RevIb*, 114/115 (1981), 83-93

—, "Literatura peruana: totalidad contradictoria", *RevCrit*, 18 (1983), 37-50

—, et al., *Literatura y sociedad en el Perú*, 2 vols. (Hueso Húmero, 1981, 1982)

Delgado, Wáshington, *Historia de la literatura republicana* (Rikchay Perú, 1980)

Escobar, Alberto, *Patio de Letras* (Caballo de Troya, 1965)

Esteve Barba, Francisco, *Historiografía indiana* (Madrid: Gredos, 1964), pp. 385-515

Forgues, Roland, *La sangre en llamas* (Studium, 1979)

Higgins, James, *The Poet in Peru* (Liverpool: Francis Cairns, 1982)

La Fuente Benavides, Rafael de (Martín Adán), *De lo barroco en el Perú* (San Marcos, 1968)

La Riva-Agüero, José de, *Carácter de la literatura del Perú independiente*, vol. I of *Obras completas* (La Católica, 1962)

—, *Del Inca Garcilaso a Eguren*, vol. II of *Obras completas* (La Católica, 1962)

Lara, Jesús, *La poesía quechua*, 2nd ed. (Mexico City: Fondo de Cultura Económica, 1979)

—, *La literatura de los quechuas* (La Paz: Juventud, 1980)

Lauer, Mirko, "La poesía vanguardista en el Perú", *RevCrit*, 15 (1982), 77-86

Lazo, Raimundo, *La novela andina* (Mexico City: Porrúa, 1971)

Loayza, Luis, *El sol de Lima* (Mosca Azul, 1974)

Lohmann Villena, Guillermo, *El arte dramático en Lima durante el virreinato* (Madrid: Escuela de Estudios Hispanoamericanos de la Univ. de Sevilla, 1945)

Losada, Alejandro, *Creación y praxis. La producción literaria como praxis social en Hispanoamérica y el Perú* (San Marcos, 1976)

—, *La literatura en la sociedad de América Latina: Perú y el Río de la Plata 1837-1880* (Frankfurt: Vervuert, 1983)

Luchting, Wolfgang A., *Pasos a desnivel* (Caracas: Monte Avila, 1971)

—, *Escritores peruanos ¿qué piensan, qué dicen?* (Ecoma, 1977)

Mariátegui, José Carlos, *Siete ensayos de interpretación de la realidad peruana* (Caracas: Biblioteca Ayacucho, 1979)

Means, Philip Ainsworth, *Biblioteca Andina* (Detroit: Blaine Ethridge, 1973)

Miró Quesada, Aurelio, *El primer virrey-poeta en América (Don Juan de Mendoza y Luna, Marqués de Montesclaros)* (Madrid: Gredos, 1962)

Miró Quesada, Carlos, *Rumbo literario del Perú* (Buenos Aires: Emecé, 1947)

Monguió, Luis, *La poesía postmodernista peruana* (Berkeley and Los Angeles: Univ. of California Press, 1954)

—, *Don José Joaquín de Mora y el Perú del ochocientos* (Madrid: Castalia, 1967)

—, "La poesía y la Independencia, Perú 1808-1825", *Literatura de la Emancipación*, 7-15

Morris, Robert J., *The Contemporary Peruvian Theatre* (Lubbock, Texas: Texas Tech Press, 1977)

Natella, Arthur, Jr., *The New Theatre of Peru* (New York: Senda Nueva, 1982)

Núñez, Estuardo, *La literatura peruana en el siglo XX* (Mexico City: Pormaca, 1965)

—, "La recepción del surrealismo en el Perú", in *Surrealismo/Surrealismos. Latinoamérica y España*, ed. Peter G. Earle and Germán Gullón (Philadelphia: Dept. of Romance Languages, Univ. of Pennsylvania, 1977), pp. 40-48

O'Hara, Edgar, *Desde Melibea* (Ruray, 1980)

—, *Lectura de 8 libros de la poesía peruana joven, 1980-1981* (Cuadernos Ruray 3, 1981)

—, *La palabra y la eficacia (Acercamiento a la poesía joven)* (Latino-americana/Tarea, 1984)

Ortega, Julio, *Figuración de la persona* (Barcelona: Edhasa, 1970)

—, *La imaginación crítica* (Peisa, 1974)

—, *La cultura peruana: experiencia y conciencia* (Mexico City: Fondo de Cultura Económica, 1978)

Palma, Ricardo, *La bohemia de mi tiempo*, in *Tradiciones peruanas completas* (Madrid: Aguilar, 1964)

Paoli, Roberto, *Estudios sobre literatura peruana contemporánea* (Florence: Università degli Studi di Firenze, 1985)

Porras Barrenechea, Raúl, *El sentido tradicional en la literatura peruana* (Porras, 1969)

Primer encuentro de narradores peruanos (Casa de la Cultura del Perú, 1969)

Rodríguez-Luis, Julio, *Hermenéutica y praxis del indigenismo. La novela indigenista de Clorinda Matto a José María Arguedas* (Mexico City: Fondo de Cultura Económica, 1980)

Rodríguez-Peralta, Phyllis, *Tres poetas cumbres en la poesía peruana: Chocano, Eguren y Vallejo* (Madrid: Playor, 1983)

Rodríguez Rea, Miguel Angel, *La literatura peruana en debate* (Antonio Ricardo, 1985)

Romero, Emilia, *El romance tradicional en el Perú* (Mexico City: Fondo de Cultura Económica, 1952)

—, *Diccionario manual de literatura peruana y materias afines* (San Marcos, 1966)

Salazar Bondy, Sebastián, *Lima la horrible* (Mexico City: Era, 1964)

Sánchez, Luis Alberto, *Los poetas de la Colonia y de la Revolución* (P.T.C.M., 1947; CAP, 1974)

—, *La literatura peruana: derrotero para una historia cultural del Perú*, 5 vols., 5th ed. (Mejía Baca, 1981)

—, *Introducción crítica a la literatura peruana* (Villanueva, 1972)

Sánchez Hernani, Enrique, *Exclusión y permanencia de la palabra en Hora Zero: diez años después* (Cuadernos Ruray 2, 1981)

Sánchez Lihón, Danilo, *El libro y la lectura en el Perú* (Mantaro-Grafital, 1978)

Sologuren, Javier, *Tres poetas, tres obras. Belli, Delgado, Salazar Bondy* (Porras, 1969)

Suárez Radillo, Carlos Miguel, "Poesía y realidad social en el teatro peruano contemporáneo", in *Lo social en el teatro hispanoamericano contemporáneo* (Caracas: Equinoccio, 1976), pp. 39-61

—, *El virreinato del Perú*, vol. II of *El teatro barroco hispanoamericano* (Madrid: Porrúa Turanzas, 1981)

Tamayo Vargas, Augusto, *Literatura peruana*, 2 vols. (San Marcos, 1965)

Tauro, Alberto, *Esquividad y gloria de la Academia Antártica* (Huascarán, 1948)

—, *Elementos de literatura peruana*, 2nd ed. (Leoncio Prado, 1969)

Urteaga, Horacio H., "Los copleros de la Conquista", *Mercurio Peruano*, 31/37 (1921), 120-42

Vargas Llosa, Mario, "Sebastián Salazar Bondy y la vocación del escritor en el Perú", in *Contra viento y marea* (Barcelona: Seix Barral, 1983), pp. 89-113

Watson, Maida Isabel, *El cuadro de costumbres en el Perú decimonónico* (La Católica, 1980)

Wise, David O., "Writing for Fewer and Fewer: Peruvian Fiction 1979-1980", *Latin American Research Review*, 18 (1983), 189-200

Zavaleta, Carlos E., "Narradores peruanos: la generación de los cincuenta. Un testimonio", *Cuadernos Hispanoamericanos*, 302 (1975), 454-63

INDEX OF PRINCIPAL AUTHORS

Abril, Xavier, 170
Adán, Martín, 121-23, 236-46
Alegría, Alonso, 304-06
Alegría, Ciro, 129-37
Alencastre, Andrés, 17-18
Amarilis, 44-45
Aréstegui, Narciso, 70-71
Arguedas, José María, 16, 17, 18-19,
    137-43, 211-20
Arona, Juan de, see Paz Soldán y
    Unánue, Pedro

Belli, Carlos Germán, 283-92
Bendezú, Francisco, 260-62
Bermúdez de la Torre, Pedro José, 48
Bryce Echenique, Alfredo, 309-16
Bueno, Leoncio, 272 n.11

Cabello de Carbonera, Mercedes, 77-78
Carrillo, Enrique A., 79-80
Carrió de la Vandera, Alonso, 33-35
Caviedes, see Del Valle Caviedes
Centeno de Osma, Gabriel, 10-11
Chariarse, Leopoldo, 258-60
Chioino, José, 294
Chocano, see Santos Chocano
Churata, Gamaliel, 126
Cieza de León, Pedro, 22-24
Cisneros, Antonio, 332-40
Cisneros, Luis Benjamín, 71-72
Concolorcorvo, see Carrió de la
    Vandera, Alonso
Congrains Martín, Enrique, 193-95

Dávalos y Figueroa, Diego, 45
Del Valle Caviedes, Juan, 39 n.16,
    48-54
Delgado, Wáshington, 276-80
Diez-Canseco, José, 123 n.14, 124-26

Eguren, José María, 102-09
Eielson, Jorge Eduardo, 246-52, 307-09
Espinosa Medrano, Juan de, 10, 11-12,
    45

Falcón, César, 126-27
Florián, Mario, 269-71
Fuentes, Manuel Atanasio, 65-66

Gálvez Ronceros, Antonio, 322
Gamarra, Abelardo, 73-74
García Calderón, Ventura, 113-14
Garcilaso de la Vega, the Inca, 24-29
Gibson Parra, Percy, 294-95
González Prada, Manuel, 72-73, 93-97
Guaman Poma, see Poma de Ayala
Guevara, Pablo, 276-77, 280-83

Heraud, Javier, 327, 328-30, 332
Hernández, Luis, 330-32
Hidalgo, Alberto, 149-52
Hinostroza, Rodolfo, 340-46
Hojeda, Diego de, 46-47
Huaman Poma, see Poma de Ayala
Huanay, Julián, 192 n.2

Jerez, Francisco de, 21-22
Joffré, Sara, 303-04

La Fuente Benavides, Rafael de, see
    Adán, Martín
La Puente, José Félix de, 116-17 n.8
Loayza, Luis, 206 n.11
López Albújar, Enrique, 114-16, 118-21

Mariátegui, José Carlos, 117-18, 119-
    20, 136, 170
Martínez, Gregorio, 322-25
Martos, Marco, 346-50

Matto de Turner, Clorinda, 74-77, 78-79
Melgar, Mariano, 56-61
Mexía de Fernangil, Diego, 45-46
Miramontes y Zuázola, Juan de, 43-44
Mogrovejo de la Cerda, Juan de, 35-36, 37
Mora, Tulio, 355-56
Moro, César, 184-90

Olavide, Pablo de, 36-37
Oquendo de Amat, Carlos, 172-78

Palma, Clemente, 80-82
Palma, Ricardo, 66-70
Pardo y Aliaga, Felipe, 63-65, 83-84, 87-89
Parra del Riego, Juan, 147-49
Paz Soldán y Unánue, Pedro, 89-90
Peña Barrenechea, Enrique, 190 n.15
Peralta, Alejandro, 170-72
Peralta, Arturo, see Churata, Gamaliel
Peralta Barnuevo, Pedro de, 39-41, 48
Pimentel, Jorge, 351
Poma de Ayala, Felipe Guaman, 29-33

Quispez Asín, Alfredo, see Moro, César

Ramírez Ruiz, Juan, 351
Reynoso, Oswaldo, 195-97
Ribeyro, Julio Ramón, 201-11, 301, 302-03
Riesco, Laura, 322
Ríos Rey, Juan, 295-97
Rojas y Cañas, Ramón, 65-66
Romero, Emilio, 127
Romero, Fernando, 127-29
Romualdo, Alejandro, 272-74
Rosas de Oquendo, Mateo, 49

Rose, Juan Gonzalo, 274-76

Salaverry, Carlos Augusto, 91-93
Salazar Bondy, Sebastián, 192-93, 262-65, 297-301
Sánchez León, Abelardo, 356-61
Sancho de Hoz, Pedro, 21-22
Santos Chocano, José, 98-102
Sarmiento de Gamboa, Pedro, 24
Scorza, Manuel, 272 n.11, 316-19
Segura, Manuel Ascensio, 65-66, 84-86, 89
Solari Swayne, Enrique, 301-02
Sologuren, Javier, 252-58

Terralla Landa, Esteban de, 54-56

Ureta, Alberto, 102
Urteaga Cabrera, Luis, 321-22

Valdelomar, Abraham, 111-13, 144-47
Valdez, Antonio, 12-13
Vallejo, César, 117 n.9, 126-27, 153-70
Varela, Blanca, 262, 265-69
Vargas Llosa, Mario, 220-35, 303 n.10
Vargas Vicuña, Eleodoro, 197-99
Verástegui, Enrique, 352-55

Wagner de Reyna, Alberto, 204 n.10
Waman Puma, see Poma de Ayala
Waraka, Kilku, see Alencastre, Andrés
Watanabe, José, 355
Weisse, María, 126
Westphalen, Emilio Adolfo, 178-84

Yerovi, Leonidas, 87 n.4

Zavala, Víctor, 303-04
Zavaleta, Carlos E., 197, 199-201

INDEX OF PRINCIPAL WORKS

Abolición de la muerte, 181-84
Afectos vencen finezas, 39-41
Agua, 138-40
Agua que no has de beber, 337
Album de familia, 355
Aletazos del Murciélago, 65-66
Algo que quiere morir, 299
Alma América, 98
Amauta, 118, 126, 170
Amor, gran laberinto, 298
Ande, 170-72
Apologético en favor de D. Luis de Góngora, 45
Arenga lírica al Emperador de Alemania, 149
Armas Antárticas, 43-44
Aves sin nido, 75-77, 78-79
Ayar Manko, 296-97

Baladas peruanas, 95
Balseros del Titicaca, 127
Blanca Sol, 77-78
Buen lugar para morir, 358

Cambio de guardia, 205-06
Canciones y otros poemas, 290-91
Cantar de Agapito Robles, 316-19
Canto ceremonial contra un oso hormiguero, 333, 334-37
Canto de sirena, 324-25
Canto villano, 267-69
Cantos, 260-62
Cantos desde lejos, 275
Carpe diem, 349-50
Cartas a un ángel, 92-93
Cartas de una turista, 79-80
Casa nuestra, 346-49
Charlie Melnick, 330
Cien años de vida perdularia, 74
Cinco (5) metros de poemas, 172-78
Collacocha, 301-02

Colónida, 144
Comentarios reales (Cisneros), 334
Comentarios reales (Garcilaso), 24-29
Como higuera en un campo de golf, 337-38
Como todos en la tierra (Los Villalta), 204 n.10
Confidencia en alta voz, 262-63
Consejero del lobo, 340-41
Contra natura, 342-46
Conversación en La Catedral, 229-33
Crónica de San Gabriel, 202-03
Crónica del Niño Jesús de Chilca, 338-40
Crónica del Perú, 22-24
Crónicas contra los bribones, 281-82
Cuaderno de quejas y contentamientos, 346-38
Cuarentena, 275
Cuentos andinos, 115-16
Cuentos malévolos, 80-82

Defensa de Damas, 45
Descripción del cielo, 150-51, 152
Detenimientos, 254-55
Diario de poeta, 245-46
Diente del Parnaso, 50-52
"Discurso en loor de la poesía", 44
Doce relatos de la selva, 127-28
Don Quijote, 295-96
Donde no se ama, 346
Dos viejas van por la calle, 299-300
Duque, 125-26

Edgardo o un joven de mi generación, 71-72
Edición extraordinaria, 273-74
El caballero Carmelo, 111-13
El conspirador, 77
El Cristo Villenas, 200
El cruce sobre el Niágara, 304-06

El cuerpo de Giulia-no, 307-09
El escarabajo y el hombre, 195-96
El Espejo de mi tierra, 63-65
El fabricante de deudas, 300
El fuego, 296
El hijo pródigo, 10, 11-12
El incógnito o el fruto de la ambición,
    36
El jinete insomne, 316-19
El lazarillo de ciegos caminantes, 33-35
El libro de Dios y de los húngaros, 337
El morador, 253-54
El mundo es ancho y ajeno, 133-37, 141
El Padre Horán, 70-71
El pez de oro, 126 n.17
El pie sobre el cuello, 283-90
El pobre más rico, 10-11
*El primer nueva corónica y buen
    gobierno*, 29-33
El pueblo sin Dios, 126-27
El rabdomante, 300
El retoño, 192 n.2
El río, 328
El Sargento Canuto, 85
El silbo de los aires amorosos, 349-50
"El sueño del pongo", 16-17
El tacto de la araña, 262-65
El truco de los ojos, 322
El tungsteno, 126-27
El viaje, 328-29
El zorro de arriba y el zorro de abajo,
    218-20
"Elegía al poderoso Inca Atahualpa",
    8
En los extramuros del mundo, 352-55
En octubre no hay milagros, 196-97
"Epístola a Belardo", 44-45
Esa luna que empieza, 294-95
Escalas, 117 n.9
Escrito a ciegas, 243-44
España, aparta de mí este cáliz, 163,
    166-67, 169-70
Estación reunida, 329-30
Estampas mulatas, 124-25
Estancias, 255-56
Evaristo Buendía, candidato, 116-17 n.8
Exóticas, 93

Fabla salvaje, 117 n.9
¡Fiat Lux!, 98
Flora Tristán, 299
Frutos de la educación, 84

Garabombo, el invisible, 316-19

Grafitos, 95-96

Habitación en Roma, 249-51
Habitaciones contiguas, 359
Herencia, 77 n.13
Historia general del Perú, 25, 28-29
Historia Indica, 24
Historietas malignas, 82
Horas de lucha, 73
*Hotel del Cuzco y otras provincias del
    Perú*, 282-83
Huerto cerrado, 312

Ifigenia en el mercado, 300
Indole, 77 n.13
Informe al Rey y otros libros secretos,
    275-76
Inkarrí myth, 17
Iras santas, 98

Joyería, 149-50
Julia, 71-72

Kikuyo, 193
Kollao, 170-71

La batalla, 199-200
La casa de cartón, 121-23
La Casa Verde, 225-28
La cena en el jardín, 258-59
La ciudad y los perros, 222-25
La Cristiada, 46-47
La danza inmóvil, 319 n.5
La endiablada, 35-36, 37
La epopeya del Morro, 99
La escuela de los chismes, 300
La felicidad ja ja, 312-13
La Florida del Inca, 25
La gruta de la sirena, 256
La guerra del fin del mundo, 234-35
*La mano desasida (Canto a Machu
    Picchu)*, 244-45
La palabra del mudo, 206-11
La Peli-Muertada, 89
La piedra absoluta, 244
La Rodoguna, 39-41
La rosa de la espinela, 236-37, 239
La sangre del pueblo magisterial, 271
La saya y manto, 85
La serpiente de oro, 129-31
La tía Julia y el escribidor, 233-34
La tortuga ecuestre, 185-90
La tumba del relámpago, 316-19
La venganza del cóndor, 113-14

La vida exagerada de Martín Romaña,
  314-16
Las comarcas, 275
Las constelaciones, 330-31
Las ínsulas extrañas, 178-81
Las voces de colores, 149-50
Libertarias, 95-96
Lima, hora cero, 193
Lima la horrible, 192-93
Lima por dentro y fuera, 54-56
Los cachorros, 228-29
Los desesperados, 296
Los gallinazos sin plumas, 207-08
Los geniecillos dominicales, 203-05
Los habitantes, 281-82
Los heraldos negros, 154-56
Los hijos del orden, 321-22
Los hijos del sol, 111-12
Los Ingar, 200-01
Los inocentes, 195-96
Los perros hambrientos, 131-33
Los ríos de la noche, 258-60
Los ríos profundos, 212-14
Los sonetos de Spoleto, 258
Luz de día, 268

Mar y playa, 128-29
Matalaché, 118-21
Mi Darío, 245
Minúsculas, 93
Miscelánea Austral, 45
Misterios de la tumba, 91
Mitología, 355-56
Museo de limeñadas, 65-66
Mutatis mutandis, 251-52

Ña Catita, 86
Nahuín, 197-98
Náufragos y sobrevivientes, 192
No hay isla feliz, 299
No una sino muchas muertes, 193-95
Noche oscura del cuerpo, 252
Nueva crónica y buen gobierno, see *El
  primer nueva corónica y buen
  gobierno*

Oficio de sobreviviente, 360-61
Ollantay, 12-15
Orilla, 330
Otoño, endechas, 256

Páginas libres, 72-73
Panoplia lírica, 149, 151
Pantaleón y las visitadoras, 233-34

Parnaso Antártico, 45-46
Pedro Palana, 271
Plantel de inválidos, 126
Poemas humanos, 163-69
Poemas y ventanas cerradas, 356-58
Poesía concreta, 272-73
Presbiterianas, 95-96

Química del espíritu, 150

Rasgos de pluma, 73
Rastro de caracol, 358-60
Recinto, 256-57
Redoble por Rancas, 316-19
Reinos, 246-49
Relación de la conquista del Perú, 21-22
Retorno a la creatura, 281
Rodil, 299

*Siete ensayos de interpretación de la
  realidad peruana,* 117-18, 119-20
Simple canción, 275
Simplismo, 150
Sombras como cosas sólidas, 263

Taita Cristo, 197-99
Tantas veces Pedro, 314
Tema y variaciones, 251
Tierra de caléndula, 322-24
Todas las sangres, 214-18
Tradiciones cuzqueñas, 74-75
Tradiciones peruanas, 66-70
Tragedia del fin de Atawallpa, 7, 17
Travesía de extramares, 236-43
Trilce, 156-63
Triunfos de amor y poder, 39-41

Un mundo dividido, 277-80
Un mundo para Julius, 309-12, 313
Una piel de serpiente, 206 n.11
Urpi, 269-70
Usca Paucar, 10

Valses y otras falsas confesiones, 265-67
*Verdadera relación de la conquista del
  Perú,* 21-22
Vida continua, 252-58
Vida y pasión de Santiago el pajarero,
  301, 302-03
Vox horrísona, 331-32

XYZ, 82

Yawar Fiesta, 140-43

LIVERPOOL MONOGRAPHS IN HISPANIC STUDIES

ISSN 0261-1538

General Editors: Peter A. Bly, James Higgins
Assistant Editors: Ann Mackenzie, Roger Wright

The Poet in Peru
Alienation and the Quest for a Super-Reality
JAMES HIGGINS
0 905205 10 3. LMHS 1. x+166pp. 1982.

Readings of the work of six modern Peruvian poets—Eguren, Vallejo, Belli, Cisneros, Moro, Adán—reveal, in spite of wide differences between the poets, a common dilemma (how to reconcile the dichotomies of their society) and a common artistic stance (that of the outcast who perceives a higher reality in a visionary, surreal world).
  "Higgins has set himself a difficult task in this intriguing volume, and to say that it perhaps raises more questions than it answers is in no way anything but an appreciation of the way in which he has carried out a complex and difficult undertaking" (*Hispanic Review* 1984).

Galdós's Novel of the Historical Imagination
A Study of the Contemporary Novels
PETER A. BLY
0 905205 14 6. LMHS 2. xii+195pp. 1983.

Professor Bly argues that in the *serie contemporánea* Benito Pérez Galdós (1843-1920) created a special type of historical novel which, by drawing subtle parallels between fictional action and political events, allegorises the political history of the recent Spanish past.
  "*Galdós's Novel of the Historical Imagination* is one of the most fruitful studies of Galdós to appear in recent years; it deserves a place in the library of every *galdosista*" (*Crítica Hispánica* 1983).

The Deceptive Realism of Machado de Assis
A Dissenting Interpretation of Dom Casmurro
JOHN GLEDSON
0 905205 19 7. LMHS 3. viii+215pp. 1984.

This reading of *Dom Casmurro* (1899) lays the basis for understanding in more 'realistic' terms the work of the major Brazilian novelist, Machado de Assis. Dr. Gledson first disentangles the 'plot' of the novel from the biased and twisted version of events presented by the narrator and central character, Bento. This leads to a new perception of Machado's veiled commentary on the contemporary political and social situation—issues such as slavery, the growth of capitalism and the influence of organised religion within the state form a vital (though covert) part of Machado's narrative structure.
  "There is no gainsaying that this is a remarkable, thought-provoking addition to the critical literature on Machado de Assis. In subtlety of analysis as well as conversancy with Machado's oeuvre in prose it bears comparison with the best work to date on *Dom Casmurro*" (*Times Literary Supplement* 1985).

The Structured World of Jorge Guillén
A Study of Cántico and Clamor
ELIZABETH MATTHEWS
0 905205 23 5. LMHS 4. x+326pp. 1985.

In this study of the work of Jorge Guillén (1893-1984), one of the greatest poets of twentieth-century Spain, Dr. Matthews argues that his vision of the world as an ordered harmonious unity is echoed in the structural symmetry of his work. Close analysis of twelve long poems, forming ideological and structural pillars of the *Cántico* and *Clamor* volumes, reveals the intricacies of Guillén's mimesis of cosmic harmony. The first English translations of the twelve poems appear in an appendix.

"Matthews offers a precise study of the poet's main themes which, without modifying in a major way earlier overviews, contributes many new insights and deepens our general vision of his work" (*Hispanic Review* 1986).

Reading Onetti
Language, Narrative and the Subject
MARK MILLINGTON
0 905205 26 X. LMHS 5. vi+345pp. 1985.

The Uruguayan Juan Carlos Onetti is one of the leading exponents of the new Spanish American novel. Mark Millington's comprehensive study traces the various stages of his existential and artistic evolution and utilises recent developments in narrative theory to illuminate Onetti's complex fictional world.

Vision and the Visual Arts in Galdós
A Study of the Novels and Newspaper Articles
PETER A. BLY
0 905205 30 8. LMHS 6. x+242pp. 1986.

The keen interest which Galdós took throughout his life in the visual arts is documented in Parts I and II of this book, which discuss his art journalism and his artistic contributions to the illustrated edition of his historical novels. But the main focus (Part III) is on Galdós' frequent use of the visual arts and pictorial landscapes in his fictional work, particularly the *seria contemporánea*. These artistic allusions not only direct the reader's interpretation of novelistic events, but also relate to the aesthetic and philosophical question of the human eye's role and reliability in apprehending physical reality. Professor Bly offers a fascinating analysis of the types of interrelationship between visual art and novelistic action; his study contributes greatly to the understanding of aesthetic and moral perception in Galdós' novels, and suggests wider implications for the literary and aesthetic theories of the nineteenth century.

A History of Peruvian Literature
JAMES HIGGINS
0 905205 35 9. LMHS 7. xiv+379pp. 1987.

Further volumes of Liverpool Monographs in Hispanic Studies are in preparation